A Research on Current Political Thought Trends in China

Conception of Political Thought Trends and Their Regularities

Wang Bingquan

translated by Zhu Jianting

CANUT INTERNATIONAL PUBLISHERS

Istanbul - Berlin - London - Santiago

Academic Research on Contemporary China Book Series

A Research on Current Political Thought Trends in China. Conception of Political Thought Trends and Their Regularities

edited by Wang Bingquan

translated by Zhu Jianting

The English version is published with financial support of the Innovation Program of the Chinese Academy of Social Sciences

Chinese Title: 当代中国政治思潮研究, ISBN: 9787516129227

Copyright © China Social Sciences Press, Beijing, 2014

Canut International Publishers

Canut Intl. Turkey, Teraziler Cad. No.29. Sancaktepe, Istanbul, Turkey

Canut Intl. Germany, Heerstr. 266, D-47053, Duisburg, Germany

Canut Intl. United Kingdom, 12a Guernsay Road, London E11 4BJ, England

Copyright © Canut International Publishers, 2018

ISBN: 978-605-9914-66-6

Printed in UK

Lightning Source Ltd. UK

Chapterhouse, Pitfield Kiln Farm

MK11 3LW

United Kingdom

www.canutbooks.com

About the Author

Wang Bingquan, Master's tutor in political sciences. Ph.D. Political Science Institute, associate editor and editor in chief of the journal "Political Sciences". His main research direction is the basic theory of political sciences, the theory and practice of contemporary China's democratic construction and contemporary Chinese political thought trends.

His representative books include: *On the Nationalism Thought Trend, China Growing Up: National Consciousness of the Contemporary Chinese Youth*. His main academic papers are: "Institutional framework for the political development of socialism with Chinese characteristics", "Trends of Contemporary Chinese Nationalism: Values and Theoretical Limitations of the Times", "Some Basic Concepts of Marxist Political Science", "Consciousness Characteristics of Social Trends", "Strong Socialist Democracy with Chinese Characteristics", "Deep Understanding of the Basic Connotation of Social Thought Trends", "Why Is Nationalism Possible?".

Editor's note

The book is authored by Wang Bingquan, one of the most renown scholars specialized in the research of political thought trends, he gave a meticulous energy to understand the development laws of political thought trends and make breakthroughs in this area. Men are in interaction with all kinds of political thought trends, how they emerge, develop, transform, vanish and re-emerge in a different historical era, how they embrace and mobilize millions for certain goals, is a vast scientific question. The book investigates this question from a Marxist view and methodology, besides other convenient methods of research. The first part of the book deals to build a systematic conception to answer this question. The second part of the book investigates into the 3 major political thought trends which most vigorously affect contemporary China: nationalism, civil society, universal values. Wang Bingquan argues that these 3 trends represent a positive effect upon the spiritual production of Chinese people. With the deepening of Reform and Opening-up and the socialist market economy, China's economic and social structures, patterns of employment and interest relations and distribution mode have become more and more diversified. And the spiritual life of people has become more complex, and the differentiation and diversity between various social consciousness forms have become more obvious, which to a large extent demonstrated by various political thought trends. In China the leading party reproduces and innovates the dominant ideology of socialist core values to support the social system and to achieve a healthy progress towards a comprehensively prosperous socialism. Numerous political trends, have complex relations with the dominant ideology, thus the catchword "guiding social thought trends with socialist core values" is the task and "showing tolerance and respect for differences and diversity" is the dealing principle set by the leading party to enable a benign atmosphere in the ideological field. The conclusion part of the book discusses the issues of "guiding social thought trends with socialist core values." We hope the readers will find abundant thought provoking material and information in this book.

Daivja Jindal
June, 2018
London, UK

Contents

CHAPTER FIVE

THE NEW VALUE MONISM – "UNIVERSAL VALUES" THOUGHT TREND

CHAPTER SIX

BETWEEN STATE AND SOCIETY – "CIVIL SOCIETY" THOUGHT TREND

Foreword

Political thought trend is a reflection of social reality. It is also the "sensor" regarding the changes the spirit of times, the "sensor" of social contradictions which become prominent, the "sensor" of social change and transformation in the social development trend. By acknowledging this important "information base", we can grasp the pulse of times and identify social contradictions and challenges. An important phenomenon in the field of social consciousness during the new period of Reform and Opening-up in contemporary China is the rise and fall of various thought trends. The research object of this book is political thoughts, and to further deepen the study of the law of political thought, to deepen the research on specific trend of thoughts so as to further improve ideological work and make a modest contribution to the task of insisting on guiding political thought trends with socialist core value system.

I. Research of thought trends in the field of political science

The research of contemporary Chinese political thought trends has always been the focus of contemporary Chinese political science research. The issues concerning different political thought trends are also among the concerns of political science research, and the study of the history of political thought trends cannot be separated from the study of political thought trends, and when studying current China's political development, this study cannot do without paying due attention to the realistic picture and theoretical inspiration and enlightenment provided by the political thoughts, on the other side the studies on western political science, cannot be separated from looking into its interaction with contemporary China's political thoughts. And, from a certain point of view, we can say that the research carried out by political science contributes to the studies on the occurrence and development of political thought trends. Therefore, political thought trends have always been an important object of political science research.

Political thought trends provide the road map for reform

Reform is the driving force behind the development and progress of all undertakings in contemporary China, it is also the core theme of current political thought trends in China. Today, what to change, and how to change is the main content demonstrated by the current political thought trends. Although their road maps vary, and sometimes conflict with each other, they all put forward important proposals after relatively careful considerations, worth our attention and best use should be made. Following the 18th National Congress of the CPC, the central government has proposed to deepen reforms with greater political courage and wisdom, and initiated major steps to promote Reform and Opening-up, consequently during the 18th CPC National Congress. Comrade Xi Jinping proposed "we need a serious review and comprehensive summarization regarding the process of Reform and Opening-up, thus have a more profound understanding of the historical inevitability of the process, consciously grasp the regularities of transformation and, more firmly undertake the responsibility of deepening Reform and Opening-up."[1] This passage clearly shows that reform is still the banner, that will be carried forward by the ruling party in the future, and that various other reform measures will be launched at a deeper level. From this view, we can say that, what to change, is still one of the main focus of various thought trends. Although there are disagreements between different schools of thought in this regard, one thing in common, their road map proposals may not be able to accommodate the mainstream ideology. But more than one kind of thinking and proposal will give people more choices. We should have a relatively peaceful and sober mind regarding reform road maps proposed by different political thoughts. Socialist society is in a constant change and reform. Engels has commented on the issue as early as in 1890: "a socialist society is a thing not immutable and frozen but often encounters changes and reforms"[2]. Reform is inevitable and at this point there are no fundamental differences, but on what to change, and what will be the objective of change there are different opinions. There is no need to give hasty judgments regarding different opinions, those who lead should also be tolerant, and examine them with an inclusive and productive attitude.

Political thoughts provide the road map of transformation.

Social development and progress, in fact, is the consequences of social transformation. The ascending process of social development is the negation of negation, i.e., the process of transformation, and this is in line with

---

1   *People's Daily*. Jan. 2nd. 2013.
2   *Selected Works of K. Marx and F. Engels*. Vol.4, People's Publishing House,1995, p.693.

the basic principles of Marxism. During the social transition periods, political thoughts are often active and vigorous, and they do not only offer a window to examine social transformation, but they are also one of the cursers of the road maps for the content, how society will be transformed. As an important part of social consciousness political thoughts tend to make judgments, and put forward looking visions regarding social development and social change, which are often different compared with the understanding of the mainstream ideology, which precisely enrich our understanding on the changes in social development and affects our thinking over the solutions that can further promote social progress.

Political thoughts scrutinize the rationality of governance.

The ruling party is an important target of political thoughts, while the rationality of their governance is often a prime concern of them. If we closely examine the major political thought trends in contemporary China, we can see that their core research often deals with the ruling party's governance problems. This is quite understandable. In contemporary China, we can say that the most prominent research issue of political science is how the Communist Party can strengthen and improve its leadership capacity and more importantly how it can achieve a perfect governance system. The concern demonstrated by the political thought trends also provides a rare, valuable reference for the ruling party to strengthen its capacity. Currently, with the comprehensive deepening of Reform and Opening-up, the ruling party faces unprecedented opportunities, but also the risks and difficulties are unprecedented.

The party needs to aggregate all possible positive energies, in order to build consensus and overcome challenges; and it needs to rely on the current good momentum of economic development, to guide the direction of transformation and development. The deepening of the reform in various fields cannot be separated from the party's leadership, control and plan. The CPC shoulders a historical responsibility and mission. Consequently, in the face of opportunities and challenges—the party—while giving full play to its political advantages and continuing to promote Reform and Opening-up, in order to promote the self-perfection and development of socialism, from time to time, it will be good to look in the mirror of "trend of thoughts" and examine them for strengthening its self-building.

Political thought trends reflect the basic layout of ideological sphere

In today's China, socialist symbolic system is still dominant in the ideological sphere and also called the official ideology. Besides, various other kind of thoughts trends coexist in the country. The relation between these ideological trends and the mainstream ideology includes both struggle and cooperation, whereas both sides maintain a relationship of mutual repulsion and attraction. They seek common points while reserving difference based on their common and divergent appeals. Thus, a basic pattern of mainstream ideology that coexists with various ideological trends has taken shape.

Political thought is a window through which we can see the social contradictions in the society.

Throughout the past 30-plus years since the Reform and Opening-up, China's economic and social structure have experienced tremendous changes; profound adjustments have been made in the pattern of interests within social strata, people's expectations to share the fruits of reform and development have general improved, contradictions between different social strata and interest groups due to their different interest appeals have become more apparent, and the contradictions among the people tend to become increasingly diversified and complicated. Different interest groups often constitute the main body and basis of certain political thought trends. Controversies and debates between different thoughts also reflect the boundaries of the social contradictions among social groups to some degree. These aspects of political thought trends, we can observe, constitute the important questions, which need be answered by the political science. Political thoughts should be a focus of the political science researches for a long term.

II. Research object

Political thought trend is an important form of social consciousness, it becomes quite active in an era of social crisis, in an era of conflict and change, it is an important witness of the history, reflecting the process of social dynamics. Since China's Reform and Opening-up, the political trend of thoughts have been very active. Trend of thoughts, which have adapted themselves to the development of the times, to a certain extent, have played positive role to enhance social, ideological and cultural level and provided certain spiritual impetus for the Reform and Opening-up, while on the other hand, those thought trends which run counter to the trend times make negative effects and endanger social stability. After ushering in the new century, political thought trends have been even more active, and several of them which have larger social impact are quite effective in the fields of thought and culture.

The research object of this book is contemporary Chinese political thought trends, and aims to contribute to the overall research and exploration of development laws of thought trends, through the study of political thought trends, i.e., and with a view of contributing to theoretical innovation and social practice, aims to examine major effective thought trends in the whole pattern of numerous thought trends. The debate on the general development law of political thoughts, cannot be restricted to the time period of "contemporary times" but should also cover the bygone ones, and pay attention to the whole world. Generally speaking, research on political thought trends can be classified into two levels: basic theoretical research of political thought trends and research on specific political thought trends. The basic theoretical research takes political thought trends as its research object, explores the general laws of its operation and relevant theoretical issues include the following: a) ideology embodiment of thought trends, b) research on the relations between thought trend and social psychology c) and the relationship between research on conscious operation of ideological trend, namely exploring relationship among thoughts, social psychology and ideological system (ideology).

Basic issues of theoretical research also explore the connotation, structure, subjects, characteristics, types, functions of thought trends. Secondly, explores the conditions of formation and development of thought trends, explores social and historical basis and conditions of thought trends. Thirdly, the effect of prominent figures in the emergence and development of thought trends. Fourthly, the unity of opposites between thought trends and so on. Fifthly, exploration on the movement of thought trends; exploration on the mode, characteristics, processes within which thought trends are disseminated.

Research on specific thought trends

The research on various specific thought trends generally includes the research on a variety of specific thought trends, together with the background of the times when this trend emerged and developed, and explores their rheological interaction processes, main demonstration forms and their representative figures and so on. The research on the law of thought trends, is a common and universal research issue, which also aims to explain specific thought trends, the research on the law of thought trends cannot be separated from the research on specific thought trends. In general, the research object of this book is political thought trends: in particular, its content covers the two levels, it does not only include the general study of political thought trends, but also includes the study of specific political thought trends.

III. Significance of the research

To further deepen the study of political thought trends has certain theoretical and practical significance. Its theoretical significance is to make political thought research more comprehensive and thorough so as to grasp its laws. Its practical significance includes contribution to improve the party's ability to guide and govern the field of ideology, so that we can do a good job in the work of guiding political thought trends with the socialist core value system. All in all, it will help to provide thought resources for promoting the process of Sinicization of Marxism in China. Both during its foundation and throughout its development, Marxism has always engaged in dialogues and debates with various thoughts of its contemporaries. Still today, when we seek to understand the classical works of Marxism more perfectly, naturally we find it necessary to study and grasp various other thoughts that appeared in historical conditions of their time and the debates between the classical writers of Marxism and these various schools of thoughts. After Marxism was introduced in China, the reason why we could continuously gain new achievements which kept pace with the times is that: our party has insisted on combining the basic tenets of Marxism with the ever-changing concrete reality in China, and the other factor is that—considering the rapid changes in the society—our party has been keen to learn from various other progressive political thoughts and at the same developed itself by criticizing the backward ones. Since any political thought trend arises from the realistic contradictions in the society, it often contains valuable and inspiring academic views and theoretical patterns, which pushes people to think more deeply on the society, social life and social problems. Exploring and discovering these spiritual resources and core ideas which are contained in these political thought trends can inspire us to solve practical problems facing us, and can enrich the theoretical system of socialism with Chinese characteristics, and can enhance its suitableness to reality. Various thought trends put forward several new issues brought by the continuous development of social life practice. By the way of including these new issues and new problems into the field of vision of Marxism view and in-depth study of these new issues with the methodology of Marxism method, and by drawing new conclusions from these studies, Marxism can be developed in contestation with various thought trends. Thus, it will also help to deepen theoretical study on the "social consciousness theory" of Marxist historical materialism. The consciousness property of political thought trends is not only a fundamental theoretical problem, but also an important aspect that needs in-depth study in regard with the Marxist theory of social consciousness. Following the rapid development of productive forces, and improvement of the practical ability of human beings, The complexity of social consciousness increases, the reaction and effect of social consciousness over the social existence becomes more prominent. A political thought trend is an important part of social consciousness, which fully embodies its characteristics. Strengthening the studies on political thought trends can deepen the understanding of the Marxist theory of social consciousness. A clear understanding of consciousness property of the political thought trends and having a clear understanding of the status of the political thought trends in the structure of social consciousness will not only provide a certain theoretical support for grasping the occurrence, development, regression and control over political thought trends, but will also provide some new ideas for enriching the social consciousness theory of Marxist historical materialism. In previous studies, a little attention was given to the social conscious property of political thought trends and also on the level of social consciousness there is less study regarding the representative figures of political thoughts.

Political thought trends, which are closely connected with human practice, are important component part of social consciousness. As a specific form of social consciousness, a political thought trend verifies the basic judgment and ideas of Marxism about social consciousness in many ways. Undoubtedly, deepening the research on the consciousness property of political thought is not only a supplement to the research on the Marxist theory of social consciousness, but also the application of basic ideas of Marxism regarding the social consciousness in practice.

Deepening the study of specific thought trends

Research results regarding the operation laws of political thought trends can provide us "guidance" when studying the specific political thought trends. The academic circles have made great achievements in the research of specific political thought trends, but different academic studies regarding specific political thought trends show different features in diverse studies. This is because most researchers, according to their own research standards, have summarized and analyzed some specific political thought trends, this means there can be alternative ways of grasping and evaluating the same specific political thought trend, On the one side, these alternative research ways help us to understand a specific political thought trend more realistically, but on the other side it shows us that it is quite impossible to grasp the "true colors" and a full image of a specific political thought trend. This paradox should make us think over, I think this objectively needs the transformation of the research methodology and research approach, and strengthen the depth of our research of specific political thought trends.

The new research approach regarding specific political thought trends. Regarding this point, we can propose is to start from the basic issues (aspects) and operation laws of political thoughts, i.e. the general law of political thoughts. And with this reference "benchmark" of study we can further deepen the research on specific political thought trends, this will to some extent help us to predict the general direction of the formation and development of specific political thought trends. If we have a deeper understanding on the general operation law of political thought trends, it will be completely feasible to guide research on specific thought trends, What we propose is as follows: our deeper cognition on the general law of political thought trends, can be deepened by making the abstraction when studying various specific political thought trends, this abstraction will be derived from research of the particular, because every particular or specific thing embodies a certain degree of generality, (character of the general). People first learn about particular things and gradually ascend to the level of abstraction through comparison, similarity, generality and universality embedded inside these specific things and in this way people advance towards general concepts, which are relatively deeper. Thus, in this way, if we have a better grasp of general law, with its guidance, our research on specific thought trends will surpass "one-sidedness" and become more comprehensive, and we can explain them more completely. This new approach will help to enhance the realistic orientation of our work of guiding political thought trends using the socialist core value system. The building of the socialist core value system has been a major theoretical innovation regarding ideological and cultural construction which was formulated in the sixth Plenary Session of the 16th CPC Central Committee. The socialist core value system is the fundamental aspect of building a harmonious culture. A political thought trend is the "mouthpiece" of social consciousness, various social consciousness forms in the society are often manifested through political thought trends. In contemporary China, the building of a socialist harmonious society necessarily requires the establishment of the guiding status of socialist core values system, only in this way can we consolidate the ideological and ethical foundation of a harmonious society, and strengthen our guidance over the diverse political thought trends. "The decision on a number of major issues in building a harmonious socialist society of CPC Central Committee proposed to guide the social thought trends using socialist core value system, and advocated the principle of " showing tolerance and respect for differences and diversity" called for the formation of consensus among social thought trends in the society. The 17th National Congress of the CPC further emphasized: "We will explore effective ways of letting the system of socialist core values guide trends of thought and take the initiative in ideological work, respecting divergence and allowing diversity while effectively resisting the influence of erroneous and decadent ideas." Insisting to guide social thought trends with socialist core value system will help to deepen our understanding of the theoretical research and strengthen our practice, will help to eliminate estrangement in the level of values, and expand consensus among thought trends in the society so that the whole nation's wisdom and strength is united around the great cause of building a harmonious socialist society. There is no doubt that constructing a socialist core value system, guiding social thought trends and perfecting our ideological work are the true inspiration of this book. The political thought trends are the core of the social thought trends therefore they are important targets of our guidance work by the socialist core value system. Only through in-depth study of the general nature of the political thought trends and studying the actual performance of certain specific political thought trends our work guiding will be a more targeted work, we should hit the nail right on the head. To grasp the general nature and basic characteristics of a political thought trend theoretically can help us to understand the overall situation of a political thought trend more deeply, this will help us to be flexible when guiding them and improve our ability to make predictions about political thought trends. For example, the social psychological component of a political thought trend is often expressed through some social hot spots, while its ideological component is often expressed by specific group of intellectuals. Therefore, in the process of guiding the political thought trends we should both pay close attention to the hot spot issues in social practice and also focus into the theoretical aspect of the political thought trends as well as to studying the ideological and theoretical trends of specific groups in order to effectively grasp the status of political trend.

The emergence of a political thought trend has complex social and historical conditions. These conditions, play different roles in the emergence of a political thought trend, and different trends of thoughts have different focal points. Through an in-depth understanding of specific historical conditions which give rise to a political thought trend, we can more accurately compare different political thought trends accurately and can better grasp the magnitude of their social role and their development direction. Examining different political thought trends which have different features, will help us in the process of guiding political thought trends with socialist core value system, thus we can adopt different approaches and give different responses to each different political trend.

It helps us to maintain social stability and promote harmony. Social stability is the premise of a benign social life and social operation. Deng Xiaoping pointed out: "in China the overriding need is for stability. We must counter any forces that threaten stability, not yielding to them or even making any concessions."[3]

The study of political thought trends, the realization of social stability and harmonious development, is the full implementation of the Scientific Outlook on Development and inevitable requirement of building a harmonious socialist society. A political thought trend is the "barometer" of socio-economic and political life and also acts as the "wind-vane" showing the development direction of the whole ideology of a certain period. A political thought trend may not only be the "horn" of social development and progress, but may also be a "catalyst" for social unrest. Both history and reality have fully proved this point. Originally, Marxism was introduced to China as a "new trend of thought", due to its great scientific and revolutionary nature, it eventually took root in the old China, and has become the mainstream ideology of the state, while some political thoughts that were unsuitable for China's national conditions were swept by the historical tide and has disappeared.

With the progress of times, with the development of the socialist cause and with the continuous adjustment of productive forces and production relations, in China the diversification regarding the political thought trends has become even more obvious and the natures of political thought trends have become more complex. The emergence political thought trends and their development is closely related with social progress and stability. Some of the political thought trends can unite people's thinking, and regulate their social behavior, while some political thought trends can cause confusion in their thought, and may become a social unrest factor. Therefore, we should intensify the study of political thought trends, grasp their essence, their laws of development and dissemination, grasp the operation of thought trends more accurately, thus help people to raise their awareness, better predict the real political consequences they may bring, all of which can also will help to strengthen the building of a harmonious socialist culture and which can play an important role in maintaining social stability.

IV. Research methods

"The Marxist method is our telescope and microscope in political and military matters."[4] The fundamental method of studying political thought trends is dialectical and historical materialism. The view that all the phenomena of the modern world are inextricably connected with each other;

---

3   *Deng Xiaoping Selected Works*. Vol.3 People's Publishing House,1993, p.286 and https://archive.org/stream/SelectedWorksOfDengXiaopingVol.3/Deng03_djvu.txt.
4   *Selected Works of Mao Zedong*, Vol.1, People's Publishing House, 1991, p.212.

the view of development; the view of unity of opposites; the view of social existence determines social consciousness; the view of the economic base determines the superstructure; the view of class and the view of people as the creators of history are all fundamental methods of political thought trends research. This book adheres to the basic methodologies of Marxism, and consciously implements the standpoint and methodology of Marxism.

But in our specific research work, we also use the following specific research methods.

The causal analysis method. This method, in its concrete application, should deconstruct all aspects of thought trends, basing itself on the basic tenets of historical materialism, such as the relationships between social being and social consciousness and economic base and superstructure and in many aspects, such as economics, politics, thoughts, culture in the synthetized role of socio-historical conditions. For example, when we analyze the basic nature of a political thought trend and its political orientation and its fate (rise and fall), we start from analysis of the social status of people that are the representatives of such trend of thoughts, the position of the class and its hierarchical status of these people in the society, and the core theoretical arguments and demands of the said political thought. We explore the main reason for the occurrence and development of thought trends from the socio-economic conditions, the political development situation, ideological and cultural conditions and other factors. We try to grasp the specific performance of the political thought trend by looking into the changes occurring regarding the main social contradictions, and try to understand the development trend of the thought trend by looking into the changes of the theme of times and into the social psychology of people. During the examination of the causes behind the emergence process of a political thought trend, we should give full attention to the specific phenomena which presents itself as "one cause leading to multiple effects".

The system analysis method. In our researches, we mainly use the system analysis method, to examine the overall state of a political thought trend in a specific stage of history. We use the system analysis method regarding the following issues: a) the overall condition of thought trends, including the trend of the overall structure, b) the scale and magnitude of development of thought trends, the dissemination situation of thought trends) when analyzing the various sub-systems of a political thought trend, including the basic elements inside each specific thought trend; d) When including the relationship between the subsystem and thought of the whole system, f) when studying the interrelationships, between large system of political thoughts and social consciousness system, g) the relationship between a thought trend and the ideological superstructure, h) the relationship between sub-systems of political thought trends and other social consciousness systems, i) the relationship between the big whole system of political thought trends and the system surrounding it, j) the relationship between thought trend system on the one side, and economic, political, ideological and cultural other external systemic conditions system, and so on.

In addition, the comparative analysis method is also an important analysis method. By using this method, we can analyze and explore the relationships between different thought trends such as Chinese and foreign thought trends, thought trends in different historical periods, thought trends in the same historical period, between thought trends with different nature and thought trends having the same nature. Other fields of comparative analysis method include the following: a) comparison between political thought trends as specific form of social consciousness and political thought trends related with other forms of consciousness, b) the relationship between political thought trends and ideology; c) the relationship between political thought trends and the dominant social thought; d) the relationship between political thought trends in their various stages of development, etc.

In our researches all methods should be applied rationally to explore the essence of things. In the process of studying the object of study, we cannot deliberately impose any method onto the study object, neither can we search a method for the sake of method. The process of research and explanation (expression) of thought trends follow the clues of history and logic which are naturally demonstrated. Whether the fundamental method of Marxism or other specific analysis methods we have mentioned above should be used naturally in the study process, which will suit the law of birth and development of things and will suit the laws of human cognition.

V. Structure and views

This book discusses the basic theoretical issues of political thought trends of contemporary China especially those recent ones, basing itself on the analysis of their basic situation, we have developed our ideas starting from concrete to abstract and from theory to reality. The whole book, except the introduction and conclusion parts, is divided into two parts and includes a total of seven chapters. Both the first and second chapter includes four chapters: The first chapter discusses the consciousness attribute of the political thought trends, the second chapter discusses the general characteristic of political thought trends, the third chapter expounds on the social and historical conditions of the formation and development of political thought, the fourth chapter discusses the dissemination of political thought trends, the fifth chapter studies the thought trend of "universal values", the sixth chapter studies the thought trend of civil society and the seventh chapter discusses the thought trend of nationalism. The conclusion part discusses the issues of guiding the thought trends. The first part of the book is the methodology, i.e. "general", while the second part of the book is the application of the methodology, i.e. "specific".

The book argues that a political thought trend is based on a certain social existence which embodies the two levels of human activity: their social psychology and ideological activities, and it is a specific social consciousness phenomenon which generates strong political and social impacts. A political thought trend not only embodies socio-psychological components, but also ideological content. Political thought trends can play both positive and negative roles: the progressive political thought trends have positive effects on social existence while the wrong or even reactionary political thought trends generate a negative effect upon the social existence. The politicalness is the most important character of political thought trends, , the (mass) group subject feature and motility feature are also important features of political thought trends.

The contradictory movement of productive forces and productive relations is an important condition for the emergence and development of political thought trends. The formation and appearance of political forces, and the formation and development of political movement constitute the political conditions of apolitical thought trend. Emergence of a political thought trend cannot be separated from its current thought and cultural environment as well as from its thought and theoretical content in the past history. The men's subjective initiative displayed by some representative figures is also an important condition of apolitical thought trend.

With the deepening of Reform and Opening-up and the socialist market economy, China's economic structures, organizational form, patterns of employment and interest relations and distribution mode have become more and more diversified. And the spiritual life of people has become more complex, and the differentiation and diversity between various social consciousness forms have become more obvious, which to a large extent demonstrated by various political thought trends. Judging from the overall situation in contemporary China, we can say that, among the numerous and complex thought trends, the thought trend of universal values, the thought trend of civil society and the thought trend of nationalism, enjoy hefty large social impacts and broader audience and they more objectively, reflect the social psychology of people mind and more vigorously attract the concern of intellectual circles, which are worthy of attention and study. This book presents an objective elucidation of these thought trends, and makes comments on them, and argues that—in the Chinese ideological field—they represent a positive effect upon the spiritual production, they help in reflecting on the problems, help to discover and solving them.

CHAPTER ONE

Consciousness Property of Thought Trends

This book aims to understand and explore all aspects of political thought trends in the field of view of historical materialism. As a specific existence form of social consciousness, political thought trends can only obtain a complete embodiment in the relationship between social existence and social consciousness. The issue of the position of political thought trends in the social consciousness structure is the fundamental theoretical issue in the study of political thought trends, and the research of this issue has a key significance in understanding the nature, characteristics and development conditions of political thought trends.

I.1. Connotations of political thought trends

In order to understand the political thought trends more thoroughly, it is necessary to make a detailed explanation of the meaning of political thought trends. To study the connotations of the political thought trends, first of all, it is necessary to clarify the relationship between the political thought trends and the social thought trends. In the academic research, on the whole, social thought trends are often equated with political thought trends, and this also conforms to the actual situation of the thought trends. In the family of the social thought trends, the political thought trends constitute their core, and although some non-political thoughts also exist, these thoughts are often relatively unimportant in the thought pattern and difficult to cause wide concern. In people's daily use, social thought trends also refer more to political thought trends. In the discussion of the consciousness characteristics of political thoughts in this chapter, the academic circles rather take the "social thought trends" as the research object, and the conclusions they have drawn are entirely suitable for political thought trends. Therefore, in the content of this chapter, we did not make any deliberate distinction between political thought trends and social thought trends and fully respect the objective situation in the academic circles' research.

I.1.1. Semantic analysis of "thought trends"

When an important concept expresses some thoughts, the meaning of the concept is both established by popular usage and developed with historical changes. It has often different meanings in different periods, different understandings in different settings of the same period, and also different interpretations in different theoretical systems. This book does not interpret the social thought trends from the etymology, but according to the standpoint, viewpoint and methodology of Marxism and by proceeding from the actual practice, puts the social thought trends in the mutual relationship of theory and practice, based on its actual application in the social and economic life, political life and cultural life so as to understand them.

When people use "thought trends" in daily life, they often confuse "thought trends" with "social thought trends", and when they treat currents of thought, they sometimes call them as "thought trends" and sometimes as "social thought trends". In the actual application, "thought trends" refers to "social thought trends", because there are no thought trends that do not belong to men, that do not possess sociality, that are divorced from men's practical activities. Social thought trends are thought trends, including "thought trends" that have spheres, and the difference lies in the different distance of different thought trends from the social life. More often, what is widely influential and attracts much attention in actual life, especially as the key content of research of thought trends, are often those thought trends that are typical and more prominent, namely those thought trends with quite strong sociality, actualness and politicality.

To be specific, the term "thought trends" has two basic meanings: one is the current of thoughts that reflect in a certain class or stratum within a certain period the then the socio-political circumstances and have a greater impact; the other is the movement of thoughts one after another[1]. Both meanings highlight the characteristics that thought trends have ups and downs. The former more distinctly and clearly summarizes the sociality and classness of thought trends and approaches the basic meaning of the social thought trends, the latter closely refers to the rather obvious psychological and ideal fluctuation, and both actually summarize respectively the different aspects in the connotation of thought trends.

The term "thought trends" has become a common vocabulary used in the Chinese academic research since the early 20th Century. It was Liang Qichao who proposed to pay attention to "thought trends of the era", and called

---

1   *Modern Chinese Dictionary*, Commercial Press (2012), p. 1230.

the thought trends "today's sayings"[2]. The first part of Liang Qichao's *An Introduction to the Learning of the Qing Dynasty* is a summary of thought trends, and although it regarded learning thoughts equivalent to the history of thought trends, namely thought trends as the flow and change of thoughts, a point of view which is different from our understanding of social thought trends, his analysis is very enlightening for the issue of generality in the research of thought trends. This book will be talked about in the later relevant parts of the book. In the period of the May Fourth Movement, the term "thought trends" was more widely used by people. During the more than 30 years of Reform and Opening-up, the term "thought trends" has been a widely used vocabulary by thinkers and theoretical circles. The *China Great Encyclopedia - Philosophy Volume* has also added an entry for the term "social thought trends".

Seen from the existing materials, the social thought trends is not regarded as an important academic concept with exact connotation in the foreign academic circles. "Social thought trends" is not recorded in some famous academic reference books[3], but phrases expressing the meaning of the social thought trends are embodied in some literature. The editor of *A Dictionary of Marxist Thought* Tom Bottomore said in the introduction: "A hundred years after Marx's death the ideas which he launched upon the world have come to constitute one of the most lively and influential currents of modern thought."[4] Here, we can see that "社会思潮" can be translated as "currents of modern thought"[5]. The entry "社会思潮" in the *China Great Encyclopedia* is translated as "trends of modern thought". Both of these translation methods' translations proceed from the Chinese "社会思潮", and it should be said that both are the understanding of the Chinese people, and this book has not yet proposed a very typical English noun corresponding to "social thought trends". Seen from a glance over some English materials, foreign scholars have quite many discussions on concrete thought trends, therefore, the Chinese and English names of concrete thought trends should correspond quite perfectly. In English, the meanings of "current" and "trend" are similar, but the former places more emphasis

---

2 Liang Qichao: Introduction to the Qing Dynasty, recorded in: *Liang Qichao's Four Historical Works*, Yuelu Press, 1985, p. 20.

3 "Social Thought Trends" is not included in *Encyclopedia Britannica, Encyclopedia Americana, International Encyclopedia of the Social Science* and *Encyclopedia of Philosophy*.

4 *A Dictionary of Marxist Thought*, Oxford, UK; Cambridge, Mass.: Blackwell Publishers Ltd., 1991, p. xii.

5 *Oxford Advanced Learner's English-Chinese Dictionary*, The Commercial Press, Oxford University Press, 2007, pp. 49, 187.

on the direction, tide and flow and the latter places more emphasis on the tendency. Some people translate "社会思潮" as "ideological trend"[6]. These three kinds of translation methods respectively emphasize the attributes of fluidity, tendency and ideology of social thought trends, and the attributes of thought trends are reflected, but on the whole, the translation of "currents of social thought" is more accurate. The term "current" has the two meanings of flow and tendency, which is more appropriate to express the tide of thought.

I.1.2. Various interpretations of "social thought trends"

Classical Marxist writers and revolutionary leaders tend to understand the thought trends often from the perspective of their revolutionariness and advancedness. Marx and Engels called the new doctrine they have established as "new idea" and "new theory".

Marx wrote in a letter to Ruge in 1843: "It is precisely this advantage of the new direction that now we do not dogmatically anticipate the world, but only want to find the new world through criticism of the old one."[7] When Lenin had just stepped on his revolutionary journey, he called on the Russian youth and students to pay close attention to and study Marxism. In the Historical Destiny of the Doctrine of Marx, he divided the development of Marxism into three periods: from the Revolution of 1848 to the Revolution of the Paris Commune of 1871; from the failure of the Paris Commune in 1871 to the Russian revolution of 1904; from the Russian revolution of 1905 to the present. He believed: "At the beginning of the first period Marx's doctrine by no means dominated. It was only one of the very numerous groups or trends of socialism." Until the second period, through development and constant struggle, "Marx's doctrine gained a complete victory and began to spread." Lenin believed that through the Bolshevik Party's and Russian Marxists' insistence on unrelenting propaganda, "Marxism became a mass social trend in Russia". The above discussion shows that Lenin regarded Marxism as a progressive thought trend, and paid special attention to the wide dissemination of this thought of trend in Russia, and also demonstrated the general development process of a progressive thought trend. In his youth, Mao Zedong showed a very strong spirit of criticism towards the prevalent erroneous thought trends and pointed out that Russell's paci-

---

6   Compiled by Dictionary Group of the English Department of Beijing Foreign Studies University: *Chinese-English Dictionary* (Revised Edition), Foreign Language Teaching and Research Press, 1997, pp. 1168.
7   *Complete Works of Karl Marx and Frederick Engels*, Vol. 47, People's Publishing House, 2004, pp. 64.

fism "makes sense in theory, but in fact impossible"[8], while he showed an enormous interest in learning the new Marxist thought trend and organized the New People's Study Society to conduct active study and discussion. Lu Xun also understood the new thought trends from the perspective of advancement. In April 1919, he published the paper "Trend of New Thoughts in the Academy" in *Weekly Review*, and argued that "a trend of new ideas is expanding day by day, generally by scholars who pretend to conserve the national essence, let's rally to attack them"[9].

From modern times to contemporary times, Chinese scholars have attached great importance to the research of various thought trends, and many scholars themselves actively promote the emergence and development of certain thought trends. In the course of studying and promoting the development of the thought trends, these scholars tend to explain the thought trends from different angles. Liang Qichao once described the process of the formation of thoughts as follows: "in a country where the culture is developing, due to changes in the environment and changes in people's social psychology, the thoughts of its citizens always tend to develop toward the same direction, thus the era demonstrates itself as being turbulent as the tide."[10] Although this thesis does not fully clarify the connotations of thought trends, it correctly points to some important conditions that lead to the emergence of a thought trend, such as psychological conditions and environmental factors, etc, thus reveals the motility of thought trends to a certain extent.

Hu Shi also discussed the "new thought trends", but his understanding of the new thought trends is completely different from the understanding of the classical Marxist writers. The new thought trends that he claimed are not revolutionary. He argued: "The basic significance of new thought trends is only a new attitude. This new attitude can be called 'critical attitude.'"[11] There are two kinds of critical attitude: "On the one hand, the discussion of social, political, religious and literary issues. On the other hand, the introduction of Western new thoughts, new science, new literature, and new faith. The former is 'issue of research', the latter is "import of theories".

8   *Letter to Cai Hesen from Mao Zedong* (December 1920), recorded in: *The Letters of Mao Zedong*, People's Publishing House, 1983, pp. 5.

9   Zhong Limeng and Yang Fenglin, editors in chief: *Compilation of the History of Chinese Modern Philosophy*, 1st part of Volume I, Department of Philosophy of Liaoning University, 1981, (Informal publication), pp. 29.

10   Liang Qichao, *Introduction to the Qing Dynasty*, recorded in: *Four Kinds of Liang Qichao's Historical Works*, Yuelu Press, ed, 1985, pp. 20.

11   Hu Shi, *The Meaning of the New Trend of Thought*, recorded in: *The Information of Hu Shi's Philosophical Thought* (Book One), East China Normal University Press, 1981, pp. 126.

These two are the means of the new thought trends."[12] The only purpose of the new thought is to "recreate civilization".[13] In the period of the May Fourth Movement, at an era when the future and destiny of the country and the nation seemed desperate, there were still many people who paid more attention to the issue of social function of the social thought trends. At that time, the first issue of the magazine *New Wave* published 4 articles focusing on the research of "new thought trends" as the following: "My View on New Thought Trends", "Origin and Background of New Thought Trends", "Social Transformation and New Thought Trends", "Ethical Basis of Modern Thought Trends"[14]. Yu Gong's "My Views on New Thought Trends" authored by argued: "new thought trends are to solve difficulties, to adapt with purposeful concept to the intentional effect of the nature"[15]. Bai Li's "Origin and Background of New Thought Trends" put forward that the thought circles have to carry out the impulse of facts, otherwise they cannot bring the subjective initiative into play and cannot bring the role of the spirit into play. Therefore, "the spirit of our cultural movement is to sing before the second cock-crowing at dawn with the message that a new time has come. The essential spirit of this cultural movement is to champion the social thought trends when it is weak. Thus, the priority for the commenter of new thought trends is to reflect himself."[16] The remaining two articles respectively put forward the issues like the mutual causality of new thought trends and social transformation, the ethical foundation of new modern thoughts. In early 1940s, in his article "Critique of Modern Thought Trends", He Lin has argued that thought trends can dominate the behavior of the people of all countries.[17] The above conclusions reveal some characteristics of the thought trends, especially the function of the "new thought trends" in the criticism of old traditions and construction of new ideas. The proposition of these conclusions is based on the comparison of old and new ideas. Although what they call the "new thought trends" may not necessarily be an advanced trend of revolutionary thought trends, the ideas they hold relative to decadent social forces still have positive and progressive meanings. Therefore, these trends of thought trends will have the function of criticism and construction. China's early Marxists' attention to the trend of social thought gives us more important inspiration.

---

12   Ibid., pp. 127.
13   Ibid, p. 133.
14   Zhong Limeng and Yang Fenglin, editors in chief: *Compilation of the History of Chinese Modern Philosophy,* 1st part of 1st volume, Department of Philosophy of Liaoning University, 1991, (Informal publication), pp. 3-52.
15   Ibid., p. 37.
16   Ibid., p. 45f.
17   Ibid., p. 153.

For example, "Fierce Battle between New and Old Thought Trends", "Material Changes and Moral Changes" and other articles written by Li Dazhao before and after the May Fourth Movement applied the materialist view of history to analyze the significance of the conflict between the new and old thought trends, and material originality of changes in social thoughts. Li Dazhao wrote: "the evolution of the universe, the whole battle of new and the old thought trends, each invading and implying each other"[18], and added: "Material must be eager to open new, morality will follow the new."[19] Qu Qiubai pointed out in his article "A New Declaration of the 'New Youth" the importance of studying social thought trends: "The social sciences are meant to determine social consciousness and excite social sentiments so that the actual movement of oppressed and exploited commons will be carried out. The flow of general thoughts and emotions needs to be correctly analyzed and reflected."[20]

The other articles such as "China's Present World of Thoughts" by Deng Zhongxia, "Marx' Doctrine and China" by Li Da[21] also provide important inspirations for us. In the confrontation of various thought trends, the controversy between Marxists and "main forces" of other thought trends also provides us beneficial enlightenment for understanding many natures of thought trends. The fierce confrontation of thoughts unfolded by issues such as "Issues and Isms", "Anarchism", "Nature of Chinese Society" objectively presented the correct way to study the movement laws, basic characteristics, social and historical origins and interactions of thought trends, as well as to identify and distinguish a variety of concrete thought trends by applying the material view of history.

In their research of social thought trends, contemporary scholars have all carried out definitions for social thought trends, but each has different emphases. In some recent research works which study concrete social thought trends, in the introduction, the authors often refer to the explanation of "thought trends" made by Liang Qichao in "An Introduction to the Learning in the Late Qing Dynasty".[22] But the analysis of "thought trends"

---

18 *Compilation of the History of Chinese Modern Philosophy*, co-edited by Zhong Limeng and Yang Fenglin, 1st part of 1st volume, published by Department of philosophy of Liaoning University, 1981, (Informal publication), Volume I, p. 4.

19 *Selected Works of Li Dazhao*, Vol. 3, People's Publishing House, 1999, p 111.

20 *Selected Works of Qu Qiubai,* People's Publishing House, 1985, p. 5.

21 *Compilation of the History of Chinese Modern Philosophy*, co-edited by Zhong Limeng and Yang Fenglin, 1st part of 1st volume, published by Department of philosophy of Liaoning University, 1981, (Informal publication), Volume I, pp. 12, 170.

22 For example: Gao Ruiquan, *Social Thought Trends in Modern China*, published by East China Normal University Press, 1996; Guo Hanmin: *The Study of Social Thought Trends in the Late Qing Dynasty*, China Social Sciences Press, 2003, etc.

made by Liang Qichao highlights an emphasis on "environmental" factors, which is also an emphasis on the era characteristics of thought trends, and fails to give a rigorous definition of social thought trends and the summary of their connotation is not very comprehensive. This book illustrates the contemporary scholars' understanding of the connotations of social thought trends with the following typical examples.

"The Preliminary Study of Social Thought Trends"[23] gives such a definition of social thought trends: "social thought trends, by their very nature, are the reflection of material economic relations and social conditions in which people exist by forms such as viewpoints of thoughts and sentiments in the consciousness of a part of people in the society. As people's economic status or the social conditions of survival are roughly the same or similar, the resulting viewpoints of thoughts and sentiments naturally merge into a general social thought trend." This definition emphasizes two important aspects of social thought trends, one is the viewpoint of thought, and the other is the social psychology. In contemporary scholars' definition of social thought trends these two aspects can be generally seen. For example, in the introduction part of the book Thought Trends in the Contemporary World it is argued that thought trends are the "unity of theoretical forms and psychological form"[24]. It should be said that thought trends are guided by a certain theory of thoughts, is combined with the social psychology of men and expresses sentiments and aspirations of a certain group of people, which is a very important understanding. In *A Probe Into Social Thought Trends, Ordinary Consciousness and Their Mutual Relationship*,[25] the social thought trends are defined as "thought tides that spring up with a spontaneous surge, have distinct ups and downs, strong political colors and with certain group features", excluding the schools of thought and theory (such as literature thought trends, historiography thought trends, philosophical thought trends, etc.) and thought movements (such as the Enlightenment thought movement in the European modern times, the "Emancipation of Mind" movement in China, etc.) in the true sense of social thought trends. This article has clearly proposed the issue that the academic thought trends and social thought trends are not the same, which is quite enlightening. Most of the works or articles that study the social thought trends include the academic thought trends in the social thought trends. This means that no

23   Wang Ruisheng, A Preliminary Study of Social Thought Trends, *Dongyue Tribune*, 1981(3).
24   Editorial board of the book, *Thought Trends in the Contemporary World*, CPC Central Party School Press, 2000.
25   Zhang Shujun, Primary Exploration on Social Thought Trends, Ordinary Consciousness and Their Mutual Relations, *Philosophical Studies*, 1992(3).

matter how pure the academic thought trends are, they cannot do without sociality, thought trends which merely have an academic character are not thought trends in the true sense, but "schools of thought" that give different interpretations to the same academic issue and will not widely spread in the society, but can only exist in different academic fields.

The entry "social thought trends" in *China Great Encyclopedia - Philosophy Volume* explains social thought trends as follows: "social thought trends are sometimes manifested as a thought guided by a certain theoretical form and sometimes as the social psychology of men in a specific environment, and it is a synthesized manifestation form of social consciousness." This definition is a quite typical way to give a definition to social psychology and social consciousness synthesized under social thought trend. When the studies in the mid and late 1990s carried out definitions of social thought trends, they generally followed the definition given in the above Encyclopedia. For example, the article "Birth, Development and Wane of Social Thought Trends"[26] argued: "The social thought trend is a kind of phenomenon of popular social consciousness, and it is a kind of movement form of social consciousness with the era as the background, the society as the place and groups as the subject. Every social thought trend is a common trend of thoughts and a psychological tendency of people in a certain social environment."

The positive exploration of the connotation and definition of thought trends made by the above studies are an important thought basis for us to continue studying this issue in depth. These studies investigate thought trends from different angles, and the definition they make of the thought trends briefly summarize the specific nature of thought trends and emphasize different levels, so it is still hard to see the theorists' key issues in the thought trends from the similar definitions on the surface and the views on important issues such as the position of the thought trends in the structure of social consciousness.

I.1.3. Scientific explanation of "social thought trends"

Social thought trends are the form of activity of the social consciousness taking a certain social psychology as the foundation of consciousness, taking the relevant social ideology as theoretical core, and which has a certain influence within a certain historical stage.

---

26 Liu Jianjun, Birth, Development and Wane of Social Thought Trends, *Academic Monthly*, 1995(2).

Social thought trends are the reflection of social existence, and are determined by the social existence. This is the meaning of "taking the relevant social ideology as theoretical core". "Historical materialism explains all historical events and ideas, all politics, philosophy and religion from the material, economic conditions of life of the historical period in question."[27] The social consciousness in different historical periods is different, and the basic reason lies in the different social existences, especially the different production modes in different historical periods. Therefore, social consciousness is of social and historical nature, and the social thought trends, as a specific form of social consciousness, are also of social and historical nature, it is certain that a social thought trend can only exist and have influence in a certain corresponding historical period. Social psychology does not need more links and can directly reflect the social existence. A certain consciousness form of social psychology necessarily exists in the social thought trends which reflect the change of social existence, otherwise the social thought trends cannot be produced and cannot spread. The core of the thought system and theoretical system of social thought trends is the social ideology, which is the most important spiritual factor when the interaction of the thought trends and the social existence occurs.

The social thought trends are a manifestation form of social consciousness. We can say that it is the social consciousness, but it has also particularity different from the social psychology and other consciousness forms, and these particularities are "has a certain influence within a certain historical stage", "taking a certain social psychology as foundation of consciousness", "taking the relevant social ideology as theoretical core" and "form of activity". This shows that the social thought trends not only manifest the general of the social consciousness, but also has its own particularities. Of course, the definition of the social thought trends does not reflect the whole face of the thought trends, nor can it reveal the whole connotation of the thought trends, it is only a description of the main characteristics of the thought trends, so it cannot substitute the concrete analysis of thought trends. The comprehensive grasp of the social thought trends stems from the concrete investigation of the social thought trends, the understanding of their connotation, and is concluded from the concrete social thought trends in the scientific cognition.

The social thought trends have the unity of the opposites of quality and quantity. In terms of a concrete thought trend, the quantity of the social thought trends refers to the scale of the occurrence, the degree of the influence and the speed of the development of the social thought trends. Without

---

27   *Selected Works of Marx and Engels*, Vol. 3, People's Publishing House, 1995, p. 209.

a certain quantity, it is not sufficient to constitute a thought trend; if the quantity of a social thought trend reaches a certain scale, can it become the guiding thought of the society. Under such circumstances that the quantity of a social thought trend is not enough to make the social trend of thought "qualitatively change", this change only affects the display of the basic functions of the social thought trend, and does not affect other natures of the thought trend.

Seen from the epistemological angle, the social thought trends are the spiritual product and cognition process of the mankind, which is both the result of the cognitive activity and the dynamic process of cognitive activity. The social psychology component of the social thought trend is the cognitive activity of the daily psychological level of the cognitive subject and is the attitude, opinion, mood and viewpoint, etc. that the people form based on the direct or indirect observation and feeling of all kinds of natural and social and cultural phenomena in the everyday society, and has the nature of intuition, flow and change, group, region and even nation; the component of thought and theory of the social thought trend is the cognitive activity of the theoretical level of the cognitive subject, and the advanced cognition form, and provides the theoretical basis and value orientation for the spiritual world of the mankind.

I.1.4. Differentiation and analysis of "social thought trends"

Although social thought trends are a quite new research topic, the use of this term is already very common, and there is the issue that a certain concept is not clear in terms of use, so it is necessary to clarify the association and difference of the social thought trends and various consciousness forms.

Social thought trends and social popularity.

Social popularity is rather used in the sociological sense, and does not refer to a concrete consciousness form, therefore it is necessary to distinguish it from a social thought trends. A new manifestation of some kinds of habits and customs of life, necessities of life in a definite stage and definite period spread in a quite large range of group of people, followed suit by a considerable number of members of the society, thus become popular in the society, namely social popularity. A fashionable hair style, fashion style, fashionable mode of entertainment and content of entertainment and so on are all common contents of social popularity. It is obvious that the social popularity mainly expresses the change of a mode of life, and is the manifestation of the change of people's basic necessities of life. It the partial content refracted by the psychological aspect of the social thought trend from one side. The social thought trend is a thought trend which is popular in the society, but not the content of social popularity, not the content of sociology, but is more a thought concept concerning politics.

Difference between the social thought trends and social trends.

A "social trend" manifests the concrete manifestation of the objective laws of social development in a specific historical period. Social thought trends are the conceptual reappearance of social trends. Social trends are of material nature and rank in the first place, while the social thought trends rank in the spiritual, second place; the former determines the latter, and the latter reflects the former. The latter can conform to the trend, but also move against the trend. If the socialist trend of the era is a "great scourge", then the thought trend of "returning to old ways" (a Confucian tradition) moves against the trend, while the Marxist doctrine, as a thought trend, conforms to the major tendency of the historical development, and moves alongside with the trend.

Social thought trends and gossip, rumor.

Gossip refers to groundless remarks, and rather refers to talking behind the back, slander or provocative words, while rumor refers to deliberately fabricated gossip that has no factual ground. Gossips and rumors rather occur in periods when the society is in turmoil, the politics owe clarity and the dissemination channels cannot normally guide the public opinion. Gossips and rumors mainly embody certain socio-psychological phenomena of people, are often their subjective imagination of things and events and have the characteristics of emerging and perishing on its own and embody expectations in people's psychology, but are not the result of scientific cognition. In wrong thought trends gossips and rumors are often at work, which are the composite elements of thought trends, and play a role in the formation and development of them.

Social thought trends and public social opinion.

Social opinion and thought trends often occur synchronically, and the vivacious era for the social opinion is often also the era when the thought trends are vivacious. Generally speaking, social opinion refers to sentiments, views, opinions, attitudes, etc. with a tendency and expressed by a certain number of people, groups or organizations on the social existence and development. On the whole, social opinion belongs to the consciousness level of social psychology, and manifests the common tendency of some kind of psychology, and as Marx and Engels pointed out, the social opinion is "the general state of the public opinion"[28].

---

28   *Complete Works of Marx and Engels*, Vol. 12, People's Publishing House, 1962, p. 658.

Although the social thought trends have two aspects of social psychology and theoretical consciousness, its symbol and core is the specific theoretical consciousness with a quite strong ideologicalness, which is the point where thought trends differ from the social opinion. The thought trends often derive "nutrition" from public opinion and promote the development of different opinions, so as to try to solve the more important problems of social trends. It is precisely because a kind of thought trends often mingles with public opinions that focus on different issues that it is feasible for the public, especially the ideology departments to regard the thought trends and public opinion for a long term as "social public sentiment". This is reasonable from the perspective of general knowledge and concrete work, but this does not mean that the thought trends are the social public opinion.

Social thought trends and social "hot spots".

"Hot spots" refers to those issues that arouse widespread concern in the society. The common point between the social trend of thought and the "hot spots" is that the public's attention is relatively high. "Hot spots" can rapidly turn hot or cold, with a wide range of issues involved on different levels. Social thought trends constantly emerge grow and fall or extinguish. "Hot spots" are mostly specific issues that a group of people are highly concerned about, but thought trends are thoughts and theories with a quite deep level. The relationship between the thought trends and "hot spots" is close. The thought trends are embodied in "hot spots", and hot spots are borrowed by thought trends. "Hot spot" is one of the "platforms" where a thought trend is expressed, and the thought trends will often draw support from the "hot spots" in the social life, especially express themselves in some outstanding contradictions and problems in the society, and obtain an opportunity to spread widely.

The existing outstanding contradictions that are originally in the social life may also form a "hot spot" or make a "hot spot" heat up again due to the encounter between the latent thought trends and accidental incidents that break out. The thought trends make use of the "hot spot" issues to become widely popular, which is one of the laws of the generation of thought trends. The thought trends are often the "soul" of the hot spots, and a hot spot that is "left and right" for the thought are often more influential. Sometimes a social thought trend also embodies the social "hot spots" characteristics of the coming and going in a hurry, so these short-lasting thought trends can also be called "hot spots".

Social thought trends and thoughts.

The subject of thought trends has often the nature of groupness, and the subject of thoughts is often an individual. In a certain period of time, a certain thought may develop into a thought trend, infect and influence more people. At this moment, the thought moves from the individual to the group, and becomes a social phenomenon, thus the thought of a few people becomes the thought shared by a mass of people, a person or a few number of people become the representative of the thought trend, and its thought becomes the theoretical core of the thought trend. The thought trends cannot be divorced from the independent existence of thoughts, but a thought may be divorced from the independent existence of thought trends, but not all thoughts can become the thought core of a thought trends.

Social thought trends and thought movements.

A thought movement usually refers to a very vivacious state in the field of social consciousness in a particular historical period, and often refers to a certain historical event with wide influence, such as the Enlightenment movement and the Renaissance movement, or the May Fourth movement, and social thought trends are often the spiritual bearers in the thought movements. A period when such a thought movement occurs is often a period when a social thought trend is vivacious and appears concentrated and if the thought trend is not concentrated, then there is no thought movement, the social thought trends will still exist, but the quantity is not as much as in the period of thought movement, and the influence is not as strong as in the period of thought movement.

Social thought trends and dynamics of thoughts and theories.

"Dynamics of thoughts and theories" is the situation of change of thoughts and theoretical viewpoints and it is an important issue our propaganda of thoughts and theoretical work pays attention to. Dynamics of thoughts and theories describes the ideological part in the social consciousness form and pays attention to the situation of change in the thought superstructure, is a description of the changes in the system of thoughts in the social thought trend, and rather pays attention to their sociality and politicality. In a certain sense, the dynamics of thoughts and theories can be equated with thought trends, because the external manifestations of thought trends are often embodied in all kinds of remarks, but the dynamics of thoughts and theories is bound to be a set of remarks. What needs to be noticed is that parts of the remarks cannot be simply regarded as a thought trend. Whether or not part of the remarks is a trend of thought should be concretely analyzed. The relationship between remarks and thought trend should be determined according to the basic elements in the connotation of thought trends.

Social thought trends and academic schools.

The social thought trends and academic schools have a lot in common, and the relationship between the two is also relatively close. They all have themes of long-term concern, have one or more generations of representatives (from the founder to his disciples, to the synthesizer, sometimes inherited and carried forward by several generations), basic standpoints and viewpoints and a course of rise and fall. Academic schools make great contributions to the emergence of the social thought trends. Social thought trends often take the viewpoints of academic schools as the core, but the influence of the academic schools is not as wide as that of the social thought trends. After the core theoretical system of the academic school becomes the core of a thought trend, it becomes a spiritual resource that is shared universally and has sociality. The participants in the activities of academic schools are often "insiders" participating in the research of this discipline, its members are relatively "pure", and its thoughts and theories are more systematic, and the recipients and disseminators of thought trends are quite "miscellaneous", from professionals to people from all walks of life in the society. The viewpoints of thoughts between them are same in the main aspects, and within its parts a variety of small schools that are mutually complementary and divergent are still included. School activities are academic and rational, which is also a form of social consciousness, belonging to either ideology or non-ideology, often quite distanced from social psychology, while the thought trends are a specific social consciousness phenomenon, stretching across the two levels of social psychology and ideology, combining some schools of thought with social psychology, have a quite strong ideologicalness, and rational, sensual, irrational, psychological and emotional factors are intertwined. Although the popularity of a thought trend is related with the activities of an academic school, there are still more profound social reasons. So sometimes the doctrine as the core of the thought trend does not follow its decline, but continues to spread. For example, pragmatism, as an academic school, has already been on the decline, but pragmatism as a trend of thought is still in vogue even today.

Social thought trends and "academic thought trends".

Seen from the concrete study of "academic thought trends", there are two cases in referring to "academic thought trends": first, we conduct an abstraction of the part of the thought and theoretical system of a social thought trend and conduct a discussion of a social thought trend from a "purely academic" angle, and basically not involve the sociality and politicality of the thought trend. Positioning the social thought trends from this angle, they can be equated with schools of thought. But, in fact, there are no pure, abstracted "academic thought trends". There is also another case that when the non-ideological part in the social consciousness form, such as languages and words, are studied, different views emerge, which are purely different academic viewpoints and it cannot be considered a thought trend. Thus, it can be seen that "academic thought trends" are the position of a concrete thought trend put forward because of the different research angles of the social thought trends and emphasizes the characteristics of the aspects of the systemic and academic nature of a thought trend, i.e. ignores the political and social nature of the thought trend and it is not the comprehensive summary of a thought trend. Sometimes, some academic thought trends do not even mainly take "social thought trends" as their research object, have their own object of discipline, research results and research process, and it can also manifest as a social thought trends. To put it in this way, there will be a distinction between "thought trends of politics", "political thought trends" and "economic thought trends", all of which emphasize the different aspects of thought trends and are caused by the different division criteria of social ideological trends, are all social thought trends, but cannot be juxtaposed with social thought trends as a separate kind of thought trend. Among the many categories related to social thought trends, ideology is the most important category. This chapter will be dedicated to exploring the relationship between social thought trends and ideology.

I.2. Social thought trend as a dynamic synthesis of social psychology and ideology

The position of social thought trends in the structure of social consciousness is a key aspect of the social consciousness features of social thought trends.

I.2.1. Social thought trends and the structure of social consciousness

In academic circles, there are two different conclusions or judgments in the research about the position of social thought trends in the structure of social consciousness: one argues that thought trends has both social psychology and social consciousness, which can be summed up as the "theory of synthesis"; another argues that social thought trends is the intermediary of social psychology and social consciousness, which can be called as the "theory of intermediary". Both theories provide important enlightenment for the further research of social thought trends, but there are also some areas that need to be deepened and the "theory of intermediary" seems to need more explanation. This book argues that a social thought trend is a dynamic synthesis of social psychology and ideology. In the following, we will make an objective description and evaluation of the "theory of synthesis" and "theory of intermediary".

The theory of synthesis argues that the social thought trend is the synthesis of social psychology and ideology. In the article "A Preliminary Study of Social Thought Trends", the author wrote: "social thought trends, by their very nature, are the reflection of material economic relations and social conditions in which people exist by forms such as viewpoints of thoughts and sentiments in the consciousness of a part of people in the society. As people's economic status or the social conditions of survival are roughly the same or similar, the resulting viewpoints of thoughts and sentiments naturally merge into a general social thought trend."[29] The entry "social thought trends" in *China Great Encyclopedia - Philosophy Volume* gives the following definition: "social thought trends are sometimes manifested as a thought guided by a certain theoretical form and sometimes as the social psychology of men in a specific environment, and it is a synthesized manifestation form of social consciousness." The two explanations emphasize two key aspects of social thought trends—social psychology and thoughts/ ideas and are quite typical for the "theory of synthesis" about the relations between social thought trends and social consciousness.

The "theory of synthesis" reveals the position of social thought trends in the structure of social consciousness, showing that the manifestation of the consciousness form within the social thought trend is complex and is a synthesis composed of various consciousness forms that are blended with each other. Some theorists who hold this theory fail to notice to differentiate between theoretical consciousness and social psychology in the consciousness structure of the social thought trend in terms of what is primary and what is secondary, to give sufficient explanation on the dialectical relation of the two, nor to emphasize that theoretical consciousness is the symbol and core of a thought trend. Any social thought trend has the two elements of social psychology and theoretical consciousness. However, it is not always manifested as theoretical consciousness, not always as social psychology, but throughout as a dynamic combination of social psychology and social consciousness. I basically agree with the "theory of synthesis" but thinks that its content needs to be supplemented.

---

29   Wang Ruisheng, A Preliminary Study on Social Thought Trends, *Dongyue Tribune*, 1981(3).

The "theory of intermediary" argues that a social thought trend is the intermediary of social psychology and ideology. In the article "A Brief Study on Social Thought Trends", the author Liu Defu makes a quite clear discussion of the intermediary position of the social thought trends in the structure of social consciousness: "In the multi-level, complex structure of social consciousness, we can find three basic levels in the order from lower to higher: social psychology, social thought trend and social ideology. There is both is difference and association among them, while the social thought trend is at a status of linking the lower and upper level."[30] This formulation places social thought trends between social psychology and social ideology, making it the middle layer in the structure of social consciousness, which is the typical explanation of the theory of intermediary. It should be said that the "theory of intermediary" sees the difficulty of locating social thought trends as a specific form of ideology in the dual structure of "social psychology" and "consciousness form" and wants to break the dichotomy of sensuality and rationality by taking the dialectical materialist epistemology as the basis of argument and turn the dichotomy of social psychology and ideology into a trichotomy, so as to give the social thought trend a middle link position. The middle link of social consciousness should be relatively stable, but the social thought trends rise and fall, sometimes flourish and sometimes wither and if they are the middle link of social consciousness, this link will also sometimes be and sometimes not. How to solve this problem? Some scholars have suggested such a solution: in case of absence or lack of thought trends, "ordinary consciousness" is the intermediary of social psychology and social ideology. Ordinary consciousness is a general form of the intermediary of social consciousness, while the social thought trend is a specific form of intermediary of the ordinary consciousness, which manifest itself under specific circumstances, such as crisis and revolutionary times.[31]

If we deem ordinary consciousness and its specific manifestation—the social thought trend—as the intermediary of social psychology and ideology, there is still room for discussion and since ordinary consciousness is usually used as a concept of the same level of social psychology, it is like we are treating 1 as the intermediary of 1 and 2, if we treat social psychology as the intermediary of social psychology and ideology. This shows that ordinary consciousness and social psychology are equivalent and quite complicated, and it is necessary to start with the concepts of social psychology and ordinary consciousness and the classical Marxist writers'

---

30   Liu Defu, A Brief Study of 'Social Thought Trends', *Qiushi*, 1988(1).
31   Zhang Shujun: Primary Exploration on Social Thought Trends, Ordinary Consciousness and Their Mutual Relations, *Philosophical Studies*, 1992(3).

understanding of social psychology and ordinary consciousness in order to get a more thorough explanation of the issue.

The scientific analysis of various social psychological phenomena dates back to Marx and Engels. The concept of "social psychology" never appears in the works of the Marx and Engels, but there are some usages that are equivalent to social psychology. This concept and usage elucidate the basic connotations of social psychology, i.e. the primary form of spontaneous and intuitive social consciousness in men's life and production. For example, Marx and Engels once used "the phantoms formed in the human brain", "consciousness of existing practice"[32] and "pure" theoretical consciousness to make a distinction in referring to social psychology, and still used phrases such as "mental feeling", "practical feeling" (will, desire and so on)[33], and used such comments as "limited sense of art"[34], "habits of small shopkeeper"[35], "manners and customs"[36], "feeling of reverence for money"[37] and so on.

Plekhanov revealed the basic connotations of social psychology more deeply, and clearly distinguished "social psychology" from the thought system in the social consciousness. Some of his thoughts can enable us to further grasp the structure of social consciousness, providing important enlightenment for us to study the internal relations between social psychology, ordinary consciousness and social thought trend. In his articles such as "The Development of the Monist View of History", "Materialist Conception of History", "Materialism" and "Fundamental Problems of Marxism", he revealed the relation of social psychology and thought system during his deep analysis on the issue of social structure. He emphasized the significance of the study of social thought trends: "To understand the history of scientific thought or the history of art in any particular country, it is not enough to be acquainted with its economics. One must know how to proceed from economics to social psychology, without a careful study and grasp of which a materialist explanation of the history of ideologies is impossible."[38]

32 *Selected Works of Karl Marx and Frederick Engels,* Vol. 1, People's Publishing House, 1995, pp. 73, 82.
33 *Complete Works of Karl Marx and Frederick Engels,* Vol. 42, People's Publishing House, 1979, p. 12.
34 *Selected Works of Karl Marx and Frederick Engels,* Vol. 1, People's Publishing House, 1995, p. 110.
35 Ibid., p. 113.
36 Ibid., p. 117.
37 *Complete Works of Karl Marx and Frederick Engels,* Vol. 2, People's Publishing House, 1957, p. 411.
38 *Plekhanov's Selected works in Philosophy,* Vol. 2, SDX Joint Publishing Company, 1961, p. 272.

Plekhanov used "all habits, manners, feelings, views, aspirations and ideals"[39], "intentions and interests of a class"[40], "popular sentiment and interest"[41], etc. to express social psychology. He argued that man's psychology is "determined in part by the economic conditions obtaining, and in part by the entire socio-political system which has arisen on that foundation."[42] As for the relationship between social psychology and thought system, he argues that social psychology as kind of ordinary consciousness generated spontaneously during men's daily practical life activities and intercourse (*Verkehr*) and originally not remolded by thinkers' processing is, compared with strict and complete thought systems, still the primary form that belongs to social consciousness and becomes as such the indispensable and important link between the thought system, socio-economic relations and political relations. He said, "all ideologies have one common root – the psychology of the epoch in question"[43], and "the 'social man' has a certain psychology and the characteristics of this psychology determines all ideologies they build"[44] and "the psychology of society is always expedient in relation to its economy, always corresponds to it, is always determined by it."[45]

The core of Plekhanov's thoughts about social structure—the "five factors formula"[46]—clearly shows that social psychology exists as the intermediary and bridge between the thought system and social being. He attached great attention to this element of social psychology. He ranked social psychology as the fourth of the five basic factors, deeming it as the indispensable middle link between socio-economic relations, political system and social thought system. He pointed out that, socio-economic relations and the political system determine various thought systems through social psychology, while various thought systems reflect men's economic

---

39 *Plekhanov's Selected works in Philosophy,* Vol. 1, SDX Joint Publishing Company, 1962, p. 715.
40 *Plekhanov's Selected works in Philosophy,* Vol. 2, SDX Joint Publishing Company, 1961, p. 189.
41 Ibid., pp. 273.
42 *Plekhanov's Selected works in Philosophy,* Vol. 3, SDX Joint Publishing Company, 1962, p. 195.
43 Ibid, p. 196.
44 Ibid, p. 734.
45 *Plekhanov's Selected works in Philosophy,* Vol. 1, SDX Joint Publishing Company, 1962, p. 715.
46 "1. The state of the productive forces. 2. The economic relations these forces condition. 3. The socio-political system that has developed on the given economic 'basis'. 4. The mentality of social man, which is determined in part directly by the economic conditions obtaining, and in part by the entire socio-political system that has arisen on that foundation. 5. The various ideologies that reflect the properties of that mentality." (*Plekhanov's Selected Works in Philosophy*, Vol. 3, SDX Joint Publishing Company, 1962, p. 195.).

relations and political relations through social psychology. In his opinion, social psychology is of great significance to the formation and development of various social thought systems. Therefore, in order to understand various thought systems, as well as the development history of human thoughts, it is necessary to deeply research social psychology based on the investigation of socio-economic and political relations. For this purpose, he proposed the important view to establish "the science of social psychology" with social psychology as its object.

Plekhanov argued that he did not deny that various thought systems have their root cause in the social being when he said that thought systems have their root cause in social psychology. His emphasis on the factor of social psychology stems from the formal incorporation of social psychology into the composition of the consciousness, and highlights the richness of social consciousness forms. When he discussed aesthetic taste during his analysis on issues of aesthetics, he said, "even in primitive hunting societies, technology and economy do not always directly determine the aesthetic taste. What often happens there is a considerable amount of and various intermediate 'factors'. But, even an indirect causal relation is still a causal relation. If in one case, A directly generates C, while in another case, A generates C through B that it had previously generated, is it therefore possible to say C does not come from A?"[47] This above can also explain the true relationship among social existence, social psychology and thought system. Social being is always the root source for social psychology and thought system. Generally speaking, social psychology refers to men's feelings, sentiments, motives, habits and so on, which is developed directly under the impact of the concrete conditions in social being and men's activities, and not represented by a generalized thought system. Compared to various systematized forms of social consciousness, social psychology locates at a lower level of social consciousness. Based on such a definition of social psychology, we are able to further explore its relationship with ordinary consciousness.

Marx and Engels once mentioned some concepts similar to ordinary consciousness, but they were all at the socio-psychological level, such as daily consciousness, common consciousness, ordinary daily consciousness and ordinary people's daily consciousness.[48] Marx pointed out: "The exchange between capital and labour at first presents itself to people's sensation in the same guise as the buying and selling of all other commodities. The buyer gives a certain sum of money, the seller an article of a nature different from

---

47   Plekhanov: *Unaddressed Letters: Art and Social Life,* People's Literature Publishing House, 1962, pp. 148-149.
48   *Complete Works of Karl Marx and Frederick Engels,* Vol.3, 23, 20, 22, pp. 145, 592, 17, 384.

money." "this same labour is, on the other hand, the universal value-creating element, and thus possesses a property by which it differs from all other commodities, is beyond the cognizance of the ordinary consciousness."[49] In other words, both "people's sensation" and "ordinary consciousness" can only cognize the imagination of labor force commodity, but cannot cognize the specific nature of its connotations. Evidently, Marx used these above two concepts at the same level, while the concept of "people's sensation" just belongs to the level of social psychology. Marx once also pointed out: "… The various forms of capital, as evolved in this book, thus approach step by step the form which they assume on the surface of society, in the action of different capitals upon one another, in competition, and in the ordinary consciousness of the agents of production themselves."[50] It is not hard to find that "ordinary consciousness of the agents of production" mentioned by Marx is actually the unadorned daily empirical consciousness, namely what we call social psychology. It seems impossible to find any clear evidence that Marx and Engels deemed ordinary consciousness as the intermediary of social consciousness. The Soviet textbook of philosophy *The Fundamentals of Marxist-Leninist Philosophy* also treated social psychology equivalent with ordinary consciousness, arguing that, "social psychology is a kind of ordinary consciousness formed directly during people's daily practical activities and intercourse (*Verkehr*) by other people"[51] and "one part of man's ordinary consciousness."[52] But domestic scholars seem to pay less attention to the "ordinary consciousness".

Another ground for the "theory of intermediary" is that "social thought trends have more rational factors and less psychological factors than social psychology, but less rational factors and more psychological factors than thought systems", thus social thought trends shall be at the intermediary of both social psychology and thought system.[53] However, the fact is that social thought trends in the reality are rich of both rational and perceptual factors, and its theoretical and perceptual components are no less than those in the pure thought system and social psychology. In fact, social psychology and thought system are a relatively stable structure of social consciousness. No matter how intensive and extensive the practice field of human

49   *Complete Works of Karl Marx and Frederick Engels*, Vol.23, People's Publishing House, 1972, pp. 591, 592.
50   *Complete Works of Karl Marx and Frederick Engels* Vol. 25, People's Publishing House, 1974, p. 30.
51   Konstantinov, editor in chief: *Textbook of Philosophy Principles of Marxism-Leninism*, People's Publishing House, 1985, p. 376.
52   Ibid., p. 375.
53   Xiao Jinquan, On Social Thought Trends as a Concept of Social Consciousness, *Modern Philosophy*, 1997(1).

activities is social consciousness is always manifests as two aspects: social psychology and thought system, while at times there are no social thought trends. In some periods, the social thought trends may be very vivacious, while some periods they may be very silent. In the period of Renaissance, the Spring and Autumn period and the Warring States period, the May Fourth Movement, and the early period of China's Reform and Opening-up, the social thought trends were very vivacious. During the long period of feudal patriarchal autocracy, either the Middle Ages of Europe or the feudal society of China, social thought trends were not vivacious. Social psychology and thought systems exist throughout in any era. This point also shows that it does not conform to the practice to consider social thought trends as the intermediary of social psychology and thought system.

If the intermediary of social consciousness is divided into two forms: general intermediary and specific intermediary, then, when the social thought trends become as specific intermediary, does the ordinary consciousness as a general intermediary still exist? What does it then relate to social thought trends? Can we say that in case when social thought trends exist, there will be no ordinary consciousness? Obviously, in order to incorporate social thought trends into the structure of social consciousness, it is still not quite scientific to fill up the gap with ordinary consciousness, when there is no social thought trend or when the social trend of thought is not active.

There are often certain gradients or different links inside a thing. These links are often interim links inside the thing, but are not regarded as intermediaries of the thing. For example, perceptual cognition includes different levels and links such as sensation, perception and imagination, and we do not deem perception as the intermediary of sensation and imagination; rational cognition also includes different levels and links such as concept, judgment and reasoning, but we do not deem judgment as the intermediary of concept and reasoning. Likewise, there is no need to look for an intermediary and bridge for perceptual and rational cognition, because they naturally and intrinsically have an association. The same is true between social psychology and ideology. As different levels of social consciousness, they also intrinsically have interim mechanisms and links, so we do not have to artificially arrange an intermediary to bridge them. Therefore, it is lack of sufficient evidence to locate ordinary consciousness as the intermediary of social psychology and ideology, and based on that, it can be inferred: it is difficult to establish that the social thought trends are the specific manifestation of ordinary consciousness, are the specific intermediary form in the structure of social consciousness.

To sum up, the theory of synthesis that treats social thought trends as a synthesis of social psychology and social consciousness and the theory of medium that deems social thought trends as a separate level in the structure of social consciousness both provide important reference for our further study on the consciousness features of this trend. The social trend of thought keeps shifting and is not an independent level within the structure of social consciousness. It is a specific consciousness phenomenon which acts at two levels of social psychology and ideology and includes elements of social psychology and ideology.

It is an important reference for us to further study the consciousness characteristics of social thought trends by considering the social thought trends as a theory of synthesis of synthesizing social psychology and social consciousness and as a theory of intermediary of placing social thought trends in the social consciousness structure as an independent level. The social thought trends undergo frequent changes and are not a separate level in the social consciousness structure, but active at two levels of social psychology and ideology and have the specific consciousness phenomena of the components of both social psychology and ideology.

I.2.2. Composite elements of social thought trends

The composite elements of social thought trends are perceptual social psychology and rational ideology. A social thought trend involves both social psychology and ideology. If it has not a social psychological base, a social thought trend cannot popularize and spread, nor be able to exert a wide social influence and can hardly become a thought trend. Meanwhile, a social thought trend is also is a great spiritual strength which pushes ahead conceptual changes and social movements. Such strength often stems from the theoretical charm of the ideological part in the thought trend, even more in advanced thought trends. As Liang Qichao said, "not all thoughts can form a trend, but only those with great value and suitable to the requirements of the era can achieve this."[54] Lenin pointed out that advanced thought trends have a major function of social transformation: "But there can be no doubt about the vigorous growth of the "new spirit" and the "European currents" that are stirring in China, especially since the Russo-Japanese war; and consequently, the old-style Chinese revolts will inevitably develop into a conscious democratic movement."[55] It can be inferred that, without a powerful theoretical system of ideology, as theoretical kernel, the transformative

---

54   Liang Qichao, Introduction to the Qing Dynasty, recorded in: *Four Kinds of Liang Qichao's Historical Works,* Yuelu Press, 1985, p. 20.
55   *Collected Works of Lenin,* Vol. 15, Progress Publishers, 1973, p. 184.

effect of the social thought trend on the society will necessarily be limited. The wide the range of the social psychology of a social thought trend and the universal and typical it is, the easier for it to bring about the relevant theoretical system; the ripe the thought of a social thought trend and the complete its theory is, the more can it consciously and actively become a socio-political movement; the close the relations a social thought trend maintains with the real life and real movement and the more it has a certain theoretical form, the extensive and profound its social influence will be.

The social psychology and ideology components of the social thought trend permeate mutually and feature consistency, commonality and compatibility in essence. Any social psychology and ideology which are in essence inconsistent, uncommon and incompatible cannot be combined into a trend of thought. The element of social psychology is not a purely psychological content but the psychological constituent which has certain theoretical colors. Since it is inevitably led and "nurtured" by corresponding ideology, this makes it more concentrated and summarized. If the ideological factor does not participate, the social psychology will never be sublimated and will not be able to form a social thought trend. The vigorous tide of thoughts in the period of the May Fourth Movement shocked the country and the world. The reason why its potential was so violent was that the social psychology of the Chinese nation has been strongly stimulated by the oppression, slavery and insult of the imperialist powers and the Beiyang Warlords' policy of selling out the country. Without such stimuli, it will not cause the psychological changes of the general public, and there will be no social trend of thought. If there was no such stimulation, any change in the psychology of the broad masses would not be evoked and a social thought trend would not emerge. However, the reason why such thought trend formed cannot be separated from the amassment of progressive rational power. If Marxism-Leninism was not introduced, if the thought of communism was not disseminated, if the thought of science and democracy was not advocated, the thought trend in this period would not be so lively. Therefore, the social psychology as one content of social thought trend and consciousness cannot only boiled down to sensations, sentiments or popular likings, but also includes viewpoints and thoughts, and these viewpoints and thoughts are seized by the masses and become the stimulant of their belief and activities. Meanwhile, the ideology as another element of social thought trend is inspired and restricted by social psychology, which brings it closer to the wishes of the masses of people and the demands of the era. Therefore, social thought trend is not the simple addition of social psychology and ideology, but an organic whole forged by mutual influence, mutual restriction and mutual permeation of the two sides.

Ideology and social psychology have a discordance to a certain degree. Such discordance is prominently displayed in advanced social thought trends. In the mass psychology vis-à-vis advanced ideology there is a process from non-adaptation to adaptation. In Cheng Xiao's book "Rural Consciousness of Late Qing", he believes that the mass consciousness with regards to the then advanced thought social trend had a promoting, propelling role but they were also in a discordant state. On the one hand, the mass consciousness restricts and influences advanced thinkers' reasoning on historical themes. The mood, demands and voices of millions of masses in the bottom of society are the nutrients and evidences for them to construct various doctrines. On the other hand, because of the historical limitation of the then advanced social thought trend and the rural consciousness and the huge gap between the two, the advanced thought trends in the late Qing Dynasty failed to grasp the masses. The tremendous strength of customs of the rural society restricted the advanced thought trends in a narrow social range. Cheng Xiao has argued that the fundamental cause why that advanced socio-political thought trends in the Hundred Days' Reform, Xinhai Revolution and other movements could not be extended to the people was that the agricultural natural economic system and the socio-psychological environment which lasted since the Middle Ages had not changed substantially. This analysis shows that under different socio-historical conditions, the mass psychology restricts not only the birth of social thought trends but also that they play their role. How to make the masses accept the advanced thoughts and consciousness depends, on the one hand, on the changes of socio-economic and political conditions, and more importantly on the groups of thinkers to give play to their subjective initiative, publicize their thinking and educate the masses.

Social consciousness has diverse forms. The systematicness and profoundness of various consciousness forms vary, so does the theoretical level of the social thought trends reflecting these consciousness forms. The systematization and systemization level of the theoretical core of some social thought trends is high, while the theoretical contents of some social thought trends are relatively simple, with lower degree of systematization and embody more perceptual colors and psychological components. Generally speaking, the mark for the degree of maturity of a social thought trend is the degree of maturity of its theoretical core. The vitality of a social thought trend is, to a certain extent, related to whether its theoretical core is scientific and mature. The development process of a social thought trend is the gradual maturation process of its theoretical core. Those trends with scientific, mature and advanced theoretical core will finally defeat those trends with outdated and reactionary theoretical core.

When we emphasize that the social thought trends are an organic unity of social consciousness and ideology, what we emphasize more is the ideological factor of the thought trend, the core role of ideology in the composition of the trend's consciousness. This is because that a thought system that systematically and consciously reflects the modes of production is able to systematically embody features of the era and the trend of society, while the social psychology of the community can only vaguely sense the changes of the society. Both, affirming the syntheticity of the composition of the social thought trend's consciousness and affirming the core role of the theory in it—this is dialectical unity, the combination of the doctrine that everything has two aspects and the doctrine that everything has a key aspect. When we actually use the concept of social thought trend, we often take its theoretical core as mark and pay less attention to the psychological components So that there are such concepts as political thought trends, economic thought trends, cultural thought trends as well as philosophical thought trends and ethic thought trends. In the process of social development, specific strong cliques will appear. Intellectuals often play the role as "spokespersons" in expressing the interest claims of these strong cliques with social thought trends. In such case, the consistency of social psychology and thought consciousness in the social thought trend will be more obvious.

I.2.3. Social thought trend is the form of activity of social consciousness

"When we consider and reflect upon nature at large or the human history or man's intellectual activity, at first, we see the picture of an endless entanglement of relations and reactions, permutations and combinations, in which nothing remains what, where, and as it was, but everything moves, changes, comes into being, and passes away"[56]. The whole social consciousness that is composed of various factors unceasingly changes and develops. This stems from the unceasing changes of the social existence and the unceasing progression of the human society. Social consciousness is not the addition of static social psychology and social consciousness forms, but is manifested as the actual form of activity that these factors activate and form, within an era as the surrounding environment. As social psychology is manifested as dynamic social sentiments, social moods, social tastes, social manners, social customs, will, faith and so on, social consciousness forms are manifested as a series of relatively stable but unceasingly and dynamically developing concept-category system expressed by language

---

56 *Selected Works of Karl Marx and Frederick Engels,* Vol. 3, People's Publishing House, 1995, p. 359.

and writing. The dynamic development of social psychology and social consciousness forms is often manifested through the form of social thought trends.

"Change characteristics" is one of the key features of social thought trend, and characteristics such as era characteristics, politicality and groupness. Marx said, "The same men who establish their social relations in conformity with the material productivity, produce also principles, ideas, and categories, in conformity with their social relations. Thus, the ideas, these categories, are as little eternal as the relations they express. They are historical and transitory products. There is a continual movement of growth in productive forces, of destruction in social relations, of formation in ideas; the only immutable thing is the abstraction of movement—mors immortalis [eternal death]."[57]

If the thought trend is not the form of activity of social consciousness, it is difficult for it to generate huge social effect. The activity characteristics of social thought trend can be explained at least from the following respects.

Firstly, the determination of social consciousness by social material activity is active. Social material activity always determines the origin and development of social consciousness. This is the most fundamental drive of the activity of the thought trends. When discussing the origin of social consciousness, Marx and Engels pointed out that "the production of ideas, of conceptions, of consciousness, is at first directly interwoven with the material activity and the material intercourse of men, the language of real life. Conceiving, thinking, the mental intercourse of men, appear at this stage as the direct efflux of their material behavior. The same applies to mental production as expressed in the language of politics, laws, morality, religion, metaphysics, etc., of a people."[58] This means that whatever primary or advanced form of social consciousness, its generation and development is determined by the direct material activity of men and the social thought as a major consciousness phenomenon exactly embodies this activity characteristics of social consciousness and that its activity characteristics is inevitably determined by human material activity. There are no social thought trends existing without the character of activity.

Secondly, the changes of the production relations are the direct cause of the activity of social thought trends. The vivacious times of social thought trends occur often in times of crisis, transformation and shift. Productive forces as the finally decisive force of social development will,

---

57   *Selected Works of Karl Marx and Frederick Engels,* Vol. 1, People's Publishing House, 1995, p. 142.
58   Ibid., p. 72.

once developed into a certain stage, bring about the adjustment of production relations, engendering social transformations, shifts and crisis. This
turmoil of society is mainly reflected in the field of social consciousness,
and the social thought trend which mutually combines specific social psychology and ideology is also enlivened. Although the thought trend has
ups and downs, sometimes cosmetic changes, its movement direction seem
impossible to grasp, it changes, generally speaking, along with the change
of the production relations. The adjustment of production relations, social
transformation and crisis are often manifested as interest adjustment among
various social classes and strata. "The 'idea' always disgraced itself insofar
as it differed from the 'interest'."[59] And in a society where classes exist, the
class is still an important form of subject of thought trend. Lenin believed
that the "class [which] stands at the hub of one epoch or another, determines
its main content, the main direction of its development, the main characteristics of the historical situation in that epoch."[60] At a time when the mankind
still not stepped out of class society, in order to finally become the core of
the epoch, various interest groups will for the sake of their interests inevitably impel their theoretical system to combine with the social psychology,
promote the development and strengthening of the thought trend, attempt to
take the place of the predominating traditional ideology. If at this time, the
people also generally hope for social transformation and look forward to a
theory that is able to guide the social transformation and solve the crisis to
emerge, the specific socio-psychological atmosphere will combine with a
theoretical form that requires changing current situation, develop into various thought trends and a vivacious status will emerge at the level of social
consciousness. It can be said that the crises, transformations and shifts are
the horn to awaken and enliven social thought trends. In periods when production relations are stable, social thought trends with relatively big and
long-lasting impact often do not exist. In periods of socialist reform, one
main cause for the flourishing of trends of thought is that the changes of
production relations are relatively vivacious in this period. In periods when
production relations are relatively stable, sometimes there are also fluctua-
tions in the ideal and theoretical field and one or another social thought
trend also exists. For example, the widely criticized ultra-"left" thought
trend which was in vogue some time before the contemporary China's
Reform and Opening-up was a bias which occurred in the understanding
within the predominant ideological field, caused by a certain deviation
which occurred in the understanding of the social life by the ruling party.

59   *Collected Works of Karl Marx and Frederick Engels,* Vol. 1, People's Publishing
House, 2009, p. 286.
60   *Collected Works of Lenin,* Vol. 21, Progress Publishers, 1917, p. 143.

Of course, it can also be not ruled out that some people within our party become subjects of some social thought trends and turn into opponents of the predominant ideology. This is manifested in eras when multiple social thought trends emerge simultaneously at all times and in all countries. In the new period of Reform and Opening-up, this phenomenon has occurred frequently. When the leading ideology fully displays its leading and ushering function, the probability that a thought trend emerges is relatively small and, fundamentally speaking, in this period, the changes in productive forces and production relations are not big and will also not give a fundamental impetus to the thought trend. Under such circumstances, it will be more difficult for a social thought trend to exist.

Thirdly, as components of the conscious composition of social thought trends, social psychology and ideology are in an unceasing interaction. Lenin pointed out: "Without 'human emotions', there has never been, is not now, nor ever will be any human search for truth"[61] As the soil of the activity of consciousness, social psychology is the primary "nutrition" and material of the generation and strengthening of a specific theoretical consciousness. In turn, sublimated and theorized social consciousness actively influences the social psychology, making it to renew and deposit new psychological components with theoretical colors. In different historical stages, the degree of the role that the two play in the development process of the thought trend is different, or is manifested more as psychological component, or is manifested more as ideological component, or both sides play a relatively significant role. In the interaction between them, the social thought trend develops and strengthens. When a concrete thought trend grows to a certain stage, due to the changes of the social life practice, it will face or become a big trend, main trend, or even mainstream ideology, or it will perish because it no longer tallies with the historical trend. The process of becoming mainstream ideology is one in which social psychology and theoretical form show a positive and benign interaction. If the development tendency of a social thought trend is in a gradual decline, it means that social psychology and the corresponding theoretical form are in a gradual detachment, and the accordance between the two is greatly reduced. Of course, the fading and vanishing of a thought trend does not mean that all the elements composing it completely vanish and just as the vanishing of the waves does not mean the vanishing of the seawater, some of factors will still persist at some corners and, awaiting a proper soil to "stage a comeback" again. Many thought trends of the period of Reform and Opening-up do not appear out of thin air, but have deep theoretical and historical sources.

61   *Complete Works of Lenin,* Vol. 25, People's Publishing House, 1988, p. 117.

Fourthly, the dissemination is an important mode for the social thought trends to exist and social thought trends are always in an unceasing dissemination. To be generated and developed through dissemination and further to amass strength through dissemination, the thought trend has to return to the social life practice and form a social movement. In the dissemination process, the thought trend has to constantly create "fame and power" and unify thoughts by the way of evaluation, propaganda and education. The dissemination process is both the process of amassing energy and of dissipating energy. The prominently a social thought trend embodies the theme of the era, the vivacious its manifestation, the powerful the expansion ability and the profound the social impact. If the theme of the era as the basis for the thought trend to exist has already been solved or surpassed, its theoretical core may go towards logical end and can no longer be able to solve the actual problem, which means that the said thought trend's energy has been exhausted and the dissemination is about to cease, namely that it faces the destiny of quitting the big stage of social thought trends.

I.3. Social thought trend and ideology

Clarifying the relationship between social thought trend and ideology is an important aspect of deepening the understanding of social thought trends. In the actual social life, social thought trend and ideology are related inclusively. In order to further explain the social consciousness attribute of a thought trend, we need to discuss their association and difference after drawing a distinction and an abstraction. The following analysis is based on abstraction and detachment of the two basic elements of a social thought trend: social psychology and ideology. Such an analysis is mainly intended to demonstrate the difference and association between a concrete social trend of thought and another ideology which not its own. The relationship between a social thought trend and ideology is an important issue in the consciousness attribute of a social thought trend and also an important issue in the theoretical research and ideological work. Ideology is both the core part of a social thought trend and differs from the manifestation of the social thought trend in the level of social consciousness. The rise and fall of a social thought trend is the signal of the unceasing adjustment of ideology and superstructure. In the actual social life, the process in which we sense social thought trend is often the process of sensing ideology. Without the participation of ideology, it is impossible to grasp the essence of the social thought trend.

I.3.1. Association of social thought trend with ideology

The association of the social thought trend with ideology is manifested in two aspects: first, the theoretical core of the social thought trend is ideology. Second, investigating the relationship of social thought trend and ideology respectively from the angle of independent systems, ideology has to draw support from the dissemination of the social thought trend. Ideology is the system of thoughts in which people consciously and directly reflect the economic base and the political superstructure and belongs to the category of thought superstructure. In the class society, ideology has class nature, intensely embodying the fundamental interests and demands certain social classes. The display of the active role of ideology depends on its understanding, recognition and grasp by a broad number of the members of the society and only by this way can ideology control the behavior of the members of the society and realize its real purpose. To achieve this point, ideology must appear in form of social thought trends through propaganda, agitation or other modes of dissemination. As comprehensive and dynamic manifestation form of social consciousness, social thought trend is able to make ideology as the core of the trend to be disseminated and popularized among the masses, make it blend into the social knowledge, sentiments, motives and attitudes of the masses, thus guide the social behavior of broad masses. Otherwise, ideology as the embodiment of the will, viewpoint and policy of certain classes will hardly merge with the social psychology of the masses and also hardly transform into their practical activities.

Social thought trend is both the objectification process of social spiritual activities and the result of the objectification, both social spiritual resource and social spiritual strength. The convolution of the social thought trend forms, within a social scope, the "gravitational field" of a specific psychological atmosphere and thought and the members of the society within the field, making the individual psychological status of the members of society partially converge, laying the foundation for ideology to turn into the cognition criterion and value benchmark of the members of society. Through psychological exchange and collision among social members, they gradually tend to be basically in line with each other in respect of their emotions, wills and beliefs, which is the basic social foundation for ideology to be put into practice and react on the social practice.

For different social consciousness forms in the same kind of social ideology, the strength, velocity and scale of influencing social psychology are different, which is directly reflected in the different strengths of integration of different social thought trends towards the social being. The political and

legal thoughts in ideology are the most important factors that affect the social psychology, and will often quickly and extensively exert their influence
on the social psychology, which is not unrelated with the clear-cut politicality and actualness of the social politico-legal thought trends. The impact
of morals, art, religion, philosophy, etc. on social psychology is, relatively speaking, an imperceptible impact, while being continuous and stable,
which is closely related to the profoundness nature and historicalness of
morals, art, religion and philosophy. For any ideology, the size of its impact, the length of its impact time and strength of impact force with respect
to social being are to a certain extent related to the breadth and depth of corresponding social thought trends' development. Associated with the above
issue, the relationship of social thought trend with superstructure also needs
to be clarified. There is not too much disagreement in academic circles' cognition of superstructure, including political superstructure and thought superstructure, while there has been disagreement as to whether in the thought
superstructure the ruling class ideology is included, whether under socialist
system wrong and reactionary ideologies are included, and whether language and science & technology, etc. are ideologies.[62] Marx said: "Upon
the different forms of property, upon the social conditions of existence,
rises an entire superstructure of distinct and peculiarly formed sentiments,
illusions, modes of thought, and views of life"[63] In other words, the general
status of the economic base determines the general status of the superstructure. Different ownership forms and production relations correspond to different superstructures. If in a specific historical period of a society multiple
production relations exist, and multiple ideologies are necessarily reflected
in the thought superstructure, differentiated into mainstream ideology and
non-mainstream ideology. In the new period of Reform and Opening-up,
with the common development of multiple ownership forms, the field of
thought superstructure necessarily reflects the situation that multiple ownership forms coexist. It should be said that the composition of the thought
superstructure during this period is complicated, being a situation in which
the mainstream ideology and non-mainstream ideology coexist. Ideology
is thought superstructure, thus the relationship of social thought trend and
superstructure is intensively embodied as the relationship of ideology and
superstructure. Economic base determines superstructure and necessarily
determines ideology; ideology reacts on political superstructure and necessarily affects economic base, and social thought trends also follow that path

---

62   In the mid-1950s and early 1980s, the journal *Philosophical Research* has published
numerous articles discussing this issue.
63   *Selected Works of Karl Marx and Frederick Engels*, Vol. 1, People's Publishing House,
1995, p. 611.

to be associated with superstructure and economic base. Different thought trends correspond to different ideologies in the superstructure, some are consistent with the mainstream ideology and some are in accordance with the non-mainstream ideology. Within a period of time, the general status of social thought trends presents a complicated situation, which is exactly related to the complicated situation within the thought superstructure.

Treating social thought trends and ideology separately as independent systems, the following several aspect issues need to be grasped. The relationship of social thought trends and ruling class ideology is an important aspect in the issue of the relationship of social thought trends and ideology. Summarizing the social thought trends as the vivacious relationship of social thought trends in different periods and ruling class ideology, there are probably two circumstances: opposition and accordance. Opposition or accordance, either one is dynamic. With the unceasing adjustment of the productive forces and production relations and the unceasing change of the economic base, the ruling class ideology is also restricted by socio-historical conditions and among them, some thought trends are opposite to the ruling class ideology, while some thought trends defend ruling class ideology or are even the direct representation form of ruling class ideology, but are, in content and representation form, not completely consistent with ruling class ideology, also properly raise questions to the ruling class ideology, basically defend the wills and demands of the ruling class.

In the discussion of the relation between social thought trend and ideology, the relation between social thought trend and mainstream ideology and non-mainstream ideology shall also be studied. Dividing ideology into mainstream and non-mainstream is more often aimed at contemporary China, especially at the ideological status of contemporary China since the middle and late period of 1990s, where the mainstream ideology refers particularly to contemporary Chinese Marxism. Though the studies of our party's literature and scholars don't give a clear definition of "mainstream ideology", this does not preclude the use of such a phrase when elucidating the issue. Any thought and theoretical system that has wide social impact and produces tremendous impact on social practice in a certain historical stage can be called mainstream ideology, the thought and theoretical system of the ruling class may not necessarily be mainstream ideology, and social thought trend "in opposition" may not necessarily be mainstream ideology. In two cases can an ideology be called mainstream ideology: One, if the thought and conceptual system of the ruling class is recognized by society, then it is mainstream ideology, such as the theoretical system of socialism with Chinese characteristics; two, thoughts and concepts of the non-ruling class, yet widely accepted by society, as in the period of the new democratic revolution, Marxism together with the unceasing success of the Chinese revolution and the growth and expansion of the Communist Party of China was accepted by the vast masses and all sectors of society, as on the eve of the founding of New China, become the mainstream ideology of the then society to a certain extent. Seen from a historical perspective, all the mainstream ideologies within a certain period are not scientific and progressive. The ideology outside of mainstream ideology is non-mainstream ideology, their divide into primary and secondary is relative, and the one that conforms to the historical trend will eventually become the mainstream ideology. The relations between social thought trends, mainstream ideology and non-mainstream ideology have a different manifestation in different historical periods. Since the social thought trend is a system, there are diverse concrete thoughts with different directions in it, thus, as a matter of fact, the relation between social thought trend and mainstream ideology and non-mainstream ideology refers to the relation between a concrete thought trend and mainstream ideology and non-mainstream ideology. Generally speaking, the relations between a social thought trend and mainstream ideology manifests itself in three cases: equivalence, similarity and opposition. Equivalence means that the thought system upheld by some social thought trends has the largest social impact and lasts for a long time in a specific period; though it is not the ideology of the ruling class, it is the mainstream of the ideology field, and in such a case the ideology of the ruling class turns to a tributary; similarity means that in a specific historical period, a social thought trend is in major demands close to the ideology of the ruling class that seizes the ruling position, and differs in individual aspects; what opposition refers to is that a social thought trend is the "opponent" of the ideology that seizes the dominant position; the "opponent" may be the ideology of the ruling class, or may be other social ideologies. It should be noted that the mainstream ideology that seizes the ruling position could also be manifested in diverse thought trends of different forms and dissimilar content. In contemporary China, there are: socialist thought trend, socialist reform thought trend, Marxist thought trend, etc., which embody the main content of the mainstream ideology in contemporary China, and are each one of its concrete manifestation forms.

Many concrete thought trends within the system of the social thought trends are under the same circumstances, some may have big impact, be mainstream thought trend, even become mainstream ideology, some may be a tributary and non-mainstream ideology, or all the thought trends are non-mainstream ideology. In the new period of Reform and Opening-up, the relations between social thought trends and mainstream ideology are an important aspect to examine contemporary social thought trends. Although during this period, a part of thought trends in the family of social thought trends have big social impact, they, together with other thought trends with quite weak impact, belong to non-mainstream ideology in the society. Such an objective situation of thoughts determines the relations between various thought trends and mainstream ideology, as well as the relations among each other. Clarifying the relations between social thought trends and mainstream ideology and non-mainstream ideology is of positive significance for us to grasp the basic situation of contemporary China's ideology and basic pattern of social thought trends.

I.3.2. Differences between social thought trends and ideology

There is a close and complex association between social thought trend and ideology. Seen from the perspective of social consciousness, social thought trend and ideology belong to the phenomenon of social consciousness, but they two are not equal. It is not correct to completely separate social thought trends from ideology or completely equate social thought trends with ideology. Judging from their constituent elements, as a kind of thought movement and thought trend, social thought trends sweep along the social psychology much, and are the organic unity of social psychology and thought system. Compared with social thought trends, ideology does not have socio-psychological factors, but is only a systematic and complete theoretical system and belongs to the level of the thought system in the social consciousness. Social thought trends and pure ideology—political and legal thoughts, philosophy, religion, morality, literature and art, etc.—also differ in the required degree and mode of reflecting the economic base and superstructure, that is, to a certain extent, social thought trends are, in terms of manifesting ideologicalness, not as strong as pure ideology.

Seen from their development direction, any social thought trend must always seek to perfect its own theoretical system, and strive to become the guiding theory of some economic base and political force. Therefore, any social thought trend basically follows a development path from low to high, from bottom to top. In terms of ideology, no matter which ideology of what society, the force that supports it always tries hard to spread and disseminate it to the society, seeks to expand its scope of influence and socio-psychological basis, to infuse its own political and legal thoughts, moral ideas, etc. into people's behavioral motives, inner convictions, aesthetic taste and other social psychologies.

Seen from their social status and mutual effect, social thought trends often do not have the function of controlling and guiding the entire social activities and the operation of the state apparatus, instead it objectively influences the ideological sphere in two aspects: positively and negatively. The negative influence is that it will exert some impact and threat to mainstream ideology, impair and erode its authoritative status and guidance function, even shake its status of the core idea as superstructure; the positive influence is that it will provide abundant thought materials for the development of mainstream ideology and make the mainstream ideology constantly supplemented and perfected. Mainstream ideology has a certain influence and status in the society, even a guiding and controlling status in the society, determining that it bears the role of supporting the regime, integrating the society, bring together people's souls and regulating life in the society, and to fulfill such functions, it is not enough to rely solely on some material forces and organization methods. An important way is to convert it into social thoughts through various channels so as to be understood and grasped by the most number of members, and influence their behavior. At this point, social thought trends act as the intermediary for the social ideology to transform into social psychology. Meanwhile, due to the positive and negative effect and influence of social thought trends on ideology, the ruling classes in any society, for the sake of maintaining their ideology and notions, often conduct an analysis and differentiation of social thought trends, absorb the beneficial and positive factors in the social thought trends, remove the factors unfavorable to them, and interferes in those social thought trends that threaten their status by various methods and means, even declare them illegal and directly ban them.

Seen from their relations with social existence, social thought trends positively reflect the reality, and transcend the "social existence" based on reality. Social thought trends may surpass or may lag behind the real social existence, but it is always based on the real social existence. There is a considerable synchronicity between social thought trends and social existence. However, in terms of synchronicity, ideology is inferior to social thought trends. Due to the relative stability of ideology, between an ideology and the corresponding social existence, asynchronicity is more prominent. Even if its social existence has disappeared, an ideology, as a spiritual and cultural achievement of mankind, can still amass.

CHAPTER TWO

Basic Characteristics of Political Thought Trends

This chapter will mainly discuss characteristics, structure, classification, subject, functions, etc of political thought trends. These factors are the basic issues of the theoretical aspect of political thought trends and display their basic nature.

II.1. Characteristics of political thought trends

"Every form of society, every form of ideology, has its own particular contradiction and particular essence."[1] The aim of investigating the characteristics of political thought trends is to reveal their particularity distinguishing them from other social consciousness. Our academy has conducted profound studies on the characteristics of political thought trends and have made many generalizations. Among these achievements, there are some investigations on the characteristics of a particular thought trend and some on the general characteristics of thought trends and different research achievements have different generalizations of the characteristics of the same thought trend. Each of these generalizations makes sense and makes in-depth analysis of the basic characteristics of political thought trends. However, these achievements have not generalized the common basic characteristics of political thought trends to a certain extent and need to be further deepened.[2]

---

1   *Selected Works of Mao Zedong,* Vol. 1, People Publishing House, 1991, p. 39.
2   *Six Major Thought Trends in the Research of Contemporary Foreign Marxist Theories* (Liao Huihe, National Defense University Press, 1992) argues that the thought trends have the qualities of openness, extensiveness and guidance. Openness means that each kind of thought trends is an open problem domain, which can be widely embedded and covered in social and human sciences, even each scientific domain of natural sciences, but not arbitrarily for any discipline. Extensiveness means that a thought trend does not often have the specific academic research tradition, and there is no clear definition of the concept system,

The basic characteristics of political thought trends can be analyzed from two aspects. One, from the angle of thought trend itself, having the qualities of politicality, groupness, and the nature of theory, practice, movement, etc., and these characteristics follow general laws of social consciousness; two, from the relations between thought trends and social existence, having the era characteristics, sociality, nationality and territoriality, internationality, etc.

II.1.1. Political nature of political thought trends

Political thought trends have a clear value orientation, embodying apparent or hidden nature of political tendency. Lenin pointed out: "There is no middle course (for mankind has not created a "third" ideology, and, moreover, in a society torn by class antagonisms there can never be a non-class or a supra-class ideology)."[3] Qu Qiubai elucidated the class factors in the struggle of thoughts: "While any era changes from new to old, the arguments of various schools of thought all contain a class background."[4] Political thought trends have an obvious nature of political tendency. There is no political thought trend that has no political characteristics at all. The politicality of different political thought trends is manifested not unitarily and differs in strength too. The "main trends" of political thought trends within a certain period of time are often thoughts with politicality, and are the thoughts worth the most attention within a certain socio-historical period. The politicality of political thought trends stems from social relations of interests. "The 'idea' always makes a fool of itself insofar as it is different from 'interests'"[5]. The most basic reason why a political thought trend can obtain the recognition of a particular class or stratum and yield a wide influence is that it always represents the interests of such class or stratum, and embodies a clear political tendency.

---

and there is also not a complete theoretical framework. A thought trend at the same time or successively has a lot of theories and factions. The quality of guidance means that the thought trend has not been fully theoretical and systematic, and it is often more easily accepted by the public with greater influence and visibility. These three characteristics summarized by the author illustrate some cases of thought trends, give people inspiration, but these three characteristics are still not the essential characteristics of thought trends. If any thought trend is quite single, with fewer issues to be covered, this is the case with the philosophical thought trends; the theoretical core of the influential thought trends is often systematic, not "extensive"; the quality of guidance can seize the people and seize the people just because of the maturity of theoretical core of a thought trend.

3   *Selected Works of Lenin*, Vol. 1, People's Publishing House, 1995, p. 327.
4   *Selected Works of Qu Qiubai*, People's Publishing House, 1985, p. 144.
5   *Collected Works of Karl Marx and Frederick Engels* Vol. 1, People Publishing House, 2009, pp. 286.

From the outset, the Marxist doctrine emerged in the form of an advanced thought trend, became the ideal weapon for the proletariat and the broad masses of working people, in uniting them for the revolutionary struggle passed to them by the efforts of advanced intellectuals, and has become the theoretical cornerstone for the establishment of the system of scientific socialism. Seen from the perspective of content and tendency of political thought trends, it often represents interests and demands of a certain social group. For example, generally speaking, the contemporary Western political thought trends all reflect the political views and political attitude of various social groups to varying degrees. Since sometimes one political thought trend reflects the interests and wishes of more than one social group, it will gain wide social response. From the perspective of practical role of political thought trends, the generation and development of one kind of political thought trends is always beneficial to some social group or class and social stratum objectively. For example, the vigorous development of the socialist thought trend will eventually benefit the fundamental interests of proletariat of the world. The ultra-"left" thought trend interfered and obstructed the healthy development of our cause of socialist modernization construction, and violated the fundamental interests of the broad masses of working people and contradicted the trend of history.

Does any political thought trend without politicality exist? Generally speaking, the overwhelming majority of political thought trends have very apparent politicality, while among the social thoughts family, there are really some thoughts with inconspicuous political characteristics. Their reflection of the social nature and direction are not obvious, and the manifestation of the influence of the social production relations is not full, the social influence is relatively quite weak, and some different research orientations and academic schools in the scientific field and purely academic field (such as the linguistic research mentioned above) belong to this type. There are also some researches that regard some political thought trends with quite obvious politicality as the so-called "pure academic thought trends" without politicality, but this does not mean that the political characteristics of such thought trends do not exist. As a matter of fact, what the researches that claim to be "purely academic" and conduct so-called "keep away from politics" flaunt is another kind of political discourse in a sense. The political characteristics of political thought trends is one of the properties of thoughts, is objective existence, and the basic properties that thoughts as objective things possess cannot be obliterated due to differences in angle of research.

Sometimes, the thought trends of some specific fields are sometimes a kind of synthesized social thoughts with wide influence, and the politicality is often quite obscure, instead of expressing out in straightforward way. Just like the thoughts in literature and art field. They are also products of social idea system and ideological principle, which refract and express the spiritual excitement of some social group in aesthetic and perceptual way, namely components and specific form of political thought trends of a certain historical period, being one of multiple political thought trends, or "reflection" or "presentation" of political thought trends. Although the political nature of literary and art thoughts may not be straightforward, it could publicize its political orientation with specific expression form in a wider range than other political thought trends. The humanistic thought trend in the late 1970s and early 1980s belongs to the philosophical thought trends, and is in fact a purely academic thought trend, but one with very strong politicality. Meanwhile, the potential political orientation of this thought trend is centered on the issue whether there is alienation in socialism and how to treat the errors in the construction of socialism, even the so-called issue of the "legitimacy" of socialism. This thought trend, on the one hand, calls for the humanist view of history and world, emphasizes that Marxism is "human-centered", "man is the starting point of Marxism", conducted translations and comments on the state of research of foreign humanist thoughts, and launched a discussion of the issues of humanity and humanism on an unprecedented scale. On the other hand, it raised enlightenment again and criticized the phenomenon of "alienation" in the socialist society. In early 1980s, this thought trend had become synthesized political thought trends that involves each field of social sciences and has wide influence, and has manifested itself in literature, aesthetics, economics, historiography, ethics, philosophy, sociology and other fields or subjects.

The "Cultural Fever" of 1980s and 1990s in China could be classified as a kind of cultural thoughts. At the phenomenal level, the ideological nature of such thoughts are not strong, while some actual claims of them, do have obvious political tendencies. The national nihilism, attitude or claim of wholesale westernization expressed by "Cultural Fever" rose in the middle of 1980s had a profound impact in ideological and cultural field. For the "Cultural Fever" of 1990s, some people conducted "introspection" or "self-questioning" to the cultural strategies of 1980s and sought to establish a new kind of cultural strategy, they gave up radical social and political criticial discourse words, and adopted a mild discourse, and advocated to "collude" with mass culture, however its political content was still very apparent, and kept a tense relation with the mainstream ideology. During the discussion of "Cultural Fever" in 1990s, some important topics appeared, such as problems in transformation and reconstruction of culture, the humanistic spirit, the Chinese learning, the standardization and localization of social science, and intellectual issues. Part of discussion on these problems were converting "words" positively, adjusting "cultural strategy", emphasizing the independence of culture and academic, to strip the relations between culture and ideology. However, this is not the standpoint of "pure academic" in any case. "Postmodernism" thoughts rose in art and literature field in 1990s, there were some theories claiming themselves as the "means to fight against the ideology of the state".[6]

The oil painting "My Dream" expresses a scene that a young man breaks through a broken red wall and a head portrait symbolizing the falling of Marxism, and he runs forward. The oil painting A Gratified Young Man expresses a scene that tears apart lives bloodily and enjoy the satisfaction. Such two oil paintings won Excellence Award and Silver Award of The First National Oil Painting Exhibition respectively, while the reason was not for skills, but the awakening of "some kind of consciousness" these art works have transmitted.[7]

In recent years, the outstanding "Chinese Confucianism" thought trend is also a kind of cultural thought trend, but it claims that the Confucianism thought trend shall be the dominant idea of the state and society, and being also a thought trend with very strong political nature in essence, it is a distinctly political thought trend. Obviously, "no matter which kind of force or cultural work by which faction, they all serve the political task"[8], "the cultural work of various forces are all connected to the political task closely, and the so-called over-political cultural is not exist"[9]. Mao Zedong said: "There are two criterions for literary and art criticism, one is political criterion, and the other is artistic criterion."[10] One cannot regard one kind of literary and art thoughts as a kind of thought about literature and art itself only. The political orientation of some political thought trends could be judged from the speech situation of the literary and artistic works.

The political characteristic of political thought trends is like "storm-glass", they forecast climatic change of the social and political life, reflecting trends in people's political attitudes, political ideas and political behaviors.

---

6   Qian Haiyuan, *Art Theorists That Influence the Development of Contemporary Chinese Fine Arts*, http://arts.tom.com/Archive/1004/2003/10/17-61761.html.
7   Liu Shulin, *Analysis and Forecast of the Trend of Social Thoughts among the Youth*, zisi. net http://www.zisi.nGt/htrm//ztlw2//whyj/2005-05-11-21410.htm.
8   *Selected Works of Deng Xiaoping,* Vol. 1, People's Publishing House, 1994, p. 22.
9   Ibid., p. 23.
10   *Selected Works of Mao Zedong,* Vol. 3, People's Publishing House, 1991, p. 868.

As some scholars pointed out, through objective and overall analysis and research to political thought trends, to obtain political information, make political prediction, and reveal political development trend, and it is very important for proletarian party who has been in power to consolidate the obtained fruits of victory and lead people to realize the set goals amidst constantly changing international and domestic political environment.[11]

II.1.2. Groups as carriers of political thought trends

Political thought trends have a clear quality of groupness. The characteristics of groupness stems from the basic situation constituted by the subjects of political thought trends. As group consciousness, political thought trends have specific groups as subjects and carriers. Without the recognition of a certain social group, it is impossible for a thought to be converted into a political thought trend, and without such these grouped carriers, political thought trends cannot be developed.

The formation and development of political thought trends have broad social mass basis. Some scholars have conducted in-depth analyses of this. Whether a political thought trend can be spread widely, can be seen besides in the degree to which it is required by the then society, more importantly in whether this political thought trend arouses people's mental and psychological resonance, and whether it can grasp a considerable part of the masses and make them admit, accept, and embrace. Political thought trends cannot be formed if there is no approval, acceptance and dissemination by a social group. Once a political thought trend becomes a thought trend with a certain influence, it will widely spread in the society in form of grouped dissemination and influence. The political thought trends are also a kind of specific group consciousness, macroscopically expressing common wishes and interests/demands of considerable scale of social groups in a synthetized way. These social groups themselves may be single, or maybe very complicated. The reason why a kind of political thought trend can be commonly accepted by so many households, collectives, groups, classes, strata and nationalities, and affect their thoughts and behaviors, lies in the fact that the political thought trends themselves are synthesized and constituted by factors such as thoughts and viewpoints, emotions and wills, desires and demands, and reflect people's thoughts and wishes, as well as interests and demands with their wider universality and bigger sociality.[12]

---

11   Deng Zhuoming, On Types and Characteristics of Social Thought Trends, *Journal of Southwestern China Normal University*, 1995(5).
12   Ibid., p. 3.

For example, one of the reasons why the Marxist thought trend could be widely spread in China, lead the Chinese revolution to victory and become the guiding thought in achieving the unity of our country, lies besides its own advanced nature and distinctive collectivity, also in that it could be widely spread and enjoy a significant impact worldwide. In the early days when Marxism was introduced to China, it was spread among advanced young intellectuals. During May Fourth period, with the deepening of China's crisis, more and more young intellectuals have awakened and kept searching for the proper prescription that could save the nation and people. At this juncture, Marxist thoughts started to acquire greater attention from young intellectuals, who believed that Marxism complied with the historical trend of China's development, and that Chinese revolution could achieve victory under its guidance. Hence, Marxism started to spread widely among these specific groups, the young advanced intellectuals, and was highly valued. Under the guidance of Marxism, this specific group have launched a series of activities, and conducted three debates against non-Marxist trends, in order to further augment the position of Marxism.

In the process of spread, recognition of the working class and the broad masses of peasants were obtained, and wide social mass basis was achieved, forming powerful social trends sweeping the whole China quickly, and the victory of China's revolution was obtained under its guidance. During the spread process of Marxism thoughts, we could realize its characteristic of of group deeply. For thoughts, in its spread process, it shall be accepted by specific groups firstly, and turned into specific group consciousness, and then expand the influence of such thoughts constantly, and become thoughts with wide social bases eventually. The characteristic of group is the base for political thought trends to generate and develop. The thoughts without characteristic of group is as a tree without roots and water without sources, which is hard to stand and exist.

Secondly, political thought trends possess an inherent affinity to group activities, which can affect to a certain extent the development direction of the society. For instance, the socialist thought trend with biggest influence in modern world is widely spread all over the world. It represents the fundamental direction of development of human society, and promotes continuous development of the socialist system in the practice. Since 1990s, the rise of cultural conservatism is a good interpretation for dominant role to group activities. The cultural conservatism is introduced to our country from Japan, Singapore, etc., and accepted by part of groups in the society rapidly. Under the influence of this thought, the traditional culture start to obtain attention, and more and more people turn to traditional culture research, forming national culture fever and classics reading fever in the society. So to speak, the generation of this national culture fever and classics reading fever shall not be unrelated to the rise and spread of cultural conservatism. Exactly under the influence of such thoughts, people begin to feel that the development of present society is not only simple economic development, political development, nor only simple acceptance of output from the western culture, absorption of advanced experiences from the western. During modernization process, we should pay equal attention to develop our traditional culture, and the power and spirit of traditional culture must be implemented in every stage of state and society development all the time. Just because such thoughts bring renewal to people's idea, which transforming people's actions subtly, and it is not hard to understand the cultural phenomenon of traditional culture fever and classics reading fever. While just because this dominant role to activities of subject of political thought trends, people are able to renew their inherent ideas constantly, and bring forth new ideas to practical activities of subject continuously, and promote constant progress and development of the society.

In the end, the operation of political thought trends possesses liquidity among groups. Political thought trends are the reflection to social life in dynamic form, it always spreads from one group to another group during its development process, and constantly searches for new soil suitable for its breeding and reproduction, and brings influence to people of different times and ranges in flow and diffusion mode. At the beginning when Marxism thoughts was spread in China, the major audience were young intellectuals, whose scope was limited, and the level of the accepted subject was relatively narrow. With unceasing development and deepening of its spread in China, Marxism was gradually accepted by the vast working class and peasants masses, and obtained new breeding ground for spread and development. The subject accepting the Marxist thought trend gradually became the vast peasants and proletariat, and the influence it generated grew greater and greater.

II.1.3. Theoretical nature of political thought trends

Political thought trends possess a profound theoretical property. Any thought trend, no matter how complicated and scattered, has a relatively stable conceptual core or theoretical core. The development of the thought trend is the process of the core from nothing, from unshaped to shaped, from immature to mature. Some thought trends already have a basically shaped conceptual core, while some not, but only have a kind of quite obvious universal tendency of psychological mood and some fragmentary ideas.

With the further development of the thought trend, its theoretical core is condensed and formed in people's psychological tendency and fragmentary ideas, constantly enriched and formed through the collection process and argumentation of theorists and representative figures, which makes the thought trend obtain the nature of a conscious guidance. Generally speaking, the theoretical cores of current political thought trends are quite complete.

Political thought trends embody a philosophical thought, and this is an important mark of their theoretical characteristic. All kinds of political thought trends take thought system as their core, and especially often embody a philosophical view deeply. Philosophy is the essence of the era spirit and also the inner core of a specific social culture. As a kind of ideology, philosophy is the reflection of interests and wishes of particular class or social groups. Mao Zedong has commented on the class property of philosophy: "All philosophical theories have been created by men belonging to a definite social class. The ideas of these men have moreover been historically determined by a definite social existence. All philosophical doctrines express the needs of a definite social class and reflect the level of development of the productive forces of society and the historical stage in men's comprehension of nature. The fate of a philosophy is determined by the degree to which it satisfies the needs of a social class."[13] Political thought trends often evolve from philosophical thought trends to political thought trends with wide range of influence. "Once a kind of philosophical thought and theory got understood and mastered by a certain class or social stratum, or a certain social group, and as they become fundamental principles, methods and actions recognizing and reforming external objects, then this kind of philosophical thought and theory will become a kind of political thought trend, thus it will rise and develop."[14]

As the scientific world outlook and methodology of the proletariat, Marxist philosophy with its high degree of unity of scientificalness and value quality becomes the spiritual weapon of world proletariat as well as the essence of the era spirit, and a political thought trend popular worldwide with enduring strength. Chinese modern philosophy revolution ever became the forerunner of political revolution, hence the modern philosophical thought trends usually possess wide social influence, and they break through the walls of the academy and directly evolve into political thought trends. There are many political thought trends that contain deep or shallow philosophical implication. The liberal thought trend in old China has

---

13   *Selected Works of Mao Zedong*, Central Party Literature Press, 2003, p. 17.
14   Deng Zhuoming, On Types and Characteristics of Social Thought Trends, *Journal of Southwestern China Normal University*, 1995(5).

adopted the Anglo-American empiricism or positivism as its philosophical base; while the inner core of scientific socialism thought is Marxist historical dialectics. The philosophical base of the liberal thought trend in the 1980s was "subjective practical philosophy", which analyzed and evaluated the mistakes made in the past with the humanist view of history and theory of socialist alienation.

The diversification of the social development and the growing complexity of practice also necessarily lead to the emergence of many different thoughts. For the spread and development of thought trends themselves, it is inevitable that each political thought trend must publicize its legitimacy, correctness, advanced nature, etc. at all costs, in order to gain the recognition from social groups, and obtain better spread and development. Since the interest classes and strata they represent are different, it is certain that basic claims of various thought trends will be greatly different, even completely opposite situations may arise, and mutual collisions and frictions are unavoidable in the process of dissemination. Hence, in the spread of various thought trends, disputes and debates happen usually occur among them. In the debate process, all the political thought trends will start from their most basic theoretical core to argue the correctness, and the thought trends they debate with will also necessarily carry out their dispute from their theoretical core. Therefore, if one kind of political thought trends does not possess a basic philosophical basis, or theoretical property, it will inevitably lack of effective point of view to refute, and defend its own existence in the debate process. For various political thought trends throughout the world, the theoretical property is the root of doctrine and source of development, only if a certain philosophical basis exists can the development and progress of the thought trend be guided.

II.1.4. Actual nature of political thought trends

The functions of political thought trends embody their strong actual relevance. The formation and development process of political thought trends is the process of putting their claims and demands into practice and affecting the social reality. Political thought trends have a clear goal orientation, namely participating in social transformation, solving focal points of the society, even affecting the social development trend, which requires constant practice. Once mastered by the masses, theory will turn into material force, and as a group consciousness with wide range of influence, political thought trends can exactly turn into such material force, become an important thought weapon in the transformation of the society, so as to realize the promotion of social practice by thought trends. Not only advanced and progressive thought trends have the property of actualness, backward, retrogressive or reactionary thought trends also possess such characteristics. In the Renaissance period with its vivacious thought trends, period of China's May Fourth Movement, period of China's Reform and Opening-up, major advanced political thought trends have all possessed a very strong actual relevance, and have had huge impact on social transformation.

The Middle Ages in Europe was called "Dark Ages", and the Christian theology became the spiritual pillar of the then feudal society, and established a rigorous system of religious theology which regarded God as absolute authority. Any culture, including literature, art, philosophy, had to to follow Classics of the Christian teaching–the Bible doctrine–for interpretation, nobody could violate it, otherwise would be severely punished. Under such circumstances, whole Europe lost its vitality, and no one dared to speak out, the social development tended to stagnation. This institution which went against the human ethics and social development was broken through in the Renaissance period. In the literary world, "Three Literary Heroes" of Italy, Shakespeare of Britain, Cervantes of Spain, etc. have emerged successively. In the fine arts, da Vinci, Michelangelo and Raphael as the three greatest artists of the Renaissance appeared; as well as Copernicus in astronomy, and Cardano in mathematics, etc. The appearance of a series of new thought trends with them as core figures had an extremely significant impact on the social development at that time. Under the influence of the spread of thought trends, people generally demanded to break the shackles of religious theology, to restore humanism under a free status. Moreover, along with the constant development and spread of such thought trends in Renaissance, they have been accepted by more and more people who lived under "dark state", and such theoretical thoughts eventually grasped the broad masses, becoming huge material force for social transformation, and eventually made Europe break the shackles of European Medieval theology, and opened a new period of rapid development after the Renaissance.

In 1976, the Central Committee of the CPC crashed the domination of the "Gang of Four" successfully, and ended the 10 years of chaos caused by the "Cultural Revolution". However, after this success, where China would head has become a huge question in people's minds. Would China stick to the wrong thought of "Two Whatevers", and insist to adhere to the mistaken thoughts of Mao Zedong in his later years, or break the chains of old thought habits boldly in order to explore a new path of developing socialism, became an urgent problem faced by the new central leadership should resolve. At this time, Deng Xiaoping, Hu Yaobang, etc. initiated and led "A great debate on the question of criterion of truth", which greatly liberated people's minds, and a new trend of sticking to the principles of seeking truth from facts swept across China. The ideological emancipation thought and movement which advocated seeking the truth from facts as its core, laid the ideological basis for the convocation of the Third Plenary Session of the 11th Central Committee in 1978, in which the Party and nation turned the focus of work to economy construction timely, and made the great historical decision of the Reform and Opening-up. At the initial stage for Reform and Opening-up, there were still a lot of people whose thinking remained rigid, and they were unwilling to support the reform and obstructed Reform and Opening-up in every possible way. Especially after the political disturbance of 1989, many people stood out to criticize and doubt Reform and Opening-up publicly, and completely attributed those various new social contradictions and problems which had appeared to the Reform and Opening-up, itself. Considering these trends, in 1991, the Liberation Daily of Shanghai published multiple articles under the name of Huang Fuping, which triggered a heated discussion, and a new trend to adhere to Reform and Opening-up swept across the society. At the same time, this trend also has been a strong and powerful responsive stroke to those various thoughts blaming and opposing Reform and Opening-up. The political thought trends adhering to Reform and Opening-up in 1990s had a significant influence on the deepening of market oriented reforms, they have pushed the opening-up, and played a pioneering role in cracking various adverse thoughts and doctrines.

As a kind of social consciousness, the political thought trends, their generation necessarily stems from the actual social practice, hence their generation and development has an inseparable association with the social environment of their time. When a kind of political thought trend emerges according to the requirements of social practice, it will also necessarily have a dynamic effect on the social practice. What's more, as a kind of doctrine with certain goal directionality, political thought trends will inevitably have an impact on the development of the whole society. As the saying goes, thoughts guide the action that is the actualness of political thought trends.

II.1.5. Motile nature of political thought trends

The motility property of political thought trends has two integrated aspects. Firstly, as a specific form of social consciousness, political thought trends are active on two levels of social psychology and ideology, and sometimes there are more socio-psychological components, sometimes there are more ideological components. Since 1990s, along with the expansion of globalization and marketization, the neoliberal thought trend has been spreading constantly, showing a trend of politicization and globalization. Along with the constant deepening of Reform and Opening-up, the economic, political and cultural communication with countries in the world has got closer and closer, and the neoliberal thought trend has also begun to spread in China, advocating market economy, opposing government's intervention in the market, argued that the essence of market economy lies in free competition without intervention, and worshipped the regulatory role of the "invisible hand" on the market, propagated modes of thinking and value ideas different from the past, and advocated liberalization, marketization, and privatization. It denied public ownership, socialism, and state intervention, possessing a clear ideological nature. Different from the ideological components of neoliberalism, the rise and spread of nationalism are mostly socio-psychological factors. For example, the upsurge of nationalism that began in the 1920s and 1930s was due to the disunity and oppressed status of the country and the dual oppression by imperialism and feudalism, the country plunged into a state of getting trampled, especially after the 9/18 Incident, which stimulated the national psychology of Chinese masses immensely, and influenced by this kind of social psychology, the nationalist ideology developed rapidly at that time. Since the 1980s, the reason for the appearance of nationalist thought trend was also inspired by socio-psychology factors. At the beginning of Reform and Opening-up, the masses, especially the youth, absorbed the ideas and thoughts of Western humanism when getting rid of the influence of "left" thoughts, paid attention to individual liberation, demanded self-development and self-realization, and laid the foundation of a new type of state and national idea taking ego as starting point to change the tradition. Along with the development of the commodity economy, out of hope for the prosperity of the country, the people were concerned about and participated in the Reform with a high patriotic enthusiasm; the patriotic enthusiasm declined when the demands and participation were frustrated. In people's eyes, the high material civilization of Western developed countries contrasted with the relative backwardness of the Chinese economy, resulting in the emergence of a sense of national inferiority. In the late 1980s, some topics of discussion involving nationalities' and nations' rise and fall/honor and disgrace appeared, and among them there was no lack of voices that advocated learning from Western capitalism and criticized socialism. Driven by a strong sense of national crisis, awareness of urgency and sense of mission of era, the patriotic awareness was expressed in a radical mood, and further developed and converted into the radical nationalist thought trend with critical nature and theoreticalness. But the appearance of such thought trends were directly related to masses' social psychology.

Secondly, seen from the mode of motion of political thought trends, the motility of political thought trends embodies characteristics of radiation and wave motion. As far as the dissemination process of political thought trends is concerned, once thought trends that meet the needs of the era are put forward, they will often start to radiate rapidly, be recognized by broad masses, become a powerful force, as if "one stone stirs up thousand waves", forming a very strong impact force on the society. The wave motion is with regard to the development process of thought trends. In the initial stage, political thought trends are often very weak, while expand gradually with unstoppable surge, being great in strength and impetus, and then exit the stage of thoughts competition gradually with the change of social conditions, and replaced by new thoughts which will experience the same process, fluctuating as if surge. Political thought trends are in motion, while this does not mean that there is no relative stability. Thought trends with greater influence always exist for a long term. That is because thoughts always run along with changes of relations of production, no matter by means of revolution or reform, and the changes of production relations and its thorough transformation is not accomplished in one move, but a longer historical process, hence the existence of thoughts is also for a long term, even though the relations of production adapting to some thoughts stays in a more stable status till disappears, the thoughts will not disappear immediately, which will be inherited and maintained as one kind of man's intellectual products, and still have a certain vital force. Its theoretical core is more mature, being important spiritual wealth for the society. As thought trends, both the Marxist and the Western liberal thought trend follow this development mode of motion. From the publication of Marx's *Communist Manifesto*, passing through over half a century, the Marxist thought trend has become the programmatic thought to guide the world revolution. Under the guidance of this thought trend, the Soviet Russia established the first socialist country in the world. After this, the Marxist thought trend swept the whole world, setting off a red cyclone in the worldwide, especially at the later World War II, a series of socialist countries were established one after another. In the end of 1980s and the beginning of 1990s, socialist countries experienced severe setbacks, however the Marxism did not decline accordingly, and China started a new development in higher level under its renewed leadership. Marxism is an ideological system which brings to light the laws governing the development of the history of human society. Its basic tenets are correct and have tremendous vitality and it accords with the laws of social development, as well as the trend of the times, therefore, it must be inherited, carried forward, enriched and developed constantly. Just as Deng Xiaoping said, as times proceed, more and more people of the world will embrace Marxism".

II.1.6. Era nature of political thought trends

The consciousness component of political thought trends has a marked time stamp, thus they have obvious era characteristics. The background of the era in which the specific thoughts are produced is specific, and different thoughts correspond to different times. In different times, different mode of production and different social environment will form a wide range of political thought trends. Marx said: "Upon the different forms of property, upon the social conditions of existence, rises an entire superstructure of distinct and peculiarly formed sentiments, illusions, modes of thought, and views of life"[15] The reason why political thought trends have epochal characteristics is because they are always related with the mode of production of the specific times, and always expresses requirements of the times determined by the mode of production. Just as Engels said: "all theories that appeared in history can be understood only if social conditions of existence of each corresponding times is understood, and they are derived from these material conditions".[16]

Political thought trends are the product of the times. Those kind of political thought trends popular in an era are often closely related with both people's ideological consciousness and their theoretical level. The epochal changes in the political thought trends are caused by the development of the times. "With the development of the times and the progress of science and technology, political thought trends will also be changed subsequently. The rise and fall of political thought trends is closely related to the need of the development of the times, and the nature of some political thought trends will change with the evolution of the times. Even those political thought trends, which had the correct, progressive and revolutionary significance in the past, is transformed into political thought trends with incorrect, backward or reactionary significance, today."[17]

Political thought trends tend to reflect the changes of the times. People's ideas, psychological expectation and theory request on the contradictory situation, the social tendency, the social focus and the political atmosphere will be expressed by political thought trends. Democratic and scientific thoughts during the May Fourth Movement period expressed the struggle by people against the feudal and backward and ignorant, and the search by

---

15 *Selected Works of Karl Marx and Frederick Engels*, Vol. 1, People's Publishing House, 1995, p. 611.
16 *Selected Works of Karl Marx and Frederick Engels*, Vol. 2, People's Publishing House, 1995, p. 38.
17 Deng Zhuoming, On Types and Characteristics of Social Thought Trends, *Journal of Southwestern China Normal University*, 1995(5).

the new intelligentsia for the thinking method to save the country and the people. Nationalism thoughts set off in the 1920s and 1930s expressed the wishes from people of all walks of life to defend for the survival of the nation under the situation when the country was on the verge of extinction. Reform thoughts at the beginning of China's Reform and Opening-up urgently reflected people's desire for a stronger country and better-off people. After the ten chaotic years of the "Cultural Revolution" and two years of wandering period, people began to pursue ideological emancipation, demanded changing and surpassing the original rigid economic system and release of the development of productive forces.

This reform thought reflected people's demand and expectation for new social mechanism after the 3rd Plenary Session of the 11th Central Committee. The humanism thoughts during the period of European Renaissance reflected the wishes of the new bourgeoisie to oppose the feudal autocracy and the religious oppression, and demand the development of capitalism and get ruling power. Liberalism thoughts, which has risen and developed in modern Europe, concentrates on the inherent essential demand of the development of capitalism, and the pursuit of market competition and the appeal of the value idea of individualism.

The formation and evolution of a political thought is not necessarily through the whole times. The life cycle of political thought trends with different nature is different, and the formation and disappearance of some political thought trends can be quite short. Therefore, the epochal characteristics of political thought trends can manifest themselves as being prevalent for longer period of times or for shorter period of times.

II.1.7. Social nature of political thought trends

"Consciousness is, therefore, from the very beginning a social product, and remains so as long as men exist at all… The production of ideas, of conceptions, of consciousness, is at first directly interwoven with the material activity and the material intercourse of men, the language of real life."[18] First of all, the formation of political thought trends are directly restricted and influenced by social factors. Some studies have suggested that certain political thought trends are always related to the mode of production and social relations under certain historical conditions, and their formation contain profound political and economic motive forces. Any kind of political thought trend, in the final analysis, is the refraction and echo of social and

---

18 *Selected Works of Karl Marx and Frederick Engels,* Vol. 1, People's Publishing House, 1995, p. 81.

historical progress in the field of ideology. When the movement of social contradictions in a society reach a certain degree, it violently stimulates people's psychology, reorganizes and forms a common psychological tendency among people within a certain range, combines with the corresponding social ideology, and often evolves into political thought that widely spreads.[19] After the Opium War, the gates of ancient China were opened, and it began to lose its status of independent development, and was forcedly drawn into the colonial system of world capitalism. In order to adapt to the changes of the situation, part of the people in the ruling class of Qing government started to promote the Self-strengthening Movement aimed at the resurgence of the dynasty, and in the society the general self-strengthening reform thought trend took shape. The basic reason for such a thought trend to rise is that after the failure of the two Opium Wars, the social life had encountered profound changes under the influence of Western colonialism. The advanced western technology was continuously transmitted into China, and the traditional Chinese social life began to go bankrupt. People's ideas and views gradually began to change, and the rule of the Qing Dynasty was challenged to some extent. Under such circumstances, the Self-strengthening Movement thought trend with the purpose of "Chinese learning as the essence, Western learning as the tool" mounted the stage of history, and changes in social factors were the most direct reason for the generation of this thought. Because the Chinese society at that time was still a feudal society, the traditional feudal Confucianism was still at the dominant position in people's ideology. In the aspect of economic life, while the traditional way of life and production in coastal areas started to vanish, new types of life and modern factory production emerged. But from a national perspective, self-sufficient small-scale peasant economy was still dominant, and the traditional feudal system was still at the leading position in society. In this case, restricted by the social environment, the vision of the Self-strengthening Movement thought trend was necessarily limited in a certain range, and the leading part was only to learn some advanced technology, and its vitality was also bound to be short-lived. Along with the deepening of the social crisis and the constant change of social environment, the reform faction began to see that it was far from enough to just rely on the Self-strengthening Movement to learn western technology, what they should learn was the western advanced system, so in the society the thought trend of the constitutional reform and modernization was set off, Kang Youwei, Liang Qichao and a large number of leading reformer leaders that led the wave of constitutional reform and modernization emerged.

---

19   Deng Zhuoming, On Types and Characteristics of Social Thought Trends, *Journal of Southwestern China Normal University*, 1995(5).

Compared with the thought trend of the Self-strengthening Movement, the thought trend of constitutional reform and modernization was a big step forward in history. The reason for the emergence of this situation was mainly because after the Sino-Japanese War, the social crisis deepened, people needed a new thought trend for the reform and development of the society, the thought trend of constitutional reform and modernization reflected people's common psychological mood in those days.

Secondly, political thought trends are a reflection of people's social life. The complexity and diversity of human's social practice determines the complexity and diversity of life style and life state, and the aspect of interest direction is also bound to show a variety of different results. At present, there are many kinds of political thought trends in the society, which are the representatives of the interests of different classes and strata, and they are also a reflection of people's real life. Especially in recent years, some emerging political thought trends have shown this trend. For example, the feminist thought trend that rose in late 1960s and early 1970s, and the reason is that the social status and rights of women in the West was oppressed and exploited, they were unable to enjoy equal rights in the society, and they were subject to discrimination and unfair treatment in different levels and aspects. The situation of this kind of social life made women urgently need and demand changing this inequality. So, the feminist thought trend with the aim of defending and emancipating women and showing women's rights have spread vigorously in the western society. For another example, green pacifist thought trend that rose in the late 1960s was also a profound reflection of the social life of people. In the 1960s, the social economy rapidly developed, and the rapid expansion of modernization, industrialization and urbanization brought a series of negative consequences. With the continuous development of science and technology, the industrialization has developed with leaps, and the ability of people to transform nature has become stronger and stronger. However, correspondingly, the natural environment got worse and worse, the depletion of the ozone layer has become increasingly serious, global warming, air and water has been polluted, and chemical waste was diffused. In addition, the swelling population, food crisis and the crisis of water resources and other issues became more prominent. People's social life began to face all kinds of difficulties. Under these circumstances, people began to deeply reflect on the social life. In the face of these problems, the green pacifist thought trend has come into being. Therefore, in essence, political thought trends are people's understanding, thinking, judgment and evaluation of society, with the performance of people's desire, will, ideals and so on, but human beings (men) are the ensemble of social relations. It can be seen that political thought trends is the epitome of society in a certain period, therefore social, ideological and cultural conditions of the society are well reflected by the mirror of political thought trends.

Thirdly, political thought trends have a significant active role in social development. "Revolutionary, advanced and correct political thought trends have a tremendous promoting effect on the development of the society because they are consistent with the direction of development of the era. Backward, wrong and even reactionary political thought trends have a hindering effect on the human progress and social development because they go against the direction of social development. Even those political thought trends that are not revolutionary and the reactionary, progressive and backward, positive and negative or those thoughts which waver between the two will also play an implicit or explicit, direct or indirect role in promoting or hindering the development of the society because of the change of flow direction in the development or the deviation in people's acceptance and other factors."[20] As a kind of progressive thought trend that conforms to the historical trend, the Marxist thought trend has had a positive impact on the world scale, has guided the Chinese revolution towards victory, made the majority of working people emancipate themselves, and became the masters of the new society and the new country, this is a role played by a correct, positive and progressive thought trend. On the contrary, currently there are some thoughts in the society, for example, historical nihilism, which fundamentally denies the historical achievements of revolution, construction and reform of our country; anarchism which advocates absolute freedom without any restriction; and those negative thoughts including mammonism and hedonism that hinder the process of social development. The practicalness aspect of political thought trends emphasizes the dynamic aspect of thought trends, and the dynamic role emphasized here focuses on the object of the dynamic role of thought trends and emphasizes the social attribute of the dynamic role of thought trends.

II.1.8. National nature and territorial nature of political thought trends

If we say that era characteristics of political thought trends is to explore the natures of political thought trends from the time dimension, then the nationality and territoriality of political thought trends is to explore the characteristics of political thought trends from the spatial dimension. In

---

20   Deng Zhuoming, On Types and Characteristics of Social Thought Trends, *Journal of Southwestern China Normal University*, 1995(5).

the history people have formed a stable national community, acquiring a common language, a common geography, a common economic life and common psychological qualities with the common characteristics of the national culture. As different peoples live in different natural environment and social environment, their mental qualities and cultural traditions with their own nationality characteristics will inevitably form. Therefore, the political thought trends with full psychological factors has a clear property of nationality. Different countries and different peoples have different psychological and cultural traditions, and they often appear in thought trends. The performance of psychological and cultural traditions of different countries and peoples tend to have large differences, and the difference in performance of thoughts is even larger, even though international thoughts are unequivocally of its national and regional characteristics in different countries and peoples. Just like the looks of mythical figures around the world studied by Marx, European gods look similar to Europeans, and Asian gods are similar to Asians, the results reflect that the consciousness is decided by the material, and at the same time, they also reflect the influence of ethnic culture on the consciousness of thought trends. For example, in China, because the Chinese nation is a unified nation, the highly centralized imperial system was established in an early period of time, the Confucianism was the main trend to dominate the society in political thought trends in ancient China, and clearly reflected the unique nature of the Chinese nation. In Europe of the same time, the mode of economic development of the ancient Greece and Athens was mainly about overseas trade because they were near the sea and their land area was relatively scarce, and the organizational form was the city-state style with small territories and population, and this national characteristic contributed to the creation of special city-state culture of the ancient Greece and Athens. For another example, the thought trends in the modern Europe and US have taken liberalism and free development as their goal, and the countries throughout Asia take the establishment of an independent nation as their goal due to their traditional national customs. Different ethnic groups and different regions create different political thought trends and this fact is closely related with Marx's view of practice. In the creation of historical materialism, Marx made it clear that material life of men determines their consciousness, and social life practice determines the existence of society. Different peoples live in different areas, the innate natural conditions and development levels are different, which determine that each nation has its own development characteristics, and those unique causes lead to diversification of practice. And political thought trends are inevitably produced on the basis of a certain kind of society. Therefore, this kind of complex and diverse social practice is the fundamental reason for the creation of different political thought trends in different national groups and within different regions. In addition, people work and live in different natural environment and social environment, form specific social relations and life style, and political thought trends with regional characteristics will form. It is manifested in two aspects. One is the specific needs, emotions and desires of the people living in different regions arise from some special interests, which form some specific political thought trends. The other is the performance of the same political thought trends is also different in different regions. For example, in the economically developed areas, the market system tends to be mature, the policy system is relatively perfect, and the free competition of the market economy makes the society full of vigor and it continuously develops, people worship the power of the "invisible hand" and promote the market economic system with completely free competition. Liberalism thoughts in these areas tend to hold high the banner of reform of the political system, and constantly stress that the political system must be compatible with the free and open market economy. But in some economically less developed regions of the world, liberalism thoughts will be more interested in economic freedom. This shows that the development process of thoughts in developed regions and underdeveloped regions of the world are not synchronous, and there is even no trace that those thoughts which are popular in the developed regions will enjoy great popularity in the underdeveloped regions of the world.

II.1.9. International nature of political thought trends

The internationality of political thought trends is not contradictory to nationality and territoriality. The international characteristics has a close relationship with the depth and breadth of the international exchanges. Compared with the developing countries, the developed countries have a high degree of development, rapid modernization and great influence on the ideology and culture, and have obvious advantages in spread. In the process of building modernization, whether or not taking the path of western modernization, developing countries cannot avoid numerous social problems the west ever experienced and is experiencing. With the deepening of economic globalization and the deepening of exchange between people in different countries, political thought trends caused by these problems will undoubtedly be influenced by western ideology. Western ideas on these issues will become the theoretical support of these ideas or the target of criticism. In the worldwide, the socialist production relations are in a weak position, and it is a fact that to a certain extent, some thoughts in the socialist countries are influenced by the ideology of capitalist countries. Some of political thought trends as opposed to Marxism ideology in the socialist countries that are carrying out reform are more obviously of internationality, the core theory of some thought trends originates from certain western ideas, and some thoughts are directly exotic. The exchange of ideology and culture is bidirectional. Thoughts in developing countries will also move towards international. But from the perspective of international flow of thoughts, the western developed capitalist countries tend to be the source of some thoughts. For example, various kinds of thoughts including liberalism thoughts are currently popular in some countries and regions, we can observe that democratic socialism thoughts, the thoughts of cultural imperialism, thoughts of selfish interest seeking, money worship thoughts and ethnic separatism thoughts are originated and spread from the western capitalist countries, when the world socialist movement is at a low ebb, western political thought trends has more powerful effect across the whole world, in general. Under the conditions that the Reform and Opening-up has been carried out in China and China has more contact with the capitalist countries, some western political thought trends inevitably spread in China and have an impact, which is an indisputable fact. The theoretical and practical significance of the political thought trend is an important criterion for measuring the degree of its development. The more thoughtful and theoretical a thought trend is, the more mature the thought and the complete theoretical system are, and the more it shows that it is at a higher stage and a higher level of thought trend development. If a kind of thought trend is not limited to the scope of pure theory, but widely socialized and deeply realized, combines with actual activities and actual struggle, it will show that it is on a higher level of development and maturity. The more mature and complete the theory of a kind of thoughts is, the more consciously and voluntarily can it transform into some certain social and political movements; in turn, the more contact it maintains with real life and social movement and draws strength from the reality, the more it will continue to develop in theory. The interactive relationship of mutual promotion is clearly reflected in the process of the development of scientific socialism thoughts. Scientific socialism itself is a scientific and complete theoretical system, but its mission is to guide the socialist movement in real practice. The two aspects are closely related, and the unilateral development separate from the other side is difficult to imagine. Of course, due to complexity of the historical conditions, and because of characteristics of thoughts, some thoughts cannot develop in two aspects, but often only develop only in one aspect. For example, the German classical philosophy, as a philosophical trend of thought system, has circuitously expressed the interests and needs of the German bourgeoisie which fought for a political reform in Germany, but was just a "philosophical current", and could not go beyond the scope of an academic philosophy, and could not directly affect and form a realistic political struggle. On the other hand, classical German philosophy has made a great progress in the historical development of philosophical theories, thus it has become one of the important sources of Marxist philosophy and Marxism. The above political nature, characteristic of group, theoretical property, reality, motility, era character, sociality, nationality and territoriality, and internationalism are all fundamental characteristics of political thought trends, which are mainly examined from the point of political thought trends and the relationship with social existence. In addition, a political trend of thought also has a distinct value orientation, class nature, group interest character, diversity and complexity, repeatability and other characteristics.

Political thought trends have the distinctive value orientation means that political thought trends, as a kind of unique social consciousness, is the reflection of the existence of some certain society, and as the reflection of the existence of a specific society, political thought trends is inevitably affected by this factor or that one. Some views, ideas, values, attitudes, and psychological factors that are circulating in the society will have a certain effect on it. For example, a social group needs a kind of political thought trends in line with its own interests to serve its interests, and the value orientation of thoughts reflecting the value interests of this group is bound to be consistent with it. For another example, political thought trends are numerous and varied, the kind of thinking and standard for people to adopt to examine it and decide whether to accept it or not, the selection of this thoughts also inevitably contains some certain value orientation, and under the influence of some particular value orientation, people make judgments and choices to fit value orientation contained in some political thought trends.

The distinctive class nature and group interest character of political thought trends means in the same historical development period, under the situation that productive force, class status and social level of various social classes are different, so their interests are also different, which causes the diversity for the identification and selection of political thought trends. In addition, political thought trends are also imbued with group interest character. The diversification of social practice determines that various groups strive for different interests. With the continuous development of social division of labor, there are more and more types of social occupations group interests, and the division has become more and more detailed. People's professional life has become an important part of people's life. When people are engaged in a certain social occupation and living in a certain circle of professional life, they are bound to have the specific occupation style and occupational psychology with some kind of professional life because of the difference in the field of social occupation. The particular occupational psychology, occupational preference and occupation interests affect all aspects of people's lives, and subtly influence people's ideas and views and values, so people tend to start from their own group (occupational) psychology and interest to choose political thought trends, which forms the group (occupational) interest character of political thought trends.

The diversity and complexity of political thought trends means political thought trends represents interests, appeals of various people, and each kind of political thought trends is subject to control and effect of different classes, strata and social groups, social culture, values and thinking modes. Therefore, a political trend of thought extends to every field and every corner of the society, and there are also various factions in every field, even within one kind of comprehensive political thought. For example, there are not only utopian socialist thoughts, egalitarian socialism thoughts, but also scientific socialism thoughts and democratic socialism thoughts in the family of socialist thoughts. When we briefly overview the thoughts for economic development and economic management, we can see the planned economy thoughts, Keynesian thoughts which advocate the state's macro regulation and macro control of the economy and new liberalism thoughts which advocate free markets, and so on. Repeatability of political thought trends means that certain political thought trends that do not meet the demands of social development laws and historical development are eliminated by history due to the development of society and the times. But under certain social environment, political thought trends that has been eliminated by history appears in front of people with different faces and identities, especially in the historical transformation period of rapid development of society, various social contradictions are prominent, these thoughts that have been abandoned by history are re-embraced by some people to convey some certain value orientation and to express their interest appeals and aim to affect social psychology and participate in the reconstruction of social ideology.

II.2. Classification and structures of political thought trends

There are many kinds of political thought trends and they can be classified from different aspects and different angles. The angles for research on thoughts are different, and the classification of thoughts is also different, the same political thought trends can be classified into different categories according to different standards, and different political thought trends can be classified into the same category. There are various kinds of political thought trends. The classification of political thought trends is closely related with their structures. In regard with classification of political thought trends, the structure of political thought trends is also a criterion for their classification, and making classification from different angles also deepens the analysis of the structure of political thought trends. According to different standards of classification, political thought trends can be classified differently. In the following we will summarize a variety of classification methods for political thought trends and further explain the significance of classification methods.

II.2.1. Classification according to the nature of the role of thought trends

Seen from the different natures of the social role of different political thought trends, political thought trends can be divided into progressive, correct, revolutionary, positive political thought trends and reactionary, wrong, conservative and negative political thought trends. The correct thoughts and the wrong thoughts should all be judged from the standpoint of Marxism. Throughout the formation and development of the various political thought trends at all times and in all countries, some political thought trends are of the revolutionary, progressive, correct and positive nature because of their conformity with the requirements of the development of social productive forces and apt with the development of times, and promote social development in different degrees. For example, Marxism is a political thought trend that has profound influence worldwide, which has served as the guiding ideology of the Communist Party of the Soviet Union and the CPC in leading the October Revolution of Russia and China's New Democratic Revolution to victory. It is a kind of political thought trends with revolutionary nature; Humanism thoughts in the Middle Ages was a kind of political thought trends with progressive, correct nature at the time; during the "May Fourth Movement" period in China, many new thoughts with the anti-imperialist and anti-feudal content were a kind of political thought trends with positive nature.[21]

Of course, these four aspects emphasize the nature of their role from four different aspects, some thoughts are more prominently bear only one aspect, and some political thought trends have the nature of these four aspects at the same time. For example, Marxism, as political thought trends, has

---

21   Deng Zhuoming, On Types and Characteristics of Social Thought Trends, *Journal of Southwestern China Normal University*, 1995(5).

these four properties at the same time. Fundamentally speaking, any correct thought is in line with the interests of the masses. But the correct thoughts may not meet the immediate interests of some people or some groups, and sometimes even is in sharp opposition against the interests of individuals or groups, or in conflict with the immediate interests of the masses.

The wrong thoughts are not the correct reflection of the objective reality, "it is often the case that thinking falls behind reality"[22]. And on the contrary to the correct thoughts described earlier, some political thought trends are of reactionary, wrong, backward, passive nature and produce different degrees of obstruction on the social development because they do not comply with requirements of the development of social productive forces and the direction of the development of the times. For example, ultra-leftist thoughts that spread in China was a kind of reactionary thoughts against the historical trend; feudal revivalism thoughts around "May Fourth Movement" period in China that promoted "the quintessence of Chinese culture" and went against the literary revolution were a kind of backward political thought trend. On the other hand, the "left" thoughts during the period of socialist construction in China, including the petty bourgeoisie egalitarianism, and also those ideas which were "eager and hasty to transit directly into communism", have spared respect to knowledge and discriminated against intellectuals, can be evaluated as a series of political thought trends having erroneous and backward qualities.[23] In fact, some political thought trends possess these four properties simultaneously, which is true for the "ultra-left" thoughts. The qualities of backwardness, erroneous, conservative and reactionary are intertwined, in fact some trends of thoughts often possess these qualities simultaneously, and they cannot be simply separated. We observe that, in contemporary China a variety of political thoughts have emerged in the practice of building socialism. in contemporary China. The majority of these thoughts belong to the category of "various controversial ideas and opinions that have emerged in the process of practice and exploration. But some thought trends belong to the category of thoughts hostile to socialism." Therefore, to make a correct distinction between correct thoughts and wrong thoughts has a great practical significance for the development of the socialist cause. As emphasized by Mao Zedong and Deng Xiaoping, the most important criteria for us to determine whether a thought trend is correct or not is its attitude towards the principles of "following the road of socialism and the leadership of the Party". Mao Zedong pointed out: "In the political life of our people, how should right be distinguished

---

22 *Selected Works of Mao Zedong,* Vol. 1, People's Publishing House, 1991, p. 295.
23 Deng Zhuoming, On Types and Characteristics of Social Thought Trends, *Journal of Southwestern China Normal University,* 1995(5).

from wrong in one's words and actions? On the basis of the principles of our Constitution, the will of the overwhelming majority of our people and the common political positions which have been proclaimed on various occasions by our political parties and groups, we consider that, broadly speaking, the criteria should be as follows: (1) Words and actions should help to unite, and not divide, the people of our various nationalities; (2) They should be beneficial, and not harmful, to socialist transformation and socialist construction; (3) They should help to consolidate, and not under-mine or weaken, the people's democratic dictatorship; (4) They should help to consolidate, and not undermine or weaken, democratic centralism; (5) They should help to strengthen, and not discard or weaken, the leadership of the Communist Party; (6) They should be beneficial, and not harmful, to international socialist unity and the unity of the peace-loving people of the world. Of these six criteria, the most important are the socialist path and the leadership of the Party."[24]

On September 7th, 1983, while Deng Xiaoping talked with some leading comrades about the draft of the speech in the 2nd Plenary Session of the 12th CPC Central Committee, he said: "the core of humanitarianism and alien-ation debate is opposition to socialist path and the leadership of the Party. The core of 'Four Cardinal Principles' is upholding of the Party leadership. In fact, these thoughts insist that capitalism is better than socialism, lose con-fidence in the leadership of the Party, and they think they are better than the Party, and whatever they do is legal."[25] In summary, at present, the criterion to judge whether any political thought trends is correct or not is whether it accords with the basic line of the Party. Development of a new kind of pro-duction relations consists of a process of emergence, development and de-cline, when they no longer represents the requirements of the development of the advanced productive forces, it is wrong to support them from the level of social ideology and thoughts. From the historical perspective, we should affirm the historical progressiveness of the correct thoughts in promoting people to further understand and grasp the aspects of human society, exter-nal nature and human beings, but the historical progressiveness of a thought trend does not mean, they are exempt from making wrong judgments when reflecting on the real life. In the period of our socialist reform, under the situations that various forms of ownership commonly developed, and ideol-ogy pattern was complex, it is reasonable and necessary for the mainstream ideology to keep vigilant, restrict some political thought trends that have strained relations with it and curb the momentum of their development.

---

24 *Collected Works of Mao Zedong*, Vol. 7, People's Publishing House, 1999, pp. 233-234.
25 *Chronicle of Deng Xiaoping*, Vol.II, Central Party Literature Press, 2004, p. 930.

From the class and system represented by thoughts, progressive, correct, revolutionary and positive political thought trends are proletarian political thought trends and socialist thoughts, and reactionary, wrong, conservative and negative political thought trends are often the bourgeoisie political thought trends and thoughts of capitalism, etc. Progressive, correct, revolutionary, positive political thought trends are often the new thoughts, and reactionary, wrong, conservative and negative political thought trends are often the old thoughts. Thoughts produced under the new social and historical conditions are often referred to as the new thoughts. The development and evolution of thoughts is like waves behind drive on those ahead. In order to constantly solve ideological problems, new thoughts tend to break through the defects of old thoughts to replace them. New thoughts come from old thoughts and transcend them at higher levels or "reaction of old thoughts and negation of old thoughts"[26]. The criterion of dividing the old and new thoughts does not only refer to the time period of their generation, but also the nature of these thoughts. In the research of specific thoughts, the new thoughts are often used to refer to thoughts that are different from the declining or decayed old thoughts or thoughts trends and to thoughts that favor the new production relations, the new class, interests of the ascending class."[27] This is consistent with people's common sense and application of "new thoughts" and "old thoughts" in reality. In a certain period of time, the time for successive generation of thoughts has not always been consistent with the advanced and backward of thoughts. From the actual situation of thoughts, some new thoughts are not necessarily correct and advanced thoughts, and the existing thoughts are not necessarily backward and wrong thoughts. Some new thoughts are the version and new performance of the backward thoughts in the new historical conditions; some thoughts are always the new and advanced thoughts through a long-term inspection of history, such as Marxism thoughts. During the "May Fourth Movement" period and at the beginning of Reform and Opening-up, new thoughts occurred repeatedly, but not all the new thought trends were correct thoughts which were in line with the laws of social development. Only those new thoughts which conform to the objective laws of social development and represent the fundamental interests of the people are the correct thoughts.

---

26   He Lin: *Critique of Modern Trend of Thoughts*, Zhong Limeng, Yang Fenglin as editor in chief of *Compilation of the History of Chinese Modern Philosophy*, 5th part of 3rd volume, Department of philosophy of Liaoning University, 1982 (Informal publication), p. 153.

27   Some classical writers of Marxism have looked upon the new trend of thought from this point of view, which partially ignoring the principles of Marxism. The first chapter offers a brief description of this issue.

II.2.2. Classification according to the theoretical foundations of thought trends

According to the theory, thought trends can be classified as philosophical thoughts, economic thoughts, literary and artistic thoughts, religious thoughts, and so on. Before talking on the division according to the subjects (individual, group, class) of thought trends, we deem it is necessary to explain the differences between political thought trends and academic thought trends. Political thought trends are highly concerned about the deep problems of social life, and show strong political participation with strong practicality; while academic thought trends have a strong color of theory, and are more on the academic level. Academic thought trends may offer important theoretical guide for political thought trends. Of course, this distinction is relative, and some thoughts are politically and academically prominent. As mentioned above, any thought is more or less related with politics, and there is almost no academic thought trend that has no relationship with politics. Some academic thoughts are political thought trends themselves, and it is also common that academic thoughts turn into the social political thought trends at the end. But this division is almost established in the study of thoughts with a ready market. Strictly speaking, political thought trends reflect the interests and demands of a certain class, stratum, group or part of people in society. They are based on the cognition of social and political phenomena, and political theories, beliefs, opinions and ideas, expressed by a group of thinkers and cognized by some people in society; they are often linked to a political party, political organization or political movement, and it is the ideology to guide and explain their political action. There is always a variety of political theories, political views and theories in the social and political life of every era. Once a certain political thought has evolved into a kind of thought trend, it will certainly affect choice and pursuit of the people's political awareness, political emotion, political value and political ideal. In fact, in the social life, people are exposed to the radiation of all kinds of political thought trends, and consciously or unconsciously accept their suggestion and influence. The scientific socialism, as the mainstream of political thought trends in the contemporary world, has experienced evolution processes in which its theory was founded, it was accepted by the world proletariat and became the dominant ideology in the labor movement, spread widely all over the world, and merged into the worldwide tide rich in connotation.[28] For example, the current constitutionalist thought in China which call for constitutional reforms is a typical political thought

---

28   Deng Zhuoming, *On Types and Characteristics of Social Thought Trends*, *Journal of Southwestern China Normal University*, 1995(5).

trend, which has clear political views, and reflects the interests and requirements of the newly emerged social strata and groups in the society. Another example was the rise of bourgeois constitutionalist thought trend in modern China. They all have clear political views and political ideas. They also hope that through the dissemination of ideas, they can express their own demands, achieve certain political goals, and have great influence on the society. In general case, thought trends with politicality is to be understood as the political thought trends, and this book is also to understand political thought trends from this relatively broad significance. Philosophical thoughts, economic thoughts, literary and artistic thoughts and religious thoughts are not only based on the basic knowledge system of this subject but also related with the real life, especially the political life, and they are active in the academic and political life.

II.2.3. Classification of political thought trends according to classes and social system they represent

Classification according to the class they represent

A political thought trend can be divided into the feudal landlord class political thought trend, or a petty bourgeoisie political thought trend, or a bourgeoisie political thought trend and proletarian political thought trend.

In China, political thought trends representing the feudal landlord class had developed intensively in the middle and late periods of 19th Century, advocating the political slogans of "beat someone by playing his games only better" and "Chinese essence and Western utility". In the middle and late periods of 19th Century, with the opening of gate of ancient China, China was forced to be part of the world capitalist colonial system, and the crisis of Qing Dynasty rule had intensified. In order to maintain the rule of feudal landlord class, the Self-strengthening Movement aiming to promote the resurgence of the dynasty was raised inside the ruling class, whose purpose was to thrive western science and technology massively, maintain the ideological crisis of Qing Dynasty, and maintain the governance of the feudal landlord class. A typical characteristic of petty bourgeoisie political thought trends is their utopian nature, and such utopian nature was demonstrated thoroughly in the Taiping Heavenly Kingdom Movement. The programmatic document of the Taiping Heavenly Kingdom peasant movement Celestial Field System intensively expressed peasants' longing and pursuit of land ownership for thousands of years. In Taiping Heavenly Kingdom Movement, the peasant class opposed oppression from the feudal landlord class to peasants, and asked for egalitarian distribution of land plots, and such social demand expressed desire of the peasants. However, their demands and scheme possessed obvious utopian nature, such thoughts reflected the idle dream of peasant class for land, while real practical feasibility could not be defined. The bourgeois class political thought trends had been very popular in China at one time, especially in modern China. In order to find a way out for the Chinese society, countless men and women with high ideals have made various efforts, and many people could not help but turned their attention to the western developed capitalist countries, hoped to realize the independence and prosperity of China through learning from the west. Since modern times, bourgeoisie reformist thoughts, bourgeoisie revolutionary thoughts, complete Westernization thoughts, etc. took the stage of China's history, successively. The proletariat thoughts mainly refer to thoughts represented fundamental interests of the broad masses of the proletariat, with Marxist thoughts as their main representative. Since the establishment of Marxism, it has placed the interests of the proletariat in the fundamental position all the time, and guided proletarian movements in the world with its progressiveness and correctness, being the strong and powerful tool for proletarian struggle.

Classification according to the system they represent

They can be divided into capitalist thoughts and socialist thoughts. At present, the regime in the worldwide could be divided into capitalist system and socialist system principally. With the division of such two systems, the system attribute of one kind of political thought trends could be distinguished very well. Capitalist political thought trends mainly refer to those bear and grow under western capitalist system, and the main contents of them are publicizing thought value viewpoint of capitalist society, such as neoliberalism thoughts, neo-conservatism thoughts, humanitarianism thoughts, postmodernism thoughts, and behaviorism thoughts, although they have various forms and types, the essence of their contents all praise and publicize the capitalist value system. Meanwhile, the socialist thoughts are not always correct and advanced, course hundreds of years has become necessary for socialism to transform from an idle dream to science, and socialist thoughts of each era have also showed diversity. For example, there were utopian socialism thoughts represented by Thomas More of England, Campanella of Italy, etc., equalitarianism political thought trends represented by Marbury and Babeuf from France, and scientific socialism thoughts represented by Marx and Engels.

II.2.4. Classification according to the cause of emergence of political thought trends[29]

According to causes of political thought trends formation and development, political thought trends could be divided into crisis type thoughts, advocacy type thoughts, transformation type thoughts, etc. This classification focuses on causes of thoughts, which is meaningful to understand causes of formation for different thoughts. It involves in three aspects: one, drastic changes of social and historical conditions; two, relations with mainstream ideology; three, relevant thoughts resources in history. Such three aspects could be causes of different thoughts respectively, or maybe reasons for one same kind of thoughts.

Crisis type of trend of thoughts refer to the case that a society appears crisis, when social contradictions develop to a certain degree, people need new belief and pursuit of goals generally to obtain self-support, seek for theory could reflect their interests, wishes and demands, and be eager for significant revolution under the sense of crisis, and some social problems need to be solved urgently. At the same time, the society in the turmoil and crisis also needs to find a way out of the predicament. Under this case, some new political thought trends emerge as the times require among social crisis and turmoil usually. Since 20th Century, a lot of western capitalist countries have experienced two world wars and ups and downs of economic crisis, numerous and diverse thoughts and theories were bred and publicized during these period, which formed various political and economic thought trends, such as Keynesianism thoughts. Around the May Fourth Movement, the Marxism thoughts spread in China could be classified as the crisis type thoughts to some extent. Its generation was related to China's social crisis which had reached to a considerable degree, and because multiple ways which had aimed saving the country and the people had failed. People with broader vision finally gave up the method of seeking effective prescription saving the country from old tradition and the western colonialism, and Marxist thoughts spread in the land of China gradually by virtue of key element-" October Revolution" of Russia. While at that time, the revivalism and conservatism thoughts had been seeking the advocacy of warlord rule in China.

---

29   Deng Zhuoming made deep analysis of the crisis era type of trend of thoughts, the transformation type and advocacy type trend of thoughts (apologist type) in his article *On Types and Characteristics of Social Thought Trends* (recorded in *Journal of Southwestern China Normal University*, 1995(5), and the following discussion in the book draws ideas from this article.

Transformation type of thought trends refer to those new political thought trends which rather reflect the changing realistic conditions, which win people's acceptance and recognition and which encourage them to discard and transcend the limitations of the previous thought trends. They are formed due to the improvement of people's cognitive ability and changes in the needs of the society. For instance, the rising of New Freudianism among contemporary western philosophical thoughts is developed from the processing and transformation process of Freudianism. For the generation of various political thought trends, beside this primary cause of major changes in social economy and political life, there is the starting point of ideology datum, namely they are not created out of thin air by some people, but relying on ideological theory materials left by predecessors, and conduct inheritance, transformation, amendment, supplement and development to them, turn them into new thoughts embodying features of the times, expressing interests, will and demands of their own class, social stratum or some social group. Take another example, the liberalism thoughts popular after Reform and Opening-up greatly absorb and transform contents and traditions of liberalism thoughts before liberation, and the thoughts serve for Reform and Opening-up and socialist market economy construction could also be called as transformation thoughts. Advocacy type of thoughts embody a certain kind of social ideology which shows tendentiousness and biased nature which may become the motive force of a political thought trend. When some ideology tends to advocate the interests of some class or stratum, the advocacy will be gained from such class or stratum in most cases, obtaining their approval and advocacy, so that it can spread in the society more widely, and further to form political thought trends. In general case, political thought trends with tendency conforming to direct or indirect interests of the ruling class will receive support from the government. Otherwise, it will gain interference and opposition from the government. Accordingly, it is much easier for the thought advocated by the class occupying the dominant position to form some political thought trends and expand its influence scope. For instance, the economic thoughts with greater influence in contemporary western society are usually popularized and promoted by the advocacy and practice of ruling governments. As it should be, such advocacy could also come from some ideologists or social groups, its specific influence among people urges political thought trends to germinate and develop within a certain scope. Although this method is rarely used for the classification of thought trends in the actual research, the "advocacy type" criterion can be very enlightening for the research of contemporary Chinese political thought trends. The development of thoughts in reform period of socialist society has close relation with mainstream ideology, or policy and measures of the governing party and government. The acquiescence, support or opposition by the mainstream ideology will determine the rise and fall of certain other thoughts.

II.2.5. Classification according to the degree and scale of influence[30]

When classifying political thought trends, based on their social influence, they can be divided into minor thoughts, branch thoughts, main thoughts, big thoughts, while these types are not paratactic division in fact, just a direct description to the social influence degree of multiple thoughts within a certain time period. Meanwhile, such division facilitates to the analysis of the basic situation of different political thought trends influence within a certain time period. When studying the specific thought, we mainly research those important thoughts, which are big thoughts and main thoughts mostly. The standard for judging the thoughts which are major ones is objective. The comprehensive performance of a kind of thought determines whether it is a kind of major thought trend that is worth attention. Minor thoughts are thoughts have certain partial influence which affect quite a number of people in some regions of a country, or influence part of people in some regions of various countries. They may be a prelude to a kind of major thought trends, may also be epilogue of major thought trends. These kind of political thought trends have obvious academic colors in most cases, and play the role within specific professional range or corresponding social groups mostly. For example, in 1980s, some philosophy thoughts of the modern west have a great influence on intellectual circles of our country, especially young college students. Branch thoughts are supplement to comprehensive thoughts. Any kind of thought trend contains many different claims and schools internally. For instance, liberalism thought trend, contains not only classical liberalism, but also neoliberalism; and conservative thought trend also includes new conservatism and old conservatism which co-exist, etc. There are scholars summarize the major thoughts of present China as: neoliberal thoughts in the economic field, democratic socialism thoughts in the political field, historical nihilism thoughts in the historical research field, etc. These thoughts exist in multiple fields, and not simply active in one field.

For thoughts pattern of contemporary China, they are all branches of major comprehensive thoughts of contemporary Chinese liberal thoughts, and specific branches with outstanding performance in different fields are the

---

30   Ibid.

specific manifestation of liberal thoughts from different aspects. The major thoughts are thoughts have greater influence upon the majority of people in a certain historical period within a region, a country or a national scope. This type of political thought trends reflects social development situation and major contradiction of such region, country or nation within a certain historical period. In 1980s, the liberalism thought trend with huge influence has been a kind of major social thought trend which has made great influence upon our society within a certain historical period. Big thoughts are thoughts with wide influence within the scope of world and last a long time. Some of them keep thriving for dozens of years, some last for centuries without falling, and some even last for thousands of years continuously. For example, Marxism thought trend guiding the world proletariat movement has always stood in the forefront of times from the date it was created till today, and guides proletariat movement in the world, and has a long practice of over 160 years. Again, for instance, the imperial power and autocratic thought of feudal society, bourgeois democracy and free thought, religious thought of capitalist society, etc. all ever be spread and developed within longer period and worldwide.

In current China, we can also see the shadow or revival of those "feudal thoughts of restoring ancient ways" inherited from the late Qing Dynasty and the early Republic of China periods, revisited, which is called as "modern Neo-Confucianism" by the scholars and the media. In addition, we could also divide thoughts as per scale of thoughts into large-scale political thought trends, middle-scale political thought trends and small-scale political thought trends. This kind of division is mainly from the view of influence scale, which could be regarded as a beneficial supplement to the division mode of small thoughts, branch thoughts, main thoughts, and big thoughts. The characteristic of large-scale political thought trends is having influence to most people in the worldwide and lasting for a long time. The characteristic of middle-scale political thought trends is having the greater influence on most people within a certain historical period in a region, a province or a nation-wide scope. For example, the political thought trends opposing imperialism, feudalism and bureaucratic capitalism in the new democratic revolution period of our country, and reform thoughts with goal of realizing socialist modernization in socialist construction period. These are all political thought trends with greater influence within the scope of our country in a certain historical period. The characteristic of small-scale political thought trends is having greater influence on quite a number of people in some fields of a country, or having influence on part of people in some fields of many countries. Such type of political thought trends belongs to academic and cultural thoughts mostly, and only plays effect among specific professional range or corresponding social groups.

II.2.6. Classification of political thought trends according to historical eras within which they were formed

Based on the historical periods they were created, political thought trends could be divided into ancient time political thoughts, recent time political thoughts, modern political thoughts, and contemporary political thoughts. During the Spring and Autumn Period in China, all schools of thoughts had contended for attention, such as legalism advocating severe criminal law, Confucianism denying self and returning to propriety, and Taoism governing by doing nothing that went against nature. The spread of these thought trends in that age all generated a profound impact, and these thoughts could be classified as ancient politics thoughts based on time. The Westernization thoughts promoting revitalization of dynasty raised in China, constitutional reform thoughts and modernization thoughts saving the country so that it may survive, as well as science and democracy thoughts of May Fourth period belong to recent times thoughts. On the other side, the current thoughts of Reform and Opening-up period belong to contemporary thoughts. But, some political thought trends have longer spread time, which is very difficult to be divided according to historical period. For example, Marxism thoughts, which is established based on historical materialism, represents the correct forward direction of human society development, and guides the occurrence, development and deepening of the world socialist movement with its correctness and progressiveness. Since its founding in the middle 19th Century, it had been activating in the worldwide and walking in the forefront of the times, for this kind of political thought trends lasts for one and a half centuries long maintaining progressiveness, it is very difficult for us to classify it by a specific historical period. Nowadays, Marxism is still playing a huge role of theoretical guide, and it is foreseeable that Marxism will still influence the whole world as an advanced political thought trend in a long period. For another example, the western liberalism thoughts and conservatism thoughts both have co-existed for over hundreds of years of history, and at present, with the continuous development of the times, their influence is still not weak worldwide. Therefore, it is very difficult to divide them into some specific historical periods, furthermore, there are also some religious thoughts which display the same nature.

II.2.7. Classification of thoughts according to where they have spread: regions or countries

Firstly, according to this division criterion, political thought trends could be divided into domestic political thought trends and international political thought trends. Since, the degree of the spread of some political thought trends, is limited within the scope of a country, such as the reform thoughts generated in 1980s of China, which was generated under specific historical background and practical environment of China at that time, and the main purpose of its generation and development were both to promote the Reform and Opening-up of China's society, and to complete the transformation of economic and political system of contemporary China society, and the spread and influence were mainly generated and developed inside the country, not wide spread internationally. While the so-called international thoughts, such as democracy thoughts, especially after World War II, the democracy thoughts swept over the whole world, and raised three waves of democratization surge successively, and multiple emerging national independent countries of Asia, Africa and Latin America walked on the democratization road. Here, we do not look at the pros and cons brought by democratization thoughts itself temporarily, only from the aspect of spread range, it could be deemed as a kind of international political thought trends. Secondly, it could be divided into western political thought trends and eastern political thought trends. From the formation of human civilization, the two worlds of eastern and western were stay in independent and closed development for a long time, and nearly in separation status for history of human civilization up to thousands of years, and such two worlds got connected till the opening of the New Route in modern times. For eastern and western, they are not only different in natural environment and geographical climate, etc., but also greatly different in cultural tradition, national character, and way of thinking formed for thousands of years. Therefore, there is unique rationality to divide so-called political thought trends into western thoughts and eastern thoughts. From the perspective of the regional location, this is the difference between east and west, which also implies differences in thought, thinking, and value pursuit. For example, traditional Confucianism thoughts is a typical eastern political thought and conservative Christian thought trend in the Western countries is a typical western political thought. At last, this division mode could divide it into China's political thought trends, America's political thought trends, Japan's political thought trends, France's political thought trends, etc. based on country. In essence, this division mode is a refinement of eastern and western political thought trends, and conduct further division according to the concept of country. The so-called Chinese thoughts refer to thoughts generated, developed and spread within the territory of China, also thoughts initiated from China. So are US's political thought trends and Japan's political thought trends.

II.2.8. Classification of thought trends according to manifestation forms

Classified according to their expression forms, thought trends can be divided into synthesized political thought trends and singular political thought trends. The Marxism thought trend can be regarded as a synthesized political thought trend and since it covers a wide range of areas and is manifests itsels in many fields such as politics, economy, philosophy, literature and art and military, etc., and becomes a system, it can be called a synthesized political thought trend. Other examples are the liberalism thought trend, conservativism thought trend, democratic socialism thought trend, which are all-embracing thought systems and possess synthesized characteristics. The so-called singularity mainly refers to the range it covers is narrower, such as the subjectivity philosophy thought trend and the practical materialism thought trend. The subjectivity philosophy thought trend was a question raised by China's aesthetics circles in 1980s, which soon expanded into various fields of philosophy, but its range of dissemination and research of was limited to the field of philosophy and related disciplines and it did not form a fairly broad manifestation. Such thought trends whose dissemination field is singular and which have a certain specialization are called singular thought trends.

II.2.9. Classification of thought trends according to their relation towards the mainstream ideology

According to their relations towards the mainstream ideology, political thought trends of a country in a definite period can be divided into three types: same direction type of political thought trends, differential type of political thought trends and hostile type of political thought trends. The same direction type of political thought trends mainly refer to those trends in accord with the current mainstream ideology, which is in China mainly manifested in conformity with the socialist core value system and with the main melody of the society, such as the thought trend of patriotism and the thought trend of Reform and Opening-up; the differential type of political thought trends means that the overall value orientation of the thought trend can be accepted by mainstream ideology and that in some aspects friction and collision occur, but such friction and collision will not seriously contravene the main viewpoints of the mainstream ideology; the so-called hostile type of political thought trends refers to those thought trends which completely departs from the mainstream ideology. With regard to socialist countries, all kinds of non-Marxist and anti-Marxist thoughts will be included in the ranks of hostile thought trends, such as the historical nihilism thought trend and separatism thought trend. However, the division into such three types is not absolute. In fact, some political thought trends fall in the middle of two types; some political thought trends have different relations with mainstream ideology in different periods; and some political thought trends have, due to the complexity of the evolution of their historical status, a quite subtle or quite controversial relation with the mainstream ideology, and are hard to classify for the time being, such as the Confucianism revival thought trend that currently exists in China.

Besides the above classification modes, there are many other modes of classification. For example, the classification according to the age and gender of the representative subjects of the thought trend as youth political thought trends, college students political thought trends, older people's political thought trends, female political thought trends, etc.; or according to the span of time as political thought trends with small time span and short duration and political thought trends with big time span and long duration. There are many classification criteria and various types of political thought trends, indicating people's different understanding and approaches towards them. As the basic characteristic, politicality is the primary criterion for the classification of types.

II.2.10. The structure of political thought trends

The classification of political thought trends and the structure of political thought trends are closely related. The structure of political thought trends is always specific to some thoughts of some type. We can look at the problems of the structure of political thought trends from two angles. Firstly, we should treat political thought trends as a whole, analyze their basic composition, and reflect the complete picture of the political thought trend in a specific society and a specific period. Secondly, we should analyze the concrete thought trends, look at their basic composition, and present the relations of various elements inside concrete thought trends. Systematic analysis of thought trends can reveal their present components, constituent elements, as well as the mutual relationship among thought trends and that between the whole thought trend and social environment and play an active role in mastering "the true face of Mount Lu"[31] of thought trends. Taken as a whole, political thought trends are composed of various real and different concrete thought trends, which become core part and peripheral part of the whole of thought trends respectively due to differences in their social influence.

The whole of political thought trends is a complex and intricate system composed of numerous political thought trends with different qualities, different reflection fields, areas, and influences. Within such a system, there are advanced and correct thought trends, also backward and wrong political thought trends, as well as thoughts about politics, economy, literature and art, philosophy, etc., and domestic and overseas thought trends. Each concrete thought trend has a self-formed system, becoming the sub-system of the big system, of the whole thought trend. The whole and part, big system and small system cross, contact, influence and effect each other.

The inner composition of the whole of political thought trends has the feature of multiple levels and complicated contents. Multiple concrete thought trends are all different parts of the whole of thought trends, and the bond that makes different thought trends unify organically is the main theme of the era that various thought trends face together. Different political thought trends examine such theme of the era from different angles of view and combine the theme of the era as the clue with the big system of political thought trends. The whole of thought trends is a complex organic structure, and multiple thought trends inside such structure contact and effect each other, forming a complex and intricate organism. Therefore, such interaction among political thought trends usually urges the whole system of thought trends to rise and fall, and the up and down of one important thought trend influences the development of the whole system of thought trends.

As a system, thought trends are open. They constantly carry out exchange of information and communication of energy with the social environment they are located, and interact with different systems. The whole of political thought trends is so, so is their sub-system as well. Investigating the circumstances of thought trends, especially of those in contemporary China historically, we can see that the big system of thought trends often contains "main trend" system and "auxiliary trend" system, where the energy of such sub-systems varies from big to small, the relations between

---

31   Mount Lu holds a special place in the hearts of the people of China, since it has a history as one of the country's original spiritual centers, being revered especially by Taoists and Buddhists. Countless writers, artists, calligraphers, and other famous personages from China's past have written in homage to Mount Lu.

each other are complementary or opposite to each other. As a sub-system in the big system of political thought trends, a concrete political thought trend often has a smaller sub-system within it, such as subjects of thought trends, psychological and theoretical appeal of the subject, and the platform for the dissemination of the thought trend.

Although a kind of thought trend can be subsumed under different thought trend categories according to different classification criteria, and different thought trends can be included into the same category according to the same classification criteria, but in the overall structure of political thought trends, the concrete thought trend takes the degree of social influence as criterion to determine its position in the structure of thought trends. In the totality of thought trends of each society, there are main thought trends and secondary thought trends. The main thought trend or mainstream thought trend is at the center of the thought trends system, the secondary thought trend or non-mainstream thought trend is at the periphery of the thought trends system. Within the main thought trend system, or taking one kind of thought trend as the center, or taking several thought trends as the center, multiple thought trends are complementary or opposite to each other. The secondary thought trend or non-mainstream thought trend exists either as the sub-system of the main thought trends system, or as the sub-system opposite to the main thought trend. Within a period of history, the amount of thought trends with big influence is not many, which makes one or several centers in the solid system of thought trends more obvious, becoming the focus of attention, and compared to them, other thought trends will "lose their splendor" .

II.3. Subject of political thought trends

Subject is the key element of political thought trends. Only by starting from the basic principles of Marxist historical materialism, can we make an accurate analysis of the subjects of political thought trends. The members of the society in a certain historical period are the material undertakers of thought trends, i.e. subjects of thought trends, and they are also the key when thought trends play their social role. The term "subject" has three basic meanings: firstly, it refers to main part of things, speaking in the sense of the amount of things, secondly, it refers to men who possesses the ability of cognition and practice in philosophy; thirdly, it refers to the natural man, legal man or nation who enjoy rights and bear obligations according to law in law.

II.3.1. The subject of political thought trends is the subject of practical-cognitive activities

A thought trend is a tide of thoughts, and the flow and change and ups and downs of thought trends embody the cognitive subject's cognition of social life and the constant conceptualization and systematic summary of their social life practice. The subject of thought trends is does not mean the subject in "public ownership as mainstay", "distribution according to work as mainstay", the main meaning of the two refers to the major parts and has a quantitative meaning. The subject of political thought trends refers to the undertaker thought trends and has no quantitative meaning.

In his monograph "Reflections on Cognition", Professor Tian Xinming has defined the relations between the subject in the epistemological sense and the subject in the substantive sense. He argued: "the subject we speak of in the epistemological sense refers precisely to the cognizant, and it is not necessary to trace what original relation it has with the subject in the sense of substantive subject or in the sense of main part, but only to distinguish them."[32] The subject of political thought trends we speak of here refers to the subject, namely undertaker of practical and cognitive activities. According to Marxism's practical point of view, man is the undertaker of social practice and of cognition, i.e. subject, and the cognition comes from practice, man obtains cognition on the basis of practice, after mastering such cognition, it is verified through practice, and the constant progress and development of cognition is pushed forward. Here, the subject of political thought trends is the subject of practice and cognitive activities, namely refers to "man" speaking from a broad angle, only that the quantity of men engaged in practical and cognitive activities is extremely enormous, and the practical activities engaged by individuals vary greatly, not every individual will access political thought trends or be effected by their influence. Therefore, the subject of political thought trends refers actually to man who is related with the emergence, development, spread, etc. of political thought trends in society.

Political thought trends are both the result of a kind of cognitive activity and a process of cognitive activity. Political thought trend is a trend of thoughts which reflects the interests of a certain class or stratum within a certain period, it is based on a certain social existence, reflects changes in social life from a certain aspect, and its mutual influence, mutual restriction and mutual permeation with some social psychology is a quite mature trend of thoughts, but such quite mature trend of thoughts is necessarily

---

32   Tian Xinming, *Reflection on Cognition*, People's Publishing House, 2000, p. 63.

the cognition o thoughts obtained based on a certain social life practice, hence, looking from this angle, we can say that a political thought trend is the result of a kind of cognitive activity. As a kind of ideal consciousness, political thought trends are not static and immutable to some extent, on the contrary, political thought trends are a dynamic and constant movement and change process. The vitality of political thought trends lies in its quality of dissemination, while a kind of political thought trend itself may also keep changing along with the constant deepening of practice. For example, in its development process, the liberalism thought trend gradually evolved from old liberalism to neo-liberalism and its internal theoretical claims have continually changed along with the changing times. Another example is the socialist thought trend that developed from the thought trend of utopian socialism to the thought trend of egalitarian socialism, to the foundation of scientific socialism by Marx and Engels, which all prove that after the formation of a political thought trend, it is still inherently changing along with time and the deepening of practice, hence, it can be said that political thought trend is both a kind of cognitive process and a kind of cognitive result.

The process of emergence, development and decline of a political thought trend is just a kind of concrete practical and cognitive activity. Through the cognition of social life practice, the subject of cognition obtains quite abstract ideal conceptions, i.e. "regular knowledge" by analysis and induction, and the practice is guided by such subject of cognition. In essence, political thought trends belong to the category of consciousness or category of cognition. Consequently, once a thought trend is formed, it will have an active effect on real practical activities, and such an active effect may be positive or negative. Therefore, the correct thought trend is the correct cognitive result obtained by cognition, and has a scientific guidance effect on practice; wrong thought trend is the opposite. During the appearance and development process of a political thought trend, the subject will conduct re-cognition effort regarding the already existing cognition results again and again, and conduct corrections and development, etc., which reflects the inheritance and innovation openness attribute of political thoughts. As it should be, as a kind of social consciousness, a "political thought" is not only "cognition" result of the subject, but also embodies feelings, social psychology, the will of subject and effect of other consciousness factors, such as currently popular money worship thoughts and hedonistic thoughts, whose spread is not only "cognition" result of subject, but also intertwined with many personal emotions, desire and wills of subject and other factors.

Nowadays, we can observe some kind of blind worship of consumerist behavior among the young people, who favor to purchase and own most popular famous brands,, seeking for easy life and pleasure as the arch value of their lives, thus they fear facing any kind of hardship and suffering. They like to show off their advantages and wealth and they are afflicted by "vanity". Under the effect of such unpleasant habits and weird psychology this section of the young people will start from their own emotions consciously, to accept money worship thoughts and hedonism thoughts these kinds of thoughts concept going against socialist core value system, which exacerbates the spread range and degree of influence to society of such bad thoughts.

II.3.2. Specific thought trends and specific groups

Certain kind of political thought trends always reflect the basic standpoint, core idea, interest appeal, etc. of certain social groups, hence these specific thoughts are mentally attached to specific groups, specific social member groups are always spread their political appeal and theoretical claims by way of thoughts, and they connected to each other closely. For instance, some green new energy companies in the west, the industrial chain where they developed are green and environmental protection, under driving and support of their own company interests, they actively promote the spread and development of green pacifism thoughts in western countries, since the more such political thought trends are accepted by government, society and the public, the more maximization of its own development interest appeal to be realized. Again, as we observe in the current world, the movement of capital keeps growing rapidly, and many western developed capitalist countries vigorously promote the spread of neoliberal thoughts and other western thoughts across the world, and especially target the socialist countries, the reason is that the spread of such political thought trends conforms to the free movement of capital owned by monopolies of the western countries. These monopolies supported by western governments not only pursue capital export and squeeze the developing countries economically, but also impose western values and western way of thinking, in order to effect the field of ideology and culture, in the final analysis, their aim is to realize their own economic and financial interests.

The destiny of thought trends and their ups and downs are always determined by the historical fate and strength of the relevant social groups they represent, and the changes in the historical circumstances and historical conditions of the social group determines the position and direction of political thoughts they support. Various political thought trends that have appeared in modern China is a good explanation, the Westernization Movement and Reform raised by feudal landlord class generated the political thought trends of "beat someone by playing his games only better" and "Chinese essence and Western utility" in the society, however due to the its own class limitations, its development is not consistent to the trend of history forward, and such thoughts saving revitalization of the dynasty disappeared along with disintegration of the feudal landlord class, mainly due to its failure to comply with socio-historical trend. For another example, after the 1911 revolution in China, the view of democratic republic had gained support among the people, Yuan Shikai engaged in restoration, and promoted the adverse trend of "respecting Confucianism and restoring ancient ways" and he even attempted to restore the monarchy, and such political thought trends withdrew from the stage of history soon due to the elimination of its corresponding social subject. While Marxist thoughts is caused by the progressiveness of its accepted subject, the proletariat entered into the stage of history as an independent political force along with its constant awakening and simultaneously proletarian class movement has spread to many regions of the world, which served as the basis that Marxist thoughts started to gain great vitality across the world and they spread to every corner of the world.

In most cases, the appearance and development of a new class are accompanied by the emergence and development of new thoughts, while the classes eliminated by history are always accompanied by old thoughts. When a class exit naturally or be ejected from social history stage, the thoughts representing its interest appeal will leave the stage of social awareness finally. According to the Marxist view of social formations and social development, the human society will experience five basic social formations according to five modes of production(s), i.e. the classless primitive community, slave society, feudal society, capitalist society, and finally the communist society, which will foster free and all-round development of men. As mentioned in the previous chapter where we dealt with the issue of classifying political thought trends (see the section 2 of the Chapter II), we have elucidated that the political thought trends could be classified as per their class attributes, and the essence means that each class will generate political thought trends belonging to its own class for declaring its own interests and claims in every social development stage. Meanwhile, with appearance of new class and exit of old class, the political thought trends will also present state of replacement of old and new. During political thought trends development historical process, no matter the east or the west, with the overthrow of the feudal autocracy, the feudal class was gradually replaced by the bourgeois class, and simultaneously the political thought trends reflecting the interests of the feudal class also exited the historical stage, and became a kind of "historical relic "exhibited in museums. In contemporary times, with the constant growth of the proletariat class, various political thought trends which reflect the demands and ideals of the proletarian thought are spread widely in the world, furthermore, according to Marxist idea regarding the law of social development, we can predict that the political thought trend of the proletariat will defeat political thought trend of the bourgeois, and the political thought trends of the bourgeois class will become the "antique object" of history along with the perishment of the bourgeois class.

"The social totality or human totality as subject shall not be comprehended as a unified and independent subject of cognition."[33] Generally, the subject of a specific political thought trends is less the whole social members or human totality. There are no such political thought trends taking social member totality and human totality as subject. A kind of political thought trend is usually sum of various concrete thoughts, while the addition of various concrete political thought trends subject does not equal to the totality of social members. The subject of political thought trends is the subset of subject of social history. Generally speaking, political thought trends always stay in the situation of "out of office", the various "weak zone" left by mainstream ideology serving regime in life are not dominating thought of society yet. Nevertheless, there are also some political thought trends already become social dominating thought, namely so-called "holding the office", while still being political thought trends with huge influence, which is not appropriate to say the mainstream ideology and dominant social thoughts are not political thought trends anymore. The development of Marxism in China is a typical example: during the development process of Marxism in China, it emerged and developed as one kind of political trend of thought and gradually turned into a mainstream ideology, thus became both the guiding thought of our party and nation. While the Marxist thought trend has risen to a kind of mainstream ideology in our country, in the other parts of the world it remains to be in a subordinate, status and exists as one of the various political thought trends, although it keeps spreading and has important social influence. On the other side some western political thought trends, such as western liberalism and parliamentary democracy thoughts, which are the main pillars of the mainstream ideology in the western countries, we see that these two political thought trends still keep spreading all around the world, especially in some burgeoning developing countries, and the spread of them still have certain vigor.

---

33   Tian Xinming, *Reflection on Cognition*, People's Publishing House, 2000, p. 65.

II.3.3. Group subjects and individual subjects

Prof. Tian Xinming has argued: "Subject is not an isolated individual. People are all engaged in cognition and practice activities who live within specific social relations, and form their own cognition or thought from a certain social relation, hence the subject is the real men, who are essentially "ensemble of certain social relations". While in this way, not only individuals are subject, but also various social groups (such as scientists group, school of thought, political party, class, nation) formed by bonding a certain social relation could be the subject. In this way, there are two forms of subject: individual subject and group subject, where the group subject further contains multiple social groups of different natures, forms, scales, levels."[34] Here, such concrete analysis to subject of cognition is heuristic for us in studying the subject of political thought trends.

There is no doubt that people (men) are the subject of political thought trends. However, these "men" are not abstract men in general case, but real men in life, and they are "ensemble of social relations". The social men, as ensemble of social relations exist in two ways, firstly as individuals in an individual mode, and secondly in a collective existence mode. The collective existence mode is the existence mode of a social group. The subject of political thought trends could be individuals, and can also be various groups, as the unity of an number of groups, and a nation can be seen as one of the most big groups of men. Even though when leaving thought of social individuals, there will be no political thought trends, the political thought trends are not simple addition of individual thought, but present in a general form which have transcended the specific, complex and variable factors of individual thought to a great extent. The political thought trends embody emotions, wishes, theoretical direction and interest appeal of social members within a certain scope relatively concentrated in dynamic form, which is group consensus.

In concrete real social life, different social member groups possess hierarchy, having difference of family, collectivity, class, nation, country, and all mankind. As social consciousness with widespread influence, the subject of political thought trends could reach to the scale of class usually. With the development of human spread ability, the subject scale of political thought trends also has very big extension, and the influence of thoughts is widened unprecedentedly.

---

34   Ibid., p. 64.

When discussing the problem of thoughts subject, the role of ideologist in thoughts has to be considered. The ideologist or the theoretician plays important role during thoughts generation and development process, which will be further explained in the Chapter III of this book. Among specific performance of thoughts, the most striking is "performance" of ideologists or representatives, their speech, their active participation to social affairs all impress people very much, they are the real "initiator of evil" of some thoughts, the subject of thoughts. Notwithstanding the ideologists or those other people "representing" certain thoughts pay great attention to social reality with stronger cognition ability and explore theoretical solutions to social problems, having excellent performance, even possess many "followers", but they should be evaluated as organic embodiments of thought subjects, being individual subjects of thought trends, which should be evaluated separate from the big group of subject of the thought trends.

Although men's thoughts of daily life, seem quite apart from "class outlook", from the view of world scope, the social group form of class is still the most important subject of thoughts. With the world scope, the existence of class is an objective and unavoidable social fact. The proletariat and the bourgeoisie are still the two big classes of human society. Both the Marxism and socialist thoughts reflecting interest appeal of the proletariat and various capitalist thoughts reflecting the bourgeoisie interest appeal are taking class as subject. Lenin believed: "We cannot know the speed and success with which individual historical movements of a respective era will develop. We can and in fact do know, which class is at the center of this era or that era, what determines its essential content, the main direction of its development, the most important characteristics of the historical situation of the respective era, etc"."[35] "Since history is mentioned, various concrete questions should be explained, by illustrating the class origin of various thoughts."[36] Mao Zedong once pointed out: "In class society, everyone lives as a member of a particular class, and every kind of thinking, without exception, is stamped with the brand of a class."[37]

Throughout the main thoughts with global influence of stage of thoughts occur repeatedly in Chinese and foreign history, where the important form of subject is groups, classes and strata in most cases. For thoughts from "Westernization" and "Constitutional Reform and Modernization" thoughts in the late Qing Dynasty, to "reform" thoughts of revolution of 1911 period, the subjects are all concrete social class, either landlord class, or the new

---

35 *Complete Works of Lenin*, Vol. 26, People's Publishing House, 1988, p. 143.
36 *Complete Works of Lenin*, Vol. 25, People's Publishing House, 1988, p. 213.
37 *Selected Works of Mao Zedong*, Vol. 1, People's Publishing House, 1991, p. 283.

bourgeoisie of China. After May Fourth movement, the socialist thoughts with Marxism as core take the new proletariat as the subject. Since modern times, the western important thoughts all embody cognition to society trend and other important issues of bourgeois class in different period of bourgeois development, which is expression of bourgeois will.

Political party is the centralized representative of class, being the core subject of thoughts in sequence. Marx believes that the essence of political party is centralized representatives of specific class interest, is the leading force in specific class political force, is a political organization formed by political hard-core of each class to seize or consolidate the political power of the state. The class basis of political party is a certain class groups. These free class groups become class for itself by organization of political party, and the thought system and social psychology reflecting whole class interest and wish shall be expressed by such political party intensively. The functions of political party are to condense class interest demand and political consciousness, aggregating and developing class force, influencing and leading social politics, cultivating politics backbone of own class, etc., where such functions determine that political party will publicize the class or stratum it represented to realize its own purpose and functions inevitably. A kind of political thought trends possessing specific political standpoints is formed accordingly, and certainly the political standpoints of such thoughts may be recessive in most cases. For instance, the green party established by western countries rises rapidly as a kind of new political force in recent years, driven by green party, the concepts of "priority of ecology" green environmental protection", etc. are developed rapidly, and the green party also becomes the main undertaker and pusher of green pacifist thoughts. In this perspective, the core subject of political thought trends should be political party.

In most of the time, it seems that many political thought trends possess a certain characteristic of all the people, being psychological reflection and theoretical appeal of the majority of social members. However, this characteristic of all the people is visional in fact, the core subject still possesses a certain nature of class, the reason is that "every newly emerging class attempting to replace the old ruling class status have to say its own interest into the common interest of all the social members to achieve its own purpose, that is to say, when expressing on concept: give general form to own thought, and describe them into the only thought conforming ration and having general sense"[38]. This is similar to western political parties who raise the flag of "serving all people" when conducting their election

---

38   *Selected Works of Marx and Engels,* Vol. 1, People's Publishing House, 1995, p. 100.

campaigns and try the best to label themselves as the representative of social people, which confuses the masses by such campaigns, so as to publicize their own justice, representative and advanced nature, etc., and obtain
more support from people. As a matter of fact, according to the basic views
of Marxism, such "characteristic of all the people" does not exist in a class
society, as long as we are in a class society and classes exist, there will be
difference for sure, the non-harmony of class contradiction, class antagonism will generate differentiation of peoples' interests, and every stratum
or class will generate political party, groups, etc. representing its own interests. The more recognition and support one kind of political thought trends
obtain from social subject, the better it develops, the vitality and influence
will be stronger, and hence various political thought trends will show its
correctness, representative nature, etc. with all force when publicizing its
value viewpoint and theory connotation, so as to gain more support. Those
denying existence and antagonism of class publicized by political thought
trends are just a kind of means of publicity of themselves.

In addition, for any class political party and core figure would like to develop their theory system into thoughts form of wide influence, the recognition of majority members of own class must be obtained firstly, and then it
is possible to spread to other social people from this class, to obtain acceptance and support of different social members, strata, classes and groups.

Under same period and same mode of production, different class and
stratum will form different political thought trends due to different class
status. Marx and Engels believe: "The existence of revolutionary thought
under a certain time has the premise of existing revolution class."[39] Such
as the rising and spread of Humanism in Renaissance period, it appeared
based on capitalist mode of production, being the thoughts reflecting wish
and demand of newborn bourgeois; Before generation of Marxism, the utopian socialism thoughts have reflected the voice of the exploited people.

II.3.4. The subjects of contemporary political thought trends in China

In contemporary China, the subjects of political thought trends have
roots in different interest social strata or groups. Our party leads Chinese
people of all ethnic groups to hold highly the great banner of socialism with
Chinese characteristics, continue to emancipate the mind, adhere to the
Reform and Opening-up, promote the concepts of scientific development
and social harmony, and advance by full steps along the path of socialism

---

39   Ibid., p. 99.

with Chinese characteristics. All the people in the great course of socialism with Chinese characteristics have the common ideal and common interest of socialism with Chinese characteristics. However, with profound changes of social structure, social organization form, and social interest pattern, the social gap between the rich and the poor is widened, and different social stratification and interest groups have appeared. Such different groups have different cognition to social practice, which accompanying the whole process of Reform and Opening-up all the time. Among these cognition, some become thoughts have huge influence and wide attention, some are political thought trends with small influence, some are still staying in the level of social psychology, and not "appear on stage" in theoretical and systematic form yet. These thoughts possess a certain political nature even class nature.

So far, in the over 30 years of Reform and Opening-up, the thought trends with huge influence and wide attention have quite obvious political nature and class nature in most cases. The reason is that in most cases major political thought trends of contemporary China have close relation with "discourse" of western developed capitalist countries. For example, the liberalism thought trend in China inherits both the partial legacy of the Chinese liberalism before the founding of new China and the current western liberalism thought trend as its theoretical source. The bourgeois nature of liberalism thought system is clear. The liberalism is ideology has been constantly adjusted by western bourgeois in different periods since modern times; also in old China, it has showed apparent class consciousness. Additionally, the political nature and class nature of these main thoughts all possess a certain realistic basis. They reflect political thought trends of ownership system of different natures, which embodies different political nature and class nature to some extent. Our socialist basic economic system takes public ownership as the mainstay, and allows a variety of ownership systems to develop jointly. People's views and values are different under ownership system of different natures. The existence and development of non-public ownership economy are determined by basic national conditions in the primary stage of socialism, which are necessary and beneficial supplement for public ownership economy. The views and values corresponding to non-public ownership and public ownership economy will show a certain political nature and class nature objectively. The existence of views and values, and political thought embodying non-public ownership economy demand shows characteristics of ideology in the primary stage of socialism, which are objective and normal, and we cannot regard it as "dreadful monster" due to a certain political nature and class nature. We should positively explore the effective way to lead the social thoughts with the socialist core value system following the spirit of the 17th National Congress of the CPC, and conduct ideological work actively, namely respect for differences and tolerate the diversity.

In most cases, political thought trends appear earlier than the corresponding stratum, or still continue to exist after the fall of that specific stratum. There may be not a concrete stratum corresponding to a kind of thoughts with apparent class consciousness in social life, while this cannot indicate that thoughts have no class character, and not take class and stratum as subject, the class subject of thoughts just exists potentiality at this time, or already withdrawn the historical stage, falling and even disappear. Such existence of political thought trends earlier than or behind social stratum is determined by the characters of political thought trends itself essentially. To a certain extent, political thought trends belongs to a kind of specific social consciousness, as which the development of political thought trends possess relative independence, and the direct performance of such relative independence could be divided into advance nature and hysteretic nature. The advance nature of political thought trends means that a kind of political thought trends could appear earlier than the class it corresponded. For instance, during European Renaissance period, bourgeois thoughts opposing feudal ruling generated, while the generation of bourgeois itself was in the bud, this political thought trends belonging to bourgeois generated earlier than this class, and played a role of theoretical forerunner for the generation and development of such class. The hysteretic nature of political thought trends refers to a class which has been eliminated by history with times development, while some thoughts reflecting such class are still spreading on society and having a certain influence. For example, the feudal superstition thoughts exist in Chinese society at present, although the feudal class had fallen apart long ago and banished into the cage of history, there are still many thoughts reflecting vestiges of feudalism spreading.

Generally, the political thought trends reflecting interest appeal of different social stratum and groups in contemporary China exist under the premise that the primary interests of all the people are consistent. As for such political thought trends reflecting different interest appeals, we should treat them dialectically. On the one hand, the rationality of the existence shall be affirmed. At that time, our country stayed in the crucial period of social transformation, a series of various problems and contradiction were brought along with rapid development of social economy, the whole society generated different stratification either, and people representing different strata would generate political thought trends reflecting their own stratum interest appeals, which is a necessary phenomenon that social development faced. On the other hand, we should also notice that the divergence among them does not mean fundamental divergence inside people, and the overall interests and fundamental interests of Chinese people are consistent, every Chinese desire to complete the construction of great socialist modernization country at an early date, and realize great rejuvenation of the Chinese nation. Accordingly, the contradictions embodied by political thought trends reflecting different voices are basically contradictions among the people, rather than contradictions between us and our enemies.

II.4. Functions and capacities of political thought trends

The functions and capacities of thought trends reflect and demonstrate the initiative and active role of social consciousness. Historical materialism advocates social consciousness being determined by social existence, in turn social consciousness can also counter react on human social existence. Therefore, during the research on functions of political thought trends under the guidance of historical materialism, it is required to explore the particularity in these functions based on general functions of social consciousness. Functions and capacities of the political thought trend can be examined from various aspects, below we will mainly discuss their guidance function, social cognitive function, conceptual integration function and social practice function.

II.4.1. Guiding function of political thought trends

All existing research results emphasize on the issue of social role of political thought trends. In the series of books "Thought trends in Modern Chinese Society" edited by Wu Yannan, Mr. Dai Yi, the impetus effect of political thought trends on social history has been emphasized as follows: "any thought trend derives from the material life of society, this does not hinder its proactive guidance capacity and function. Once a thought trend is generated and formed, it will mobilize a huge social feedback power. People will use the political doctrine they are inclined to or believe in as a guidance for their current activities. Thought trends can impede the development of history, significantly. The outline for further development of society can be predicted through observation and research on the main trend in some political thought trends."[40]

---

40   Wu Yannan, editor in chief, *Modern Chinese Social Thought Trends*, Hunan Education Publishing House, 1998.

In the introduction of the book *Marxism and Contemporary Thought Trends: Debate on Thought Trends in Contemporary Social Trend*, it is indicated that political thought trends can "significantly impact social development," "in human society, political thought trends normally goes ahead of the society, and it often predicts that some social change will occur" "under the cover of thought trends, the history in deep layer is surging and developing." This book also indicates that both correct and wrong trends will have social effect: "once grasped by the mass, a social thought trends will turn into a material power that can affect social development and directly impact people. When the trend is correct, it will push ahead the society. But when it is wrong, it will undoubtedly cause adverse and even destructive effect on the society."[41] Just as the great initiative effect of political thought trends, people keep researching on it constantly. Without such initiative, our study on political thought trends will lose its realistic base.

Although researchers extremely highlight the powerful guidance function, they need to further study its specific role. In this book, the author believes that we should continue to deepen the knowledge on the guidance function of political thought trends in the following respects. First, we shall focus on the whole situation of political thought trends, and not only research the social role of each specific trend from the perspective of intellectual history, but also make overall discussion on social function of political thought trends. Second, we should not only study political thought trends from the perspective of academic thought trends, but also focus on its political nature, as well as political and social issues embodied by the trend. Third, we should separate research on functions of political thought trends from the study upon the effect of social science on society. Social science is not identical to political thought trends. Their social roles are not the same. The social role of political thought trends is not a subset in that of social science. The political thought trends may be intensely embodied as the generation and development of one category of social science in certain historical period or as the rising and falling of synthetic change in multiple categories of social science in certain social historical period. Therefore, during a period when dramatic changes are occurring in economic, political and cultural life of society, the role played by political thought trends will normally greater than that of general categories of social science. The social roles of political trend of thought and social science both specifically reflect the reaction of social consciousness on social existence. They have both difference and association, but they are not identical.

---

41 Wang Ji, editor in chief, *Marxism and Contemporary Social Thought Trends—the Debate on the Trend of Thought in the Contemporary Society*, China Renmin University Press, 1994.

Fundamentally, the guidance function of political thought trends reflects the reaction on social existence. As a form of social consciousness, the thought trends can exert material power under corresponding social and historical conditions to react on social existence and affect social material and spiritual life. As for various trend of political though, their guidance function has difference in respect of quality and quantity. In respect of quality, an advanced political thought trends plays a positive and promoting role on social existence, while an outdated trend will play a negative and hindering role. In respect of quantity, the role of the political thought trends can deepen or lightened in degrees, large or small in scope and long or short in time.

II.4.2. Cognitive function of political thought trends

A political thought trend is a specific form of social consciousness, it naturally counter react to social existence and thus can affect it. One key aspect of this reaction is its reflection function. The reflection function can directly embody the effect of social existence on political thought trends. A kind of thought trends would change social existence at some level only when it can reflect social existence. The thought trends are the cognition of its subject (as cognitive subject) on social existence. The subject of a thought trends is a group comprising of individuals. During the process of cognition on social existence, the thought trends, as a cognitive result, represents common opinions of the members in the group. But the formation of these opinions are realized by the creative contributions of a certain relatively small political group and some thinkers. Specifically, the cognitive object of the thought trends mainly refers to hot or hard issues in economic, political and cultural life of society, containing both problems in material field and focuses on spiritual level. Basic features of thought trends are also deemed as characteristics of the cognition of this trend on social existence. The political feature of thought trends means that political thought trends will pay more attention to these realistic issues, since it is often an indicator of the sensitivity of national conditions and public opinion. The movement feature of thought trends means that it normally expresses the cognition on society by means of ideological trend and tide, which is surging and flooding and will turn to the most powerful voice of the era. The practice feature of thought trends means that its cognition on society is forward-looking. It can reflect social movement by means of ideological trend, performing as an alarm.

Specifically, in a real society, the cognitive function of political thought trends can play its role by being use as "barometer" and "reference system". The political thought trends are much surging and massive, but wild wind normally rises from gentle breeze. Political thought trends are a represen-tation of public psychology. The change of society leads to various emo-tions, desires and demands among the mass. And political thought trends just come from such public psychological opinion. Social change may induce splits of public social psychology. When a new common psycho-logical tendency emerges, it will combine with a certain ideological ele-ment or ideology, evolving to political thought trends that is widely spread and responded. Generally, political thought trends manifest social change. Under a kind of political thought trends, there must be some social con-tradiction that has exited or occurred. Just because people's psychologi-cal consciousness and appeal has not been expressed publicly or achieved, which is then restricted and depressed into civil pains and complaints, such pent-up social sub-consciousness will surge and gather quickly and lead to political thought trends. This shows that the generation and spread of political thought trends corresponds to a dialectic process in which a social contradiction grows from its potential status to intensified status and ac-cordingly the social change develops from a stage of quantitative accumu-lation into a qualitative change. It is said that "any thought trend within an era is caused by "continuous mass movement". A movement is not neces-sarily conscious, planned and an organized. We cannot tell who is active or passive in the movement. People involved in the movement may not possess a common plan or know one another. Their posts and purposes to in the movement are also different. Within a movement, there exist numerous small factions, which envy and exclude one another. However, there must be one or several common ideas as the basis of thought trend."[42] Through the role played by cognitive function of political thought trends as barom-eter and reference system, one political party and country can analyze and understand the mentality, social psychology, social demand and ideological trend of each class and stratum, and also find focuses and issues in social contradiction, so as to seek out common concerns of the mass, grasp the appeal of thought and interest of the public, and timely adjust its own route, principles and policies.

II.4.3. Political thought trends pursue to integrate ideas and concepts of the group

The subject of apolitical thought trend, especially the subject at the core of it, will inevitably strive to get the support of "masses" by means of pub-licity, education, guidance. In this way, the core subject will pursue to in-tegrate the ideological cognition and understanding of a group (a part of

---

42   Liang Qichao, *Introduction to the Qing Dynasty*, Zhonghua Book Publishing, 2011, p. 2.

masses) to enhance its cohesive group strength. By using the scale provided by standards in the thought trends reflecting their own interests, major
members in political thought trends may not only preach to social members
agreeing with their thoughts, but also make efforts to affect, transform and
absorb more social members to identify with and insist on their core theories and values. Besides, these major members will criticize all opposite
or rivaling ideologies and the social system they support and advocate and
publicize their own ideology and practical demands.

Mao Zedong once commented: "the birth of a new social system also ac-
companies screaming and shouting, which aim to advertise the superiority
of the new system and criticize the backward character of the old system."[43]
The spread of a thought trend includes a process of publicity, education and
ideological integration, which aims to unite and gain active members, unify
their thoughts, thus achieve cohesiveness in the group subject. Political
thought trends not only integrate people's thoughts at the level of theoretical cognition, but also pursue to integrate people's social psychology, their
emotions, wills, demands and ideals. Therefore, political thought trends are
a key mirror which reflect social consciousness. The social influence of the
thought trend depends on the depth and scope of its idea integration. Marx
pointed out: "in order to play this role of liberating (the whole society, note
by the quoter), any class must arouse instant fanaticism among itself and
among the masses. In such instant, this class and the whole society share
a relationship of close brotherhood. This class unites with the whole of
society as one and is deemed as the general representative of the whole of
society. The class making a revolution appears from the very start [...] not
as a class but as the representative of the whole of society"[44] This is why the
political thought trends can gather strength from various different groups,
in certain socio-historical periods. The idea integrative function of a political thought trend is reflected in the following aspects:

First, as one form of social consciousness, a political thought trend provides
some social members with common value orientation, idealized goals, even
moral rules and even a religious faith. Common value orientation and ideal
target are a kind of social ideology, which can reflect and adjust various interest relation between social members in real life and which, by relying on people's inner belief, value orientation and ideal target, also can affect people's
living and production order, adjust the relation between human and nature,

---

43 *Selection of Important Documents Since the Founding of China,* Vol. 7, Central Party
Literature Press, 1993, p. 231.
44 *Selected Works of Karl Marx and Frederick Engels,* Vol. 1, People's Publishing House,
1995, p. 12.

and encourage, restrict or guide individual act. This pursuit on common value idea by political thought trends makes human inner spiritual life orderly and reasonable, and forms a sense of belonging, which shows the interest integration function of the trend. Second, conceptual and ideological integration function of political thought trends is reflected by its guidance on people's political thinking and political inclinations. Generally, a political thought trend has a "political nature". It achieves conceptual and ideological integration by the "guidance" of politics. Any social person will spontaneously accept the cultivation by some ideology since his birth. During such influence, the person will be indoctrinated, assimilated and finally completely controlled. As a social consciousness with political nature, political thought trends will inevitably publicize its political tendency during its spread. Whether the tendency is "recessive" or "dominate", it will unconsciously change people's thoughts, thinking and ideas, and make them be integrated into the system of the political thought trends. Third, the idea integration function of political thought trends is reflected by that the trend absorbs, inherits and develops other thoughts. Any political thought trends grow up based on certain cultural background and ideas, and it is an outcome from combined action of various social cultural thoughts and ideas. Therefore, during its formation development, the trend inevitably integrates with original social ideas, thoughts and faiths, turning into a political ideological system with unique features. Fourth, the conceptual and ideological integration function is also embodied by the thought trend's social and political ideals, which greatly unify the purpose and goals of its social members regarding their behaviors. To some degree, political thought trends can be deemed as a flag for different people in the community or society, directed by which the purpose and action of social members can be unified. For example, during the May Fourth Period, stirred by the "democracy and science" thought trend, there formed and grew a political trend to bring down Confucianism and oppose feudal ethics. The spread of Marxism trend in China was another example. Countless revolutionary martyrs struggled bravely and doggedly, under the guidance of Marxism and with common political ideals. Finally, led by Chinese Communist Party, the victory was won, which enabled that people become the masters of their county.

II.4.4. Political thought functioning as the generator of social practice

A political thought trend possesses, distinct and strong, reality nature, thus all political thought trends will strive to become the spiritual driving force for a certain social change, and lead some social members to engage in practical activities so as to change the social reality. The realistic nature of political thought trends represents its powerful practical function.

No matter what kind of political trend, it must have certain social influence and be accepted by some social members, leading to calling ability in different degree. Although a kind of political thought trends shows no mandatory or restrictive nature, it obtains certain influence and strong initiative once it has emerged, with great impact on society. Marx and Engels said: "Just as in France in the 18th Century, so in Germany in the 19th Century, a philosophical revolution ushered in the political collapse."[45] Lenin said, "Without a revolutionary theory, there can be no revolutionary movement."[46] Mao Zedong also pointed out: "Once the correct ideas, characteristic of the advanced class are grasped by the masses, these ideas turn into a material force which changes society and changes the world."[47]

No matter what kind of political trend, it will lead some social members to identify the circumstance, direction and road, organize spontaneously or consciously and take actions to maintain or reform reality. As for the political thought trends that roots in spirit of the time and meets the development trend of the era, its cognition on the society is objective and has the nature of truth. Its integration of people's ideas is advanced, which can really motivate people. Therefore, it can help people to solve the issues of world view, view on life and values, indicate the direction of society and propose active and effective theoretical resolution for the practice task of society change. It is a spiritual power to achieve social reform.

As for an outdated thought trend that deviates from the main trend of society and opposes historical trend, it has no the nature of truth as it cannot correctly reflect the law of social development. Its integration of people's ideas is backward, even reactionary. Therefore, it cannot positively guide people to go along the right way in social production and life, but cause negative and harmful effect, such as confusing and corrupting people's thoughts. Prof. Xu Qixian has made an profound analysis in this respect: in the reform of new and old society, an advanced political thought trend functions as catalyst for the birth of new society and elegy for the old society, such as Marxism thought trend in the period of May Fourth Movement; while a reactionary trend of thought is the cardiotonic for a dying society to linger out its existence and the stumbling block for the birth and advance of a new society, such as "pursuit for the old democracy trend" and individualist

45   *Selected Works of Karl Marx and Frederick Engels,* Vol. 4, People's Publishing House, 1995, p. 214.
46   *Selected Works of Lenin,* Vol. 1, People's Publishing House, 1995, p. 153
47   *Collected Works of Mao Zedong,* Vol. 8, People's Publishing House, 1995, p. 320.

liberalism thought trend and the third road liberal trend thought before the birth of New China. In history, a large-scale stormy thought trend generally functions as the precursor of social reform and change, such as humanism thought trend that formed since the 16th Century in Europe, bourgeois democratic revolution trend that formed in China's modern history era, the May Fourth (New Culture) trend, and the patriotic trend in the War of Resistance against Japanese aggression. In a relative peaceful historical period, political thought trends normally do not assume such violent or stormy forms or do not hold simple affirmation or negation attitude when attempting to solve social issues. A progressive political thought trend such as the socialism thought trend often pushes ahead the development of society by enhancing the progressive content in social life of people and actively develops and emancipates the social productive forces. On the other side, erroneous and reactionary political thought trends, such as the anarchistic trend and the ultra-left trend which we have seen we have encountered during the "Great Cultural Revolution" often cause social turmoil, consequently such negative stormy thought trends are not precursors of progressive social reform, instead constitute a dangerous mine that can paralyze the society and hinder its normal advance and development. Because of this complexity, when we examine political thought trends, we should first analyze their nature and identify whether it is a progressive and revolutionary trend or a wrong and reactionary trend.[48]

The social practice function of political thought trends is reflected by its maintaining nature and critical nature. As a specific social ideology, the political thought trends normally play a great role of initiative in the field of social ideology. In the development of the current society, no matter in a capitalist country or a socialist country, there all exist a social ideology suitable for its regime, pleading for the rationality and legitimacy of the regime. As previously discussed, based on its relationship with the dominant ideology, the political thought trends can be divided into three categories: same-directional trend, differential trend and hostile trend. The maintaining nature means that the political thought trends maintain the rationality and legitimacy of the current regime. It is mainly reflected by that the political thought trends can basically match the dominate ideology of the society. The spread and development of such trend can enhance the trust of people on present regime and is beneficial for the stability and development of the society. The critical nature means that the political thought trends criticizes and satirizes the real society by mirroring current social problems, causing

---

48   Xu Qixian, Research on Social Thought Trends, *Journal of Hainan Industrial University,* 1999(2).

certain influence among the mass. Some political thought trends may induce a large-scale mass movement, so as to express the interest appeal of the mass.

The exerting of above functions of political thought trends is mainly determined by how deeply and extensively it has grasped the mass. The more people it grasps, the greater role it can play. The number of the mass grasped by the thought trends relies on whether it can seize the law of social and historical development, its class subject's status and strength in the society, as well as other factors, such as publicity.

The magnitude of the above functions of political thought trends is also affected by the state of interactions among different thoughts. Such interactions not only affect the functioning or function of the thought trend as macro system but also affect specific thought trends embodied (as subsystems) in this macro system. The paradoxical movement of the specific thought trends (as sub-systems) within the macro system of the political thought trends, can in some cases strengthen and solidify the whole system, conversely in other cases weaken it. In the case that specific thought trends within the macro system are in a state of mutual cooperation and mutual promotion, the function of the whole system will be greatly enhanced; contrarily when specific thought trends are in a status of mutual opposition and confrontation, they will offset each other, the function of the whole system will be weakened. Consequently, the social function of those mutually promoting and supporting thought trends will be enhanced, in a reverse case the social effect of mutually opposing thought trends will weaken.

CHAPTER THREE

Basic Conditions for the Formation and Development of Political Thought Trends

The formation and development of political thought trends have complicated causes. The contradictory motion of productive forces and the relations of production is deemed as the root cause among all causes. Additionally, there are many other important affecting factors as well, such as the existence and activity of multiple economic forms and social powers that rise and fall, as well as the surging of various ideological trends and resources.

III.1. Economic, political and cultural conditions for the formation and development of political thought trends

The formation of any political thought trend finds its roots in social existence. The general relationship between social existence and social consciousness provides an important basis for the analysis regarding the social and historical conditions for the formation of political thought trends. The production mode which is a summation of productive forces and the relations of production is the key aspect of social existence. The main form of social consciousness is the ideological and cultural conditions. Therefore, the social and historical conditions for the emergence of political thought trends may be analyzed based on economic, political, ideological and cultural conditions of a certain society. Changes in these conditions reflect the contradictions between the productive forces and the relations of production, as well as between economic foundation and superstructure. By these changes, social psychology, social tendency and the epochal theme of specific era is protruded. Among all these conditions, economic conditions plays the dominant role, while, generally speaking, political, ideological and cultural conditions often constitute the direct cause for the rise and fall of the political thought trends.

III.1.1. Economic conditions

Historical materialism "explains all historical events, ideas, all politics, philosophy and religion from the material, economic material conditions of life of the historical period in question."[1]

When we study a political thought trend, we must understand its economic conditions within which it comes into being. The fundamental cause of why people form one motive or feeling instead of another is buried deeply in the economic process. It is the economic conditions and the conflict of material interests among men that drive people to generate various consciousness forms and desires. The economic conditions for the formation of political thought trends is a sum of all economic factors in the field of material and economic life of the society that lead to such formation. Some researchers believe that, such economic conditions also include the level of productive forces in a certain given social stage, the composition of the relations of production, the nature of economic system, and "people's daily material life conditions. Liu Jianjun wrote: the level of productive forces is the most fundamental and crucial condition.[2] This analysis is very enlightening, but we still need to pay sufficient attention to the role of the relations of production, and focus on the influence of the dynamic influence of productive forces and the relations of production on political thought trends. We can analyze the connotation of changes of economic conditions affecting the two political thought trends at tree levels: productive forces, the relations of production and daily material life.

The productive force factor: The productive forces are the most fundamental factor that affect and restrict the formation and development of a political thought trend. Productive forces ultimately determines the overall form of a society, including the difference of social development stages, the replacement of one social form with another, the structure of the relations of production, the level of economic development, the condition of material life, and the development degree of spiritual life. Therefore, it can be concluded that the level of productive forces is the decisive factor in the formation and development of political thought trends. Generally, the development degree of political thought trends is determined by the level

---

1   *Collected Works of Karl Marx and Frederick Engels*, Vol. 3, People's Publishing House, 2009, p. 320.
2   Liu Jianjun, On the Formation, Development and Regression of Social Thought Trends, *Academic Monthly,* 1995(2).

of social consciousness, which is further determined by the development status of productive forces. Although the three items—productive forces, the relations of production and daily material life—do not always keep pace with one another, the development of political thought trends is always determined by the level of productive forces. Fundamentally, political thought trends reflect the development and changes in the productive forces through multiple intermediate links. Plekhanov indicated, "People get accustomed to the prevailing beliefs, concepts, modes of thought and means of satisfying given aesthetic demands. But should the development of productive forces lead to any substantial change in the economic structure of society, and, as a consequence, in the reciprocal relations of the social classes, the psychology of these classes will also change, and with it the "spirit of the times" and the "national character" will change. This change is manifested in the appearance of new religious beliefs or new philosophical concepts, of new trends in art or new aesthetic demands."[3]

Plekhanov did not clearly explain the relationship between productive forces and the relations of production, but the paragraph above from him also discuss the meaning of thought trends, such as "popular faiths", "ideas", and "modes of thought" and "means of satisfying given aesthetic demands requirements". The relationship between all these factors mentioned by him and the development level of productive forces can also be applied to the relationship between political thought trends and productive forces level.

The level of productive forces can affect political thought trends, which can be observed intuitively. For example, the speed and scope of spread of political thought trends are directly determined by various levels of material conditions provided in different stages of productive forces development. This is typically reflected by the fact that, since the later 1990s, the innovation of internet technology and the popularity of its application had greatly accelerated information dissemination and information rapidly spreads across the whole world, which objectively push political thought trends to diffuse worldwide at an unprecedented rate. The development of information technology is gradually weakening the concept of time and distance in the spread of political thought trends, enabling certain unique political thought trend which rises in some countries rapidly spread to others, although they have different realistic basis, they can attract the attention of other countries and affect them. The internet and IT technology is

---

3 *Plekhanov's Selected Philosophical Works*, Vol. 2, SDX Joint Publishing Company, 1961, p. 273, http://www.newyouth.com/archives/classics/plekhanov/materialist_conception_of_histor.html.

undoubtedly the product of relatively developed productive forces in the current stage of the world, and the constantly improved productive forces will inevitably create a higher level of material conditions, which will accelerate the spread of political thought trends and extend their influence scope.

Generally, the changes in the relations of production is the immediate cause for the activity of a thought trend, while the development of productive forces is the fundamental driving force pushing the changes in the relations of production. The different development stages of productive forces have determined that human society has undergone or is undergoing through five types of the relations of production: primitive communist relations of production, slavery relations of production, feudal relations of production, capitalist relations of production and communist relations of production in sequence from lower to higher levels. Pushed fundamentally by the advancement of productive forces, the development level and activity of political thought trends shows an increasing tendency on the whole. Besides, the formation and development of political thought trends is more immediate and become prominent during the period when the relations of production are in an era of change. The relations of production determined by the development and emancipation of productive forces are the direct factor which affect the formation, development of the political thought trends. The influence of productive forces on political thought trends is grasped normally through abstractions made by the cognitive subject.

For example, the development requirements of and development direction of productive forces determine the nature and fate of a political thought trend. In the early 1990s, as a result of the collapse of socialist camp, and the communist movement entering a period of low tide, the residual psychological effects of the 1989 Tiananmen student upheaval, as well as the chronic economic turbulences and rising inflation the "left wing" thought trend had once more arose in China. This "left wing" thought trend, under the disguise of rejecting peaceful evolution towards capitalism and fighting against bourgeois liberalism, has doubted the ten-years plus Reform and Opening-up practice, and questioned whether its nature was socialist or capitalist. However, the economic achievements in this period have evidently proved that the Reform and Opening-up was in conformity with the requirements and orientation of developing the productive forces of our country. Those political events were triggered by economic issues, and economic issues, like the price inflation, occurred as a result of specific causes, in fact the Reform and Opening-up was not the underlying cause. Therefore, since Deng Xiaoping's Southern Speech in 1992, China firmly deepened and extended the Reform and Opening-up, and decided to establish a system of socialist market economy. The "left" thought trend which flourished in the 1990s finally perished as it could not hinder the development of productive forces.

In general, the influence of productive forces on the formation and development of political thought trends is based on the general principle of the relationship between social existence and social consciousness. Compared with other economic factors, this effect of the former is more abstract and indirect. The formation and development of political thought trends at the level of social consciousness of broad masses is fundamentally and undoubtedly determined by the development of productive forces. However, as mentioned above, the decisive influence of the productive forces factor is abstract and indirect. This factor provides different levels of material life conditions for people in the certain development stages of productive forces development, which in turn affect the changes in the relations of production. And it is grasped by abstraction of cognition subjects. In a nut shell, the productive forces abstractly and indirectly affect the formation and development of political thought trends.

Compared to productive forces, the relations of production factor affects the formation and development of political thought trends more specifically and more directly. The changes in the relations of production directly influence the formation and development of a thought trends. The changes in the relations of production is driven by the development of the productive forces. Therefore, during the formation and development of a thought trend, this factor is reflected as a paradoxical movement of the contradiction between productive forces and the relations of production. The dominant production relation determines the nature of a society, as well as the economic and political status, historical fate and interests pattern among the existing classes in the society. The dominant production relation is also the decisive factor in the formation of the political superstructure (such as political and legal system) and the ideological superstructures (such as philosophy, ethics and religion.) Social groups, strata and classes enjoying different economic and political statuses adopt different attitudes towards the basic economic and political system of the society, and people's opinions towards social life and reform is inevitably reflected in political thought trends. At the level of direct cause, the paradoxical movement of the contradiction between productive forces and the relations of production, bring about either vigorous or gradual changes in the relations of production, which in turn becomes the fundamental cause for the formation, development, perishing and revival of certain political thought trends. In both Chinese and world history, there existed many thought trends which have emerged and developed just because of the changes in the relations of production caused by the paradoxical movement of the contradiction between productive forces and the relations of production in respective periods. In the Chinese history many new thought trends ascended to the historical stage and were promoted during the Spring and Autumn and Warring States Period, and their competition was regulated by the principle of "Let The Contention of a Hundred Schools of Thought".[4] The same can be said for Renaissance era[5]

---

4   If we examine the "contention of a hundred schools of thought" principle in the Spring and Autumn period, all thought trends surged, and contested, which was the embodiment specific development requirements of history. In 594 BC, the State of Lu officially and legally recognized and promoted private land lord ownership of land plots. Subsequently, the State of Chu and the State of Zheng carried out similar reforms, which promoted the development of feudal production relations, and the landlord class gradually gained the political power. Towards the end of the Spring and Autumn period, the emerging landlord class had gained the upper hand in the political life of the State of Lu, State of Zheng, State of Qi, State of Jin and others , thus within the Warring States period, the social reform was basically completed in all the states. The rule of the slave owners class was replaced by the landlord class. Farmers became the dominated class in the feudal agricultural production and they were the social force which possessed the qualities of promoting social progress. The slave owners were the corrupt and reactionary social force that hindered the social development in this period. During this period, the class contradictions and class struggles found their reflections in the field of ideology, and the "contention of a hundred schools of thoughts" principle was formed. A number of schools ascended to the stage of history, there were both ideological confrontations and ideological convergences or integrations, and the flow of thoughts was spectacular.

5   The Renaissance is an important period during which modern Western thoughts had occurred repeatedly. On the surface, the Renaissance was a revival of the ancient Greek and Rome culture, but it was actually a great anti-feudal movement carried out by the emerging European bourgeois class in the ideological field in the form of the revival of classical culture. Through the investigation of the reason of the surge in the thought trend in this period, we can also clearly see that the development of productive forces, and the changes of production relationship and class relationships are the main condition of the surge of thoughts. The Renaissance brewed in the 14th Century, and reached a climax in the 15-16th Century. In the 13th Century, the productive forces of feudal society in Europe developed greatly, the social division of labor had expanded, and the city and town economies became more and more prosperous. On the basis of the improvement of productive forces, the capitalist production relationship began to form. In the class structure, in addition to the old feudal lords and peasants, there were the emerging bourgeois class including merchants, business owners and the early proletarians supporting their lives by selling their own labor force. The reform of the economic base had a deep impact on the feudal superstructure. The emerging bourgeois class, as the representative of the new production mode within the feudal society, tried to break through the ideological shackles by the feudal rulers and the church, criticized the theological view of feudalism, advocated the life philosophy and natural philosophy of bourgeoisie, advocated the dissemination of scientific knowledge, and cleared the way for the development of capitalism. At the same time, as class contradictions inside the feudal society continued to intensify, anti-feudal uprisings by farmers, urban workers and poor people flared up, which supported and promoted the anti-feudal struggle of the emerging bourgeois

from the 14th to 16th Century in the West. The major cause for such surge of new thought trends and the struggle between the old and new ones in these two periods was that the development of productive forces which had led to changes in the relations of production and in turn new social classes have merged. These new classes in their formation and development have proposed a series of political, economic, and cultural ideas, which have served as the basis of emergence of new trend thoughts. Historical facts affirm that these new trend of thoughts have fought against those reactionary forces that hindered the development and emancipation of productive forces. In modern and contemporary China, many thought trends' great development were closely related with the contradictory motion between productive forces and the relations of production. After thousands of years of its development, the natural economy mode prevalent in rural China had suffered internal and external crisis, which began to decay and failed to provide a solid foundation for the development of society. The bourgeois class grew with the emergence of the new production mode, i.e. the modern capitalism. At this time, with the increasing relations between foreign and domestic Chinese capitalism, there emerged and formed the new type intellectuals, modern media and social groups one after another, which provided core members and carriers for the popularization of new thoughts and the formation of new political thought trends. New production mode, new classes and strata, new social groups and new interests and demands were generated. New thoughts and ideas reflecting such interests and demands were created gradually, forming a great number of political thought trends which pushed the society to reform and change. The Westernization Movement, Reform Movement, Constitutionalism Movement and Xinhai Revolution have occurred successively. All these movements, in turn, boosted these thought trends, forming a surge.

The rise of political thought trends in the period of Chinese Reform and Opening-up after 1978, are also closely related with the contradictory motion between productive forces and the relations of production. The transition from planned economy to market economy has pushed the development of productive forces, which in turn caused changes in the relations of productions of the Chinese society, which has laid the key historical condition for the formation and development of contemporary political thought trends in China. The research done by Prof. Tian Xinming has also revealed this truth. When Xinming studied on the economic causes of the present-day philosophical thought trends and live values among the university students,

---

class. In this way, the new thought trend of anti-feudalism including humanism and natural philosophy has gradually formed and developed, forming this grand thought trend.

he asserted: "the origin of current philosophical thought trends is deeply rooted in socio-economic facts. While the emergence of a new philosophy echoes the demand of current society, its popularity is based on a certain historical condition as its background. Material production and economic relations are the most effective factors which determine various ideologies. In recent years, pragmatism thought is favored by people once again when a socialist commodity economy started to flourish in China. This is not a coincidence. There must be an essential linkage."[6] In the new stage of the Reform and Opening-up, the proper adjustment of the relations of production will further release productive forces, and in turn, the further development of productive forces will promote greater change in the relations of production and ownership structure, and activate multiple political thought trends. In real life, there are many organizational modes of production in China, including the outdated agricultural individual economy and manual processing industry, new industrial economy with high level of socialization, as well as modernized information industry and high-tech industry; there are also various forms of ownership systems, including public ownership and private ownership. All these modes of production, are the basis for the development of multiple political thought trends in today's China. Any individual within a thought trend is able to find a "fellow traveler" in realistic economic life and also to support his own standpoint and viewpoint within such realistic economic life. Undoubtedly, different ownership types which have been jointly developing in today's China are the most prominent cause for the rise of these political thought trends. In addition to the dominant public ownership and the main distribution mode according to labor contribution, there exists non-public ownership and other distribution modes, in tandem. In the field of social consciousness, this is reflected by the fact that there are other kinds of social consciousness forms than Marxism. The changes in the relations of production may change the pattern in which diverse ownership forms develop side by side, which will be reflected in superstructure. Especially, there will emerge some divergence in the ideological superstructure, which is generally shown as the surge of political thought trends and lead to the complication of ideological pattern.

The development and change of political thought trends does not always keep pace with the change of productive forces and the relations of production. This is generally reflected in two respects. Firstly, political thought trends may fall behind the change of production mode and hinder the development of the production mode. This is why we should actively carry out a

6   Tian Xinming, Guo Baoping, *Trend of Philosophical Thoughts of Contemporary College Students,* Shaanxi People's Publishing House, 1990, p. 140.

proper ideological work. We must respect differences and tolerate diversity among the people, as well as strive to resist various wrong and decadent ideas. Secondly, political thought trends may also come into being ahead of a production mode, and correctly represent the progressive trend in the law of social development at some level, thus guide and push social development forward. This is why scientific political thought trends can promote social existence and why we should vigorously strive to prosper philosophy and social sciences, build an advanced level of socialist moral civilization, greatly push ahead the construction of an advanced culture and strengthen our cultural soft power.

The factor of daily material life conditions is a reflection of daily life with economic life as its core. It is normally the most direct and realistic economic activity that people can feel and the most intuitive economic condition that affects political thought trends. Based on their economic status and with the interest and its achievement as standard, people will compare and evaluate the changes in the surrounding economic system and relations, etc. caused by the development of productive forces and reform of the relations of production. Accordingly, such comparison will generate or form some forms of social consciousness, which constitutes the social psychological basis and the most immediate economic condition which generates political thought trends.

People's daily life directly reflects the adjustments in the relations of production and the changes in productive forces. The main component part of the relations of production is the economic relation among people and its changes. The changes in ownership forms and distribution modes will directly affect the status of people in daily economic life and their interests. In current stage, China adopts the basic economic system with public ownership remaining in the dominant position and which co-exists and co-develops with other forms of ownership, besides the basic distribution mode as according to labor contribution remains as the mainstay, which coexists with other various forms of distribution modes. Such socialist relations of production, bearing unique Chinese characteristics, is suitable for the realistic conditions of today's China and provides a good prospect for the development of productive forces. They also give full play to the obviously enhanced subjective status of people in daily economic life, which also serve and maintain the fundamental interest of the vast majority of people. Besides, the development speed of productive forces also affects people's material life and its level directly. Since the implementation of the basic grand policy of Reform and Opening-up by the Third Session of the 11th Central Committee of the CPC, China's economic development has demonstrated an overall tendency of rapid and leapfrog growth, except some zigzags caused by local adverse factors. As indicated in the Report to the 18th National Congress of the CPC, the rapid development was the most prominent achievement in the last 30 years of Reform and Opening-up. Chinese economy has been greatly advanced. 30 years ago, the economy was teetering to collapse, but now our total import and export has leapt to the 2nd place in the world respectively. The number of impoverished population has decreased from 250 million 30 years ago to 20 million recently. People's living standard has been improved from lacking of basic living necessities to general prosperity.

In general, people cannot directly feel the results of adjustments in the relations of production or the development of productive forces. It is an accepted fact that "the economic relation of each given society is first displayed as interest or benefit relations."[7] In daily life, especially in their economic life, the strongest feeling demonstrated by the people is the gain and loss of immediate material interests, Despite the fact that the subjective status of people in their economic life was enhanced by the basic economic system and distribution mode, or with the rapid development of productive forces in the past 30 years, although the Reform and Opening-up has increased the economic prosperity and reduced the number of poor population, the most intuitive and profound, feeling and sense of people in daily life is a series of gains or losses regarding their direct material interests, such as the increase of their incomes, the improvement of direct living conditions. This is just the response of people within the daily material life level to the changes in the productive forces and relations of production. Undoubtedly, the realistic changes in material life and the gains and losses regarding interests directly affect the formation of the emotions and attitudes of individuals. As a result, these promote the emergence of a certain social psychology, which is the psychological basis for some thought trends and which push them ahead. For example, in early 1990s, the "left" trend of thought had surged in China, which demanded the termination of the Reform and Opening-up and called the restoration of planned economy system. The immediate cause for this trend was the price inflation, stagnancy in economic development and other issues caused by temporary and local management drawbacks in this period. This thought trend was supported by some social sectors whose interests were harmed in daily economic life and led to a social psychology which doubted the reform strategy. These daily material life conditions have also formed the social psychological basis for the re-surging of ultra-left thought trend at that time.

---

7   *Collected Works of Karl Marx and Frederick Engels*, Vol. 3, People's Publishing House, 2009, p. 320.

Of course, the relationship between various levels of socio-economic conditions and political thought trends is neither isolated and still nor unvarying. Each part of economic conditions is interlinked and inseparable, forming unified whole and jointly effecting the formation and development of political thought trends. As for the actual influence on a specific thought trend, different aspects of economic conditions play different roles. The influence of some elements may be more prominent while that of others may be weaker. The green-pacifism thought trend which is popular in the world finds its most direct cause in the development of productive forces. The major development of productive forces and the major advance of science and technology have directly led to the emergence of this thought trend. This shows that the productive forces not only have indirect effects on political thought trends as the most fundamental factor, but also have direct effects occasionally. However, some economic or political thought trends which have extensive influence and attract much attention depend rather on the adjustments made regarding the relations of production. In many cases, the formation and development of one thought trend is a product of the combined effect of multiple thought trends. The individualism thought trend in contemporary China is closely linked with the major adjustment of the relations of production and the improved level of daily material life over the years of Reform and Opening-up, while the hedonism thought trend which declares "Amusing Ourselves to Death" was aroused and flourished even more due to the major improvement and increase of daily living conditions.

In addition, there also exist some political thought trends which have weak relations with the economic conditions, such as some literary and artistic trends of thought and some philosophical thought trends that have obvious political feature. However, in view of the general situation of political thought trends, the main part in the family of political thought trends are closely related to the changes in the relations of production, which have extensive influence and attract much attention, and normally have a profound effect on the formation of government policies and spiritual life of the society. This suggests that the changes in the relations of production often play a key role in economic conditions of people that affect the formation of a thought trend. This is the major reason for the formation of those thought trends with obvious political feature.

III.1.2. Political conditions

Engels once said that "according to the materialist conception of history, the ultimately determining element in history is the production and reproduction of real life. Other than this, neither Marx nor I have ever asserted.

Hence if somebody twists this into saying that the economic element is the only determining one, he transforms that proposition into a meaningless, abstract, senseless phrase."[8] Engels also explained why such a misunderstanding occurred: "Marx and I are ourselves partly to blame for the fact that the younger people sometimes lay more stress on the economic side than is due to it. We had to emphasize the main principle vis-à-vis our adversaries, who denied it, and we had not always the time, the place or the opportunity to give their due to the other elements involved in the interaction. But when it came to presenting a section of history, that is, to making a practical application, it was a different matter and there no error was permissible. Unfortunately, however, it happens only too often that people feel that they have fully understood a new theory and can apply it without more ado from the moment they have assimilated its main principles, and even those not always correctly. And I cannot exempt many of the more recent "Marxists" from this reproach, for the most amazing rubbish has been produced in this quarter, too..."[9] This shows that the economic factor is not the only element that determines political thought trends, and that the effects of other factors also deserve keen attention.

Political factors have tremendous influence on political thought trends, especially for their development direction. Political conditions for the formation of political thought trends are mainly reflected in the following aspects:

First, the change course and practical activities of the political groups, organizations and parties determine the rise and decline of a political thought trend that reflects their interest orientation and theoretical demands. Any political thought trend is the product of certain social and historical condition. Although the formation and development of a political thought trend need to adapt to the political, economic and cultural demands, at the mean time they are also determined by the status of the relation of productions they rely on and by the different economic and political positions of the class they represent. As Plekhanov pointed out, "Generally, the history of an ideological system must be explained through the formation, change and collapse of the combination of ideas, which is affected by the formation, change and collapse of the combination of certain social forces."[10]

---

8   *Collected Works of Karl Marx and Frederick Engels*, Vol. 10, People's Publishing House, 2009, p. 591 [Engels to J. Bloch In Königsberg, London, September 21, 1890].
9   Ibid., pp. 593-594; Engels to J. Bloch In Königsberg, London, September 21, 1890.
10   *Plekhanov's Selected Works in Philosophy*, Vol. 2, SDX Joint Publishing Company, 1961, p. 290.

Normally, political groups, organizations and parties adopt a certain ideology as their faith and guide of action. Their political programs often form and improve with the changes in political thought trends. Since its birth, CPC has always deemed Marxism as its faith and guide of action. "The sound of artillery of the October Revolution has delivered Marxism-Leninism to China."[11] Influenced by the October Revolution in Russia, Marxism started its spread in China. Then, the May Fourth Movement in 1919, further promoted the spread of Marxism and worked on to combine it with China's labor movement. In the early stage of CPC, many leaders, especially Li Dazhao and Chen Duxiu, published a series of articles to introduce and analyze Marxist ideas about the social problems at that time, which formed a strong political trend of Marxism. It was the spread of Marxism and its profound effect in China which then developed into the indispensable driving force for the birth and growth of the CPC. Marxism turned into the fundamental guiding ideology of CPC to lead the revolution, construction and reform in China. Besides, based on the change of actual situation and by adherence to Marxism as fundamental guiding ideology, the CPC also made new breakthrough constantly on the localization of Marxism in China. As an extremely important thought trend in modern Chinese society, innovation of Marxism continuously consolidates and enhances the ideological and theoretical basis of the CPC.

During the formation of political groups, organizations and parties, their core figures gradually come up from their own groups, strata and classes. These core figures organize and undertake the struggle in the ideological field and actively bring their initiative and subjective ability into play, which constitutes a major subjective condition for the formation and development of political thought trends. The first generation of Chinese communists, represented by Mao Zedong, were the main leaders in the period of the New-Democratic Revolution, Socialist Revolution and early socialist construction. They organized the Yan'an Rectification Campaign (1942-45) and the ideological reform of intellectuals after the establishment of new China, as well as many other effective campaigns. Although these movements were radical to a degree, they have maintained the absolutely authoritative position of Marxism in the field of ideology and helped to achieve a unified leadership under the flag of Marxism. The second generation of Chinese communists, represented by Deng Xiaoping, were the main leaders in the road of socialist construction with Chinese characteristics. Deng Xiaoping who played a decisive role in the ideological emancipation, was the chief designer of the Reform and Opening-up in China. Deng Xiaoping

---

11 *Selected Works of Mao Zedong,* Vol. 4, People's Publishing House, 1991, p. 1471.

gave a clear support to those political thought trends which can meet the development requirement of developing productive forces and which accord with the direction of social progress. He also answered the issue of what socialism is and how to establish it, scientifically, which ensured the advancement and development of Chinese Reform and Opening-up. The third generation of Chinese communists, represented by Jiang Zemin and Hu Jintao, were the main leaders who have continued to lead the building socialism with Chinese characteristics further. Many strategic thoughts in the new stage, such as the important thoughts of Three Represents and the Scientific Outlook on Development, has firmly gained the dominant position in ideological field. These thoughts, along with the Deng Xiaoping Theory, have realized the second historic leap in the Sinicization or localization of Marxism in China.

During the development of political thought trends, all groups, organizations and parties always strive to affect social psychology by various media organs, so as to publicize main propositions of their own ideological systems. By the way of a powerful indoctrination, they consolidate a social cognition in their own groups, classes, strata and even in the whole society, so as to serve realistic political practice and achieve interests and satisfy demands. The typical method for this attitude in China is to conduct public ideological and political education, which will adopt ideological ideas, political opinions and moral values of socialism with Chinese characteristics to make purposeful, planned and organized effect upon the members of society, enabling them to form an ideological belief and values that meet the requirements of building socialism with Chinese characteristics under the leadership of CPC. This is not a phenomenon peculiar to China. In western countries, numerous institutions also infiltrate thoughts and propositions of a number of groups, organizations or parties by means of public education, so as to achieve their realistic purposes, lead their political practice and realize their interests and demands. It should be noted that, in the current society with rapid development of informatics, the Internet has become another key media and battlefield where various groups, organizations and parties can publicize their thoughts and push ahead certain political thought trends which meet their interest appeals. When compared to the traditional media, such as newspapers, journals, books, magazines, radio and TV, the Internet has many advantages, including rapid spread of ideas, broad coverage scope, and rich and abundant formats for displaying. However, it also has many disadvantages, such as having a mixture of both useful and misleading contents and low level of controllability. The Internet can effectively enhance the spreading capacity and enhance the influence of political thought trends, and also can cause certain challenges. Overall, media outlets can provide a realistic carrier medium for the political groups, organizations and parties to publicize their thoughts and push a thought trend much further to meet their interests and demands. As an essential link in the practical activities of the political groups, organizations and parties, the media has become one of the main political conditions in the formation and development of political thought trends.

A political party that represents the ruling class will utilize the power of the government to defend the dominant position of the ideology of its own class in the whole society by soft or hard methods. Once a political party, group or organization dissolves, the political thought trend upheld by it will weaken, "step down" or gradually perish. When the ruling party loses its power, the influence of its ideology will accordingly decline, perish or continue to exist in the form of political thought trends, waiting to rise again in a proper situation. For example, during the period of the Republic of China (1912-1949), the ruling party KMT represented the interests of the big landlords and big bourgeoisie. Therefore, the dominant political thought trends in China had the nature of feudalism and colonial capitalism, embodying and maintaining the interest of the class of landlords, bourgeoisie as well as imperialism. The establishment of New China has marked that the CPC has become the ruling party and the Marxism political thought trend has completely obtained the dominant position in the ideological field. The political thought trend that advocated capitalism has retreated to Taiwan and lost its voice in the mainland. But this outdated thought trend which had formed in old society may surface in various forms occasionally in the new society. For example, the trends of feudalistic superstitious thoughts still exist in some fields of today's society as a kind of adverse effect.

In conclusion, guiding ideology, core figures, media outlets and ruling position of political groups, organizations and parties are the key factors for practical activities and development of political thoughts, and those thought trends that reflect their interest orientation and theoretical demands play a decisive role among various political factors.

Secondly, the occurrence of certain political situations and movements is one of the objective prerequisites for the formation of political thought trends. The emergence of certain political movements, including some political events, is related to the activities of political thought trends. Political movements and political thought trends have reciprocal causality and are interdependent. The formation and development of the reform thought trends in late Qing Dynasty was based on the political background of a general national crisis. Since the Opium War, China had stepped into a semi-colonial and semi-feudal society. After the Sino-Japanese War from 1894 to 1895, the national crisis had intensified. An overt clique inside the ruling class and certain figures with insight were faced with the task of saving the country and saving the race. The call for reform had surged. Against such a general background, the reform thought trends pushed the reform movement to develop. Those thought trends which emerged and surged with the May Fourth New Cultural Movement in 1919, had made a deep impact on the backward thoughts and lifestyles formed in thousand years of feudal patriarchal despotism and broke up the dam of ideology and culture built by feudal despotism, providing spiritual inspiration for the grand May Fourth Movement. In turn, the rise of the May Fourth Movement pushed the new thought trends into a new realm and opened a new chapter for them. From then on, Marxism and Leninism climbed to a peak in the ideological field, driving the old China to start a thorough change.

During the implementation of reforms in socialist countries, there emerge various thought trends that act energetically. At that time, the development of thought trends was closely related to the ruling status of ruling party in the field of ideology. When the ruling party insists on pushing the reform by socialist self-improvement and development, and defends the leading and dominant position of socialist ideology, it was assumed that the wrong thought trends would be weakened while the socialist thought trends would be developed. If the ruling party fails to lead the reform towards the right direction, it will inevitably affect the socialist ideology and impair its roles. The authority of socialist ideology will be greatly reduced and its leading role and charm in the ideological field will decline significantly. Henceforth, non-socialist or anti-socialist thought trends will prevail to a certain level. When the ruling party in a socialist country voluntarily abandons socialism with all of its aspects, especially in the aspect of ideology, various wrong ideological trends would surge and flood, and will eventually win the dominant position in the ideological field.

Since the era of Khrushchev, the Communist Party of the Soviet Union (CPSU) started to deny the Marxist doctrines of class, class struggle and the proletarian dictatorship, and got increasingly clearer that it begun to adopt the idea of "abstract humanism" as its flag and as its main ideological weapon. From then on, the abstract humanism thought trend has spread rapidly, greatly affecting many other ideological fields, such as philosophy, political economy, historiography, and literature. The change in the political and ideological field was finally reflected in the New Thinking proposed by Gorbachev and his relevant political program. This program has inherited the former programmatic goals of All for People, All for People's Happiness and the slogans of the Whole People's State, the Whole People's Party which were proposed by Khrushchev in the 1960s. Meanwhile, Gorbachev presented the slogan of Democratization, Openness and Pluralization, which can be deemed as the three knives in dismembering the Soviet Union. The slogan of Democratization led to the flooding of various wrong and reactionary thought trends which have corrupted people's thoughts. The slogan of Openness rejected all the past achievements of the revolution and the socialist construction in the Soviet Union and all the Soviet Union history was befouled, thus people's confidence on socialist cause was destroyed. The slogan of Pluralization (Diversification) actually meant to voluntarily abandon the guiding position of Marxism and Leninism and the leading role of the Communist Party in building socialism. The ruling power was given up and eventually, the socialist country, the Soviet Union has perished.

Political struggles lead to certain political situations and political campaigns. In the class society, the political struggles are mainly characterized as class struggles. The thought trends which emerge and evolve within a turbulent political ecology represent the posture in the thought and culture fields especially for the political struggles in the ideological level. The bellicose and revolutionary natures of French materialist philosophical thought trends in the 18th Century had emerged based on the violent political struggles and thought struggles (political) between the bourgeoisie and clergy as well as the nobility and the autocratic monarchy. This paradigm was adapted to the struggle situation between the proletariat and the bourgeoisie with the emergence of Marxism. During the 1830s and 1840s, the capitalist mode of production had become dominant in the advanced countries in Western Europe and the inherent irreconcilable basic contradictions within the capitalist society had been more obviously exposed. A periodical economic crisis of overproduction arised, which had worsened the living conditions of working-class and intensified the contradictions and the struggles between the proletariat and the bourgeoisie. The Europe-shocking 1831 and 1834 Lyon Textile Workers' uprisings (the Canuts) in France, the Chartist movement of 1836 to 1848 in Britain and the 1844 Silesia Textile Worker's uprising in Germany have successively erupted since 1830s, which have indicated that the proletariat's struggles against the bourgeoisie have entered to a new stage, the proletariat had stepped on the stage of history as an independent political force and directly pointed its arrows the against the bourgeoisie and the capitalist system. However, the rising labor movement was in urgent demand of scientific theories to guiding their revolutionary practice. The proletarian revolutionary mentors

Marx and Engels have adapted former socialist thoughts to the struggles of the times and created the scientific socialism. Therefore, along with the struggles between the proletariat and the bourgeoisie, Marxism has finally matured and gained the leadership position in the working class movement.

Some major thought trends often center on the theme of the times. There are scholars who primarily discuss such topics as "which modernization pattern China has chosen?" and "how to understand modernization to analyze various political thought trends".[12] The theme of the times is the principal social contradiction of a society in a certain historical period, which corresponds to the comprehensive reflection and understanding of the economic, political and cultural conditions and the main content of thought trends. Marx has said: "The issues are just the public, fearless epoch voice mastering everything and just the slogan of times, which reflectthe most realistic cry of its own mental state."[13] Obviously, the issues that actually become such slogans are neither irrelevant or trivial things nor false fabricated ones, rather they are systemically important having major practical significance and theoretical value and arise from the practice of millions. For example, while several political thought trends frequently embraced the "salvation of state and national prosperity" in modern China, And, a number of influential thought trends have focused on the issue of "How to realize Chinese modernization" in the new period of Reform and Opening-up. Among which, the "modernization of thoughts" is the topic of most concern. A different interpretation of the "modernization of thought" is to emancipate our minds.

In contemporary China, our Party emphasizes to constantly emancipate our minds during the whole process of the cause of socialism with Chinese characteristics. However whenever the Party stresses this cause, there are some public figures who publicize and express the core concepts of some alien thought trends in the name of "emancipating our minds". Those newly emerged thought trends since the Reform and Opening-up mostly have a nature of "Self-examination" and "Critique" adopting the premise of criticizing the certain past ideas, and try to change and re-establish some values by boosting the attitude of "emancipating the minds." The 17th CPC National Congress put forward the idea of "continuing to emancipate the minds", the discussions on what to be freed and how to emancipate them became a hot discussion topic at that time. Some articles and "public letter"

---

12   Zhou Jiming, Guo Ying et al., *Concussion and Conflict – The Thought Trends and Society during China's Early Modernization Process*, Commercial Press, 2003.
13   *Complete Works of Karl Marx and Frederick Engels*, Vol. 4, People's Publishing House, 2nd ed., 1982, pp. 280-290.

distribution network brought forward the political reform and restructuring issue, a remarkable fuss about upholding "universal democracy" occurred, they advocated that the values of freedom, democracy, fairness and justice are universal for all countries and emphasized the implementation of western mode of "separation of powers" and "constitutionalism" principle. Such thought trends have raised their ideological claims and have tried to influence the ideological field and advocated their ideological appeals with the flag of "emancipating the minds".

As the political factors influence the development and progress of thought trends, the political parties and political groups converge with different interest groups to a certain extent as their pattern of expression in contemporary China. Such development and progress of contemporary Chinese political thought trends have a close relationship with the formation of interest differentiation and formation of new interest groups. In the new period of Reform and Opening-up, the constant adjustment of productive relations have begun to readjust the social interest relations, thus various social classes and interests groups have appeared. There were no such numerous interest groups in socialist China before the Reform and Opening-up. In the past interests of the people were highly harmonious, they adhere to collectivism and argued that personal interests should be subjected collective interest while the local interests should be subjected to national interests, therefore a group or an individual pursuing partial interests was not allowed to freely exist. After the Reform and Opening-up, diverse interest groups have appeared along with the development of socialist market economy, and the members belonging to an interest group started to be increasingly aware of the commonality of intra-group interests, and began to express their interests and demands through multiple ways in a more active manner. As Comrade Jiang Zemin had pointed out at the 80th Anniversary of the founding of the CPC: "The overall interests of the masses of people are always composed of the specific interests in all directions", and especially emphasized: "Since the Reform and Opening-up, new changes have taken place in the stratum composition in China."[14] This indicates that the Party has realized the existence of different social interest groups. There are numerous research results regarding social interest groups in the new period of Reform and Opening-up; some scholars have categorized the society as ten strata (classes) in detail according to their social resource possession powers: from top tobottom they include the following: state and social administrators, management personnel, private business owners, specialized technicians, clerks, self-employed industrialists and businessmen,

---

14   *Selected Works of Jiang Zemin*, Vol. 3, People's Publishing House, 2006, pp. 279, 286.

personnel in commercial catering industry, industrial workers, agricultural laborers and urban jobless or unemployed and semi-unemployed persons.[15] Whether such an analysis is correct still remains to be discussed, but this authoritative research shows the basic fact that there objectively exists a differentiation and re-grouping among the people in contemporary China, and the newly emerged entrepreneur groups and the group of highly specialized technicians groups have gained an ever increasing social status while the status of the laboring groups have continuously declined.

Different interest groups actively express their own interest appeals, thus different thought trends have taken shape. The direct communicators of such political thought trends are mainly the intellectuals. As the reform is being deepened continuously, some intellectuals seem to start "representing" different strata and classes[16]. The more remarkable one is the emergence of an intellectual group who represents some powerful groups in the society. Over the 30 years of Reform and Opening-up, the so-called "mainstream economists" group was formed and deemed as the representatives of the powerful interest groups, who have influence some media outlets. If it is true that some interest groups are formed in a period of time, those economists who can influence government's decision-making will become a shining star and will dedicated themselves to represent certain interest groups. The "mainstream economists" in China spare quite tiny efforts

15 Lu Xueyi, et al., Research Report of Contemporary Chinese Social Strata, *Social Sciences Academic Press* (China), 2002.
16 In recent years, some experts and scholars have raised numerous "theoretical arguments" to promote private economy. One argued: "To shine a light on the entire", borrowing from Marx, I can certainly say that, there is always one dominant mode of production in all social formations, which dominates the status and influence of other modes of production, according to this premise there is no more exploitation by the private economy under socialism. The theory which advocates "private is public", says when the private wealth has accumulated so much that a person cannot spend them all, is it not this wealth of the society? "When the private economy develops to the zenith, in fact it becomes public". Another, advocates the idea of "privatization is reasonable", which says: in the past, socialist public ownership offered "a lifelong job", and produced "lazybones", only privatization can enable people to act with more initiative, gain enthusiasm, thus productivity can develop. Another, advocates the idea of "personal ability", which says under the free competition of market economy, a person with good abilities can be rich, but the poor people do not feel convinced about it, so there is nothing to blame if you are poor and have no ability. In a life of an individual, the cause behind a disadvantageous status often boils down to your own incompetence, so no need to blame the private economic system. A fifth, idea argues for the "consistency of interests of labor and capital", so as the private enterprise prospers and the cake becomes bigger, everyone can earn more from it, hence laborers should "be kind to entrepreneurs". Quoted from research report titled as *The Study of Contemporary Chinese Intellectuals and Public Opinion Elite* that has a subtitle of "The New Changes of Social Structure in Contemporary China" published as internal reference material by CASS.

into on the scientific research on economic issues but too hard-working to speak for certain interest groups."[17] The Strategy and Management in its issue 2002/2 has published a long article which analyzed the interest group issues in contemporary China, and the article has also argued that the intellectual elites in China are increasingly becoming dependent on the powerful groups and capital owning groups.[18] As some economists have openly asserted: "Economists are just to serve the interest groups."[19] Such a statement, clearly illustrates that the intellectuals such as the ideologists often play a role in the activity of thought trends by serving interest appeals of certain interest groups. A famous author has argued that the new rich strata or powerful groups actively look for a "spokesman" with such a justification: "the socialist market economy just summons those are 'clever and capable, prudent and reliable and well-managed' who can become 'new lucky knights'"; however the 'new lucky knights' are consciously or unconsciously looking for "thought" advocates."[20] Some intellectuals also belong to the group who "have become rich earlier than others", it seems that their ideological position suits their new economic status.

Thirdly, certain political superstructure inhibits or promotes the formation and development of political thought trends. The political superstructure includes the political system, legal system, state organs, party organization, army, police, court, penal institution and other political organizations; and this complex state apparatus is based on a certain economic foundation. Political and legal systems as well as relevant policies which reflect the will of the ruling class will inevitably play the role of controlling political thought trends which violate and threaten the interests of the ruling class and which risk their social influence. The state can also properly formulate targeted policy measures to regulate the ideological and culture field based on the general conditions of social ideology and culture, which also includes restricting or banning the promotion of some thoughts, the state also needs to ensure that people would continue to uphold some thoughts, and that the legal political organizations should cooperate in publicizing some thought trends in a certain design and plan. In such occasions, certain thought trends will normally, remain quiet for a period but will revive again under proper

17   Ding Xueliang, *Real Economists in China is Five at Most, Lianhe Zaobao,* October 3, 2005; Ding Xueliang, *Domestic Economists Bend the Mind to Endorse for Interest Groups, China Business Times,* October 26, 2005.
18   Wan He, Interest group, reform path and legitimacy Issue, *Strategy and Management,* 2002(2).
19   Fan Gang, A talk when accepting a press interview during "99' Shanghai Fortune Forum", *Economic Reference,* 1999(12).
20   Zhang Xianliang, *Novel China,* Economic Daily, Shaanxi Travel & Tourism Press, 1997, pp. 32-45.

situations and circumstances. Currently in China we implement the system of multi-party cooperation and political consultation under the leadership of CPC, we uphold the Four Cardinal Principles, which includes, adhering to the leadership of the CPC; the socialist road, the people's democratic dictatorship, and Marxism-Leninism and Mao Zedong Thought. Thus, it is certainly clear that uphold the Four Cardinal Principles and the attached thought trends is absolutely legitimate, this means implementing strict control and absolute prohibition of such political thought trends, which advertise the western multi-party system, within which a number political parties compete for the helm of the state, i.e. the government and which rule in turns, it is also clear that the state would try to weaken and even eliminate its social influence in the long run.

The promotion of certain political and legal systems as well as relevant policies against the background of newly emerging or a developing political thought trend, are mainly manifested in the following two aspects: firstly, some policies and guidelines are formulated by the state which allow and provided the basis for the formation and development of some thought trends. Secondly, the state ideology (dominant ideology) will support the development of some thought trends, which it deems necessary. In such cases, those ideologies that favor the ruling class will smoothly flourish and greet the "golden age" of their development. Comrade Hu Jintao has underlined this view it his Speech in the meeting to Commemorate the 90th Anniversary of the Founding of the CPC: "Our basic political system includes the system of People's Congress, the multi-party cooperation and political consultation system, the system of regional ethnic autonomy and the system of grass-root level self-governance."[21] The corresponding system and relevant laws therewith provide the basis and the guarantee for the formation and development of relevant political thought trends which also provide a favorable theoretical basis and social environment for the improvement and practice of political and legal systems in line with the requirements of national development regarding relevant aspects. Thus, certain political and legal systems as well as certain policies can maintain themselves, by promoting the development of favorable political thought trends. The political superstructures include certain political systems, legal system, relevant policies as well as the governmental sector, party organizations, political organizations and state apparatus, which play the role of inhibiting or facilitating the development of political thought trends. Those political thought trends which violate the will of the ruling class are often

21   Hu Jintao, *Speech at the Meeting Commemorating the 90th Anniversary of the Founding of the CPC*, People's Publishing House, 2011, p. 8.

firmly controlled or eliminated by the coordinated action in various ways by the elements of the political superstructure. Reversely, those in line with the interests and demands of the ruling class are supported and encouraged by the ideological work implemented by the political and legal systems as well as supported by relevant policies.

In general, a) their practical activities, development and changes regarding a political groups, political organizations or political parties including their guiding thoughts, core leading figures, their public media outlets and others; b) certain political situation, political movements including political campaigns and the ruling conditions, political struggles, the theme of the times, interest groups and ideologues and theoreticians of the ruling party in the ideological field; c) the political superstructure which includes certain political systems, legal system, relevant policies and the government organ, party organizations, political organizations and state apparatus; all in all, the organic combination of the above three components constitute the political environment of an era, which is the objective premise of the formation of political thought trends, which determines the rise and decline of those trends which reflect the interest orientation and theoretical demands of the ruling class and at the same time inhibit or facilitate the formation and development of political thought trends.

III.1.3. Ideal and cultural conditions

As Liang Qichao mentioned: "Not all 'times' have 'thought trends', those times with abundant thought trends are certainly the ones wherein cultures blossom."[22] The formation of various political thought trends certainly rely on a certain cultural environment, not only rely on the current thoughts and current cultural conditions, but also the past ones and theoretical backgrounds and also includes both the edifice of the traditional culture and the affection of foreign cultures. On this account, Mao Zedong has called them as "Source" and "Stream" in his Speech made at the Forum of Literature and Art in Yan'an.[23] Some studies regarding the thought trends have revealed important aspects, a scholar has written: "After all, people's material life conditions determine their thoughts. However, the formation of theories of political thoughts is like the formation of other kind of thoughts which have their unique characteristics. That is to say, they can be formed only by depending on or inheriting the previously existing thoughts, ideas, as

---

22 Liang Qichao, *Introduction to the Qing Dynasty, Recorded in Four Kinds of Liang Qichao's Historical Works*, Yuelu Press, 1985, p. 20.
23 *Selected Works of Mao Zedong*, Vol. 3, People Publishing House, 1991, p. 850.

roots or inputs."[24] Another scholar has stressed that we should enhance our study on western political thought trends.[25] In other words, certain domestic political thought trends may well have an international background, and it is even the same for the interaction of international and domestic thought trends in the current context of increasingly deepening economic globalization process. The monographic study on the liberal thought trend, the "On the New Liberal Thought Trends"[26] in Contemporary China" has argued that the theoretical sources of bourgeois liberalism thought trends in 1980s and the liberal thought trends in 1990s are, respectively, rooted in modern era Chinese liberalism and Western liberalism. I should say that, our book does not diverge remarkably with the existing research results regarding the ideological and cultural conditions for the formation of political thought trends. The cultural conditions of a certain society constitute an organic system which influences political thought trends, greatly.

The influence of the traditional thoughts and cultural resources on political thought trends

The historical and traditional culture resources and the growth and development of currently existing political thought trends are inseparable from each other. This "genetic factor", i.e. traditional culture of a country, region often affects the formation and development of political thought trends in a positive or negative manner. The positive influence refers to absorbing the component part needed from the traditional cultures and including that part into the current ideological system, by improving and sublating the said component part during the formation and development of political thought trends. The negative influence refers to that the system of ideological ideas of a certain political thought trend negates the traditional cultural roots. In such case, the latter will, in the long term inhibit the publicity and development of the former in a negative manner. No matter its role is positive or negative, there is no doubt that the traditional cultural resources and existing political thought trends will inevitably interact, collide and coalesce.

Any political thought trend possesses blood relationship with the cultural tradition. Although the political thought trend is characterized by an exceptional or a specific era, the inheritance relationship, a thought trend possesses is certain. The differences regarding the value orientation among

---

24   Guo Hanmin: *The Study of Social Trends of Thought in the Late Qing Dynasty Period*, 2003, China Social Sciences Press.
25   Qu Hongzhi, Discussion on the Development Law of Social Thought Trends, *Journal of Studies in Ideological Education*, 1995(2).
26   Mei Rongzheng, Zhang Xiaohong, *On the Thought Trend of Neo Liberalism*, 2004, Higher Education Press, p. 14..

different political thought trends often need to be scientifically explained through delving into their respective cultural traditions and national characteristics. Of course, political thought trends take specific demands of the times as the rational basis to develop and discard the existing (inherited) thought/idea stock and add to them the new content, spirit of the times. As Engels once pointed out: "But as a definite domain within the division of labor, the philosophy of every age has as its presuppositions a certain intellectual material which it inherits from its predecessors and which is its own point of departure. That is why philosophy can play first violin in economically backward countries.... Of itself economics, produces no effects here directly, but it determines the kind of change and development the already existing intellectual material, receives, and even that, for the most part, indirectly, since it is the political, judicial and moral reflexes which exercise the greatest direct influence upon philosophy."[27] Marxism was developed on the basis of three main trends of thought including German classical philosophy, British classical political economy and French utopian socialism of the 19th Century. Marx and Engels abandoned the idealism while absorbing the rational kernel of the dialectics from Hegel's philosophy, criticized the idealistic conception of history in general, and cleared the metaphysical views of the old French materialism, and also absorbed the reasonable materialist thoughts in the philosophy of Feuerbach, thus established the philosophy of dialectical materialism; he opened the way to utilize the dialectical materialist point of view to study the history of human society. Marx and Engels critically inherited the thoughts on class struggle from the French bourgeois historians Thierry and Mignet, and founded the historical materialism; while absorbing the theory of labor surplus value from British bourgeois classical economist Adam Smith and David Ricardo; Marx and Engels have sublated their economic theories that concealed capitalist exploitation, and put forward the theory of surplus value and created the political economy of the proletariat; while absorbing the reasonable elements of utopian socialism from Saint-Simon, Fourier and Owen; Marx and Engels abandoned their idealist and utopian historical views and founded the scientific socialism thought trend through the practice of participating in the labor movement and crude communist movement, personally. Therefore, Marxism has been the product of the excellent cultural heritage of mankind, and no major theory of Marxism has been established through negligence of previous theoretical research fruits of natural science, philosophy and social science.

---

27 *Collected Works of Karl Marx and Frederick Engels*, Vol. 10, People's Publishing House, 2009, pp. 599-600 [Engels to Conrad Schmidt in Berlin London, October 27 1890].

In the contemporary society, cultural heritage, as a spiritual product of mankind, increasingly assumes some kind of material power. As a special form of social consciousness, the traditional cultural heritage has been embodied in the whole process of human social development, which has a great impact on the formation and development of people's ideological views. As a complex system, ideological system which is involved by the traditional culture is broad and profound, of which many value ideas and ways of thinking have profound practical significance, and it provides onebasic source for ideological theory for the development of the political thought trends. On the one hand, the traditional culture, as a spiritual force, gradually and deeply plays an important role in promoting social development, and on the other hand, it constitutes a source which is inherited in different ways. Once the cultural tradition is formed, it becomes a powerful ideological and theoretical resource, and binds, harmonizes and affects people's values and modes of behavior. The progressive thought trends often reflect and inherit the positive part of traditional culture. "This part of excellent cultural resources form the cultural basis for the formation of progressive thought trends and the spiritual foundation for the further development and social recognition of the progressive thought trends. The backward thought trends often inherit and absorb negative parts of the traditional culture and even a number of sediments, and become an obstacle for the formation and development of progressive thought trends.[28]

There are many reasons for wide publicity of the socialist thought trends in China, but the idea of great harmony in the Chinese traditional culture has played a cohesive among the people in the process of socialist publicity. As it is recorded in the *Book of Rites*: "When the truth is implemented, the whole world is shared as one community.... As a result, the treacherous plan won't happen, theft, rebellion and harmful things won't happen, so every family will not need to close the door. It is called the great harmony." The thought of great harmony advocated by our Confucianism was produced since the Spring and Autumn period, inherited along the long river of Chinese history and civilization; it has an important influence upon the thinkers of the past dynasties, and has effected a sense of identity among the people as the main essence of the Chinese traditional culture. The idea of great harmony advocates the sharing of the means of production, there is no status difference among the people, no exploitation or oppression, instead equality and harmony, everyone has his own income and enjoys life, it is highly consistent with the public ownership of the means of production, the

---

28   Luo Huiyu, A Tentative Analysis of Social and Historical Conditions for the Generation of Chinese Trend of Political Thoughts, *Journal of Chongqing Institute of Commerce*, 1999(8).

elimination of exploitation and oppression, equality and freedom are generally advocated by the socialist thought trends, therefore, the thought of great harmony is deeply rooted in the thousands of years of traditional culture and has laid a benign mental and spiritual foundation for a solid social identity for the formation and development of the socialist thought trends in China, and has become an important impetus for its publicity in China.

After the wide publicity of the Marxist thought trend in China, the Marxists in China have strived to find some basic ideological material from the traditional culture. On the one hand, they have continuously developed and improved their ideas regarding the traditional culture; on the other hand, they promoted the localization of the Marxist thought trend, thus they have developed "native" characteristics and get the support and recognition from the people. Mao Zedong was an outstanding representative who drew "nourishment" from traditional culture for promoting the Marxism thought trends. "Seeking truth from facts" is the quintessence of Mao Zedong Thought, and also an important composite part of the Sinicization of the Marxism thought trend. "Seeking truth from facts" is merely the nourishment drawn from the traditional culture. "Seeking truth from facts" can be traced back to the attitude of thinking by seeking truth from facts advocated by the ancient Chinese philosophers in their research. "Admit what one really understands and what one does not know" was recorded in the Analects of Confucius for Governing.[29] The term "Seeking truth from facts" was originated from Ban Gu's "Hejian Xian Wang Zhuan" from Book of Han: "we maintain the good old practice, seeking truth from facts." Chinese thinker Yan Shigu interpreted it as: "trying to get the truth". For the so-called "Seeking truth from facts", the original meaning of "facts" is "straight", "here" and "now"; it means the live things happening here at the moment, and refers to the process of practice. It contains a kind of understanding to underline the legitimacy of practice. The true meaning of "now" in Chinese is exactly just right now, and it is the "right time" and "right place" when an action is taking place. Deng Xiaoping pointed out that the Mao Zedong has summarized the dialectical materialism and historical materialism founded by Marx and Engels four words as "seeking truth from facts", so that it has a stronger vitality.[30] In October 1938, Mao Zedong used the concept of "seeking truth from facts" for the first time in his report to the 6th Plenary Session of the 6th Central Committee of the CPC. Mao Zedong has believed that only the CPC has insisted to seek truth from facts, therefore it would mostly likely complete the task of revolution,

---

29   Zhang Yiwen, *Imperial Full Translation*, Hunan University Press, 1989, p. 7.
30   *Selected Works of Deng Xiaoping*, Vol. 2, People's Publishing House, 1994, p. 278.

and the Communist Party should always become a model of thinking and studying way of "seeking truth from facts".

"Facts" are all the things that objectively exist, "truth" is what we seek and explore as the law of the development of things and "seeking" requires people to strengthen research. Mao Zedong had pointed out that the Chinese revolutionary practice needs the attitude of seeking truth from facts, and this attitude can also be popularly understood as the attitude of shooting the arrow at the target. Here, the "target" refers to the China's revolution in the then status quo of China, and the "arrow" is the guiding ideology of the CPC—the Marxist theory. The Chinese revolution should use Marxism as the "arrow" to directly solve the problem of "target" in the Chinese revolutions.[31] So that, Marxism can take root and effect in China, it should be combined with Chinese traditional culture, and the Marxist way of thinking should be internalized into the way of thinking of the Chinese nation through maintaining the excellent part of the traditional thoughts. The process of introducing Marxism into China has been a process of mutual integration and selective relation between Chinese and Western culture. Any culture has a certain time dimension and a space dimension, and it is the unity of national space and times. Mao Zedong creatively put the idea of seeking truth from facts as the fundamental view point and the fundamental methodology for the whole ideological theory, he regarded seeking truth from facts as the universal law of practice, and thus he guided the Chinese revolution to a new stage. On the other hand, in the development process of Chinese society since the Opium War, there were always some backward or even erroneous thought trends, and the negative factors of the traditional culture were inherited which caused great depression and obstacles for the progressive thought trends. For example, since the Western learning thought trend spread to the East and China, under the impact of slavishly following the Western thought and Western power politics, the backward thoughts in the traditional culture was promoted and began to rise, the feudal backward thoughts have revived in modern China, staged the scenes of "feudal restoration" farce; in addition, there was also the historical nihilism thought trends, which held a completely negative attitude in our own national history and strongly advocated complete westernization. Still today, the dross of traditional culture is inherited by some thought trends and have become tools for publicizing wrong and evil theories.

The political thought trends inherit the traditional culture in different ways. Some, such as "the revivalist thought trend", advertise the posture of "revival" with regard to traditional cultural sources; some others, such as,

31   *Selected Works of Mao Zedong,* Vol. 3, People's Publishing House, 1991, p. 801.

numerous thought trends during the May Fourth Movement (1919), have displayed "denial" and "negative" postures against the traditional thought trends. The forms of "revival" and "negation" have quite commonly occured in the long history of thoughts. Of course, what the "revival" and "negation" describe are the external appearances of thought trends. In its real development, history cannot be restored, so both of them—the "revival" and "negation"—transform and renovate the traditional cultural sources. The Renaissance thought trend started in commercially developed cities of Italy and other regions at the end of the 13th Century. Advanced intellectuals of the emerging bourgeoisie promoted humanistic spirit (humanism) through literary and artistic creative works by means of studying the culture and art of ancient Greek and ancient Rome. They affirmed men's value and dignity, advocated the liberation of men and personality, and opposed the theological thoughts of ignorance and superstitions. The Renaissance thought trend tried to break through the medieval culture, which contained the full disarray of religious colors, through the revival of the ancient civilization of ancient Greece and Rome, the so-called "Renaissance" was only the external appearance of this thought trend, which seems as it was trying to restore the progressive thoughts of ancient Greece and Rome, but in fact it was an unprecedented liberation and creation of the knowledge and spirit that reflected the interests and development requirements of the emerging capitalism. As the May Fourth Movement (1919) took place in the turning and changing era of the development of Chinese history, many political thought trends "contended for drawing attention", mainly including the reformist socialist thought trend, democratic political thought trend, anarchist political thought trend, utopian socialist thought trend, and Marxist political thought trend. The representatives were: the enlightenment thought trend of New Culture Movement, the Three Principles of the People by Sun Yatsen, the Pragmatism by Hu Shi, and the Guild Socialism, Marxist thoughts employed by the intellectuals who had preliminary accepted the communist ideology, and other thought trends. Political thought trends during this period had something in common since they were created on the same economic basis, and the most significant point was that they had opposed to the feudal autocratic rule to a certain extent and had carried out an extremely hard and bitter struggle against the feudal forces, which—in the ideological and cultural fields—appeared as criticizing and denying the two traditional cultural thought and criticizing and denying that political thought trends that served the interests of the feudal class. However, it appeared that the so-called "negation" of the Fourth May, was against the "defects" of the feudal backward thoughts as the component part of the traditional culture, but the Fourth May had actually developed and publicized the advanced ideas and the advanced political thought trends "democracy" and "science" for the proletarian class and other progressive classes. In general, "the tradition of all the dead ancestors haunts the living mind like a nightmare"[32], no matter how they "breakaway" from the tradition, the change of the ideological system contained in the thought trends can always intertwine with traditional cultural sources.

Political thought trends always reflect the social existence of society, so as long as there are still social material conditions generating political thought trends, the similar thought trends will reappear. However, since other social living conditions have been greatly changed, the reappeared thought trends may not be able to play the progressive role like before; as what professor Tian Xinming said: "looking back to the history, we can see that the popular Pragmatism emerged in recent years is not a new culture and thought of the world brought by the Opening-up, but the old thought trend revived in the new period after a while of silence."[33] Thought trends are the result of human practice, which in turn has positive effects on practice. Review and remembrance of history by many thought trends often represents a "special" expectation on "today". History after all belongs to "the past", and cannot be replicated, so opinions on history from the thought trends were usually to use the past to satirize the present or to draw parallels from history.

Some thought trends in the new period of China's Reform and Opening-up are intertwined with the movement of thought trends over a hundred years in modern China. Over the one hundred years in modern China, with the disintegration of traditional society, the deepened national peril and national awakening, and the intersection between Chinese and Western cultures, a lot of political thought trends emerged intensively. In a very short period, the political thought trends emerged are numerous with broad impact. Today, to some extent, these varied thought trends are more or less, implicitly or explicitly repeated by many contemporary cultural debates and ideological divergences, and became the pioneer of the contemporary thought trends.

For the influence of foreign ideological and cultural resources on political thought trends, Luo Huiyu believes that when the nation is at a time of crisis or change, various kinds of foreign ideological culture will publicize rapidly across the nation with a considerable impact. As foreign ideological

---

32 *Collected Works of Karl Marx and Frederick Engels,* Vol. 2, People's Publishing House, 2009, p. 41.
33 Tian Xinming, Guo Baoping, *Trend of Philosophical Thoughts of Contemporary College Students,* Shaanxi People's Publishing House, 1990, p. 140.

cultures provide the new theoretical coordinates, which are completely different from local ideological culture, to solve social problems and ease the hardship of livelihood, they often become the catalyst for theoretical innovation of thinkers and important causes for the formation of the new thought trends.[34] Foreign ideological cultures play an important role in crystallizing the birth of new theories and new thoughts. They tend to be introduced or applied as new theory and new method, which are used as "the ready-made panacea" by some "forerunners" to solve domestic problems.

Since the Opium War, the reason why the political thought trends have been surging successively in China lies in not only the domestic crisis but also in the communication stemming from foreign cultures. In the history of Chinese thoughts of late Qing Dynasty, there was a surging tide of political thought trends, which was mainly due to the fact that the various thoughts, ideas, theories and doctrines, from liberalism to socialism, gradually established throughout hundreds of years in Western society flooded into the Chinese ideological circle, which "captured" modern Chinese thinkers and enabled them to put forward a variety of salvation plans based on the Western ideological system, promoting reform or revolution, which resulted in several political thought trends in different tendencies in a certain time. For example, the Chinese statecraft thought trend, the opening-up-to-the-world thought trend, the Taiping Heavenly Kingdom revolutionary thought, the Westernization thoughts, the early reformist thought trend in modern China, the constitutional reform and modernization thought trend, and the bourgeois democratic revolution thought, Marxist thought trend and other political thought trends that rose before and after the Opium War were both due to the objective impact of the influx of foreign thought trends on Chinese social ideology and theory and thought, and the inevitable results from the fact that Chinese advanced intellectuals learned the advanced science and technology, system and ideology from the West in order to seek development of China and get rid of the plight caused by domestic turmoil and foreign invasion.

Before and after the May Fourth Movement (1919), many new theories, new thoughts and new concepts, such as pragmatism, reformism, life philosophy, voluntarism etc., flooded. This was mainly due to the fact that China was in the period of great change in economy and politics, while the world capitalism was in a great development and prosperity process, which enabled the various ideas and political thought trends that represent the

---

34 Luo Huiyu, A Tentative Analysis of Social and Historical Conditions for the Generation of Chinese Trend of Political Thoughts, *Journal of Chongqing Institute of Commerce*, 1999(8).

interests of different classes and different walks of life to break through the old curtain of the thought of "ancient empire", and flood into China as well as rapidly combining with China's actual situation and ideological tradition to seek further development in China. The political thought trends during this period mainly included the bourgeois reformism thought trend, the political trend of bourgeois revolutionary democratic thought, the anarchism thought trend of petty bourgeois, utopian socialism, etc. Marxism-Leninism was also introduced in this period, which triumphed over the various non-Marxist thought trends by virtue of its scientific nature, and gradually developed and became the guiding ideology of the CPC in leading the Chinese people to carry on the revolutionary conflict and social construction, which had a great impact on the history of China. The diverse political thought trends got rooted in China during the May Fourth Movement, and became a wonderful landscape in the process of being welcomed or rejected by intellectuals from different walks of life all over the country. The people who pursue progress explored the way of saving the country and people through this wide range of various thought trends.

When it comes to modern society, with the constant boost of economic globalization and innovation of information communication modes, the politics, economy, ideology, culture and environment of a country are more or less bound to exchange information with the international environment, which will lead the economic, political and cultural conditions generated from political thought trends to become more and more international. In the new period of China's Reform and Opening-up, the development of political thought trends is also influenced by the foreign ideology and culture. The numerous and complex modern Western political thought trends made a complicated impact on Chinese society, a considerable part of which played a negative role in social development and socialist ideology of China. This is because, in essence, globalization is a process of capital accumulation which keeps expanding and is often in the state of a financial explosion"[35], and it is the phenomenon and process that uses capital to conquer the whole world, which is guided by capitalist and aims to realize the interests of a small number of people in the world. The popularity of liberalism thought trend in China in the 1990s was closely related to the essence of globalization. With the rise of high-tech revolution and the great development of productive forces, the impact of the tide of globalization on human society was expanded comprehensively, involving economic, political, cultural and social aspects after 1990s. However, the early 1990s was the period when the Eastern Bloc got collapsed; the international communist movement sank

---

35   Paul Sweezy, Talking about Globalization, *Monthly Review*, Vol. 49, No. 4.

into the low tide, while the Western capitalism made great achievements in economy and politics, a time when "the West prevailed over the East". The liberalism thought trend which originated from the Western capitalist society, was mainly about the neo-liberal thought trend. It developed rapidly as it solved the economic stagflation appeared in the capitalist countries in the 1970s in a widespread manner and refilled the capitalism with vitality of development, and became popular as an important part of the theoretical system of globalization thought publicized by the US and Britain for the interests of their international monopoly capitalist groups, in the 1970s and 1980s in China, who had experienced more than ten years of Reform and Opening-up and was facing the choice between the two economic paths. From the other point of view, if today's globalization is the one of socialism, there would be no space for the rise of the liberal thought trend. At the time international communist movement was at low tide and the capitalism was "rising", liberalism, as a capitalist ideology, will inevitably take this opportunity to fully display itself.

For the impact of the real ideological and cultural conditions on political thought trends, "as soon as any ideology comes into being, it will develop based on the combination with the existing concepts and materials, and further process these materials; otherwise, it is not ideology."[36] As a phenomenon of social spiritual culture, political thought trends cannot be separated from the cultural matrix, the society, and generated directly from the political and economic conditions. The formation of any political thought trend must rely on a certain cultural environment, as the level of political thought trend is consistent with the overall level of the social culture, and the value tendency and the core of the concept of thought trend are also closely and deeply associated with social ideology and culture.

The real ideological and cultural conditions, as the spiritual and ideological atmosphere of the whole society, restrict the formation and development of political thought trends. The relationships between political thought trends and traditional ideological and cultural resources and foreign ideological and cultural resources reflect its inheritance and compatibility, but there is no doubt that the most basic ideological and cultural soil for the political thought trends is still the real ideological and cultural system, as it is the most direct cultural cause of the political thought trends, originated from the fact that real ideological and cultural system is the "limiter" to the theoretical level of thinkers and the value preference of the members of the society, and the "filter" for the traditional ideological and cultural factors and the Western ideological and cultural

---

36 *Collected Works of Karl Marx and Frederick Engels,* Vol. 4, People's Publishing House, 2009, p. 309.

factors. The foreign or traditional ideology and culture must be combined with the internal cause of realistic ideology and culture to get rooted and grown.

In the mid-to-late 1990s, the liberal thought trend emerging in China considered itself as it is inherited from the liberalization thought trend in the 1980s and Chinese liberals in the first half of the 20th Century. As liberals have admitted, "the liberalism of the 1990s basically held the positive attitude toward humanism and enlightenment thought trends in cultural craze in the 1980s, and has a relationship of inheritance and development with it"[37], however, at the beginning, it could take the theoretical symbols of other theories as reference"[38]. Liberalism did not begin to be more fully "expressed" until 1990s, and make some adjustments all about the liberalism thought trend in the 1980s. The modern Chinese liberalism, especially the liberalism thought trend in the first half of the 20th Century, also supported the flourishing of the liberal thought trend in the 1990s, which is also known as "the current Renaissance of liberal tradition originated from Peking University"[39].

What occupies the dominant position in the real Chinese culture is neither the Confucianism in the traditional culture, nor the Western or any other foreign ideology and culture, but the socialist culture with Chinese characteristics with the Marxism as its guide. As the report of the 15th CPC Party Congress pointed out: "The construction of a socialist culture with Chinese characteristics is the national sphere, scientific and popular socialist culture that takes the Marxism as the guide, targeted at cultivating aspiring, moral, cultivated, and disciplined citizens, in view of the modernization, the world and the future." The socialist culture with Chinese characteristics set the tone for the whole social spirit and ideological atmosphere, and established a clear direction for the cultural value tendency of thinkers and social members, by which it constituted the most direct cultural cause for the formation and development of the mainstream political thought trends, especially the cultural thought trends. The socialist culture with Chinese characteristics itself becomes rich and perfect not only based on the modern culture but by inheriting the excellent national cultural tradition, and not of our country but fully absorbs the outstanding cultural achievements of the world, therefore, the traditional or foreign political thought trends and other ideological cultures enrich and develop both themselves and the socialist culture with Chinese characteristics on the basis of conforming to the basic value orientation of the socialist culture with Chinese characteristics.

---

37   XuYouyu, *Liberalism and Contemporary China*, *Open Times*, 1999(3).
38   Ibid.
39   Li Shenzhi, Preface of *Peking University Tradition and Modern China*, *Journal of Methods*, 1998(8).

The cultural conditions for the formation and development of many thought trends are not separated but integrated and comprehensive. It's all of the traditional ideology and culture, the foreign ideology and culture, and the realistic ideology and culture which constituted the organic system of certain social culture to provide the conditions and influence for the political thought trends. We explain the influences of the traditional ideology and culture, foreign ideology and culture, and realistic ideology and culture on the formation of the thought trends, respectively, to highlight their specific configurations. As the realistic ideological and cultural system itself is the organic integration of the three parts, which as a result impacted collectively on political thought trends, which simply presented differently in particular, as some are prominent, some are weak, the same case as the different levels of political conditions which impacted collectively on thought trends. In the study of a specific thought trend, although it focuses on the study of the condition in a certain aspect, it is also necessary to see the influences of other factors.

III.2. The role of thinkers in the formation and development of political thought trends

As Liang Qichao said, "the thought trends of the times are all originated from the 'continuing mass movements'. It is not necessarily that, the so-called individuals which take roles in the movements should have the consciousness or should make plans and be organized, moreover they should not be divided as those who have an initiative or those who are passive."[40]

This view is rightful, but the relationships between the formation and development of the political thought trends and the influence of thinkers are closely related, since the organizing and planning property of some thought trends are always originated from the initiative and creativity of their core thinkers in most of the thought trends.

III.2.1. Thinkers promote the formation and development of thought trends

A political thought trend expresses a common social psychology and a common theoretical demand of a group men in the society, and represents a common "rejection", "recognition" and "expectation" by a group men in the society in specific social and historical conditions. They have consensus due to people who live in a common living environment who make their

---

40   Liang Qichao, *Introduction to the Qing Dynasty*, recorded in: *Four Kinds of Liang Qichao's Historical Works*, Yuelu Press, 1985, p. 20.

psychological desires and theoretical appeal reached an agreement through extensive communication, which is one of the premises for the formation of a thought trend. As Marx once pointed out: "the common desire and intention of the working class is generated from the actual conditions of the working class. Because of this, this kind of desire and intention is shared by the whole class."[41] But the psychological consensus of the members of society is only one of the reasons for the formation of the thought trends. Another important element of the thought trend is the ideological theory system, namely the ideology. Ideology, as an abstract and complete summary of theory, should be complemented by a thinker who has a summarizing ability, expressive ability and foresight. A political thought trend is not a spontaneous result, but it is originated from an activity of conscious theory creation. Creation comes from the special efforts of thinkers. As Marx and Engels pointed out on the ideology of the ruling class, "in this class, some people appeared as the thinkers of the class, and they are the positive ideologues with the generalization ability in the class."[42] Lenin pointed out from the perspective of the advanced intellectuals in the society with the creation of theory: "the reason why the 'thinker' is called thinker is that he walked in front of the spontaneous movement, pointed out the road for the movement, and was good at solving all kinds of theoretical, political, strategic, and organizational problems spontaneously encountered by the moving "substance factors" earlier than others."[43] In general, the theoretical creation of thinkers is intensively embodied in the grasp and re-creation of the psychological will of some members of the society. Thinkers can keenly get aware of new social psychological trend, and consciously improve the theory to an ideological system that meets social psychological demands, and make it develop into the political thought trend through communication among the masses.

We take the Marxism as an example of the promotion of an advanced thought trend to illustrate the influence of thinkers. There is no doubt that the working masses will spontaneously tend to socialism, but they cannot spontaneously create the ideological system of scientific socialism, which requires theoretical creation by the proletarian thinkers (including some leaders). Marx, a great master of the world proletariat, founded the theory of scientific socialism. The Marxist theory system, created by Marx and Engels who learned from organic integration of the German classical

41   *Complete Works of Karl Marx and Frederick Engels,* Vol. 32, People's Publishing House, 1975, p. 68.
42   *Collected Works of Karl Marx and Frederick Engels,* Vol. 1, People's Publishing House, 2009, p. 51.
43   *Complete Works of Lenin,* Vol. 5, People's Publishing House, 1986, p. 326.

philosophy, the British classical political economy and the rational core of French utopian socialism based on the practice of the labor movement in the 19th Century, became the theoretical weapons, action guideline and guiding ideology of the world socialist movement of the proletariat. Marx devoted all his life to the cause of communism, and the ruthless disclosure and criticism of the landlords and the bourgeoisie subjected him to the curse and expulsion of all the reactionary forces. From 1842 to 1882, Marx created the *Introduction to Critique of Hegel's Philosophy of Right* (1843), *Theses on Feuerbach* (1845), *German Ideology* (1845-1846), Poverty of Philosophy (1847), *Manifesto of the Communist Party* (1848), *Class Struggles in France, 1848 to 1850* (1850), *Introduction to Critique of Political Economy* (1857), *Preface to the Introduction of Critique of Political Economy* (1859), the first volume of *Capital* (1867), *Comments on the Draft Program of the German Workers' Party*, namely, *Critique of the Gotha Program* (1875), *Anti-Dühring* (1876-1878) and other numerous books and articles. During this period, Marx also drafted declarations, programs, articles for the unity of the Communist movement in the world, and actively devoted himself in the revolution of the real political struggle and the workers movement. The combination of the real struggle and the creation of theory not only provided rich real data for scientific theory but also guided the correct direction for the revolutionary struggle. Marx, as the greatest thinker for thousands of years, played a crucial and irreplaceable role in the development of a world communist movement and the promotion of the Marxist thought trend. The significance of his talented theoretical creation for the socialist movement in the world is obvious.

Before Lenin, the positive work of Plekhanov and others played an important role in the introduction of Marxism in Russia. G. Plekhanov was one of the leaders and founders of Marxist political Party in Russia, an important organizer of Russia and the international labor movement, and the earliest thinker to publicize Marxism in Russia and Europe. In 1882, Plekhanov translated the Manifesto of the Communist Party into Russian. In 1883, he founded and led the first Russian Marxist group in Geneva-The Emancipation of Labor Community. After the foundation of the Emancipation of Labor Community, he had done a lot of work by successively translated and published *Wage-Labor and Capital*, P*overty of Philosophy*, *Theses On Feuerbach*, *On the Question of Free Trade*, and other books in order to publicize the Marxism in Russia. In 1886, Plekhanov carried out a debate and struggle against Bernstein's Revisionism and its variants of "Economist Faction" in Russia. In 1900, he started the proletariat-oriented journals of *Spark* (Iskra) and *Dawn* (Zarya) together with

Lenin and drafted the party program of Russian Social Democratic Labor Party. In 1903, he was elected as the chairman of the General Committee of the Russian Social Democratic Labor Party, and led the Russian Marxist political parties to carry out various activities and struggles. In addition, during the period of the establishment of the Labor Liberation Community, Plekhanov created *Socialism and Political Struggle*, and *The Development of the Monist of History*, Papers on the History of Materialism and other series of works to fight against populist current, the doctrine of Bernstein and the Russian economic faction and publicize Marxism. Objectively, Plekhanov's theoretical works and activities publicized a lot of principles of Marxism, which played an important role in the publicity of the Marxism in Russia, as it promoted the combination of the Marxism and the workers' movement in Russia, and they founded and led labor movement of the Russian Marxist Communist Party and cultivated a whole generation of Marxists in Russia.

As a thought trend, the rise of Marxism in China is closely related to the promotion and advocacy by some advanced intellectuals. Li Dazhao was the first to raise the banner of Marxism thought in China. In July 1918, he published the article titled View of Comparison between the French and Russian Revolutions in China, which first publicized and praised the October Revolution. Based on a scientific comparative analysis of the October Revolution and the French Revolution of the 18th Century, he suggested that the two Revolutions represent different spirits of their times, the natures of which are "incomparable with each other", as the French Revolution was a bourgeois revolution, while the October Revolution led by Lenin was "a revolution based on the socialism", "the great change to affect the civilization of the future century", and "the new trend in the world". He predicted that the trend initiated by the October Revolution is unstoppable, and "the world will be dominated by the Communist Party in the future".

Li Dazhao then published successively the Victory of the Common People, Victory of Bolshevism and New Century and other articles, which further analyzed the influence of the October Revolution and the tendency of the world changes. In May 1919, Li Dazhao transformed the magazine New Youth under his chief-editorship into a special issue to publicize and study Marxism, and personally wrote the long dissertation titled My Views on Marxism, which fully affirmed the historical status of the Marxism and systematically and thoroughly introduced the three parts of the Marxism, which marked that Marxism had entered a fairly systematic publicity phase in China. Following the My Views on Marxism, Li Dazhao published many articles on the Morning News supplement, Weekly Review and other publications under his general editorship to publicize the scientific socialism, by which he eulogized the great victory of the October Revolution with great enthusiasm, while resolutely and thoroughly criticized reformism, and presented Marxist classic works and theoretical viewpoints in detail. At the same time, he taught in Peking University, Beijing Female Higher Normal College and Chinese University as a part-time job, while at the same time he opened Historical Materialism, Socialism and Social Movements and History of Workers' International Movement and other courses to publicize the theory of scientific socialism to the college students. Based on the systematic publicity of the theory of scientific socialism, Li Dazhao established the "Seminar on Marxist Theory" in Peking University in March 1920, and initiated and established the Beijing Communist Group and the Socialist Youth League in October and November of the same year, by which he made a significant contribution to the wide publicity of Marxism in China. In addition to Li Dazhao, Mao Zedong, Zhou Enlai, Chen Duxiu, Qu Qiubai, Cai Hesen, Deng Zhongxia, Li Da, Chen Wangdao and other advanced intellectuals also made important contributions to the publicity of socialist ideology in China. Especially Mao Zedong, as a great Marxist, realized the qualitative leap in the publicity and development of Marxism thought in China. Mao Zedong was one of the earliest Chinese intellectuals who accepted and practiced Marxism, and in November 1920, he founded the communist group in Hunan. In July 1921, he attended the first National Congress of the CPC and participated in the creation of the CPC. In June 1923, he was selected as the Central Executive Committee of the CPC, and began to participate in the leadership work of the central government. In 1935, he actually became one of the core leaders of the CPC at the Zunyi Conference. During the period of leading people to carry on the new democratic revolution, he succeeded in combining Marxism-Leninism with the reality of the Chinese revolution, by which he opened up a road of fighting beginning from rural areas to urban areas and seizing power by armed force which was different from that of Soviet Russia, and achieved the historical shift to the fact that Chinese nation had become independent and the Chinese people had taken their own leadership. Then he led Chinese people to achieve the victory of the socialist revolution and construction. In general, in the long-term practice of revolution and construction, Mao Zedong had always adhered to the stance, viewpoint and method of Marxism. He not only applied Marxism in practice, but also made a series of creative developments according to the actual situation of China, and ultimately formed Mao Zedong Thought, the great thought with the characteristics of the times and Chinese characteristics. This was undoubtedly the development of Marxism thought at the highest level, the establishment and consolidation of the dominant position of Marxism and socialist ideology in China.

In addition to the thinkers, the world of intellectuals also played a very important role in the formation, publicity and development of the political thought trends. Reviewing the history, we can see that the majority of patriotic intellectuals sought the truth of saving the country and the people with great enthusiasm, publicized the new thought trends, fought against the archaic politics, and many men and women with high ideals sacrificed their lives since the beginning of modern times of China. For example, during the period of Wu Xu political reform, facing the crisis situation of domestic trouble and foreign invasion, the bourgeois reformists led by Kang Youwei issued a strong voice for national salvation. In 1895, Kang Youwei, Liang Qichao and thousands of patriotic scholar-bureaucrats had initiated the "Gongche Shangshu Movement", and the reformists boarded the stage of history. Kang Youwei organized the Society for National Strengthening in Beijing and Shanghai, and founded the Chinese and Foreign News and Qiangxuebao, to introduce the Western capitalist countries and publicized reform; besides, he wrote books and published the Reform of Confucius Exam, which provided the theoretical basis for the ideological and political reform. Yan Fu translated the Theory of Natural Selection, published Yuanqiang, On the Original Incident, Salvation and other articles to publicize the biological evolutionism and the theory of natural rights, which fought against the feudal autocratic monarchy and advocated bourgeois democracy; in addition, he started the Guowen Daily in Tianjin, published daily current events from home and abroad to broaden people's horizons. Liang Qichao published Reform through Discussion and a series of articles on the Chinese Progress in Shanghai, more strongly advocated reform under the circumstance of being banned and stricken by the Qing government. Tan Sitong organized the Southern Association, and founded the Xiang Newspaper and Hunan News, to advocate new learning and publicizing reform, and actively cultivating talents and reformers; it published the Study on Benevolence, which fiercely attacked the autocratic monarchy and cardinal guides and constant virtues, and called upon "burst" feudal "trap". Under the pressure of the campaign organized by the majority of reformist patriotic intellectuals, Emperor Guangxu finally issued a series of edicts to get rid of the old rules and make way for the new rules, when the reform thought trend reached the peak. But the old school led by Empress Dowager Ci Xi strongly opposed the reform thought trend, and launched the coup to imprison the emperor and groundlessly slaughtered the reformers. The "six gentlemen of the hundred days' reform" were killed in Beijing on September 28, 1898. The Wu Xu political reform ended with failure, and the reform thought trend also declared its bankruptcy. Lenin pointed out: "And, indeed, there could not be any other grouping among our students, because they are the most responsive section of the intelligentsia, and the intelligentsia are so called just because they most consciously, most resolutely and most accurately reflect and express the development of class interests and political groupings in society as a whole."[44] As Qu Qiubai, with a deep understanding of keen insight of intellectuals on social issues, said: "The personality is cultivated by the society; it was implied by contemporary social psychology, and was also influenced by class struggle in the society. Scholars could find the problems existing in the society at that time. Although people regarded them as a matter of course, he could pose questions; but he could not create social problems that did not exist."[45]

When it entered into the 1990s, people who have played a key role in the formation and development of some thought trends are often referred to as "leaders" or "opinion leaders" in China. Some network articles and some scholars clearly pointed out: "In the early years of the Youth Forum period, after the liberals were missing for many years, the Chinese mainland was quietly waiting for another liberal leader who emerged as the times required. In 1998, on the commemoration of the one hundredth anniversary of the Peking University, there was Li Shenzhi, the prominent personage who was the former assistant dean of the Chinese Academy of Social Sciences."[46] "Li Shenzhi who is known as a current leader of the liberal thought in China is neither because that he accepted the liberalism in the earliest period and studied it most widely, nor that he led a group of people to follow and advocate liberalism; precisely, he was the most senior person with the highest prestige and the greatest impact among the liberals in mainland China. Since, he has played an irreplaceable and unsurpassed role, and led and called upon liberalism, liberals were able to form a group with certain influence."[47] Instead of using "leaders" or "opinion leaders" when referin to the masses and the advanced intellectuals, outstanding people and the backbone figures of the socialist cause, the CPC specifies "Members of the CPC will be forever ordinary members of the working people" in the Article 2 of Chapter I in the Constitution of the Communist

---

44   *The Complete Works of Lenin*, Vol. 7, People's Publishing House, 1986, p. 324.

45   *Selected Works of Qu Qiubai*, People's Publishing House, 1985, p. 125.

46   Qiu Yueshou, *From Hu Ping to Li Shenzhi: The Hard Course of Chinese Liberalism for nearly Twenty Years*, Guantian Teahouse (http://www.tianyacommunity.com/new/ Publicforum/Content.asp?idWriter=0&Key=0&strltem=no01&idArticle=94120&flag=1).

47   Xu Youyu, *Brief Comment on the Formation of Li Shenzhi's Liberalism Thought*, "Ideological   Empire   BBS"   (http://www.thinker-empire.com/forum/printpage. asp?BoardID=32&ID=6756).

Party.[48] Therefore, in contemporary China, "leaders" and "opinion leaders" are basically used to refer to the representative figures of political thought trends, which have difference with the Marxist ideology.

III.2.2. Premises for theoretical creation by thinkers

The formation and development of political thought trends is a social and historical phenomenon. In political thought trends, the relation between thinkers and the members of society who are represented by them can be accurately grasped only through the view point of historical materialism.

Thinkers carry out theoretical production and creation based on a more extensive social experience, including their individual experience. When a thinker theoretically processes perceptual materials, he processes not only the things he saw by eye or touched by hand, but also total experience of some social members. It is a perception on more extensive perceptual materials. There is an interaction between theoretical creation by thinkers and the psychology of social members. The psychology of some social members not only promotes thinkers to upgrade their theory by facilitating the formation of political thought trends, but also restricts the theoretical re-creation by thinkers and the development of political thought trends. For example, the psychology of social members may be unified or discordant with progressive political thought trends. When a political thought trend is accepted, understood or supported by most of the social members, it would generally improve and develop, and make certain effects on social practice. Otherwise, when a political thought trend is mostly resisted, opposed or criticized by the social psychology, it would disappear in history or be adjusted and transformed so as to regain the vitality and space for its development. With the development of social productive forces and the constant change of economic base, the practice experience and perceptual psychology of social members will change dynamically, affecting the theoretical creation of thinkers. Therefore, a political thought trend will normally unify, then dis-unify and again unify with social psychology.

On one hand, the psychological expectation of social members provides most immediate nutrient and basis for advanced thinkers to ponder grand historical propositions. The impulse of thinkers to upgrade theory reflects only the emotion, demand and voice of most citizens. The two industrial revolutions led to the leaping development in science and technology, as well as a dramatic increase of productive forces. While they also damaged

---

48   *Compilation of the Documents of the 17th National Congress of the CPC,* People's Publishing House, , (2007, p. 69.

ecological environment and intensified ecological crisis. The issue of ecological environment drew more and more attention of the citizens. In the
1970s, in the Western countries, there emerged academic research communities and social communities which first brought forward "common
global issues", which mainly included the population issue, grain issue,
non-renewable energy resources issue, and environmental pollution issue.
During the 1970s, this directly led to a new large-scale social movement of
ecological protection in the West. With the increasing concern, demand and
voice of the public, many political groups and social organizations emerged
in Western developed capitalist countries. These groups and organizations
were led by the "Green Party", aiming to push ahead the green thought
trend on a large-scale basis. They advocated maintaining ecological balance, opposing the unlimited development of economy and highlighting
the principle of non-violence. They turned out to be the organizer of the
largest "New Social Movement" in developed capitalist countries at the
end of the 20th Century, blowing a "Green Whirlwind" in Western societies.
Since the commencement of the Reform and Opening-up, the social and
economic development in China has achieved remarkable achievements
that attracted worldwide attention. However, during such development, the
unreasonable resource utilization and extensive growth pattern led to many
disastrous effects, such as the intensified deterioration of ecological environment and run-out of ecological resources. The issue of environment has
become one of the most worrying and painful issues that have obtained
most concern from the public. Therefore, in the Report to the 17th National
Congress of the CPC, it was decided to include the Scientific Outlook on
Development, proposed by Chinese Communists represented by Hu Jintao
into the Party Constitution, and it was agreed upon adopting the outlook of
overall, coordinated and sustainable development based on people, as our
guiding ideology for future development. In the Report to the 18th National
Congress of the CPC, the overall layout of "Five in One" was pur forward,
by which ecological civilization was added into the original overall layout
of "Four in One" (economy, politics, culture and society) for socialist cause
with Chinese characteristics. This represented and embodied fundamental
interests and common wishes of the mass, causing the green thought trend
to be perfected and developed with Chinese features.

On the other hand, psychological consciousness, such as emotion, of
common social members shows a certain gap with thinkers and progressive political thought trends with "forward-looking on a high level". This
psychological consciousness may have historic limitations on some level.
But, there exists a real gap. It is an invisible restriction on the impulse of

theoretical recreation by thinkers. In addition, the grand inertia formed by the gap also limits the space for act of thinkers and progressive thought trends. In such "game", thinkers and the public make a thought trend develop in ups and downs and move on circuitously. For example, the 14th National Congress of the CPC first established the goal pattern of socialist market economy system combining socialist basic system with market economy, which activated the strong vitality of socialism and achieved a leap-frog development of the Chinese economy. In fact, at the early stage of the Reform and Opening-up, the chief architect of the reform Deng Xiaoping brought up an advanced idea that a socialist country can also adopt market economy system and China would develop socialist market economy. However, since the opponent status between planned economy and market economy are always regarded as the essential features of socialism and capitalism in China, there was no possibility for the existence and development of market economy in socialist system. Besides, in the initial period of socialist construction when all devastated things needed to be rebuilt, the system of planned economy indeed aroused the tremendous passion of people and achieved great accomplishment in economic development. Therefore, the traditional planned economic system occupied an absolutely crucial position in the mind of the mass, even many intellectuals. This is why people questioned, even denied the progressive idea of socialist market economy proposed by Deng Xiaoping and other thinkers in the early Reform and Opening-up and rather long time thereafter. Through over ten years of unremitting effort, Deng Xiaoping finally, by step and phase, made the mass correctly understand the relationship between the social nature and the mode of planned or market-oriented development through theoretical publicity and practical action. Eventually, the idea of socialist market economy was recognized and supported psychologically by social members.

As for a thinker who pushes those political thought trends that can correctly understand objective reality and correctly reflect the law of social development, his thoughts can follow the trend of social development and therefore are eventually in line with the willing and interests of the mass. So, his thoughts can be publicized in a relatively long time, turning into a political thought trend with long-lasting vitality, even a crucial ideology in society. Why his thoughts can form a large-scale thought trend, the fundamental cause lays on that their ideas are also based on objective society which also constitutes the base for psychological basis and theoretical ideas of such thoughts. His thoughts must go with the "tide", not resist it. Such thinkers must make their thoughts meet the general trend of social development so as to obtain the base and vitality to survive and advance. A series of thoughts and theories generated from the Sinization of Marxism can always take the unshakable dominant position in the field of ideology in China, just because they always represent the demand for the development of advanced productive forces and the fundamental interests of the majority of people. During the period of the New-Democratic Revolution and the early stage of socialist construction, Chinese Communists represented by Mao Zedong successfully combined Marxism and Leninism with the reality in the revolution and early construction of China. At this period, Maoism was generated. Under the guidance of Maoism, we realized the hundred-year aspiration: the independence of Chinese nation and the governance by people. Since the new stage of the Reform and Opening-up, in the grand practice of building socialism with Chinese characteristics, Chinese Communists represented by Deng Xiaoping, Jiang Zemin and Hu Jintao successively formed many theoretical systems about socialism with Chinese characteristics, including the Deng Xiaoping Theory, the Important Thoughts of "Three Represents", the Scientific Outlook on Development and other advanced thoughts and theories. Under the guidance of these advanced thoughts which always keep pace with the times, the good wish of prosperity and strength of Chinese nation and the well-being and happiness of Chinese people are being realized. Based on this, we can say that it is historical inevitability and people's choice that Marxist thoughts, which correctly reflects the law of social development and represents interests of the mass, can achieve great development and takes the dominant position in the field of ideology.

Undeniably, there were innumerable thinkers made their thoughts resist the "tide". Their thoughts might also be in accordance with the psychological status and the ideas of some social members by forming thought trends with multiple bustles at that time. This kind of thought trends was also able to illustrate the interactive relation between these thinkers and some social members in the formation and development of such thought trends. These thought trends would finally quit the historical stage as a result of the social base on which they stand. Since the Reform and Opening-up, people's thoughts have turned to be more diversified and volatile. This, along with the incoming of various thought trends from overseas, led to the emergence of many political thought trends that represent voices of different interest groups in the field of ideology. Some of these political thought trends attacked, distorted and slandered the dominant ideology, and normally carried out publicity by taking advantage of some pressing issues in our society. By catering the interest appeal of social members on some social issues, they tried to get support from some social members. However, these political thought trends essentially went against fundamental nature of our socialism and did not represent fundamental interest of the mass, so they would finally perish with our economic development and social advance. Engels indicated that, "the main figures that show up are representatives of certain class and tendency. Therefore, they are also some ideological representatives of their times. Their motive does not come from trivial individual desire, but the historical trend they stay in."[49] "However important personal motive is, it cannot equal the motive of groups, nations or classes; so we must investigate the source of motive of the mass when we research the cause of history."[50] Thinkers should combine with the mass if they want their thought trends to be developed. Li Dazhao wrote that, "since the May Fourth Movement, movements of intellectual class has emerged unceasingly. By now, the victory of intellectual class has been gradually demonstrated. It is our eager hope that intellectual class can become the pioneer of the mass and the mass can turn to the supporter of intellectual class. The significance of intellectual class lies on some pioneers that are loyal to mass movements."[51] This has sufficiently showed that thinkers should go back into the mass and unite with them.

To sum up, some core groups, such as some social members and thinkers, complement each other in respect of their roles in the formation and development of thought trends. Social individual accept some ideas through theoretical consensus or emotional accordance. Objectively, ideological and theoretical consensus can be reached only among a few of so-called elites, thinkers and scholars, while most social members accept thoughts based on emotion and faith so as to form an extensive social base. These elites, thinkers and scholars turn out to be representative figures or "wave riders" of certain political thought trends, the main body and core force of theoretical upgrade and ideological creation, and the explorer and leader of social civilization and epochal progress. While these social members become the carrier or reflection of these political thought trends, acting the role of "soil" or "ally" of these "wave riders", and the chooser and determiner of rise and fall of thought trend and social development. Overall, as a social consciousness phenomenon with extensive influence, a political thought trend is affected more deeply by the members of society. The key factor for the formation and development of a political thought trend is whether the idea of its core group (such as thinkers) can be widely accepted, supported and endorsed by the members of society.

49   *Collected Works of Karl Marx and Frederick Engels,* Vol. 10, People's Publishing House, 2nd edition, 2009, p. 174.
50   *Selected Works of Qu Qiubai,* People's Publishing House, , (1985, p. 115.
51   *Collected Works of Li Dazhao,* People's Publishing House, , (1984, p. 208.

III.2.3. Major approaches used by thinkers to push ahead the formation and development of a thought trend

During the formation and development of a political thought trend, thinkers often utilize association type of organizations, meetings, propagation, books, newspapers and journals to promote social acts so as to promote the growth of the thought trend.In the period of the May Fourth Movement when various thought trends surged, association activities were much active. The New Culture Movement aroused intense attraction among the intellectuals, especially youth and students, who gradually organized in the form of associations so as to implement research of encountered issues and in order to find ways out. This finally produced an upsurge of seeking truth and pursuing emancipation. In the book Associations in the Period of the May Fourth Movement edited by Zhang Yunhou et al, has described the situation of associations across the country in the Period of the May Fourth Movement in detail.[52] Among these associations, there was a representative organization "Xinmin Society", which was organized by Mao Zedong and Cai Hesen to publicize Marxism. This associations carried out extensive revolutionary activities and made Marxist publicity. This militant revolutionary organization played a key role in the leading of revolutionary forces in Hunan during the struggle of the May Fourth Movement and anti-warlord peasant movement. Besides, from this association, there emerged a generation of excellent revolutionary warriors and communists. Then, many other organizations were set up subsequently to publicize Marxism actively, including "Mutual Aid Society in Wuchang", "Awareness Society in Tianjin", "Transform Society in Jiangxi" and "Peking University Marxism Theory Society". These organizations were the most progressive and active ones among the numerous communities during the May Fourth Movement. And they have vigorously boosted the publicity of Marxism in China and trained many cadres for CPC and the revolutionary cause. In addition to "Xinmin Society" and other associations that conducted publicity of Marxism, there also existed another kind of smaller organizations, which were experimental type of new life group in the mode of partial work and partial study. For example, the Work and Study Mutual Aid Team in Beijing and Shanghai was aimed to help local youth by the mode of part work and part study to achieve the combination of education and career. Although, these organizations dissolved in short time as a result of many subjective and objective factors, such as opinion divergence and shortage of money, they objectively laid certain organizational and ideological foundation for

---

52   Compiled and authored by Zhang Yunhou: *Mass Organizations during the May Fourth Period*, SDX Joint Publishing Company, 1979, p. 13.

the establishment of communist groups in each region. Subsequently, their initiators and participants all set up communist groups, or even transformed into main force and core leaders in the following revolution and construction of China. These communities adhered to some doctrine, pushing the advance of certain thought trends. The rising of various communities illustrated, on some level, the surging of political thought trends during the May Fourth Movement is closely related to the swarming of communities.

In addition to these communities, social activities carried out by thinkers are another key mode to push ahead the development of thought trends. Society actually means the same as association, but organized relatively loose. The article The Era of Transformation in the Chinese Modern Ideological History, which is collected into the book *Thoughts and Academics*, has discussed the situation about societies (associations) during late Qing Dynasty era. After 1895, with the development of political reform, societies had bloomed in China. Based on preliminary statistics, there were about 76 societies from 1895 to 1898.Among them, the most representative included China Strengthening Society and South Society in the period of Wu Xu Reform. The China Strengthening Society was founded by Kang Youwei in 1895 at Shanghai, aiming to achieve the self-strengthening of China by "information communication, book collection, professional education, talent cultivation and establishment of Confucianism". This society advocated reform and modernization. The South Society was proposed and established by Tan Sitong, Xiong Xiling, Tang Caichang., etc. at Hunan in 1898, aiming to unite to revitalize China. This organization publicized reform and modernization by "creating new atmosphere and enlightening civil wisdom". The establishment of these influential societies triggered an upsurge of other societies. There emerged various societies with the same purpose of rescuing the nation and repelling invasion, even though their contents were different. These societies boosted the change in social climate and emancipation of intellectual thoughts, which have objectively enhanced the influence of the reform thought trends in China. Generally, as a kind of organization, society did not cost many manpower and material resources, and can be founded just through the intention of a group of intellectual. Therefore, in respect of the publicity of new thoughts and knowledge, the significance of society was no less than that of newspaper, journal and new type school at that time.[53] The influence of society on the development of political thought trends is universal.

---

53   Zhang Hao, *The Transformation Period of Chinese Modern Thought History*, Recorded in *Ideology and Academy* of chief editor Chen Yushui, Encyclopedia of China Publishing House, 2005, pp. 304-305.

Newspaper and journal are also major means to push ahead the development of political thought trends by thinkers. During the May Fourth Movement, when various thought trends was surging, there emerged multiple journals one after another as key channels to publicize these thought trends. Some crucial representative figures of thought trend played a key role in the formation and development of these journals. As expounded in the article The Era of Transformation in the Chinese Modern Ideological History: "after 1895, newspapers and journals have boomed as a result of the drive by political revolutionary movement in the early stage. Based on statistics by Roswell S. Britton, China only had 15 newspapers and journals by 1895. During 1895-1898, the number increased to 60, which further increased to 487 by the year of 1913 and shown a surge in the May Fourth Movement. According to the China Year Book of the time, there were about 840 newspapers and journals in those days. As Shanghai News believed, it was 1,134. But the American scholar, Samuel Woodbridge gave a number of 2,000 in the Encyclopedia Sinica in 1917. According to the statistics by Hu Shi, newly established newspapers and journals reached to 400 only within the year of 1919. It suggests that the increase rate of newspapers and journals in this transformation era was amazing."[54] Honored as the driving engine of new thought trends, the journal New Youth was founded in September 1915 by Chen Duxiu, a highly capable intellectual in the New Culture Movement. The journal highly raised the flag of democracy and science, advocating new literature and vernacular Chinese and resisting old literature and classical Chinese. It effectively revealed and criticized feudalistic superstition. The New Youth was written mainly by Chen Duxiu, Li Dazhao, Lu Xun, Qian Xuantong, Liu Bannong, Hu Shi, Shen Yinmo, Gao Yihan and Zhou Zuoren, forming a main soil to cultivate new thought trends. Another key place to publicize new thought trends was Weekly Review, which was established by Chen Duxiu and Li Dazhao in December 1918 in Beijing. This journal was closely linked to realistic politics and reflected pressing political issues. It mutually complemented the New Youth's focus on theoretical analysis. Before Hu Shi took the post of its chief editor, the Weekly Review fiercely criticized the political agitation by Northern Warlords and Japanese Imperialism. It highly raised the flag of democracy and science, criticized dated feudal thoughts and culture, and introduced and publicized progressive Marxism. During that period, it aroused tremendous social impact and laid important ideological and theoretical foundation for the May Fourth Movement. Besides, those journals generally took the expression of certain new thought or idea as

54 Ibid., p. 303.

their task. The first issue manifesto of the New Youth argued: "New Youth should represent the source of social thoughts and arouse the impression of revolutionary emotion..." "The New Youth should analyze the origin of these schools and point out the cause for change of social mood."[55] In the issuance declaration of Weekly Review, it was said that, "this issuance is aimed to advocate recognized truth and oppose arbitrary power, with the only hope that arbitrary power will never defeat recognized truth, and this will achieve the long live of human."[56] In the Issuance Declaration of New Trend on January 1st, 1919, it was uttered that, "the New Trend is a monthly journal edited by the students of the Peking University students who have common ideals."[57]

All classical Marxist writers attached much attention to the role of journal. Engels pointed out that, "a Communist Party first needs a political organ, an official newspaper"[58] Marx also praised that those free publications which "permeated everywhere, existed everywhere and knew everything," and "they really formed an ideal world which emerged from reality, accumulated spiritual wealth and then surged back into the reality."[59]

In China, Mao Zedong, Li Dazhao, Qu Qiubai, Chen Duxiu and many other leaders either set up newspapers and journals personally, or utilized newspapers and journals to publicize Marxism. Sun Yat-sen, the pioneer of bourgeois democratic revolution, indicated in his speech in Guangzhou at the end of 1923 that, "publicity gives ninety percent contribution for a rapid victory in revolution, while military force only gives ten percent."[60] In today's social life, we can also find such phenomenon that some people with similar ideological tendency may gradually gather around certain newspapers and journals, which are turning to bean invisible position for some thought trends. For example, Mao Zedong once served as chief editor and main writer of the Xiang River Review founded by Hunan Student Union in July 1919. In the issuance declaration of this journal, Mao wrote, "What is the biggest problem in the world? It is food. What is the strongest power? It is the union of the mass." By using compelling words, Mao Zedong deeply

55   Complied by The CPC Central Committee, Marxist-Leninist Works published by the Compilation & Translation Bureau, Research Office: *Journals Introduction of May Fourth Period, Volume I,* People's Publishing House, 1958, p. 388.

56   Ibid, ,p. 391.

57   Ibid, p. 394.

58   *Complete Works of Karl Marx and Frederick Engels,* Vol. 34, People's Publishing House, 1972, p. 360.

59   *Complete Works of Karl Marx and Frederick Engels,* Vol. 1, People's Publishing House, 1955, p. 75.

60   *Speech to the Kuomintang in Guangzhou,* recorded in: The *Complete Works of Sun Yat-sen,* Vol. 8, Zhonghua Book Company, 1986, p. 568.

diffused the semantic world of the masses. Thereafter, he released an article titled Grand Union of the Mass in the journal to call on the public to unite and stand up to fight against imperialism, feudalism and bureaucratic capitalism. The Weekly Review actually became a cultural standpoint during the May Fourth Movement in which a generation of progressive intellectuals, represented by Mao Zedong, publicized anti-imperialist and anti-feudal ideas, and eulogized the October Revolution and Marxist ideology. This aroused a political thought trend that publicizes new ideas and promoted ideological emancipation of the masses. These journals greatly boosted the publicity of Marxism during the May Fourth Movement by making significant influence on the revolutionary movement in Hunan, even the whole country.

In addition to the utilization of newspapers and journals, today, the Internet also provides a vast space for thinkers and political thought trends. Thinkers make use of the Internet's inestimable effect on the development of political thought trends. In today's China, especially since the mid-and-late 1990s, this effect has become increasingly significant. Ideological websites, online forums and individual blogs with different tendencies are becoming major platforms for the development of thought trends. Relying on advantages of vast publicity, quick update utility, openness and interaction, vividness, sufficient operation ability and other features that traditional media does not have, these websites, forums and blogs can swiftly introduce a political thought trend from anywhere in the world into China. They can also timely and accurately capture the level of psychological cognition of social members towards some political thought trends and accordingly make formal adjustment so as to seek for a more extensive and profound development. Objectively, their effect has surpassed that of traditional media. Moreover, by Internet, thinkers and social members achieve the most direct and extensive communication ever. Thinkers publish articles through the Internet or adopt other approaches provided by the Internet to express their thoughts and ideas; different thinkers and groups can debate on various ideological theories on the Internet. Ordinary social members are able to pay attention to ideas and contention of different thinkers and timely express their opinions and attitudes. Such opinions and attitudes will feed back to thinkers through the Internet, so as to achieve the most direct and effective exchange between the social members and thinkers. These opinions and attitudes can also make a great influence on the discussion. To sum up, the Internet technology had become an irreplaceable approach to advance the publicity and development of political thought trends with its application and popularization.

We can describe the communication and thought exchange among thinkers as a kind of assembly, which plays a considerable role in the development of a political thought trend. This is particularly evident in the development of political thought trends in contemporary China. Various colloquiums and thought exchange meetings have become the platform for political thought trends to express their "striking claims" for the purpose of attracting the concern of the public. In terms of the discussion on "the criterion of truth", various intellectual groups with different ideas have been organizing colloquiums, policy research meetings and public lectures or published special reports, so as to expound various policy claims about various issues upon social economy, politics and culture, intellectual groups with different ideas often held. This created a picture in which different thought trends surge against one another.

In recent years, the meetings held by some intellectuals, such as the Civil Constitutional Amendment Meeting and New West Mountain Meeting, aroused a great social influence, which can create more policy claims on various levels. These two forum meetings could make a great influence through the mere fact that participants were well-known experts and scholars, who paid attention on major theoretical and realistic issues. These forum meetings objectively promoted the development of liberal thought trend.

Besides, thinkers tend to rely on a number of striking social issues to boost the development of a thought trend. Striking social issues function as the catalyst for the formation and development of a thought trend. In the long term, a key thought trend normally continues by handling a theme pertinent to the development of history. However, in the short term, it is often reflected by various striking social issues. The so-called striking social issues refer to some major change in political and economic life of society. These striking social issues normally emerge and surface in social life spontaneously. They seem to occur accidentally but actually their emergence are historically inevitable, which are the results and reflection of complicated contradictions in various spheres of social production and their effects in people's material life. Political thought trends which are rooted in certain social economic and political system will inevitably combine with striking social issues. For example, corruption cases have frequently occurred in the recent years, which can be called as a striking social issue. Corruption issue attracts universal attention from social members as a result of a series of its new modern features, such as large amounts, permeation to high level, group corruption and internationalization. At the same time, this issue also aroused a high attention of the party and state leaders, who took multiple measures to overcome it seriously. Especially since the 18th CPC National

Congress, the General Secretary Xi Jinping has mentioned this issue several times. He said, "Anti-corruption is the precondition for the realization of the Chinese Dream". He also emphasized: "We must uphold the fighting of tigers and flies at the same time, resolutely investigating law-breaking cases of leading officials and also earnestly resolving the unhealthy tendencies and corruption problems which happen all around people".

Xi Jinping also put forward certain principles and detailed policy measures for fighting corruption, such as "enhancing restriction and supervision on exercising of power, so as to restrict power by the cage of regulations"

These ideas and measures by Xi Jinping has aroused intense response among the masses, and also caused the rapid development of the political thought trend which advocates to fight corruption and uphold integrity.

Striking social issues are complicated and numerous while involving many fields, such as economy, politics and culture. The initial rise of liberal thought in 1980s has made full use of striking social issues which attracted extensive resentment among the public, such as unfair social distribution, flooding of corruption, and rising inflation.

Liberal thought trend criticized existing economic, political and cultural systems in China and advertised and advocated capitalism. At present, these striking social issues are still used as major props by the thought trends. In 1990s, thinkers from various thought trends continued to pursue their purpose by utilizing many actual issues or striking social issues generated during the constant development of the Reform and Opening-up. Thinkers from different thought trends made entirely different interpretations about these striking issues. These striking issues became hotter through the publicity of thinkers. As the amplification of these striking issues, a thought trend will lift up its influence. By way of the involvement of thinkers, a social issue that has not obtained extensive social attention may become a striking issue, and a striking social issue may come like a bombshell and arouse a more extensive social response. Even a thinker himself may turn into a striking social issue as he actively participates in the discussion of a striking issue. For example, we can find that, since the 21st Century, some scholars energetically talked about some specific events or realistic views, forming a certain "fad" or "whirlwind", such as the fad of Zhang Wuchang and the whirlwind of Lang Xianping[61]. These so-called fads were generated

---

61   Zhang Wuchang, a famous representative figure of the western private property school, gave multiple conferences at the Graduate School of Party School of the Central Committee, China Center for Economic Research, Peking University, and several other institutions on invitation. There are also plenty of articles and comments which were published in some

through the combination of thinkers' own theoretical political views about the major issues in the Reform and Opening-up, which expanded the influence of these thinkers and also draw the attention of the public on these social issues.

In the past three decades since the Reform and Opening-up, the most concerned striking social issues were generally those new ideas, policies and measures adopted by our Party to deepen reform. In the past three decades, each step to deepen reform has become a major striking issue in social life. Especially, every National Congress of the CPC has become the hottest spot. It has always been a critical endeavor for all thought trends to expound new propositions, opinions and recommendations in order to effect the orientation of the political report to be submitted to the Party Congress. All thinkers leading various thought trends have tried their best to make such propositions, opinions and recommendations regarding the new expressions and opinions of our Party to achieve their interest appeals as far as possible.

When these new expressions and opinions have not been clearly explained in these reports, the interpretations of these thinkers would become more miscellaneous. For example, while some thinkers explained the term "Equity and Justice" contained in the Resolution of the Sixth Plenary Session of the 16th Central Committee of the CPC as a universal value; some put the emphasis on the concepts of mutual restriction and supervision on power which are expressed in the Report to the 17th CPC National Congress as the separation of powers in Western society; some explained

---

important media outlets, which propagate privatization vigorously, thus Zhang Wuchang Fever" was generated. In August 2004, Lang Xianping, Chair Professor of Department of Finance, the Chinese University of Hong Kong, Chief Professor of Cheung Kong Graduate School of Business, and Hong Kong economists, published several such articles as Orgiastic Green Cool on the Grand Banquet of "the State Economy out and the Private Economy in", Alert Private Together with the State-Owned Enterprises Legal Annexation of State-Owned Assets, etc. Wu Jinglian, Zhang Weiying, and other economists, as well as some jurists criticized Lang Xianping as holding an "anti-reform" position, Wu Jinglian wrote: "Lang Xianping, has used rumor and agitation, and "caused a mess of things". (Wu Jinglian Denounces Lang Xianping!, published in China Economy Net, March 9, 2005, quoted from China Business Times). There were ten scholars including Cheng Enfu, Ding Bing, and Zuo Dapei, published an academic statement indicating: "Lang Xianping 'walking out of capitalist society' which attacked western property rights theory and criticized the misunderstandings regarding property rights reform, and opposed those ideas which attributed all the problems which exist in enterprises, financial sector and industry, etc. to public property, and opposed those ideas which have proposed that the popular demand of shifting to private property rights could realize high efficiency was timely and correct. (10 professors including Cheng Enfu and Ding Bing Have Published An Academic Statement on the Issue of Lang Xianping, Shanghai, Social Science Weekly, September 16, 2004).

the expression "the reform cannot reverse" as that the reform cannot go ahead along the direction of socialism; and some even treated the ideological emancipation as abandoning the guidance of Marxism, and so on. Some anniversaries of important events also became striking issues used by some thought trends. For example, the 30th Anniversary of the Reform and Opening-up, in 2008 was used as a golden opportunity by many thought trends to express their opinions and propositions.

Undoubtedly, those political thoughts trends which have accompanied the whole process of the movement and paid close attention to each its step will certainly express their claims by using this opportunity. Since the early 2008, many opinions and comments on the 30-year Reform and Opening-up showed up, from which we can find the hints of some thought trends.

Practically, various interpretations of striking social issues cannot be deemed as the full reflection of thought trends. Anyone can express his opinion on a widely concerned striking issue, but we cannot say that he pushes ahead the trend. However, based on an observation on reality, those noticeable interpretations on striking social issues generally embody the core idea of a certain thought trend. This is much prominent in the social development of contemporary China.

Anyway, a striking issue can be defined as the gas station for the running of a thought trend, which can inject vigor for the development of such trend. In other words, a thought trend can consider something as its standpoints, including important theoretical striking issues, social issues and policy change, etc. By actively voicing on these issues, thinkers can explain and publicize theoretical views and value orientation of their thought trends to expand the influence.

To sum up, during the formation and development of political thought trends, thinkers will promote the rapid growth of these trends through group organizations (such as associations, societies and assemblies) and academic activities, by media outlets such as newspapers, journals and the Internet and in virtue of striking social issues and major anniversaries. Relying on the core initiative and creativity of thinkers, these group activities, media outlets and striking social issues are able to make a great cohesive effect for the formation and development of political thought trends.

III.3. Political thought trends operate in mutual agitation

It is necessary for us to analyze the ultimate basis for the formation and development of political thought trends, based on the fundamental effect of social existence upon social consciousness. But this general effect is not enough to understand the issue comprehensively. We should give due attention to such crucial effect, and also notice that, as a specific form of social consciousness, political thought trends are also relatively independent. This relative independence is not only demonstrates itself as a political thought trend re-acting upon social existence, but also demonstrates itself by the inherent law within the system of a thought trend. The interactions among various thought trends promote the operation and development of a thought trend, and this is also an important law. Therefore, the research on the interactions among political thought trends is deemed as a key approach to explore the reason for their formation and development. To some degree, a political thought trend gains its power and regularity through its correlation with other social thought trends. Engels wrote: "When we consider and reflect upon Nature at large, or the history of mankind, or our own intellectual activity, at first we see the picture of an endless entanglement of relations and reactions, permutations and combinations, in which nothing remains what, where and as it was, but everything moves, changes, comes into being and passes away."[62] Hence, we should comprehensively and dialectically consider the correlation among various thought trends.

III.3.1. Interaction among different thought trends

The interaction among various political thought trends is one of the essential conditions for the formation and development of a political thought trend. The research on the conditions for such formation and development urges us to explore those causalities which are closely related to a thought trend. The relationship between thought trends is one of such relations. Social existence correlates with social consciousness, and various social consciousnesses correlate with each other, too. This relation is reflected by political thought trends which operate at different levels of social mind and ideology. Political thought trends constitute an organic whole system. Specific thought trends has a universal correlation, as opposition, mutually supplementing or activating each other, which jointly constitute a colorful picture of thought trends. Inside the system of thought trends, a certain

---

62 *Collected Works of Karl Marx and Frederick Engels,* Vol. 9, People's Publishing House, 2009, p. 23.

thought trend normally associates with other thought trends for a specific period. And this thought trend will associate with another trend with the same or different nature, or with a relevant thought trend at domestic or aboard, ancient or modern.

In two books, *Crossroad and Tower: Research on the Liberalism Trend of Thought in Modern China* and *Awakening and Confusion: Research on the Nationalism Thought Trend in Modern China*,[63] it is respectively investigated the thought trends of liberalism and nationalism in modern China. As two monographs, these books described the pleasure, anger, sorrow, joy, understanding and feeling of various people in the two trends through the movement and change in the fields of politics, economics and culture in modern China, by which we can feel the powerful cohesive function of political thought trends. More importantly, the antagonistic relation between the two political thought trends can enlighten us in the research on the operation and development of political thought trends in conflict. In the article Brief Discussion on Social Thought Trends,[64] the author directly defines the operation of social thought trends as an antagonism among different social thought trends.

A political thought trend will advance in interactions with other thought trends, since multiple thought trends coexist in the society which share the same era. Various thought trends may emerge and generate in different fields, such as literary and artistic thought trends, political thought trends, educational thought trend, legal thought trend, philosophical trends and religious thought trends. Also, there may coexist various thought trends with different standpoints and tendencies in the same field, such as liberal thought trend and conservative thought trend in respect of economic development in age of modern West, scientific thought trend and humanistic thought trend in the field of philosophy, as well as the positivist thought trend and institutional theoretical thought trend in the field of politics. Even in the same period, there may be contrasting thought trends in various societies and countries as a result of different social development stages and levels. In general, with the rapid development of contemporary society, political thought trends also turn to be complicated and numerous. There forms a contention of different ideas in the ideological field of society. Among different political thought trends, there exist interaction, mutual collision,

---

63   Hu Weixi et al., *Crisscross Streets and Tower: The Research of Chinese Modern Liberalism Thought Trend*, Shanghai People Press, 1991; Tang Wenquan: *Awakening and Perplexity: The Research of Chinese Modern Nationalism Thought Trend*, Shanghai People Press, 1993.
64   Chen Lisi, On Social Thought Trends, *Journal of China Youth University for Political Sciences*, 1995(3).

exchange, impact and integration. Although facing the same issue, different political thought trends may propose different solutions. Through the impact and collision among various thought trends, the shortcoming of an opposite trend tends to be found, such as the shortage in its perspective, argument or demonstration. It is said that "truth will be gained through debate". So, the debate among different thought trends can help a thought trend not only to detect its own shortage and rectify and improve its theory and views, but also to absorb the virtues and merits of others by mutual debate so as to obtain "nutriment" for its own theory. This will assist a thought trend for positively enriching itself, and interacting and integrating with others. For example, during the introduction of Western learning into China at the second half of the 19th Century, political thought trends from the West collided with those political thought trends in China, which coalesced and exchanged into many other thought trends, such as the "usage of Western learning based on Chinese culture". This made a great effect on the modern and contemporary society in China. By such impact, collision, exchange and integration, political thought trends moved on. They constantly drew attentions from all sides so as to constantly enhance their own influence and vitality. When a political thought trend no longer interacts and collides with others, it will no longer attract concern from all walks of life and therefore will fall into a decline and lose its vitality. In other words, the key to the development of political thought trends can be found in constant contradictions and conflicts in the ideological field. Without these contradictions and conflicts, a thought trend will lose its vitality and energy to operate and advance.

Generally, according to the difference in social and historical conditions, the correlation among various political thought trends is embodied differently. In respect of its main content, such correlation can be divided into two forms: "opposition" and "cooperation".

It is quite obvious that the thought trends with completely contrary natures will fight against each other. Marxism grew and advanced during a conflict with various political thought trends. When it was born, Marxism was just one of many innumerable socialist schools or thought trends. In order to publicize this brand new world view into international labor movement and to forge a moral weapon for proletariat, Marx and Engels relentlessly fought against Proudhonism, "True Socialism trend" in Germany, Lassallism, Bakuninism and the opportunist thought trends held by Dühring and Bernstein. They wrote many significant treatises. Only through such a conflict and criticism practice, Marxist philosophy established by them could constantly enrich and develop, and could be publicized extensively and profoundly. Marxism advanced through its struggle and contest against various other thought trends. Besides, the revolutionary practice has finally proved that only proletariat class possesses the socialist nature. As indicated by Lenin, it had been demonstrated by history that, only when the theory of Marxism, which had expounded the role of proletariat in the history of the world as the creator of socialism, achieved a complete victory and was publicized extensively, all other doctrines supporting supra-class socialism and supra-class politics has proved as non-sense.[65]

As an advanced ideological theory, Marxism has been resisted and attacked by various non-Marxist or anti-Marxist thought trends since its introduction into China. Many figures like Hu Shi and Zhang Dongsun, once questioned and attacked Marxism successively. However, in such a violent ideological theory conflict, Marxists, in virtue of progressiveness and scientificness of Marxism, participated in the debate against Hu Shi et al. in the argument about "Question and Doctrine", as well as those debates against anarchism and democratic socialism. They defeated various thought trends successively, gained a firm foothold in China and achieved a grand development. At the same time, a new theory combined with Chinese revolutionary movement was also formed gradually based on Marxism. This had been indicated by Mao Zedong, "the May Fourth Movement advanced along with two trends. Some people inherited the spirit of science and democracy from the Movement, and transformed it based on Marxism. This was done by Chinese communists and some Marxists outside CPC. Some other people went along the way of bourgeoisie, which was a right-oriented advancement of formalism."[66]

Normally, the "opposition" and "conflict" between thought trends allow people to vividly feel the existence of these thought trends and the change of society. Those thought trends with the same class characteristics and on behalf of the same interest class or stratum often integrate together and grow into a unity. However, those thought trends on behalf of the interest of different social classes or stratum normally will collide with one another and generate amazing "sparks" which allow people to deeply feel their existence and the change of society. Therefore, in certain historical periods, people generally feel more the opposition in main thought trends in society.

Various thought trends with similar nature, especially those reflecting the objective reality and meeting the law of historical development, face the same reality. However, as a result of the difference in the influence of their thinking traditions, thinking modes, conception and category systems

---

65 *Collected Works of Lenin,* Vol. 2, People's Publishing House, 2009, p. 63.
66 *Selected Works of Mao Zedong,* Vol. 3, People's Publishing House, 1991, p. 832.

and center of interest, these thought trends propose different conclusions and solutions for discussed issues. They inform and learn from one another and enrich themselves by providing nutriment from others in debate. For example, during the Spring and Autumn period in China, "that mediocrity took high level position and all rites collapsed" is the theme of that times. With the emergence of rising landlord class, the slavery system comes to the threshold of collapse and the feudal system started to be established progressively. Under this background, to solve various issues, such as long-lasting war and destitute people in society, each school offered its own suggestion and solution to achieve social development and national prosperity. This created an era of contention of a hundred schools of thoughts in which over a hundred of schools represented by Confucianist, Mohist, Legalist and Taoist thoughts have emerged. In this ideological debate lasting a hundred years long, thought trends led by each school rose and fell while shining their brilliance in the historical stage. These thought trends have continued their debates. Meanwhile, different schools started to absorb each other and integrate with one another, forming a brilliant era in the ideological and cultural field.

Undoubtedly, in modern China, the liberal thought trend and the trend of "Chinese Confucianism" have contradicted the ideology of Marxism. But this opposition has caused a negative consequence that these two trends were pushed to stand in the same boat. There still exists huge divergence. Some representatives in the trend of "Chinese Confucianism" have advocated the ideas to establish Confucian doctrines as "national religion" and build "benevolent politics". They criticized the limitations of the political mode of Western democracy which was taken as criterion by the liberal thought trend. For example, some have argued that "the legitimacy of democratic politics lacks of historical reality, and it is a product of pure reason and conceptual fiction. The ideal of democratic politics stays outside or beyond history, not based on history". "The biggest shortcoming in democratic politics lies on the fact that it believes "the only significant thing is legitimacy of public opinion, which makes it grow into extreme secularization and vulgarization and pay too much attention to human desire and sophistication" "Another drawback of democratic politics is that its deficiency of morality. The excessive emphasis on the legitimacy of public opinion not only determines that there will be no ethics during the establishment of political authority and also that there is no ideal during its operation."[67]

67   Jiang Qing, Benevolent Politics is the Direction of Chinese Political Development Today–Reply to Questions about What is Benevolent Politics, China Elections and Governance Net (http://www.chinaelections.org/newsinfo.asp?newsid=42911.

When different thought trends with the same nature are on behalf of the interest of the same class or stratum, a cooperative relationship will be formed among them. This cooperative relationship is reflected by "complementation" in respect of theoretical demand. Every thought trend will have its own focus. For example, the new-liberalism trend and historical nihilism trend both oppose against Marxism in today's China. These two thought trends have their own points, and they complement and promote each other. The new-liberalism thought trend highlights the privatization in economic reform, while "the historical nihilist" thought trend emphasizes on the non-historical materialism in the ideology field. This unifies the non-dominant ideological elements in these two thought trends regarding the aspect of economics, politics and culture.

Thought trends with different natures have extremely contrary interests or demands. In this case, an extensive debate among these thought trends will be inevitable, in which one thought trend will disparage and suppress another. As one kind of ideology with a "spokesperson" nature, a thought trend will inevitably defend for the interests of the class, the stratum and the group represented by it. The political thought trends with different natures often seriously conflict with each other even in respect of their values, and such conflict is quite normal. For example, in the period of Enlightenment in modern Europe, the rational thought trend on behalf of the interest of rising bourgeoisie was utterly incompatible with the monarchic thought trend on behalf of the interest of feudal class. In order to gain the dominant position of right to speech, these two thought trends fought each other inevitably. With the continuous opposition against feudal monarchic thoughts, the rational thought trend on behalf of the interest of rising bourgeoisie enriched and improved its own theoretical system and proposition. Finally, as early as the 17th and 18th Centuries, a grand bourgeois cultural liberation movement rose in Europe, aiming to oppose feudalism and the power of clergy. Through constant conflict against feudal thought trend, this movement publicized the light of rationality across the Europe and enrooted the concepts of democracy, freedom and equality into people's heart, which means a great contribution to the development of European capitalism and the rise of bourgeoisie.

To sum up, the large-scale movement among thought trends and its resulting impact, collision, exchange, interaction, influence and integration between these trends is one key factor for the formation and development of political thought trends. The collision of thoughts can generate a spark of wisdom. Similarly, the collision between thought trends or inside a thought trend can push ahead the development of these thought trends. Through such collision, a thought trend can detect its drawbacks and accordingly make an internal readjustment. Besides, it can also appropriate various beneficial sparks of thoughts for reference so as to enrich and improve itself.

III.3.2. Dominant social thoughts and other political thought trends

In a certain period, the sphere of social ideology is normally sphere wherin a dominant social thought coexists with numerous other political thought trends. The dominant social thought, as the ideology representing the interest of the ruling class, takes the dominant position in the social ideology field. Some political thought trends come into being as contrasting and contesting the dominant ideology; while some as its allies and as internal reformers; and some even as its direct derivatives. In Chinese contemporary field of political thought trends, a similar scene can also be seen. Some political thought trends emerge as the opposite of the dominant social ideology, while some function as its beneficial complement, such as thought trends of patriotism and Reform and Opening-up, the existence and development of which not only maintains and consolidates the position of dominant social thought, but also functions as a beneficial complement of the dominant social thought, plays a positive role in society.

A dominant social thought may be progressive, such as when it represents the interest of the rising class that newly becomes the ruling class; it also may be outdated and reactionary, such as when it represents the interest of the falling class that has kept the ruling position for a long time. Therefore, the relationship between political thought trends and between a political thought trend and the dominant social thought will be very complicated in nature. In view of the development of a thought trend, there exist conflict and cooperation between the political thought trends and the ideology of the ruling class.

The "opposition" may be reflected by the negation of reactionary political thought trends against advanced dominant social thought, such as the negation by backward thought trends against the thoughts of the rising class, or the negation by advanced political thought trends on the outdated and reactionary dominant social thoughts. This is called as the conflict between new and old thought trends. For example, in modern Europe, both the democratic and liberal thought trends of the ascending bourgeoisie attacked the feudal autocratic thought trend and the thoughts of religion and theology, also in modern China, Marxist thought trend negated the feudal thought trend and the westernization thought trend stirred by the Chinese bourgeoisie.

It is possible that such conflicts are due to the political thought trend which negates the revolutionary nature of dominant social thought, or due to its elimination its own reformatory nature. When a political thought trend has a nature which is absolutely opposite to the dominant social thought, the conflict between them normally take the form of thorough revolution. A revolutionary thought will generally be used by a class as a theoretical weapon to topple another class. In the era of proletarian revolutions, the thought trend of Marxism functioned as such a revolutionary thought trend.

On the other hand, a conflict between certain political thought trends and the dominant social thought belongs to the conflict of different ideas in the same class; and as the fundamental target is the same, the conflict between them generally adopts the mode of a reform which will maintain the unity and the change of those outdated ideas and concepts inside the same class that do not meet the demands of the time. For example, in China during the 1980s and 1990s, the conflict between thought trends of reform and anti-reform and between the thought trends of planned economy and market economy have made their struggles in the field of ideas and thoughts, but both contesting sides have aimed to promote China's development, although the thought trends of anti-reform and anti-market economy were backward and outdated.

Dominant social thought always makes use of the state apparatus it is attached to and the publicity tool of it controls, dominant social thought performs a powerful publicity so as to unite and use some consistent political thought trends, and to suppress and attack some opposite thought trends. Meanwhile, a political thought trend also tries to enhance its outward expanding power, in order either to actively maintain the position of dominant social thought or to wait for an opportunity to replace the dominant thought.

There will be two results when a dominant social thought opposes or cooperates with a political thought trend. One result is that the dominant thought loses its dominant position. Some political thought trend may become a progressive thought trend as it scientifically reflects the nature, law and solution of certain issues of the era, represents the interests and demands of the rising class, and complies with the development direction of society. Finally, such thought trend will defeat all other political thought trends and become the main thought trend, by defeat in and replacing the dominant social thought. This can be applied to the triumph of Marxism in China. Other political thought trends have faded, disintegrated or stagnated. Of course, for a progressive thought, the path to victory is a tortuous path, and multiple setbacks may well occur. The other result is the enhancing and consolidation of the dominant social ideology. The dominant social thought may be still vital. It appropriates ideas and propositions from those political thought trends with consistent fundamental nature, and absorbs lessons in respect of pros and cons from the conflict against political thought trends with contrary nature. By this, such dominant social thought appropriates fresh content and gains more strong vitality while enhancing its dominant position. In the past 30-year of Reform and Opening-up, we have formed a theoretical system of socialism with Chinese characteristics. This scientific system was formed during the collision process of Marxism and many political thought trends.

In case of a specific historical period when some ideological theory is used as the dominant ideology, we can consider those political thought trends which have different ideologies with the dominant ideology in respect of orientation and demand as non-dominant ideologies. In those political thought trends of modern China, these political thought trends which are contrary to the dominant ideology of Marxism can undoubtedly be called as non-dominant ideologies. In the context of modern China, the relationship between the dominant social thought and the political thought trends is manifested both as the relationship between the dominant ideology and those political thought trends as its derivative, also as the relationship between the dominant ideology and other non-dominant ideologies. Considering the relationship between political thought trends and the dominant ideology, and by analyzing the relation between the dominant ideology and the non-dominant ideologies can enable us to further clear how to treat various thought trends in Party's ideological work.

CHAPTER FOUR

Publicity Aspect of Political Thought Trends

Political thought trends cannot occur or develop without assuming publicity activity. If there is no publicity, there would be no political thought trends. Only the publicized thought trends can be called as political thought trends, which will have a social influence and play a role in a certain historical epoch. Specifically, the research on the publicity aspect of political thought trends aim to investigate how they publicize and continue to publicize, so as to understand their formation process. In contemporary society, the publicity of political thought trends becomes more rapid and extensive, and the mode for publicity activity becomes more complex. The research on the relatively habitual mechanism and regularity regarding the publicity aspect of political thought trends will help us to further grasp the process of their formation and development. This is of great significance for our Party to improve its governance ability in the ideological field and do good work in this sphere. The mode, characteristics and the process of such publicity work are the key. With the development of publicity means, the publicity aspect of political thought trends is becoming more complex, while in general, there is a certain law within the process and tendency of such publicity.

Generally, the publicity of political thought trends is completed by a circle consisting of the communicator, publicity content, publicity media and the audience. In his book titled Communication Tutorial, Guo Qingguang defines the communicator as an information source which is the starting point of publicity activities and the subject which initiatively publicizes the content to public. Communicator, includes individuals, groups or organizations. The publicity content is also named as information, which can be expressed as the complete meaning by a set of meaningful symbols. It can achieve the interaction between the communicator and the audience. The publicity media which can also be called as the channel, the outfit and the means of publicity, is the transporter of information, which links various factors during the process of publicity. It includes mass publicity system (such as radio, TV and newspaper), the Internet system, and the telephone system. The audience which can also be called as the destination, is the receiver of information and the object of the activities of the communicator, which can react on the communicator through feedbacks. The audience and the communicator are not fixed, and they are interchangeable within a normal publicity process.[1] The description above has explained the publicity process of the information, which can also be applied to political thought trends.

IV.1. Publicity modes and ways of political thought trends

Political thought trends are the active morphology of social consciousness, which means that political thought trends are in a continuous flux. Publicity is the motion (motility) mode of motion of political thought trends, thus the political thought trends latter can never be separated from the former. Without a certain scale of the publicity of social psychology and ideological theories, no thought trends will exist; the publicity scale of thought trends determines the scale of their development; the breakdown of the publicity of a thought trend always leads to the silence or extinction of it. The overall course of activities of political thought trends takes publicity as the core. The basic modes of publicizing political thought trends are interpersonal communication, mass communication and network publicity, etc. The first two are traditional modes, while with the development of scientific technologies, the third, which embodies both the former two, became an important and brand-new form of publicity. There are such research achievements as *Thought Trends in Contemporary World*[2] and *Brief Discussion of Social Thought Trends*[3] which mainly discuss the publicity modes of political thought trends.

In general, the publicizing modes put forward in these research achievements have certain universality, but also some deficiencies. The latter is generally reflected in that they fully regard the publicity of political thought trends as a linear mode of simply enabling the publicizing of the information from sender to receiver, like a line segment from the origin to the end.

---

1   Guo Qingguang, *Communication Courses*, China Renmin University Press, 2011, p. 49.

2   Compilation group of the book, *Contemporary Trend of World Thoughts*, Party School of the Central Committee of C.P.C. Press, 2000, p. 24-25.

3   Chen Lisi, On Social Thought Trends, *Journal of China Youth University for Political Sciences,* 1995(3).

Thus, by having only one-way transmission of information, they do not support information loop and feedback. Instead, they regard the course of publicity as static without environment interaction and an internal activity, which ignored the objective constraints affecting the influence of publicity in the publicizing process, and the information flow as a bilateral interaction process. The neglect of the bidirectional factor in which a receiver can become a communicator is the biggest defect of linear mode of publicity. In fact, with the increasingly deepening of social and living practice as well as the booming of Internet and mobile terminals, linear publicity has shifted or will shift to the network mode of transmission. In this scattered network transmission structure, information can be generated and publicized from any knot and then flow back to the network. The linear publicity is just an organic component of the network transmission which is a structure made up of thousands of linear publicities.

IV.1.1. Mode of inter-personal communication

The mode of inter-personal communication refers to the course of information exchange during which people may convey or exchange their feelings, desires, comments and knowledge directly or via such media as letters, telephone, e-mail and network chat tools. Interpersonal communication is the most common, most abundant and the oldest phenomenon of publicity in social life. At the beginning of political thought trends, the mode of publicity is always seen as the most important aspect. At this stage, each individual plays many roles in the publicity, which may both as communicator and medium as well as the receiver. The most important feature of interpersonal communication is that the medium is often the people themselves. The communicator can use not only language but facial expressions, eyes, actions and other manners to transmit information.

This is a highly bi-directional mode of publicity with frequent interactions, by which the receivers can act sometimes as the medium while sometimes playing the role of communicator in turn. The communicator and the audiences constantly exchange their roles and correspondingly modify and improve the content and methods of publicity based on the other's feedback, so as to achieve a high quality of information publicity.

When a thought trend initially comes into being, it tends to be communicated firstly among a small circle of people. The mode of publicity then is basically due to the interpersonal communication. When a thought trend is newly generated, it tends to experience an incubation phase when it becomes impossible to carry out a broad publicity, so there are relatively outstanding features of the interpersonal communication at the phase. Transmitters communicate in their own viewpoints, opinions and propositions towards the information receivers through communications of ideas and feelings among people, and transform them into a receiver of the information or a member of the subject of the thought trend by persuasion and education. When we take the bourgeois reformist thought trend in Modern China as an example, we can see that during the publicity, the opinion leaders such as Kang Youwei and Liang Qichao separately established the Wanmu Caotang and Shiwu Academy in Guangzhou and Hunan where they collected students to give lectures so as to publicize the thought of reform and cultivate talents for the Hundred Days Reform. With the academic teaching mode of Wanmu Caotang and Shiwu Academy, Kang Youwei, Liang Qichao and other opinion leaders conducted face-to-face activities for the publicity of new thoughts and new theories, by which they could deeply impress the students, and cultivate a lot of supporters and advocators for the Hundred Days Reform, and lay a foundation for the publicity of the bourgeois reform thought trend in Modern China. Therefore the earliest core members of thought trends are formed through interpersonal communication, which make thought trends become a type of group consciousness, which maintains the group order and standardizes the group members' behavior. These members, who had intensive and common mental disposition, as the medium continued to communicate on the core concept of a certain thought trend they grasped.

The early publicity of Marxism in China has precisely showed the typical mode of interpersonal communication. Some advanced Chinese intellectuals such as Li Dazhao and Chen Duxiu conducted a interpersonal communication in such ways as giving lectures and organizing meetings, through which they advocated Marxism in a small circle and constantly enlarged the scope of the receivers. As the exchange and communication deepened, some people with supreme ideals, especially a great number of strong-willed young people, internalized Marxism thought as their system of values and became its receivers, and even actively employed Marxism to guide their thoughts and behaviors, which enabled them to be pioneers in Marxist publication and practice. Marxism seminars, communist groups and others from everywhere before and after the May Fourth Movement were the groups with strong senses of identity and belonging established via the interpersonal communication during the emergence of Marxist thought, which played a leading role in further and broadened publicity in China. Also, Mao Zedong and other early revolutionary leaders during the publicity and development process of Marxism in China had keenly realized that it was difficult for the mass communication mode such as newspaper and broadcast to play a positive role on Marxist thought since the great masses of peasants in impoverished and backward regions were at a lower educational level. The only way to convince most of the peasants to accept Marxism was to build it on the living practices of the peasants and to use a simple language and vivid explanation to make the mass peasants understand and accept Marxism. As a result, Mao Zedong successively organized the Peasant Movement Training Institute in Guangzhou and Wuhan, etc. from 1924 to 1927 and personally served as the director to cultivate peasant backbones. In these institutes, Mao Zedong publicized Marxism to the peasant activists across rural areas by his own words and deeds, and cultivated lots of Marxism defenders and communicators. It was in this mode of direct interpersonal communication that Mao Zedong and others publicized Marxism in the vast rural areas in China.

As the scientific technologies developed and the social practice deepened, the mass communication medium has developed rapidly. However, the direct interpersonal communication still plays an important role during the formation and development of thought trends. People tend to think that the interpersonal communication as it exists in a period when the communication media was underdeveloped, which is a misunderstanding. During the emergence of any thought trend, there are a few people having exchange of ideas and "collision" before the consensus. Any political thought trend in any time had experienced the course of interpersonal communication.

In addition, the relationship between interpersonal communication and mass communication is not only about the sequence of "positions", in other words, the former not only works earlier than the latter and at the beginning of a thought trend but always throughout the whole publicizing system of the political thought trend. They, both as the mode of thought trend movement, do not conflict with each other. Without interpersonal communication and the discussion and communication in small scales of people, the mass communication would not "work", and the influence would decrease sharply. The interpersonal communication is well organized, as people have the social property of social communication demand and as they live in groups. Therefore, everyone lives in a specific interpersonal communication network. Within a group, only the minority of people plays the role of important information source, namely the "opinion leader", and provides information or suggestions to influence the others. A political thought trend is transmitted to the minority via mass communication medium, who in turn play an inter-link role of information medium and transmit it to other social members via the interpersonal communication during its publicity process. For example, there are some colleges, research institutes and social organizations which regularly conduct various cultural activities, thought exchange meetings, forums and reading parties for thought communication, during which many communicators will introduce the ideas and viewpoints they just acquired to the others. It is by such face-to-face interpersonal communication that many propositions of new political thought trends attract some people to discuss about them, thus the thought trends are publicize and develop. Some social members may not pay attention to political thought trends at first; however, they know and learn the information through their interpersonal communication, especially through the face-to-face communication of the opinion leaders. Moreover, the quality of communication is much higher than the influence of mass communication.

In general, the interpersonal communication is an important publicity mode of political thought trends. No matter how the mass media and network information technology develop, the role of interpersonal communication is always unique in the course of the publicity of political thought trends. Just as Marx pointed out that "people are socialized ones", nobody can independently exist by isolation from the society. In the social life of human, communication among them is indispensable, as the emergence of thoughts and the publicity of thought trends are originated from it. Therefore, people need communication no matter how the times change and how science and technology develops. Moreover, as long as such a communication exists, the ideology and culture will be intercommunicated. That is why the political thought trends of any times must go through the interpersonal communication, without which it is difficult to take shape and grow.

IV.1.2. Mode of mass communication

The concept of mass communication refers to the course of a person or a special social group conveying information, ideology and value orientation to a larger scale of people by such more influential transmission media outlets as newspaper, magazines, books, broadcast, TV, film and Internet. With the development of scientific technology and under the promotion of it, transmission media have been increasingly developed and popularized and became an important part of the living environment for each modern people. As a result, the influence of mass communication is getting more important for the formation and development of political thought trends. Schramm, an American scholar, once said, "When we talk about the interaction of the society and mass communication, we frequently use the word "revolution". Once media appears, they would participate in all significant social reforms—intelligence revolution, political revolution, industrial revolution and those revolutions of hobbies and interests, desires and ambitions as well as moral ideas."[4] In Europe, the emergence and development of the Enlightenment in the 18th Century depended on the popularized transmission channels of books and newspapers. In China, the publication of the journals such as New Youth and Fashion in May Fourth Period brought a revolutionary change to the publicity of the thought trends, as new thought trends have rapidly developed since then. In Modern China, various thought trends and theories had contested to come to the fore in order to find a path to save the country and the people, and the mass media has played a unique role in it. For example, the Commercial Official Newspaper, Study Affairs Official Newspaper and Official Press Report, etc. publicizing the imperial constitution in modern times; the Review of the Times, The Chinese Progress and New Citizens Repository, etc. during the bourgeois reform thought trends; The Chinese Times, Politics and Art Bulletin, Zhejiang Fever, Su Newspaper and New World, etc. during the bourgeois revolution thought trends; the Tian Yi Bao, Tian Yi (semi-monthly), New Age, Heng Bao, etc. for the thoughts of anarchism; the New Youth, The Communist Party (monthly), and Weekly Review publicizing the Marxism thoughts, and so on. Nowadays, the main political thoughts have their own forward positions among the mass media, for example, the Yan-Huang Historical Review is the main carrier of the publicity of democratic socialism thought trend, the journal Reminding of the Past is the internal magazine for the thought exchange among the so-called "the Old Right", and the Flag Digest and Mao Zedong Flag are the domain for "the Left" publishing their remarks. Since Chinese government gives great right of freedom to the press and publication, there is a large number of books and articles reflecting different political thought trends sprung up, for instance, there is certain reaction from the society caused by the publication of The Futures of the Democratic Socialism and China from Xie Tao, which led to an active discussion in the world of thought and theory especially.

Besides, the mass communication played a crucial role in the three debates during the early publication of Marxism in China. The first debate was the dispute of "problem and doctrine" between Li Dazhao and Hu Shi by the Weekly Review. In response to the Study More Problems and Talk Less Doctrines! published by Hu Shi in Weekly Review, Li Dazhao successively published such articles as Problems and Doctrines, Re-discussion on Problems and Doctrines to refute Hu Shi's opinion objecting to the Marxism. Through the debate, the scientific relation between doctrines and problems was illuminated, by which the influence of Marxism was

---

4   Schramm Potter, *Introduction of Communication,* Xinhua Publishing House, 1984, p. 19.

enlarged. The second debate was about the socialism. The reformists represented by Liang Qichao and Zhang Dongsun published Present and Future, Social Transformation and Political Forces, and Guild Socialism successively by Current Affairs, Transformation, and The Eastern Miscellany to advocate the social reform though trend and which attacked Marxism. In this regard, the earlier Chinese Marxists represented by Li Dazhao, Li Da and Qu Qiubai continuously published such articles as Socialist Industries, From Democracy to Socialism and Re-discussion of the Communism and Guild Socialism in New Youth to refute the criticism on Marxism. This collision of thoughts defined the boundary between the scientific socialism and various non-scientific socialisms. The third debate was the dispute about Marxism and anarchism. Due to the combination of multiple historical factors after the Revolution of 1911, the anarchism was widely publicized in China. The books and periodicals publicizing the anarchism in the May Fourth Period added up to over 70 kinds. The anarchists represented by Huang Lingshuang and Qu Shengbai successively publicized their ideas by publishing articles on the magazines of Leisure and People' Voice. Huang Lingshuang published Critique on Marxism in New Youth in May 1919. In order to contradict the anarchism, Chen Duxiu and Li Da et al., published On the Politics, Inferior Anarchism and Why We Advocate the Communism by the magazines of the New Youth, The Communist Party (monthly). This debate on Marxism and Anarchism ended up with the victory of Marxism, through which lots of advanced young people identified the distinction and boundary between the two trends and embraced Marxism. Also, many original believers of Chinese anarchism had shifted to Marxism.

In the modern society with more and more means of communication, plenty of information is transmitted via such media as TV, film, newspapers and magazines, forums, blogs and micro blogs. Main political thought trends have their own special channels of communication, and there are clues about their own core ideas hidden behind the remarks published through them on some social events, which form an atmosphere of public opinions affecting the social psychological disposition. Advanced political thought trends should pay more attention to the work of publicity, and should not take for granted that its potential advantage on the publicity will have a natural expression due to its own scientific property. It should be seen that, just as even a very aromatic wine cannot be discovered if it is sealed tightly, if publicity and communication is ignored, such advantage is hardly to come true. Even if there are equivalent transmission forces for various thought trends, none of which is overwhelmingly standing out temporarily, the positive guidance function of advanced political thought trends may also be gradually decreased due to the large scale of frequent publicity of other political thought trends. As Lenin once said after the victory of the revolution: "The current task is just to continue to care about how to use the words which can be easily understandable by the mass in the publicity of communism in each country."[5]

The mass communication of political thought trends may be interrupted under a certain given political environment, as it is an institutionalized mode of publicity. As British scholars J. Cona et al. pointed out, "The mass communication is generated from industrial production activities of large-scale organizations whose policy and professional norm exist in the social structures of politics, economy and laws"[6]; that is, the medium of mass communication is the information industry with large-scale manufacturing and transmission capacity, thus the transmission process will inevitably produce great influence and the transmission content is directly related to the construction of social value system and code of conduct. Therefore every government employs the mass communication into the social management system to maintain the stability of social system."[7] Marx and Engels pointed out in The German Ideology that "the ideas of the ruling class are in every epoch the ruling ideas." Any government of any country in the globe attempts to monopolize and controls the information in different degrees no matter what political tendency it represents and which class or group it speaks for. By exerting various forces on the mass media to control the public's opinions on the worldly concerns especially the public affairs, the feelings and values of the people can be closed up to the directions advocated by the governments. Behind various political thought trends, they represent the interests of certain classes and stratums and imply the political aspiration and the interests and demands of those classes or stratums. However, the thought trends with political claim and interest desire often have contradictions and complaints with the mainstream ideology, thus the ruling class will have to control the social ideas and theories in order to consolidate and maintain its rules. As a result, when a thought trend which is opponent to the social mainstream value system emerges, the government chooses to control it, by limiting and minimizing it and even forbidding it from transmitting ideas by mass communication modes. It is by shielding the opponent political thought trends to decrease the factors causing unstable social mind, to maintain the ruling order of the ruling class and ensure

---

5   *Selected Works of Lenin,* Vol. 4, People's Publishing House,(1995, p. 7.
6   Liu Jianming, editor in chief: A Big Dictionary of Publicity and Public Opinion, *Economic Daily Press*, 1993, p. 290.
7   Guo Qingguang, *Communication Courses*, China Renmin University Press, 2nd edition, 2011, p. 100.

the social norms being observed. Thus the mass communication process of the political thoughts opposed to the mainstream ideology is more vulnerable to be interrupted.

Compared to the mode of interpersonal communication, it is easier for the mass communication to be affected by the social and political environments, which is mainly reflected as being easily interrupted by the outside "compelling forces", while the interpersonal communication tends more to a non-institutionalized publicity, as it appears spontaneously, independently and even silently in general with stronger resistance against disturbance. It will continue even under the circumstance in which the mode of mass communication is terminated. For example, Chiang Kai-shek and Wang Jingwei successively launched the "4/12" Coup and "7/15" Coup to steal the fruits of revolution and willfully slaughtered the communists in 1927, launching a nationwide counter-revolutionary terror. Under such conditions, the newspapers, magazines, publishing houses and broadcasts publicizing Marxism thought were closed down one after another by the government authorities. The mode of mass communication of Marxism thought trend was interrupted. However, Chinese Marxists did not give up the publicity work of Marxism. Instead they "wiped the bloodstain on their body, buried the companions' dead body and moved on". The Chinese Marxists represented by the communists started to move into workshops and wharves in the cities to work with the hardworking labor and established good relations with them. During this course, they talked about how the capitalists oppress the laborers and exploit the surplus value within the mode of interpersonal communication to publicize the Marxism thought. In villages, they, by suppressing the local tyrants and by dividing the lands of the landlords among small and middle peasants, appealed the masses that it is only by insisting on the socialist road can the workers and peasants become the master of the country and get rid of the oppression of the landlord class. After the mass communication of Marxism was interrupted, it is in the mode of interpersonal communication that Marxism thought trends could develop in China and formed the situation as a Chinese probe said: "A single spark starting a prairie fire".

IV.1.3. Mode of network communication

The emergence of the Internet promoted people's awareness about the publicity, enabled the interpersonal communication to be combined with the mass communication, thus the publicity of thought trends is broadened and has become rapid. Compared to the newspapers, magazines, broadcast, TV, etc., the Internet broke the limits of time and space of traditional media to a large extent, broke through the time lag and one-way mode of mass communication, and crossed the scope of traditional interpersonal communication developed based on genetic connections, industrious connections and geographical relations, and lots of cross-cultural and cross-stratum communication phenomena appeared. The Internet gave birth to many new media for publicity, such as the websites, blogs, podcast, short message and MMS, etc. with the advantages of high opening degree, huge information content, individuation, global communication, strong interaction and convenient retrieval.

The popularity of network facilitates the information exchange among people, changes the relationship between the communicator and the audience during communication. In addition, it granted the communicators and receivers more autonomy by taking advantage of its features of anonymity and weak obligation constraints. Its rich information and convenience make it an important channel for the communication of people with the outside world. By the end of June 2012, the number of Chinese netizens (network-citizens) reached 0.538 billion with an Internet popularity rate of 39.9%, and the growth rate tends to be stable; among which the most attractive one is that the mobile netizens reached 0.388 billion[8]. The spreading mode has broken the rules interpreted in the communication studies to some degree. In the traditional mass communication and interpersonal communication, the spreading "starting points" often begin with the ideologists with a definite boundary and then spread to the "audience", and the information flow from the ideologists to the audience is obvious. While the network communication, also known as "civilian communication", which greatly broke the pattern, is a low cost but popular mode of publicity, it also enables a "barrier-free communication" with the information transmission and receiving completed in a moment. In comparison with the one-to-one or one-to-many information transmission of interpersonal communication and the "push" of content of mass communication, the audience in the network communication can provide enormous freedom of choice while receiving the information as they can actively clicks on contents they get interested in. Meanwhile, the Internet provided technical conditions for individuals as communication subject to directly participate in the mass communication, as anyone can make open communication to the public via the special network news media, online newspaper and BBS, etc.; during network communication, people can conduct interpersonal communication with specific objects via the online chat tools, social network sites and e-mail accounts, etc. Therefore, it also has the same features of information feedback and interaction as that of interpersonal communication.

---

8   China Industry Research Netwok (http://www.chinairn.com/news/20120719/657146.html).

The emergence of the personal blogs is important for the publicity of political thought trends. Blog, the abbreviation of "Weblog", is a personal homepage with a title, message and historical records, a network information carrier without technical threshold but easily operated. It can be regarded as a personal web diary on which one can record and report and publish them to the public by dates. Individuals can freely publish comments on blog, which is open and shared with others, as all netizens can read the articles via the blog site. The content of a blog may be a person's individual ideas or a collective work of a group of people based on a certain specific theme or common interests.

The blogs provide a rapid channel for the publicity of political thought trends. Firstly, the blog registration, offering a low-threshold permit, includes extensive user groups. As a result, the users' educational level and information screening capacity are not even and most of the netizens use blog lack the ability to understand social events as they are relatively young and have little social experience, which provide lots of potential acceptable objects for the publicity of political thought trends. Secondly, the content of blog neither requires original creation nor have specific standard, thus the users can forward or link the message to this blog space. Only by correspondingly clicking can the original receiver (acceptor) get shifted to a communicator in the next communication. Finally, blog is convenient for the opinion leader playing the role of them. They have wide coverage in personal social network in reality, which can also play roles in the network. On account of the convenience of communication, the ideas of opinion leaders can be more easily transmitted to the next level. Due to the openness of blog, people can have interactions with celebrities to see their thoughts and living. Following the strengthened celebrity charm of social elites, the blog clicking amounts of some celebrities hit a hundred thousand in a day. If such celebrities act on the representative of political thought trends, the publicizing influence of thought trends will be self-evident, since they have high attention and large blog-clicking amount. As there is a large difference among the netizens in their knowledge level, if they are not able enough to identify ideas in ideology field, they may follow blindly the celebrities' theories due to their admiration. The spread scope will geometrically increase by forwarding the content, which may cause a large scale of people to unconsciously follow-ups on the Internet. Back to reality, it may have a high quality spread through social network, enabling the influence of political thought trends to get more enlarged. Today, political thought trends also did not ignore the blog, a convenient channel of publicity, for example, the left-wing alliance registered an official blog on Sina to publicize the implementation of equitable distribution and other standpoints of the egalitarian socialism.

In 2009, Sina started to operate the "Sinamicroblog", by which it opened the age of microblog. Blog is a platform for information sharing, communication and acquisition based on users' relations. Users can establish individual communities via the client-ends such as WEB and WAP, post information limited to 140 characters (7 Chinese characters), and realize instant sharing[9]. Such main blog operators as the "Sinamicroblog", "Tecentmicroblog", "Sohumicroblog" and "NetEaseMBlog" have developed lots of users within a short time. The main differences between the microblog and blog include: first, they employ different technological means. The functions of attention and forwarding of a microblog entitle the users to have more rights with easier information forwarding and recommendation. Through these two functions, we can see that they attract millions of fans and forwarded articles. The more the quantity of fans is, the more amounts of forwarded articles it would have. If the fans of the user forwarded it, those are also attracted when they read it, they would continue to forward it further. The information is publicized to the maximum extent during such a course of communication with geometrical growth. We can say that "the Matthew Effect" is generated from the course of publicizing microblog information. Opinion leaders who have numerous fans can affect the opinions and attitudes of others in the society.

Secondly, compared to other spreading modes, the microblog can spread the information with such new features as miniaturization, randomization, fragmentation, rapid spreading and high delivery. Some scholars have argued that as the microblog content is short with bright viewpoints, the audience can quickly grasp the meaning conveyed.[10] It is especially for the development of mobile phones, which realized seamless spread of microblog and enabled users to look over microblogs whenever and wherever possible, the features of which make the representatives of different political thought trends be capable of competitively expressing their viewpoints on the microblog platform, so as to attract more fans and attentions by more frequently publishing comments, expressing emotions. Thus they broadened the influence of thought trends.

Finally, the short and simple information spread via microblogs is not only easily shared, but also includes personal emotions. It can express the opinions and reveal the personality[11]. The victory and mystery of social elites are fully attractive to ordinary people. For the audiences today, with

---

9   Baidu Encyclopedia (http://baike.baidu.com/view/1567099.htm).
10   Song Hao, An Analysis of the Characteristics of "Opinion Leaders" in the Micro-Blog Era, *Emerging Media*, 2010(11).
11   Sun Weihua, Zhang Yongqing, *Analysis of Micro Blog Communication Form*, *Media Observation*, 2008(10).

the current application of microblog platform, they can track the microblogs of such elites, watch their everyday dynamics and deepen the understanding of their living, thus a psychological cordial feeling and sense of close distance are generated together with a huge contrast to the arrogant and unreachable image of social celebrities. Therefore, the celebrity microblogs can be favorable if used properly, and the audiences may be liable to be affected by their opinions and concepts imperceptibly out of trust and worship for a very long time. As a result, political thought trends which are spread by social elites will deliver a favorable effect. In other words, celebrities can become a useful channel in publicity.

The network communication features strong vitality and interactivity. It is a multimedia publicity combining multiple vivid factors such as characters, images and sound. This multimedia publicity combination is conducive to ideology communication, as it can not only seize the web users' attraction but also express the profound principle in plain terms. In traditional mass communication, interaction is rather difficult. The interaction between communicator and audience is limited no matter in terms of the newspaper, broadcast or TV. Although traditional media also pays attention to the information feedback of the audiences (for instance, there are the special discussion column and readers' letter on newspaper, the listeners' hot line program on the broadcast, and the recreation and talk shows by specifically inviting the audiences to attend on TV), the indirectness and lagging are reflected from the information feedback in traditional media because of the technical reasons and spreading mode limits. What's more, the audiences can only select in a fixed scope for the interaction organized by the media unilaterally, which is a passive participation in the feedback. Therefore, a truly independent interaction between the communicator and the receiver is still difficult to come true, while the network has realized the real-time and ongoing interaction where the audience can directly and rapidly feed the information back and instantly publish opinions. For example, the People's Forum site often holds the exclusive interview and the discussion on special issues. During the interaction, the netizens can both watch the current scenes via the computer network and read the text broadcast via the mobile phone and other mobile devices. In addition, the netizens can also make feedback of their ideas and viewpoints timely via the online message, making the figure being exclusively interviewed understand and grasp the doubts of the masses in time to respond and debate them. Such network communication mode not only changes the simple role of the thought trend receiver as "audience" but also the simple "giver" role of the communicator, making it possible for the netizens at every corner of the world to ask questions to the "giver" and express their opinions. Thus, the network communication has both the vitality and interactivity.

The network provided full space for social psychological expression and a more sufficient reflection of the social mind, which enabled communicators of political thought trends to acquire the mass' social psychological dynamics more easily via the Internet and to publicize and guide the social psychological disposition based on their psychological changes. Traditional media's expression on the social psychology is obscure while the Internet has a direct and sufficient influence on the netizen's social and political attitudes, emotions, and recognition and behavior dispositions. Some websites often obtain netizens' true feelings by means of direct netizen survey. For example, the People's Daily Online has made a network survey titled "The Most Concerned xx Problems" and showed the survey results through the website during the period of convening the National People's Congress and the Chinese Political Consultative Conference in 2008.

In the new stage of Reform and Opening-up, the development of Internet in China is rapid[12]. The age of network not only created a brand-new and vast space for human but also provided a new platform for the spreading and development of political thought trends. The features of globalization, openness and equality of the network enabled political thought trends to find their base in the network environment. Today, the debate and publicity of social thought trends in the network space are extremely fierce. The

---

12   Number of China's Internet users continue to show a rapid development trend. The Statistical Report on the 31th China Internet Development Status published by China Internet Network Information Center (CNNIC) in 2013 is as follows: up to December 31, 2012, the amount of Internet users of our country has risen up to 564 mio. remaining the first ranking in the world, and Internet popularity rate has reached to 42.1%, with an increase of 50,900,000 people in a year. This explosive increase of internet user amount provides foundation for publicity, derivation and spread of various thought trends. Internet becomes a new platform for citizens expressing their will, taking part in social economic, political and cultural life. Central leadership also pays great attention to Internet, according to Xinhua. In 2003, when inspecting Guangdong during "SARS" period, General Secretary Hu Jintao said to a doctor working on the first line of "SARS" prevention and treatment: Your opinion is very good, and I have seen it on the Internet. When inspecting anti-"SARS" work in Peking University, Premier Wen Jiabao said: I saw your students expressed determined fight against "SARS" together with the people of the whole nation in BBS, which is impressive. General Secretary and Premier also surfing in the Internet" became a hot topic among Internet users. (Sohu Net http://news.soh/.com/20060411/n242745452.shtml) Our Party and government pay great attention to the development of Internet use and the regulation of the Internet content. The report of 16th National Congress of CPC points out: "the Internet should become an important battle field propagating advanced culture", the report of the 17th National Congress of CPC emphasized enhancing "the construction and leading of the Internet culture, and building a good Internet environment".

number of political thought trend websites, forums and blogs of various kinds is increasingly growing while there appears the related figures, events and activities constantly. Various political thought trends, especially those at the edge of realistic social space, have started to rapidly seize the network bases, attempted to have a voice and generate potential or obvious influences on the space in order to extend their own development space and enlarge their audience group. Nowadays, more and more political thought trends are publicized via the network. In modern China, many thought trends are operated on the network, and almost all of them have their own bases respectively on the Internet. For instance, the thought trends advocating the full privatization of the economy; the conservative thought trends marked with "farewell to revolution"; the democratic socialist thought trends advocating the reform and rejecting revolutions; the populist thought trends extremely emphasizing the values and ideas of civilian masses and assumes the plebian discourse and popularity as their ultimate source and criterion in its all political activities and in order to maintain the legitimacy of the political system; the anarchist thought trends which think it is necessary to abolish all kinds of authority bodies including the state, church, leadership or economic elites. In addition, there are varying thought trends such as the cultural imperialism thoughts, egoist thought trends, money worship thought trends and national secessionist thought trends taking advantage of the media network to spread their comments and enlarge their influence. Along with the web portals and traditional official websites with large popularity rate in mainland China, the professional ideological websites are already booming[13]. For example, I searched for the keyword "neoliberalism" on the biggest Chinese search engine "Baidu" and found 2,480,000 relevant web pages and websites; and found 6,880,000 via the "Google". By investigating the professional websites on neoliberalism, I found that the network communication of the neoliberal thought trends are much mature in terms of both the thoughts and technology. The "figure" of such trends can be obviously seen from the content published on such sites. For example, as "Guantian Chashe" once published: "Marxism has produced the historical tragedy of crazily promoting the restoration of the authoritarianism in the name of communist revolution"[14], "The Marxism-Leninism

---

13 For example, comprehensive influential websites advocating political thought trends include: Tianya Community (www.tianyaclub.com),Free China BBS (http://218.155.24.175:9876/zyzg/index.php?sid-JsdVteF8), Xinghua BBS (http://www.1911.cn), Intermediate Ideology and Culture BBS (http://www.zhong/an.net), View BBS,Pioneer BBS (http://www.whxf.net), Spring of the Northern (http://bgzd.126.com) etc., China Review Net (http://www.china-review.com), Mao Zedong Flag Network (www.maoflag.net), Utopia Network (http://www.wyzxsx.com) etc.
14 See the article The Marxist Doctrine Advocates the Philosophy of Autocracy

brought about by the salvos of the October Revolution is both a historical lie and a misinterpretation of the history"[15], "The state under the one-party autocracy which is not implementing the party-ban is bound to lead to the downfall of the Party"[16], "Our governing party insists on the catholically faith procedure"[17], such comments give us an idea of the viewpoints of neoliberal thought trend.

Network communication features an obvious timeliness. The Internet can rapidly transmit the words, sounds and images at an extremely high speed without the restraints on printing, transportation and release, thus information can be sent to users instantly, by which it raises storms in the whole society. At this point, traditional media can hardly be compared to network media. The former is restricted by the technology and cost as well as the timeliness. For example, the publication of newspapers requires a certain period, daily at least and weekly and even biweekly at most, therefore, the newspaper is not perfect in terms of timeliness in a constantly changing modern society. It is also similar for the radio and TV station whose programs also require a certain period. It is also difficult even for the news which attaches the most importance to timeliness to broadcast the breaking news about the incidents from multiple perspectives, due to the limitation of program cycle. The live show is also affected and limited by time. While the network media have unique advantages such as the layout without the restrains of time and space, the channel renewal without fixed period and simple operations of adding or updating information. All above provide the network media a whole range of preparation conditions for spreading new information at any time.

The network has always a continuous interaction with other media especially with the newspaper, broadcast, TV and other traditional mass media in terms of the information exchange and spreading. Internet information often becomes the hotspot reported by traditional media who may use quite long and highly frequent reports with intent to attract more social public

---

of "Guantian Teahouse" (http://www.tianyaclub.com/new/Publicforum/Content. asp?idWriter-0&Key-0&strItem-no01&idArticle-100791&flag-1).

15 See the article The New Culture Movement, the May 4th Movement and the Chinese Communist Revolution Have no Cause and Effect Relationship of "Guantian Teahouse" (http://www.tianyaclub.com/new/Publicforum/Content. asp?idWriter-0&Key-0&strItem-no01&idArticle-100791&flag=1).

16 Step on the Path to Democratic Politics of Liberalism of "Guantian Teahouse" (http://www.tianya-club.com/new/Publicforum/Content.asp?idWriter-0&Key-0&strItem-no01&idArticle-95030&flag=1).

17 Extracted from article Critique of the Party System and the Comparison of the Catholic Christianity of "Guantian Teahouse" (http://www.tianyaclub.com/new/Publicforum/Content.asp?idWriter=0&Key=0&strItem=no01&idArticle=100615&flag=1).

attention to relevant events, which further increases the online information momentum and influence. Likewise, information from traditional media also becomes the focus attracting the network's attention. Traditional media such as broadcast and TV enjoy their own exceptional historical advantages and large-scale audiences in some fields. Government's major policies are always formally published via the official traditional media. For example, the broadcasted content of Network News Broadcast often attracts attention from network media and be reported in a deeper and more extensive way. The interaction between traditional media and the network also indicates that although the network publicity provides every participant a virtual communication space where the users can anonymously look for and publish information with fewer constraints from the social environment and morality. However, the participants still live in a certain social environment belonging to a certain social group with specific social mind, so network publicity cannot be separated from the real social life. Therefore, the publicity of a political thought trend in the network will not be distorted due to the virtual character of the network. Instead the interaction in many of such publicizing modes in turn has a wider influence with larger scope.

Moreover, the network communication of political thought trends will not only make a difference to the mass media and have interactions with it but also combine the virtual space of network with the reality. The websites publicizing political thought trends will rely on a non-website carrier, medium and forces for the publicity in order to extend the recognition. For example, some websites of thought trends form a communication system including such collective activities as a meeting point of exchange, reading, associations and academic exchange and organizing in specific places primarily for promoting the publicity of the thought trend. The elites of thought trends in some political thought trend websites are giving lectures in every place nationwide, and the thought trend websites are publishing these lectures and reporting the lecture content. This strategy, bonding the leading figures of thought trend figures with the websites, can both enable the figures to advocate the thought trend website in the lectures and enable them obtain more popularity. The political thought trend websites also implement directional publicity strategies, send electronic magazines to individuals via e-mail and other platforms and jointly launch or publish books with other websites to promote the publicity by combining it with the reality.[18]

---

18   Fang Fujian, Research on the Development Mode of the Social trends of thought in the Network Space - Based on the Analysis of the Ideological Trend, *Social Sciences in Ningxia,* 2013(3).

In brief, the emergence and development of the Internet have changed the publicizing modes and means to a large extent and played massive facilitating roles in the publicity and development of the political thought trends. Meanwhile, the Internet combined the publicizing modes of thought trends with each other, mixed the virtual space with the reality, and enriched the methods and modes of thought trend publicity.

IV.2. Features of publicity of the political thought trends

The features of the publicity of political thought trends are divided into two levels. Generally, the publicity of political thought trends has the features of sociality, universality and historical nature. The sociality of publicity stems from the human's sociality. As Marx said, "man is the ensemble of all his social relationships". In human society, all activities of an individual are deeply marked by the society, so does the mutual contact and information transfer between humans. The publicity of political thought trends deeply reflects the social nature of man. The universality of publicizing political thought trends is originated from the universality of human existence, which is not abstract but is the subject of information production and the channel of information communication. The publicity of political thought trends, with historical nature, means it has the features of development changes and replacement of the old system by new. In different historical periods, the approaches and modes of the publicity are greatly different. Specifically, the publicity of political thought trends has the following features.

IV.2.1. Periodicity of the political thought trend publicity

Most modes of publicity include preliminary, substantial and the decline stages. As Liang Qichao has argued: "Thought trends that influenced certain eras have generally started as a very small tendency of people who hardly aware of it; and in case of that it upsurges step by step and reaches the top, it would have a recession out of time until disappearing gradually."[19] According to the Buddhist statements, the development of a thought trend can be divided into four stages: "I. Enlightenment period (birth); II. Golden era (establishment); III. Exuviate period (variation); IV. Recession period (extinction)[20]. Such a statement makes some sense and indicates that the

---

19   Liang Qichao, *Introduction to the Qing Dynasty*, recorded in: *Four Kinds of Liang Qichao's Historical Works,* Yuelu Press, 1985, p. 20.
20   Ibid., p. 21.

development of thought trends has the periods of rise and fall as well as the periodicity to some degree.

Before the political thought trends enter their substantial stage, there is a foreshadowing preliminary publicity. During this period, various emotions, tempers and fuzzy conceptions about the common tendency start to come together and be communicated, which is the preparation period for the thought trend incubation and publicity. The substantial period of publicity of thought trends has three levels: (1) theoretical awareness spread level when such trend is known by people as a new theoretical perspective; (2) value awareness spread level when such trend enjoys popular support as a value belief; (3) practice awareness spread level when it guides people as a behavioral pattern. The last level is obviously the most important level among these three levels. If there are no responses from the audience to the thought trend value orientation, such trend should not be called as political thought trends. The above three levels are unified within the political thought trends entity; and their sequence during the publicity is in line with the audiences' law of cognition, from which it can be seen that the trend's influence on people is gradually deepened. In general, political thought trends will enter a decline or transforming period after going through the three levels of publicity. The decline and transforming period stems either from the completion of their own tasks with the transformation of position and form or their advance termination due to the inadequacy of the new social and historical conditions. The publicity of thought trends will always experience a recession or transformation either in an advanced or backward way.

Marxism became the state ideology after the establishment of new China, which changed its position and made it no longer exist mainly in the form of political thought trend. As the mainstream ideology, Marxism insists on the innovative development adaptive to China's social reality, by which it realized the localization in China. This meets the psychological need of the masses and guides China's development in the correct direction. While the liberal thought trends in modern times basically disappear after the establishment of new China, for the lack of modern market economy basis and the conditions for a law-based society as well as, more importantly, the support of the masses, which failed to provide the environment for it to survive and develop, and the liberal thought trends disappear thereupon. While currently existing neoliberalism is to some degree imported from foreign countries. After the long-time cultural imprisonment, the germination of the neoliberalism grew up along with the introduction of western works to China. Except for advocating the individual rights, free competition and private ownership, the neoliberalism absorbed the principles of fairness and justice in wealth distribution suggested by the US scholar Rawls who thinks that the government should play a necessary role as a regulator to promote social justice. Neoliberalism trend has also led the western neoliberal thoughts, and have encouraged the establishment of transnational corporations and pushed globalization.

IV.2.2. Inheritance of political thought trend publicity

The content of any political thought trend often inherits the theoretical content of relevant thought trends in the history, and the publicity of it also draws experiences and lessons from the previous publicity work and provides references for the future. The characteristic of such publicity stems from the cultural character of the thought trend itself. In a way, the formation, development and extinction of political thought trends are important cultural phenomena, since the trend itself just belongs to spiritual culture and the objectification of human's psychological state. An important characteristic of the culture is the heritage with an unidirectional cultural transmission between the generations while realizing the intergenerational transition. The next generation makes further inventions and creations based on the last generation, which merely realizes the accumulated development of the inherited culture. The cultural accumulation is also an important channel of cultural development. Although the humanity have gone through social forms of different natures, a culture is always developed and strengthened constantly based on the cultural creation of predecessors, and the original thought traces still can be seen in the new political thought trends.

Yan Fu once said that "Development relies on the innovation and observation relies on the transmission of old things", in which the "old things" refers to the traditional cultures and moral order. The inheritance of political thought trends means inheriting the predecessor's ideology and culture in a sense, only based on which new ideology and culture can be developed. Without the inheritance cultures, it is difficult to exist like "water without a source, a tree without roots". As an example, Marxism is generated on the basis of critically inheriting the fruits of relevant thought trends in history and by absorbing their rational component. By studying Classical German Philosophy, Marx critically absorbed the "rational core" of Hegelian dialectics and materialism of Feuerbach, i.e, his "basic idea" about the primariness of matter and secondariness of consciousness, and created dialectical materialism and historical materialism.

By studying the works of English classical political economists, Adam Smith and David Ricardo on "labor producing the commodity value", Marx found the "law of surplus value", thus revealed the secret of the capitalist's exploitation on the wage laborers and formulated the core of Marxist political economy. By critically absorbing their rational predictions on the future society from such utopian socialists as Saint-Simon, Fourier and Owen, he created the scientific socialism. It is based on constantly inheriting the predecessor's ideology by which a new political thought trend can be formed and developed.

As another example, the neoliberal thought trends which have emerged in 1990s inherited some ideologies and theories of the liberal thought trend in modern China and absorbed relevant publicity experience for the best publicity effect to a certain extent. In the first 30 years of the 20th Century, Cai Yuanpei and Hu Shi et al. made contributions to the development of liberalism. As the first person who systematically introduced the western liberal thought trends, Yan Fu has brought about the classic definition of freedom to China: "The freedom is to do things with rules. Someone living outdoor alone has unlimited constraints. The good and evil both originate from it, is anyone forbidding them? While in a public place, everyone wants freedom and if there are no any limited constraints, conflicts will be arose among people who ignore others' freedom. As a result, everyone's freedom is bounded by others' freedom."[21] So we can see that Yan Fu has thought the freedom as people's inborn rights and an individual's freedom as a freedom that do not affect others' freedom. He has also advocated the western constitutional democracy system and "adoption of freedom-based democracy."[22] However, the liberal thought trends are not in line with the objective and realistic conditions and development demand of society at that time without the existence basis after the establishment of new China, and then gradually quitted the historical stage.

After the silence for half a century, the liberalism has started to step on the history stage again in 1980s. With the call of Party Central Committee on ideological emancipation, the neoliberalism claimed for publicizing the freedom, human rights, and democratic concepts and for finally establishing a constitutional democratic government. As the market economic system reform deepens constantly in 1990s, the pace of constructing a socialist law-administrated country is unceasingly boosted, and the consensus

---

21   Yan Fu, Discussion on Boundary of Public and Individual, recorded in: *Collection of Yan Fu*, Book One, Zhonghua Book Company, 1986, p. 132.
22   Yan Fu, Be Strong, recorded in: *Collection of Yan Fu*, Book One, Zhonghua Book Company, 1986, p. 132.

atmosphere of liberalism is constantly enhanced. As Zhu Xueqin has summarized the demands of the liberalism in contemporary China in 1998: The Manifesto of the Liberalism Theory: "First, it is a theory and then a realistic demand. The Manifesto demanded the representative democracy and lawful constitutional government in terms of politics "which will reject autocracy both by the individual or minority and the massive dictatorship by the majority, practiced in the name of public will. As for the ethics, The Manifesto demanded guarantees individual values: individual should not be reduced and sacrificed as the tool of abstract goals and causes after various precious values are finally, abused."[23] Here we can see that, although the neoliberalism is to a degree, a foreign product as described above, the freedom and democracy are the core ideas of the liberalism and neoliberalism with the same strain, and the neoliberalism got integrated with the western economic liberalism idea and added such new connotations as adoring the marketization, emphasizing the social justice, approving the globalization, paying attention to the social forces and objecting to corruption and bureaucracy by following the mainline.

IV.2.3. Organizer character of publicity

Essentially, political thought trends express certain interests of specific social groups, stratums or class. The core of such class or stratum, such as ideologists and leaders, will compete for the most extensive social resources for their own interest groups by way of publicizing thought trends. The important subjects of these thought trends will actively conduct publicity activities through multiple channels, to publicize psychological tendency and theoretical demands of their thought trends, and hence the spread of thought trends embodies a vivid organizer character.

This feature of organization by thought trends is relatively spontaneous., In most cases the publicity of thought trends is implemented in an organized behavior through disseminating self-consciousness. Traditional mode of mass communication shows more organizer characteristics, which are reflected in publicity medium control, publicity steps making, etc. The mode of interpersonal communication also features organization, embodied in organizing partial social members to collect information intensively, spreading political thought trends by speeches or setting up forum online, etc. Since there are both mass communication and interpersonal communication, the organizational characteristic of the mode of network communication is also outstanding, and much timelier with a wider influence scope. The organizational characteristic of political thought trend publicity is mainly embodied in its strong purpose and stable members of spread subjects, as well as the diversification and flexibility of publicity medium utilization during spread process, etc.

Evaluating from the aspect of publicity subjects, the communicators of political thought trends conduct thought trends dissemination activities purposefully, to expand influence of thought trends constantly. At the initial stage, the publicity of thought trends mainly relies on interpersonal communication, such as speeches, to expand their acceptance scope. After forming stable acceptor groups by publicizing in a small range, such acceptors will compose formal or informal organization supporting thought trends development. In these organizations, there will be a common sense formed based on political thought trends identification as well as a definite relation of members in which the members intersect with each other and conduct a division of labor in collaboration according to their personal specialty by forming the ability to act in concert, and adjust timely to deal with external situations. When it enters the age of mass media, organizations supporting political thought trends enlarge influences through multiple ways of interpersonal communication, mass media, network communication, etc. According to their own concept of value, the communicators will conduct a certain selection with a quite strong purpose in publishing views for social events and the external world, publicize the social sectors who are for the benefit of them with an expanded processing, while not mentioning or disregarding the unfavorable part for them, and then they will publicize the results they summarized to the public, so as to influence people's cognition and judgment on realistic environment. Therefore, the spread of political thought trends have generalized randomness and spontaneity by displaying a stronger self-consciousness.

Evaluating from the view of the process of publicity, political thought trend publicity has more abundant means for spreading than normal information, and its publicizing effect is more obvious. To obtain general attention of society, the communicators of political thought trends will improve the efficiency and quality of publicity through the control of publicizing medium and making publicizing steps.

Firstly, master multiple information publishing modes. Beside the battle field of political thought trends provided by traditional media of interpersonal communication and mass communication, the new media, BBS, blog, micro-blog, podcast, etc. also provide great convenience for communication, especially for those network platforms with big influence are more attractive to political thought trends communicators. In consequence, the publicizing process of political thought trends employs a multi-level stereoscopic spreading mode which consists of seminars, the press, new network media, etc. Since the organizations of political thought trend publicity have a large number of members, who both have higher professional quality to clearly explain the core of a thought trend with articles which can make it easier to influence people's sentiment attitude. They also have the staff who have expertise in computer or media and communication and are skilled in new media operation rules and hence can publicize by taking advantage of the multiple new media such as posting messages on BBS with huge influence based on psychological characteristics of Internet users, to win high click rate and response rate by inducing Internet users' emotion with further comments, to affect cognition of netizens and make their own opinions emerge from information ocean as striking points.

Secondly, the publicizing process of political thought trends will change as changes of social reality. With the formation and development process of a social event in a specific time, the external forms of political thought trends will also change resiliently, and guide social mass psychology flexibly. As Internet became an important life-style of people, the publicity medium relying on network possesses huge audience groups, due to technical reasons and the features of different age groups, the users of network media are dominated by middle-aged and young people, which means taking the constructers of today's society as the subject. When a social event occurs, people's attention will be attracted naturally. At this time, the core thought of some thought trends will comment about the social event after being processed. Thought trends would usually appear in the presentation of public opinions, which tend to be unique in most cases. After being expressed by virtue of famous people who can play the role of an opinion leader, the attention is improved from event enthusiasts and even the general public.

In addition to timeliness, flexibility, and rapidity of new media publicity, the communicators of political thought trends could publish speeches at any time based on the developing trend of social hotspots and psychological reaction of the public, further to form public opinion field on Internet and even in real life, exerting an influence on the cognition of people to the event, and even people's model of thinking, and then change people's attitudes and behaviors.

IV.3. Spreading process of political thought trends

The publicity of political thought trends is a multi-level web spreading process sent by senders through certain publicity mediums, and then received or accepted by receivers (acceptors), and transferred to secondary receivers (acceptors) and even multi-level receivers or acceptors below in the end. The network communication covers two aspects: interpersonal communication and mass communication. The interpersonal communication process is very simple, while mass communication process is far more complex, in sequence, here will primarily discuss the mass communication process of political thought trends.

IV.3.1. Basic elements in the spreading process of political thought trends

In general, the basic elements in the spreading process of political thought trends contain communicators, receivers (acceptors), medium, and secondary receivers (acceptors).

Communicators are the source of information in the spreading process of political thought trends, who are individuals or groups diffusing and spreading out content and claims of some political thought trends. Accordingly, the political orientation, theoretical ideas, ideological positions and other tendencies of the individual communicators have a great influence on the effect, scope, etc. of political thought trend publicity. To some extent, the communicators—those who propogate—are the principal element in the spreading process of political thought trends.

The publicity medium mainly includes traditional paper print media, such as carrier of newspapers, magazines, journals, and books, as well as new electronic media, mainly including internet, electronic publications, mobile media and other carrier forms. As it shows, the publicity medium of political thought trends covers nearly all the channels of mass media, and the influence scope, degree of authority, audience level of various media vary, hence the spread influence of different political thought trends are not all the same. However, whatever the influence degree of various forms of carrier, it is no doubt that the publicity medium is an important influence factor for spreading political thought trends from the overall view.

The receivers (acceptors) are the information audience in process of publicizing political thought trends, who are individuals or groups receiving or accepting some viewpoints of political thought trends. Since the personal factors of each receiver (acceptor) are not all the same, such as way of thinking, political tendency, cultural quality, life background, while these factors have crucial influence for each receiver (acceptor) whether to agree with some viewpoints of political thought trends, which affect the spreading of political thought trends result from the angle of the audience themselves. The secondary receivers (acceptors) are the indirect and secondary information audience of the spreading process of political thoughts trends. Different from foresaid receivers (acceptors), the information source of secondary receivers (acceptors) is not direct communicators, but exactly the primary receivers (acceptors). The primary receivers (acceptors) will transfer some viewpoints of political thought trends to the secondary receivers (acceptors) after their own "processing". The same thing for primary receivers (acceptors) is relevant for that the way of thinking, political tendency, cultural quality, life background and other personal factors of the secondary receivers (acceptors) are important factors affecting the result of political thought trend publicity as well.

"Receiving" and "accepting" have apparent differences in process of publicizing political thought trends. In the first place, there are essential differences in degrees of them. "Receiving" is only the cognition and understanding of some political thought trends to some extent, although some viewpoints are mastered, which does not mean necessarily to approve or accept such viewpoints; while "accepting" refers to the audience who recognize and admit the claims of such political thought trends to some extent on the basis of cognition and understanding of some political thought trends, becoming new supporters and communicators. Therefore, from the perspective of degree, the main difference of "receiving" and "accepting" is whether to agree and support the viewpoints and claims of some political thought trends. Besides, in the actual spread process of political thought trends, there is difference on time order of "receiving" and "accepting". Only with cognition of viewpoints of political thought trends could have further approval; without "receiving" from political thought trends, there will be no "acceptance" to political thought trends. By that analogy, "receiving" is the pilot and foundation of "acceptance", on the basis of receiving some viewpoints of political thought trends, the audience will choose to accept or be not under influence of their own ideological consciousness, values, ways of thinking, political tendency and other factors, with an attitude to some political thought trends generated consciously. After a kind political thought trend is received and accepted by a partial audience as a kind of information, it will be spread to more secondary receivers by the acceptors as new communicators, by analogy, forming complex net structure of political thought trend publicity.

Generally speaking, the basic spreading process of political thought trends is: Information spread process: Communicators → publicity medium → receivers (acceptors) → secondary receivers (acceptors); information feedback process: secondary receivers (acceptors) → receivers (acceptors) → publicity medium → communicators. This mode expresses a relatively complete publicizing process, and basically answered how political thought trends are publicized. Yet in the real life, the spreading process of political thought trends is far more complicated, and the spread process will suffer influence and limitation of various factors, and the audience are not only pure information receivers, but those who will select and feedback information actively, hence the spread process is not a one-way process operating from communicators to acceptors, rather than a dynamic bidirectional way, even a multi-way process. For network communication, the difference of communicators and audience during spreading is broken to some extent. Since each participant of network communication possesses a dual-identity of communicators and audience, they could receive information from any other communicators directly or indirectly, and transfer information to any acceptors on the net directly or indirectly at the same time.

IV.3.2. Primary publicity of political thought trends

The primary spread process is as such: "Communicators → publicity medium → receivers (acceptors)". This process contains three basic elements, namely communicators, medium, and receivers (acceptors), and this is a relatively complete spreading process.

The primary spreading process of political thought trends is not a process in which the communicators keep sending and the receivers receive passively, but an interaction process of senders and receivers. On the one hand, the senders keep studying the demand of receivers, which determines the sending content and quantity; on the other hand, driving by demands, the receivers strive to find objects that can satisfy their demands. If the information sent by senders is consistent with the information that receivers need, the spreading will be very successful.[24] The process from weakness to rising of the US neoliberalism thought trend exactly shows the relationship between the demand and satisfaction during spreading process. In the 1930s, the capitalist countries led by the United States suffered a severe economic crisis, when prices and production were falling, and unemployment rate got extremely high. According to statistics, the unemployment

---

24   Zhang Lianxu, Discussion on the Mode of Trend of Social Thoughts Communication, *Panyu Polytechnic*, 2003(9).

rate of USA in 1933 reached to 25.2%. The prevalent economic thought trends prior to this was the classical liberalism represented by Adam Smith and David Ricardo, namely the though trend in which the market is an invisible hand that manipulates the running of the economy, and the government should only bear the duty of "night watch".

But, with the collapse of the stock market, and the bankruptcies of banks, the economies of capitalist countries fell into malignant running at one time, and the US President Herbert Hoover was forced to step down. At this moment, British economist Keynes proposed to manage a demand-based economy which argued for the intervention of the state to economic development, and in which the government should bear a great responsibility for the development of economic activities. This theory directly accorded with President Roosevelt's concept of New Nationalism, which put the national need before sectional or personal advantage and President Roosevelt has generally affirmed the thoughts of Keynes and conducted a widespread and public campaign through the press, publications, radio and television, etc. in the US.

After the enforcement of the policies such as expanding public expenditure, and providing full employment to working classes by the government, based on the ideas of Keynesian economics, the US economy begun to recover And by the virtue of Keynesian economics the US economy had seen rapid growth till the 1970s. Keynes' thoughts—later called as "Keynesianism"—which advocated the state's intervention in the economy was first adopted as the major economic policy by the Roosevelt administration under the name of "New Deal", in order to pull out the US economy out of the economic crisis, and the Great Depression, and lead it to a strong and healthy economic growth.

During the over 30 years, a strong contest and struggle emerged between these Keynesian policies and the economic liberalism doctrine of Friedman who was the main representative figure of neoliberalism, who was ignored and rejected for long years in the past. Indeed, his articles and books had received marginal interest among the people and business circles.

But, in 1970s, the US economy was faced with high inflation and economic stagnation. Keynesians believed that inflation and economic stagnation were reverse trends, which should normally not appear in an economy at the same time and they could not explain this event. While US economy was also faced with these economic stagnation and inflation at this period, which could not be resolved by Keynesian traditional government expenditure expansion and reduction or other kind of fiscal policies, the proponents of Keynesianism could propose no solutions for such economic conditions. At this period, the representative personages of liberalism, such as Friedman and Hayek, pointed out that the reason of inflation and economic stagnation was very-high taxes supporting higher social welfare level, leading to a sharp drop in the production enthusiasm of the entrepreneurs, while the higher social security level and coverage scope assured a considerable purchasing power for the broad masses, and then the prices were still rising. The neoliberalism thought trend advocates to develop economy through the management of supply and demand, reduce the security expenditure, improve the production enthusiasm, and the proposal of this thought trend catered to the will of President Reagan from the Republican Party and the big bourgeoisie behind him in all manners. Henceforth, President Reagan began to apply policies of interest rate cuts, tax reductions for businesses and other policies which had taken neoliberalism as guide, and US economy got some improvement. Afterwards the neoliberalism thought trend of Friedman became popular in the United States. As the process of neoliberalism thought trend advocating government decentralization and withdrawing of state intervention shows, the rising of one kind of thought depends on whether it satisfies the psychological need of the ruling class under certain social conditions and when these two tendencies match, that political thought trend will develop more smoothly.

Zhang Lianxu has argued that in the process of publicizing political thought trends, the receivers of some thought trends will turn to acceptors at the same time of receiving. Some thought trend receivers will become acceptors after a period of receiving. However, some thought trends will never be accepted even though it is received by receivers. This is because there is a process of screening and filtering of political thought trends from receivers to acceptors, namely the process of comprehending, thinking, deliberating, and comparing and the final choice by the receivers among various theories, views and doctrines in ideological systems which constitute the thought trends. Therefore, when the thought trends are accepted after a receiving period, the political thought trends which comply with the public social psychological needs will obtain wider identification usually experience a subtle process of psychological tendency change of the people.

IV.3.3. Secondary publicity of political thought trends

It is obviously impossible for everyone to receive political thought trends through publicity medium directly because of that this process is limited by personal knowledge, life experience, objective environment and many other factors, so a large number of people receive thought information through re-sending of receivers within the primary spread process. The receivers within the primary publicizing process become senders in the secondary spread process by playing a dual role in the whole process of publicizing political thought trends. The main publicizing form of political secondary spread process is the interpersonal communication which have more productive information and meanings, and information can be transmitted by language, actions, expressions comprehensively, and be presented mostly in the process in which several people get together voluntarily for a problem they commonly interested in by conducting a thought communication. Such process is initially a one-way publicity, and with the repetition of primary publicizing, the number of political thought trend receivers would be gradually increased, and the one-way publicity turns to a "bidirectional communication". In this process, the position of senders and receivers also swaps frequently, and everyone will receive some new information from the other side by causing a further spreading of the political thought trends.[25] Due to timely feedback, the topic develops towards being of interest to both sides, and the interpersonal communication is based on the consensus of both sides, other than blind and dispersive information promotion to audience in large volumes. Thus it has a better effect on changing people's attitude and behavior than that of mass communication and network communication, which is a high quality spreading activity. However, by comparison with the mass communication process, the system and accuracy of information spreading through interpersonal communication is worse such an extent that even a few words can make people suppose that they find new and fresh information sometimes. For instance, with the popularization of Internet, micro-blogs and other network platforms, more people begun not only to gain the latest information through Internet, but also to express their own view and opinions freely. As for secondary spreading of political thought trends, the Internet has already become a kind of the strongest spontaneous spreading and communication platform, and people receive and even accept some viewpoints of political thought trends unconsciously, and be able to issue their own opinions about some problems timely, which completes the re-spreading cycle of political thought trends unconsciously. As it can be seen, this kind of secondary spreading have spontaneity and informality in most cases, but it cannot be denied that it is becoming a new approach and a new mode for the spreading of the political thought trends.

The spreading process of information is a kind of social interaction process. Opinion leaders have a wide range of interpersonal communication and active performance on the Internet. Hence they play an important role

---

25 Ibid.

in the secondary spreading process. Before the new media appears, the position and knowledge of opinion leaders were important factors which attract other people's attention and trust, with the popularization and the increasing prominence of Internet applications. In modern society, the opinion leaders have been becoming online increasingly and the plebian tendency has become more obvious, which compensate the deficiency of reputation and professional knowledge by Internet interaction frequency and depth. When we look at the studies, there are scholars who believe that the opinion leaders are glad to accept new things, and acquire information by getting in touch with various types of media. They influence the audience with a lower medium contact degree, intellectual level and interest to external information by transmitting viewpoints to others, which will generate an unexpected spread effect[26] under specific social contexts. Zhang Lianxu has argued that, the receiving (accepting) of political thought trends by secondary receivers (acceptors) does not mean end of the whole process of spreading of the political thought trends. The secondary acceptors will take the role of senders consciously or unconsciously, and carry on the spread of political thought trends, forming circulatory spread. It is also the existence of such circulatory spread makes political thought trends achieve more comprehensive and accurate spread.[27]

IV.4. Controlling the publicity of political thought trends

The publicity of political thought trends is inescapable. Controlling of political thought trend publicity is also inevitable. Political thought trends possess strong spiritual strength to integrate people into an organizational form, and further create a kind of social atmosphere through interpersonal communication, mass communication, network communication, and other modes by way of affecting the social attitudes and behavioral patterns of social members. Consequently it is necessary to regulate and control political thought trends to realize the positive operation and harmonious development of the society, which are the important aspects of our party ideology field. In order to guide political thought trends with socialist core value system more effectively, we need to study the law of political thought trends spread and regulation. For managing the ideology work well, controlling means not only a restraint and limitation, specific to those non-Marxism

---

26   Peng Lan, Three Mechanisms that Affect the News Activity, *Journal of Shanghai Normal University,* 2010(4).
27   Zhang Lianxu, Discussion on the Mode of Trend of Social Thoughts Communication, *Panyu Polytechnic,* 2003(9).

thought trends, but also a leading and guidance. Controlling the spreading of thought trends mainly focuses on several major links in the spreading process of thought trends.

IV.4.1. Controlling communicators of political thought trends

Strengthening the control over the communicators (propagators) is the most important aspect of thought trend publicity control. It is also necessary to implement the principle of party control media unswervingly, and conduct politic audits towards the allocation of leadership and general staff of publicity agencies. Such two kinds of staff are the important organizers of thought trend publicity, including media managers, editors, journalists, presenters, etc. They could decide an orientation and guard a pass to ideological contents and political viewpoints of thought trend publicity by deciding which events will be reported, in which from they will be reported, whose articles will be chosen and which standpoint, ideological tendency and political tone of the media will have.

Firstly, we should improve the professional quality of media practitioners, enhance their professional cultivation, ideological and moral education, and employ practical and powerful measures to encourage the advanced and supervise the backward, cultivate a high social responsibility conscientiousness of media practitioners, who should adhere to media works' social service function and public service mission, and spread an advanced culture consciously. For very few people inconsistent with the Party and the people, even standing on the hostile position, they should be excluded from ideological publicity cultural work team by formulating the corresponding laws and codes of practice.

Secondly, we should improve the political theoretical level of media staff, and their ability to identify the nature and the dynamic state of political thought trends. As the most prominent people in the publicity work, media practitioners should ensure political sensitivity, and pay attention to collect information of different thought trends periodically and conduct analysis, research and judgment, to practically improve the level of mastering political thought trends, so as to improve the ability guaranteeing development direction of a socialist advanced culture. Media organizations should establish long-term supervision mechanisms aiming to report about thought trends and identify political thought trends of different natures correctly, to conduct hierarchical management as per classification, as well as actively filter political thought trends distorting objective facts, with obvious reaction and detrimental to the interests of the state.

Thirdly, we should improve the evaluation system and promote social supervision. Although media has its own social supervision functions, there also has to be supervision from the society. With promotion of marketization progress, under the premise of public ownership as the main body, the government encourages media to conduct its enterprise operations by itself, hence some media agencies will deviate from track of progressive thoughts to seek for profit and widen social influence, and call the tune for some thought trends affecting social harmony, so as to attract the public opinion further to purchase. Therefore, media should also has a transparent operation, accept an active supervision from all walks of life, correct its wrong moves, and establish a cultural products market which includes positive and healthy spiritual and cultural products led by the mainstream ideology.

IV.4.2. Controlling the contents of political thought trends

The content design of the spreading process of political thought trends will determine the information which is directly received by the receivers, thus reviewing ande checking the content of publicity, for example checking rumors, and making news verification is useful, thus healthy content can be promoted.   Besides, attention and support to the mainstream media should be enhanced, to strengthen their sense of responsibility, and improve its ideological sensitivity, its correct orientation should be guaranteed, and we should continue to improve the level of our leadership regarding the mass ideology and culture in the society. The mainstream media should adjust its plans based on the analysis of the dynamic state and the changes in the main tendency of political thought trends in different periods, publicize social consciousness by reflecting public opinion truly and conforming to the interests of government and the people, and be beneficial to long-term social development in a large scale, and restrain negative, backward, destructive political thought trends timely, and lead the masses' attention and enthusiasm to practice of the construction of a prosperous society. The mainstream media should construct scientific and correct base for the spreading of thought theories, improve the quality of the spreading information and widen the influence of the spreading to society at the same time when promoting the construction of a harmonious society by the means such as striking point leading, typical publicity, supervision by the masses,[28] etc. When the subject role of the mainstream media for the spreading of the social ideology is certainly ensured, the self-inspection activities of other various mediums to spread content should also

---

28   Kong Deming, Construction of Public Opinion Guidance System in Multi-Media Pattern, *China Radio & TV Academic Journal*, 2011(8).

be encouraged, to enhance the type of consciously regulated information,[29] to spread a positive thought beneficial to society construction, and explore their own characteristics and historical advantages, forming core competitiveness, other than attract attention from society by diffusing speeches against the mainstream social ideology, so as to form a functioning pattern which have a mutual supplementary relationship with the mainstream media, and a balanced and coordinated development.

IV.4.3. Efficent control of the communication media of political thought trends

The control level of the communication media directly determines the efficiency and quality of the publicity of political thought trends, thus the work of restricting those influential thought trends which are not favorable for the social development can be inhibited at the initial phase. Firstly, besides media registration, review and cancellation system, policies should be further enhanced to restrain the spreading range of some media and the broadcast frequency and TV channels, Internet and other spreading sources should be distributed according to this view. This regulation method has its necessity in order to restrict some political thought trends with ulterior motives which aim seizing key positions in the battle field of publicity and which undermine the normal communication order.

Secondly, under the current media environment, the government should define its own regulatory positioning and duty by formulating and implementing relevant measures such as laws, regulations and rules, stipulate media to bear social responsibilities and obligations, encourage various media to perform responsibilities and bear social obligations actively. Meanwhile, it also should stipulate punishment rules which clearly aim and conduct corresponding punishment to the spreading behaviors specified as breaking rules through laws and regulations, to play a guiding and indicative role for the whole media industry.

Thirdly, we should cultivate non-governmental organizations and civilian opinion leaders, and adopt a mode of government leading and civil organization indirect leading combination by virtue of a third party's force instead of a pure and direct government leading, to enhance the communication ability of the mainstream ideology.[30] Currently, the role of non-gov-

---

29   Ibid.
30   Zhou Xiao, *Shallow Analysis on the Realistic Premise and Practice Mechanism of Public Opinion Guidance - A Case Study of Network Public Opinion Guidance in Foreign Countries, Television Research*, 2012(5).

ernmental organizations are increasingly significant in social construction, especially the non-governmental organizations based on dealing with some aspects of social problems which have a more profound understanding on some social status quo, have closer relations with some social groups, obtain a deep-rooted trust and support from the relevant objects. Hence it will be more effective to transfer core values to social public through non-governmental organizations. The role played by opinion leaders in interpersonal communication is much stronger than mass communication; and it should be conducted trainings for opinion leaders based on their influence and characters by guaranteeing correct direction of opinion leaders' thought idea, which will directly influence content selection and attitude transfer to opinion leaders' next level spreading. The non-governmental organizations and opinion leaders can also collect feedback information, and reflect it to formal organizations after systemizing spontaneous and discrete public opinions, and the formal organization will adjust the spreading content timely according to the real situation. The establishment of such appeal and feedback mechanism will contribute to extend the positive value, eliminate social barriers and promote social harmony.

Fourthly, specific to the massive information brought by new media rising as well as the characteristics of no gap, no boundary, strong interaction, etc. during publicity, we need to actively utilize new technology to manage and supervise new media, to actively introduce mainstream ideology publicized by traditional broadcast and TV media into new media to publicize it, and to play an active role on leading thought trends in the fields that new media involves, so as to form a situation of benign interaction and orderly development. There are scholars who pointed out that the application of new media technology features a continuous progress, and the website itself is also the subject to ensure that wrong political thought trends not be diffused. It is also necessary to encourage websites to take self-discipline through implementing a conscious hierarchical management of online forums, to play the level filtering function of website management.[31] For micro-blogs with bigger influence in publicity field, it should be paid a close attention to the dynamics of opinion leaders. Opinion leaders could be found by their follower numbers and the number of forwards of micro-blogs, and it is usually easier to identify opinion leaders of political thought trends due to the content of their words. Paying more attention and giving more guidance are both effective methods to lead the publicity of political thought trends.

---

31   Ibid.

IV.4.4. Controlling the audience targeted by the political thought trends

Receivers are one of the important links in the publicizing process of a political thought trend, only when information reaches the targeted receiver, can mean that the spreading of a political thought trend is realized. With the increasing enrichment of media means, the new media tools are playing an increasingly important role, as society constructors, the middle-aged and young people account for a majority of new media users. Thus it is very necessary to influence the spreading process of political thought trends by controlling audience. For controlling the audience, on the one hand, it mainly embodies in enhancing the positive publicity and education, and creating a favorable social atmosphere, to lead the wide audience to accept or restrain the content spreading by medium consciously. It is also necessary to constantly enhance the building of social civilization, so as to improve social civilization degree, cultivate an environment for the spreading of good thoughts while limiting the ground for the spreading of wrong thought trends, to guide the social mass, especially the young people to form right values, by which to establish the socialist ideal and belief, follow social norms, as well as carrying forward the contemporary spirit of advancing with the times which involves pioneering and innovative, and positive and progressive. On the other hand, the cognition level of information spread by medium of wide masses should be improved.[32] Also education of masses is a must from multiple angles and by multi-level understandable knowledge, in order to improve their resistance ability towards massive information bombardment, enhance our checking ability of various media, cultivate the wide audience towards adopting the ability of grasping the initiative and resisting the decadent and wrong thought trends which use multiple spreading patterns, and vigorously restrict the unchecked spread of wrong thought trends on the level of audience.

IV.4.5. Controlling harmful thought trends that originate abroad

Currently, it is urgent to pay a high attention towards, harmful information and thought trends that originate abroad, which can easily spread via Internet, and effective measures should be employed to restrain the dissemination of these wrong thought trends. The dissolution of the Soviet Union is a wake-up call for us. Kawatake Kazuo wrote that "during the

---

32   Lu Di, Liang Fei, How to Strengthen the Social Responsibility of Radio and Television Media, *China Radio & TV Academic Journal*, 2012(7).

dissolution process of the Soviet Union, the transnational publicity of United States and the West have played a huge role, based on relevant researches, as early as 1985, there were already 63% young people of 16-30 years old people, listening to Western broadcasts, as for 1987, the ratio raised up to 83%, among which those who have listened to them over 1 hour/day reached to 46%. Where the most influential foreign broadcasts among the Soviet Union and Eastern Europe citizens were the Free Radio of the USA and the Free European Radio, which were both operated by the funds of the US government, they implemented short wave broadcasting to the East from their headquarters set in Munich and Frankfurt respectively, to spread Western information and conduct the "publicity of freedom".[33] As it can be seen, the liberalism thought trends incited by Western countries played a certain role in the great upheaval process in the Eastern Europe. Today, the mainstream ideology of our state should be disseminated and we should vigorously advocate our own values through various media means, and stay in vigilance and resistance attitude for those attacking the path of socialism with Chinese characteristics. The introduction of overseas political thought trends brings both new opportunities and challenges for leading and governing political thought trends which are active in our country. There are scholars who point out that we should walk out positively, promote international communication and cooperation, draw lessons from foreign advanced technology and management experience, enhance international spread ability construction, influence international public comments orientation actively, to build international spread coverage system;[34] make China's mainstream voice better, improve influence among international society, reduce noisy interference from the outside world, enhance understanding towards Chinese ideology among the international community, to create a good international public appreciation.

We should not comprehend the control work narrowly. The social forces controlling the spreading of political thought trends come from multiple aspects, and the control should not be merely regarded as a kind of governmental behavior. Controlling also contains other spontaneous or conscious social behaviors, for example, the opposition among the thought trends with different natures, the people who consciously restraint to wrong thought trends, self-discipline of spreading agencies as well as the containing influence of social public's opinion feedback to the spreading of the thought trends. All of these could be deemed as a spontaneous control phenomenon

33   Kawatake Kazuo, *Structural Changes in the International Communication Media, Journalism Comment,* 1992(47).
34   Lu Di, Liang Fei, How to Strengthen the Social Responsibility of Radio and Television Media, *China Radio & TV Academic Journal,* 2012(7).

for certain political thought trends. For the decadent feudal dynasty, controlling the spreading of political thought trends spread was maintaining the decadent regime. The siege and efforts of Chang Kai-shek group who represented the reactionary forces at home and abroad, against communist thoughts and other advanced thought trends have all served their own reactionary regime. In this sense, the nature of a regime determines the nature of the control which is imposed over political thought trends, as well as the very nature of political thought trends, which are the targets of control. Our regime is a regime that represents the fundamental interests of the overwhelming majority of the people. Accordingly, our control towards the spread of wrong thought trends aims to consolidate people's power, which is natural.

In general, the research of the spread and control of political thought trends within a certain scope is quite important. Theoretically speaking, it can enrich and deepen our theories regarding political thought trends theory, help that political thought trends can develop in a healthy posture. Practically, it is helpful for enhancing our current ideological work by helping social mass to establish correct ideas and thoughts, cultivate a positive and optimistic life view, and create a benign ideological and cultural environment to promote building a harmonious socialist society.

CHAPTER FIVE

The New Value Monism – "Universal Values" Thought Trend

The politicality of political thought trends is not only reflected in the considerations of the political superstructure, but also in the enrichment and development of the ideological superstructure. In recent years, "universal values" thoughts which made a wide social influence and drew close attention of the society brought up the issue of "modernization of spirit" and the theme of "enlightenment" from the ideological concept again, emphasized the "modernity" standard of human spiritual life from the perspective of "value", which emphasizes common value pursuit of human in the view of global and human beings and returns to the "value monism" in a new level.

V.1. The origin of the "Universal Values" thought trend

Early in 1988, the US scholar Francis Fukuyama put forward in his famous article "The End of History", which argued that the disintegration of the Soviet Union, drastic changes in Eastern Europe and the end of the Cold War marked the end of communism, and there was only one way for the development of history, i.e., the market economy and democratic politics of the West. Fukyama said that the development history of human society was "the human universal history with the liberal democratic system as the direction". The liberal democratic system was "the final outcome of the development of human ideology" and "the last dominant form of human". Although the term "universal values" did not directly appear in his paper, it already had reflected this mindset.

In the late 1990s, this mindset had a response in China. Li Shenzhi, former vice president of China Academy of Social Sciences said, "The world has gone through the comparison and selection of two hundred or three hundred years since industrialization, especially China has gone through the largest scale social test in human history for more than 100 years, and there has been already enough reason to prove that liberalism has the best and most universal values.

In 2005, Yuan Weishi, a professor in Zhongshan University, published the Connotation and Significance of the End of the Debate between Chinese and Western Culture in the second issue of Spring and Autumn Annals, and clearly put forward the term "universal values". Weishi said that "With the signing of the two United Nations Conventions on human rights and participation in the WTO by China as a symbol, Chinese and Western culture debate has ended in theory, and the Chinese government acknowledges the universal values of modern civilization". He also said, "At present, many Eastern countries are still wallowing in the mud. In the final analysis, they fail to break through the shackles of traditional culture system, and do not have the courage to accept the universal institutional culture (democracy, rule of law, constitutionalism and so on)". "They should not take the multi-culture as an excuse to resist the core value of universality". "The key of the success of modernization by any country or region is closely related to whether or not they accept the core value of universality."

In February 2007, Xie Tao, the former vice president of Renmin University of China, published the Democratic Socialism Mode and the Future of China, affirmed the opinion proposed by Xin Ziling that the experience of democratic socialism in Sweden "has universal values, and it is a great contribution to human civilization", and "provides a successful example for us to adhere to the socialist direction and follow the road of democratic socialism in the Reform and Opening-up."

In May 2008, the South Weekend published an article A New China out of the Wenchuan Earthquake, interpreting the great victory of earthquake relief based on the superiority of the socialist system under the leadership of the Communist Party into "honoring their commitments to the universal values to its own people and the world." It announced that China had come to a turning point. Since then, the term "universal values" became more and more popular.

Advocates of the "universal values" argue that democracy, freedom, human rights, fairness, justice, equality and humanitarianism are the "universal values", and the theoretical innovation in economic and political or social and cultural aspects should take the "universal values" as the scale, and be in line with international mainstream values including democracy and constitutionalism. There are some scholars do not agree with this view and put forward criticism. They argue that there are no "universal values", and the so-called "universal values" are the "values of the United States" and the "Western mainstream values". It is thus clear that people have different interpretations for what "universal values" mean, whether "universal values" exist and other problems, "for" and "against" are well defined, and there are distinct camps for different views. Some print media and network play an important role in the formation of "universal values" issue as the focus of people's hot debate. Spring and Autumn Annals, Economic Observer, China Business Journal and other media have published some articles to advocate the existence of "universal values" while Studies on Marxism, Journal of Ideological & Theoretical Education, Beijing Daily and other media presented different views against the advocacy of "universal values" by the former media. People's Daily, Guangming Daily and other newspapers reproduced articles to criticize the views that advocate "universal values".

V.2. Whether there are "Universal Values" or not

Advocates of the theory of "universal values" argue that democracy, rule of law, freedom, human rights and other concepts are the universal values and they do not carry out a comprehensive and in-depth demonstration on it. Some scholars have argued that democracy, rule of law, freedom, human rights, equality and humanitarianism are the achievements of civilization commonly formed in the world in the long historical process and the universal values commonly pursued by the entire human society, rather than being peculiar to capitalism[1], "since some facts we allow in the economic field can be neither socialist nor capitalist, but can be evaluated as the objective requirement of the development law of productive forces, some things in the political field are neither socialist nor capitalist, but the objective requirement of the development of political life of human beings. These things do not belong the patent right asset of the bourgeoisie, but the favorable brilliant achievements of the development of modern political civilization of human beings."[2] In general, the advocates of "universal values" evaluate the universal nature of values from the perspective of some basic ideas of the Western world. They believe that "freedom, democracy and human rights" as the mainstream bourgeois ideology of the West are "universal values" that transcends the cultures, governments and national boundaries and will suit every country.

1   Lu Liling, Ideology Needs to Advance with the Times, *Reform Internal Reference* (Decision), 2007(19).
2   Cai Xia, What Does Emancipation of Mind Require?, *Journal of Theoretic Trends*, No. 171.

Some scholars have put it more clearly: "In a few words, universal values refer to the advocacy of individual freedoms, economic independence, equality, democracy, human rights and these values are related with science and progress for the enlightenment of rationality in the history Western ideology". "These so-called universal values are the historical products of the modern and contemporary, and are supported by the modern and contemporary capitalist economy", "these universal values have led to universal suffrage which allows election of political leaders by with the principle of 'one person, one vote', the system of ruling by a multi-party parliament and other political systems" and so on, "the universal value of the world can be widely used". This scholar has specially emphasized that, there is a relatively long process from theory to practice and from the idea of universal values to be transformed to specific systems of a country, which determines that we cannot act with undue haste, and he has thoroughly analyzed both the academic position and practical political attitude of the advocates of "universal values."

The author believes that "in the course from the idea of universal values to the realistic specific system, there is not only a time course but also these two are not the same. It is known that the American Declaration of Independence has claimed everyone to be equal, but women in the United States could not enjoy equal voting rights till the last century and equality of the Blacks was gradually realized since after the North-South civil war until Martin Luther King to Barack Obama's presidency, thus affirming, advocating and publicizing universal values is not equal to the demanding the election of a president with the principle of "one person, one vote" and based on a ruling by multi-party parliament, because there are many different ways to realize democracy, even in Europe and the US, the specific systems of political democracy are not identical. So, on one hand, the universal values are the products of social and historical development during the certain period of time. During the global economic integration, they will inevitably spread to every region of the world, and guide people to a more prosperous, wealthy and happier life, and any religion, culture or traditional ideas cannot stop them. On the other hand, there is not a fixed pattern about how to realize these universal values in regions and societies with different religions, cultures and traditions. And this is the real difficulty and focus. This is also the case in China today. So I say that we cannot mechanically take the liberal way of the existing political system in Europe and the US, nor take ways of the New Left and the Chinese Culturalism School which completely deny the universal values."[3]

3   Li Zehou, On the Universal Value and the Chinese Model from the View of "Two Virtues", *Soochow Academic*, 2011(4).

Some scholars have more clearly emphasized that those "universal values" of the West including freedom, democracy, human rights, equality, humanitarianism, and the rule of law are correct ways which are the brilliant achievements of humankind throughout their social and political practice for a long time and can effectively promote the social progress, promote the harmonious society, meet people's wishes to live a happy life and realize the overall development of people in China and the world. In today's world, both in the East and the West, those countries with developed economies, strong comprehensive national strength and wherein the people live a prosperous and happy life are mostly the democratic countries. This fact can fully prove that freedom, democracy, human rights, equality, humanitarianism, rule of law, and other values are universally applicable values which are commonly shared by people of the whole world.[4] In addition to the above-mentioned views that regard freedom, democracy, human rights and other views from the West as the universal values, the views which support for the existence of "universal values" further expand the scope of the "universal values". There is a view which advocates that the cultures created by the entire humanity are the "universal values". Such as, someone thinks that caring for life valued by all the people is the "universal values". Someone even thinks that the cultures created by all human beings are "universal values", universal values are actually the common cultures created by all human beings including Chinese in the long river of history, and the denial of its existence means the denial of the existence of people as human beings.[5]

The advocates of "universal values" put forward another view against the opponents' viewpoints, emphasizing that the universality of "universal values" is not the universal recognition of people, but the universal applicability. The proposition of universal values is actually a necessary proposition rather than a practical proposition, so that the correctness of this proposition resorting to the general recognition by people is obviously the biased grasp of this proposition.[6] This is to say, "universal value" is universality, whether people admit it or not, it exists. There is quite a gap between regarding it as a very real thing and the practical demand of "universality".

There are scholars who agree with "universal values" from the perspective of Chinese culture. Some scholars argue that, there is indeed a universal pursuit in China's ancient tradition, and such a pursuit is a

---

4   Li Zhongqin, Do *"Universal Values" Require Everyone to Agree with them?, 21cn.net* (http://news.21cn.com/luiitaii/waiigyou/2008/12/03/5562460_1.shtml).

5   Wu Jiaxiang, *China Bursts out the "Civil War"?–Value Conflict, Tianju.net,* No. 19, 2008(6).

6   Li Zhongqin: "Universal value" Requires Everyone to Agree with it? 21cn.net (http://news.21cn.com/luntan/wangyou/2008/12/03/5562460_1.shtml).

transcendental idea which inspire many non-governmental organizations, and they strive for it.[7] It is also typical for this group of scholars to consider the Confucianism culture as being an "universal value". For example, some people stress that there are universal values among each national culture. For example, the Confucianism is considered through "benevolence" with the isochromatic color, and the Western Christianism is considered through "philanthropism" with the egalitarian color, though they took different logical ways, they are all of "universal values."[8] There are studies which demonstrate the "universality" of Confucian culture from the "people-oriented" point of view. Such as, someone thinks that the Confucian culture in China has a long history and what it advocates is a kind of universal culture, especially in terms of the thought in the Confucian culture that emphasizes moral education and character building by paying attention to the beginning with the governance of human heart and fundamentally solves the social problems by gradually becoming a kind of "value" necessary for the harmonious world. The social value system of contemporary China inherits and develops the essence of Chinese traditional culture; and its core and essence is "people-oriented."[9] There are scholars who take the case of the succeeding in applying the Grand Canal for the heritage to demonstrate the intersection between the Chinese culture and universal values. The standard of the world heritage Convention is the universal value firstly discovered by the western people, and we should combine it with the Chinese culture. It should be emphasized that the Chinese culture and values should be mutually blended with foreign cultures based on the publicity and historicity.[10]

Supporters of "universal values" are also looking for evidence from the texts of Marx and Engels for the existence and advocate of the "universal values". This is an important strategy to get affirmation for existence of "universal values". Accordingly, some scholars have argued that the universal values not only exist, but also are the intrinsic, inherent and profound nature of the existence of all values. They wrote: "this point can obtain strong evidence and profound enlightenment from the classic discussion by Marx on the duality of labor. Marx, with this discussion, divided the general labor of human beings from the specific labor, and in this way, has revealed the secret of capitalist relations of

7   *Prasenjit Duara Talks about "Universal Value" in Chinese Tradition, Oriental Morning Paper,* May 6, 2012.

8   Tang Yijie, *Looking for the Universal Value in Culture, Aisixiang.net* (http://www.aisixiang.com./data/23121.html).

9   "Olympic Social Responsibility" Activates Universal Value, *China Industry and Economy News,* January 30, 2008.

10   Xie Guangqian, Gao Caixia, The Grand Canal: A Debate on the Universal Values and the Chinese Way, *China Culture Daily,* February 21, 2013.

production"[11] Some scholars have also argued that, based on the texts of Marx and Engels, the concept of universal values do exist, and Marx did not deny universal values. Marx's basic idea on universal values (consensus of human civilization value) is: Existence of human, that is, the common humanity exists –so value consensus of human civilization exists– but the real identity of value consensus in the class society is an ideology of deception or the future ideal. From one point of view, the current denial of universal values is to reject the western interference in China; but looking from another point of view, scientifically it is difficult for the "universalists" to prove that Marxism is a universal which can be simply practiced by all classes and countries, Marxism is the guiding ideology of China which leades its cause of socialism with Chinese characteristics and Reform and Opening-up.[12]

Advocates of "universal values" have refuted the views of their opponents, and have argued that it is not proper to comment coarsely this or that on "universal values". Some scholars have stressed that universal values cannot be totally denied: firstly, universal values exist objectively. Secondly, universal values cannot be totally denied; thirdly, when there is an argument, it is necessary to correctly deal it with different views, from different aspects. That people are always divided into factions refers to the difference. However, besides differences, there is the common essence between people, between ethnic groups, classes, as well as the East and the West. In the past, the common essence was not emphasized enough. Human beings have a common ideal. For example, that "do not impose on others what you do not desire" can be seen as the common value of human beings. Therefore, there is "one world, one dream", which is the premise of the "harmony" we advocate. Therefore, universal values objectively exist. The objective existence of universal values cannot be totally denied because the values held by some people or the values of a place are called "universal values". The total denial of universal values is not conducive for us to learn from foreign advanced ideas and advanced mechanism, and is not conducive for the Chinese culture to step into the world, because when you have rejected the premise, it would equally mean that you have also denied the foundation of communication and dialogue. It will inevitably lead to "cultural relativism", and it also does not accord with the policy of Reform and Opening-up of the central authorities.[13] Some scholars have further stressed that the denial of universal values will pose a challenge for human civili-

11   Pi Jiasheng, Universal Value Identification, *Jianghan Tribune,* 2009(8).
12   Huang Lizhi, Karl Marx and Friedrich Engels did not Deny Universal Values, *Exploration and Free Views*, 2012(11).
13   Gao Zhanxiang, *Universal Value Cannot be Denied Wholly, Aisixiang.net* (http://www.aisixiang.com./data/27207.html).

zation and will mean the denial of the value of our civilization. Honesty and patience, industriousness and prosperity, equality and humanitarianism, freedom and democracy, tolerance and harmony and righteousness and reason (rationalism) and so on, which can represent benign natures of human beings, can be classified as the categories of universal values.[14]

There is also a more prominent point of view utilized to refute the opponents, i.e. some prominent scholars have cited certain speeches of the CPC leaders who have underlined that "universal values" cannot be totally negated or affirmed; and this scholar has argued that the "people oriented", "building a harmonious society" and "Scientific Outlook on Development" and so on proposed by leaders of the CPC have "universal" value and they can be defended as such. This scholar has argued that, in recent years, Chinese Party and state leaders have affirmed that there are "common points" and "common universal principles" or "universal values" in the international community, between East and the West in terms of "human rights" and other issues. This scholar has also stressed that there is "no unitary mode" and it is necessary to "start from the basic national conditions". Specific measures taken by every country and nation to "protect the human rights and forms of democracy should be different". This is a comprehensive and correct attitude. In contrast, are the current ideas of "fully copy the West" and "fully reject the West" biased or not?[15]

Scholars who do not believe that there are the so-called "universal values" and advocate a specific and dialectical view of democracy, the rule of law, freedom and others have made a more in-depth analysis of these concepts. They mainly put forward the following views:

Firstly, it is necessary to pay attention to the distinction between several levels to recognize the issue of "universal values". Some scholars have argued that when people use the concept of "universal values", there are three levels including mass discourse, academic discourse and political discourse. From the perspective of mass discourse, the term "universal values" was first introduced by scholars, and then gradually become the discourse of the considerable part of the intellectuals and the mass media. For example, in terms of being ready to help others, caring for the disabled, "one world, one dream", the Olympic spirits and the spirit of earthquake relief, which can easily arouse people's sympathy, some authors use "universal values" to express ideas, emotions or behaviors with the consensus. From

14   Xu Guojin, *The Struggle of Universal Value and the Direction of Chinese Culture*, China Value Net (http://www.chinavalue.net/General/Article/2009-1-22/155939.html).
15   Wu Ge, Thought Fragments about Discussion on the Universal Value, *To Pull Together in Times of Trouble*, 2009(2).

the perspective of academic discourse, when some scholars are discussing the issue of "universal values", they do not necessarily have political intention, but mainly discuss it from an academic point of view. The third level is the level of political discourse. Now, the thing to be guarded and paid attention to is promoting the abstract "universal values" at political level. The issue of "universal values" on the political level is of strong class and ideology as well as confusion. Defining a kind of "value" such as democracy, freedom, etc. with the title of "universal" to refer to and express a kind of political appeal is a logical contradiction in theory and lacks the factual basis in reality.[16]

Secondly, the "universal values" is not a rigorous scientific concept. Some scholars propose that "from the perspective of the relationship between the subject and object, the so-called universal values are eternal and universal values which are universally applied to all people. According to this definition, the things in the form of concept are difficult to be universal in the true sense. Furthermore, from the development of human history, there have been no "universal values" that have been constant since ancient times and universally applied to all people, "the so-called absolute universal values that apply to all people, all times, all locations and cannot be transferred in any conditions do not exist in fact."[17]

Besides, the scholars have proposed that people's judgment on the value of the objective things is a concept, which belongs to the category of the superstructure and the connotation of which is determined by the economic base. Therefore, the content of value concept and the standard for people's judgment of value are constantly changing with the change of social economic relations. Under different social economic relations, people give the same value idea with completely different connotations. That is to say, the value is historical, not eternal and invariable. From the perspective of the development history of human society, there is no eternal value that is universally applicable to all societies. "The judgment of some people on the 'universal values' is logically contradictory, and the 'universal values' they talk about is not really 'universal', but only the values of certain parts of the people."[18]

---

16 Hao Lixin, Awareness of "Universal Value" Issues should Pay Attention to the Distinction between Several Levels, recorded in Eight People Talk about the "Universal Value", *Journal of Ideological & Theoretical Education,* 2008(11).

17   Zhen Yan, Some Cognitive Problems of "Universal Value", *Beijing Daily*, June 16, 2008.

18   Zhou Xincheng, The "Universal Value" Advocated by Some People is Essentially the Value of the West, recorded in: Eight People Talk about the "Universal Values", *Journal of Ideological & Theoretical Education*, 2008(11).

Therefore, "it is necessary to see clearly that the concept of 'universal values' itself is very fuzzy and abstract, lack of scientificity, clarity, and serious scholars rarely use this term to characterize specific common ideas or values in the social reality."[19]

Thirdly, do not regard the Western values as universal values, and reject its being used as a label. A theory points out that "if every country or nation regards its own values as universal values and other cultures as the opposite or appendage of the universal values, the universal values will become a card at the mercy of the hands of the people, as a label, and can be randomly identified according to their own standard. In history, many people tried to impose their own values on others, and they failed in the end."[20] Therefore, "Western civilization, like other civilizations, includes both the content of the common values and the content of the special values. Different countries or regions cannot invariably clone the pattern of Western democracy and the ideal of freedom, but they should have their own unique ways to realize it.[21]

V.3. Should China accept the "Universal Values"?

The advocates of embracing "universal values" propose that China should accept the universal values based on the premise that there indeed exists universal values. They expound their propositions from three levels: Firstly, they propose that China should accept universal values. In the view of the theory, they advocate a broad concept of "rationality" and propose "we should embrace the universal values based on rational thinking," …. "There would be no factions if we think rationally. There would be only one faction—the faction of seeking truth from facts," "to embrace universal values means, affirming the reason and making the rational choice." "The core of human civilization is the value standard which embodies universal characteristics formed in the development of long term evolution by human beings and the basic system provided by these universal standards," "any nation should join this universal path of the whole world system and arrive the common final destination of system evolution", "the Party should estab-lish an affinity with the universal human civilization and display the will to bear the historical duty for such a shift while it cannot accommodate nega-tive aspects of its own characteristics, human civilization and a node edge, willing to bear the historical duty. To achieve such change the Party should

---

19   Hao Lixin, *Awareness of "Universal Value" Issues Should Pay Attention to the Distinction between Several Levels,* Recorded in *Eight People Talk about the "Universal Value", Journal of Ideological & Theoretical Education,* 2008(11).
20   Zhen Yan, Some Cognitive Problems of "Universal Value", *Beijing Daily,* June 16, 2008.
21   Ibid.

not indulge in its own characteristics, instead it should actively create the conditions to dig its own social resources, resolutely embrace the universal values of human civilization, and look ahead to join the common civilization of the future at a faster pace", "for, us the universal values should not be sacrificial offerings, just to accommodate national flavor. We should explore and find the positive elements of our historical heritage, abandon those elements that deviate from universal values, and also strive to reach the basic social and economic system affirmed by the universal values of human civilization, strive towards and firmly push Chinese nation into the mainstream of world civilization."[22]

They add that if China wants to carry out Reform and Opening-up, it must integrate into the mainstream of human civilization and recognize the universal values. "The vital source of China's social problems, indeed, lies in the despotism and its centralized system. After the Party came to power, a centralized system with unrestricted ruling power was established, and Party members and citizens were not entitled with democratic rights. This course has discarded the mainstream of achievements of modern human civilization and even deviated from it. If China wants to follow the path of Reform and Opening-up and deepen it, it must integrate into the mainstream of human civilization, democracy, science and the rule of law, recognize the universal values, and integrate with the world civilization."[23] They also argue that the rejection of the US and British democracy means using the pretext of "Chinese specificity" in order to resist democratization of China. "Both the central government and people from all walks of life have recognized the value of universal democracy. But there are also some people who resist and advocate deliberative democracy, to belittle parliamentary democracy, and advertise democracy with Chinese characteristics to block universal democracy." "Once the democracy was established achieved, it has assumed an universal significance, since the establishment of democracy in the United Kingdom, and the United States, 2/3 of the world countries have embraced democracy, which means its universal qualities are obvious. Now, some people in China argue that we do not need to use the British and US democracy, "Chinese specificity" is the subtext of their argument strategy, to reject China's approach towards universal democracy, but it is pointless."[24] "Before the 1980s, the argument against universal de-

---

22   Dang Guoying, Based on the National Characteristics to Embrace Universal Values, *South Weekend,* October 25, 2007.

23   Li Rui, Li Chang and the Generation of the December 9th Movement, *Yanhuang Chunqiu,* 2008(4).

24   Thought is breaking through, the reform needs to open — Interview record of Zhu Xueqin (Book One), Nanfang Metropolis Daily, December 30, 2007.

mocracy was mainly based on the so-called class theory, but this kind of irrational and weak argument is not worth refutation. Then the accusation wave of "Total Westernization" was fabricated against universal democracy has emerged, which created confusion among the intellectuals and young people about what is right and wrong. Now, we are in the third stage, in order to block the universal democracy, they have engages in another set of logic, the so-called "deliberative democracy."[25]

Secondly, they have argued that Chinese leadership is affirming the universal values including human rights, rule of law, fairness, justice, freedom, equality and fraternity. For example, a scholar has argued: "after 30 years of Reform and Opening-up, China has gradually been re-integrated into the world civilization; and the universal values including human rights, rule of law, fairness, justice, freedom, equality and fraternity became the core values of our civilization."[26] The process of Reform and Opening-up is the process for Chinese scholars to learn "universal values" and accept the "universal values". "Since the Reform and Opening-up, the process the CPC has been going through is, the process of constantly learning and practicing the universal values of humankind. The economic development and social progress of China has been the inevitable outcome of this process. The CPC, has abandoned the ultra-left political line and chose the statecraft taking economic construction as the central task, and gradually formed the ideology which elevated the concept of "people-oriented" development to the core status, which means that the most important connotation of universal human values has been affirmed by the CPC."[27]

Nanfang Metropolis Daily, wrote enthusiastically: "The report of the 17th National Congress of the CPC has expounded on manifested this point. "We have seen that many concepts a lot of universal values have been included written into the report of the 17th National Congress of the CPC this year, such as including democracy, freedom, and justice, rule of law, human rights and human dignity, and which have been integrated into the system of socialist core values."[28]

Thirdly, they propose that China should continue to emancipate the minds and establish the "universal values" and argue that the emancipation of mind in fact aimed to establish the "universal values". "Whether it is economic,

---

25   Ibid.

26   Yuan Xucheng, Retrospect and Prospect of China's Reform and Opening-up in 3 Years, *Reform Internal Reference*, 2008(12).

27   Dang Guoying, Based on the National Characteristics to Embrace Universal Values, *South Weekend*, October 25, 2007.

28   The National Honor System Should Be Based on Universal Human Values, *Nanfang Metropolis Daily*, December 17, 2007.

political or social, cultural or theoretical innovation, we must take the universal values as the scale, that is, view development in tandem with freedom and common happiness as our criterion."[29] Emancipation of minds should have the main goal; the main goal is the value system, and the emancipation of minds is to establish universal values. Emancipating the minds from the people-oriented level. People-oriented approach is an outline, and to implement this outline, we need a set of universal values including democracy, freedom and human rights, and the transformation of values. If the universal values cannot be established, the result will not be people-oriented. So the question of values is a fundamental problem for the destiny of China.[30]

They argue that the focus of the emancipation of minds is the reform of the political system, and the overall goal of the reform of the political system should be the establishment of constitutionalism: "regarding the emancipation of minds in China, there are not great obstacles in the economic field, and people are free to discuss anything. There are only obstacles in the political field. The focus of the emancipation of minds is to solve the problem of the reform of the political system." "What should be the goal of political reform? The overall goal of the new round of political reform, of course, should be the constitutionalism. Then, what is constitutionalism? There is a basic consensus among jurists about that constitutionalism is the combination of democracy, rule of law and human rights."[31] "Change the "people-oriented" expression into the "civil rights-oriented" expression, and establish a civil rights-oriented society. In this way, we can begin to integrate with a series of mainstream concepts such as democracy and constitutionalism in the world."[32]

Scholars who have argued that there are no so-called "universal values" in the world have criticized the view that China should get close to and accept the "universal values". They put forward the following main points. Firstly, they have pointed out that the discourse promoting the "universal values" have a clear political orientation. Some scholars have suggested in recent years that the public opinions which promote the "universal values" are concentrated on

---

29 Zheng Yanchao, To Emancipate the Mind Requires Courage, Determination, and Dedication–View Collection of Ideological Emancipation Forum, *South Weekend*, March 27, 2008.

30 Wang Zhanyang, Emancipating the Mind Requires Courage, Determination, and Dedication–Views Collection of Ideological Emancipation Forum, *South Weekend*, March 27, 2008.

31   Cai Dingjian, Emancipating the Mind Requires Courage, Determination, and Dedication —Views Collection of Ideological Emancipation Forum, *South Weekend*, March 27, 2008.

32 Wu Si, Emancipating the Mind Requires Courage, Determination, and Dedication — Views Collection of Ideological Emancipation Forum, South Weekend, *South Weekend*, March 27, 2008.

democracy, freedom, human rights and privatization and other issues, and this is not accidental. In the process in which we adhere to perfecting and developing of the socialist system through reform, this is a means by which some of the forces at home and abroad instruct us their propositions and demands of Total Westernization under the banner of "universalism" in their attempts to change China's socialist system. While some of the articles interpret the "emancipation of minds" stressed by the 17th National Congress of the CPC as "we should pursue the "universal values"; some indiscriminately interpret the socialist democracy and the rule of law, fairness and justice, poverty alleviation and realization of modernization underlined in the Party's documents into the selection of "universal values"; some even say "the universal values should not be toward sacrificial offerings to accommodate the national characteristics", it is necessary to turn our face to the "universal value system" and "embrace the universal values". "This is certainly a confusion and wrong proposal, inconsistent with the basic theory of the Party, and it is also contrary to the spirit of the 17th National Congress of the CPC."[33]

There is a theory advocating that the notion of "universal values" is not a purely academic issue, but has a clear political purpose. Since the Reform and Opening-up, there has been a sharp struggle in the ideological field, and this kind of struggle will exist for a long time. Advocating the "universal values", and elevating democracy, freedom, equality and human rights in the capitalist countries in the West to the "universal values", then using the standard to measure the practice of socialism with Chinese characteristics, accusing that it does not work, requiring transforming China in accordance with the strategic intent of the West, regarding the multi-party system in the developed capitalist countries in the West as universal, unique democratic system, attacking the multi-party cooperation, joint consultation system under the leadership of the CPC, saying it "goes its own way", requiring the "constitutional reform"; declaring the democracy, freedom, equality, fraternity of the bourgeoisie as core values shared by all human beings means to give up the socialist core value system guided by Marxist ideology. "In fact, this point of view does not discuss academic issues, it demands total westernization.[34] Secondly, it is argued that the key for promoting the idea of "universal values" is to negate national characteristics. Some scholars point out that the essence of "universal values" proposal is to negate Chinese characteristics, and attempt to use a model to plan the path for development of all countries and the nations in the world. "In fact, the national conditions of different countries are different, the

---

33 Feng Yuzhang, How to Understand the So-called "Universal Values", Research on Marxism, 2008(7), *People's Daily*, Reprinted and extracted on September 10, 2008.
34 The Research Center of Deng Xiaoping Theory and the Important Thought of "Three Represents", Ministry of Education: Some Problems of "Universal Value", *Qiushi*, 2008(2).

paths for development are different, and the values are also diverse, full of their own characteristics, the so-called 'universal values' of the West cannot be applied for all countries."[35] Some scholars have argued that the "democratic universal theory" is not consistent with the trend of China's political development path and the elements relationship. "The practice fully proves that the political system of China is the organic unity of the class nature, practicality and scientificalness of the Marxist democracy. It is the inheritance and development of the Marxist democratic theory in the new era. Since practice is the sole criterion for testing the truth, we have no reason for not sticking to the system model that has been proved to be successful. It is very clear that the proposition of "democratic universal theory" cannot meet the practical needs of the path of socialist political development with Chinese characteristics and the construction of democracy and legal system.[36]

Scholars have argued that the significance of the "universal values" debate should deepen study of and use the basic views and methods of the Marxism, clear the fog on the issue, establish China's basic views on this issue, to help to disclose the essence of the wrong trends of thoughts cloaked with the mantle of "universal values", which means we should develop our initiative in ideological work and consolidate the guiding position of the Marxism.[37]

Thirdly, analyzing the reason for the formation and development of the theory of "universal values". Typical view is that in the process of the rise of the "universal values", the domestic factors play a major role, and the international impact aggravates the situation. The main reasons are that the exchange, blending and confrontation of all kinds of ideology and culture in the world is increasingly frequent, and the struggle between infiltration and anti-infiltration is still acute and complicated. In China, the reform of economic system is profound, the changes of social structure are profound, the adjustment of pattern of interests is profound, the trend of pluralistic, diversity and changeability of the domestic social thoughts is more prominent, the independence, selectivity and changeability and difference of thought activities of people are significantly enhancing; modern media including the Internet change rapidly and became the important channel for domestic and foreign hostile forces to manufacture and spread anti-China public opinion and carry out ideological penetration, they spread a lot of harmful

35 Mao Xiaogang, Whether The Key of "Universal" Determines the Characteristic, *Beijing Daily* June 15, 2008.

36 Chen Hongtai, How to Understand the Essence of "Democratic and Universal Theory"?, Eight People Talk about the "Universal Value", *Journal of Ideological & Theoretical Education*, 2008(11).

37 Feng Yuzhang, How to Understand the So-called "Universal Value", *Research on Marxism*, 2008(7), *People's Daily,* Reprinted and extracted on September 10, 2008.

information, try to discredit China, slander and demonize China. In addition, the weak link in the field of ideology is also an important reason for
the rise of the trend of "universal values": misunderstanding of "no debate"
in the political field, ambiguity in the ideological struggle; the tendency of
Westernization in the academic field, and some scholars blindly following
the Western thought trends; dilution of ideology in the social field weakens
the influence of Marxist ideology and socialist values and blurs the distinction between socialist values and Western values among some members of
the Party, cadres and the masses, especially young students.[38]

Some scholars have stressed that the "universal values" theory makes use
of some social striking points, which is a new feature of the recent publicity of the thought trends of the "universal values". For example, distortion
of "four advocates" in the report of the 18th National Congress of the CPC
and misinterpretation of winning speech by Mo Yan and so on, campaigns
through the current events, and tries to confuse the public.[39]

Fourthly, revealing the essence of the "universal values" theory. The typical view is that the essence of "universal values" is to challenge the socialist
core value system, and try to change the path of China's political development. Its political essence is attempting to change the guiding ideology and
socialist orientation for China's development of democratic politics and the
deepening of the political reform, using the "universal values", which consists of Western political philosophy and system modes, to transform the political system in China; Its ideological orientation aims to abolish the guiding
position of Marxism, replace with the construction of socialist core value
system with the Western bourgeois values, and carry out a diversification
in the guiding ideology; its orientation of economic system aims to create a
public opinion for an overall privatization, demolish the economic foundation of the primary stage of socialism with public ownership as the main
body.[40] Some scholars have argued that the "universal values" idea works
as a political tool of Western hegemonism. Western hegemonism describes
democracy as the only correct and rational universal value, and demands that
all countries—especially socialist countries—should follow and imitate. It is
clear that hegemonism aims to achieve the goal of overthrowing socialism

38 Yu Fan, *To Clarify the Fog of the "Universal Value", Adhere to the Guiding Position of the Marxism*, Longevity News Network (http://www.ccs.cn/jrgz/xxxdzz/news/2010-11/2460_61810.shtml).
39 Liu Shulin, "Contraband" coated by Theory of "Universal Values", *People's Tribune*, 2013(1).
40 Yu Fan, *To Clarify the Fog of the "Universal Value", Adhere to the Guiding Position of the Marxism*, Longevity News Network http://www.ccs.cn/jrgz/xxxdzz/news/2010-11/2460_61810.shtml.

and dominate the world.[41] Some scholars have pointed out that the "signifier" of the "universal values" is very broad, and a direct rejection of the "universal values" seems causing China to lose the right to speak in many ways and puts it into a passive position. But the "implication" of such a discourse is obvious, which means to carry out a subversive publicity against the political direction of our country, against its basic path and fundamental system, and its discourse coincides with the current hostile forces which use value infiltration to heat up the plot of "Differentiation" and "Westernization" against China.[42] Some scholars have further pointed out that the essence of the problem of the "universal values" theory, "aims to strengthen its demonstration power by trying to declare the values it believes or prefers as "universal values", to persuade or force others to accept its own values and political ideals". This is a common strategy for people to try to change the existing value system and political order, and it only selected other concepts including logos, concept, natural reason, God and natural law when the concept of "universal values" was not created. From a historical point of view, these values under aforementioned banners are only the values of a certain age, a certain class or a certain tradition.[43]

Fifthly, views debating against and pointing to the errors of the "universal values" theory. These views can be mainly analyzed from three aspects:

Firstly, the "universal values" theory ignores the complexity of the value issue. Some scholars have stressed that the value problem is highly complicated, and the concept of universal values obscures this complexity. First, it easily regards the value with specific social attributes and the content that is formed on a certain historical stage as the value of surpassing time and space Secondly, it easily simplifies the values which are full of differences and inner conflicts, thus ignoring the differences, contradictions and conflicts about them. Thirdly, it easily confuses the difference between scientificalness criterion issue and value criterion issue. Fourthly, it easily develops the metaphysical thinking by viewing the problem from a non-historical or ahistorical view, thus falls into a misunderstanding of universalism, consequently arrives new kind of dogmatism. Fifthly, it easily provides an excuse for despotism and hegemonism.[44]

---

41   Eight People's Talk about the "Universal Values", *Journal of Ideological & Theoretical Education*, 2008(11).
42   Hou Huiqin, To Break the Illusion with Truth: Why the View of "Universal Values" must be Criticized, *Research on Marxism*, 2009(3).
43   Ma Depu, Walk out of the Logical Dilemma of "Universal Values", *Chinese Social Sciences Press*, April 23, 2012.
44   Ma Depu, The Complexity of Value Problem and the Misleading of the Concept of "Universal Value", *Political Science Research*, 2009(1).

Some scholars have made their criticism from a philosophical level. They have argued that the "universal values" discussed here belong to the philosophical value theory. Value has its objective basis, but the difference between people's perceptions of value and the pursuit is too great. When "democracy" is taken as an example, the democratic model in the United States is known as the model of Western democracy. What is the so-called universal model of democracy? The democracy, as the dominant form and the form of the State, has always been hierarchical and historical, and there is no pure democracy, universal democracy that is non-hierarchical and trans-historical. It is claimed that democracy will die out and it will be replaced by "the association of free men" with the perishing of classes and the state. Obviously, the absolute and eternal "universal democracy" or "universal value" of democracy does not exist at all. Scholars have stressed that there has never been a "abstract democracy", "pure democracy" or "universal democracy."[45] There has only been a kind of hierarchical democracy under certain historical conditions. So in Marxist words, there has always been a distinction about the concept of democracy such as the bourgeois democracy, proletarian democracy, capitalist democracy and socialist democracy. These prefixes of democracy are essential, they underline the class nature of democracy and the essence of democracy.[46]

Secondly, the "universal values" becomes the captive of the "Western centralism". Some studies have stressed that some scholars insist on "west-centered theory" by completely identifying the Western civilization with the universal values, and regarding the non-Western civilization as authentic values, just as Huntington said "the concept of universal civilization is the unique product of western civilization", which exaggerates the universal value in the Western civilization and also universalizes the authentic values. Outstanding performance in the reality is that some countries assume themselves as the inventor, monopoly owner and exporter of the universal values, including human rights, freedom and democracy. The Western civilization was established on the theory of absolute universalization of Western values while on the one hand, regarding various non-Western civilizations and values as its anti-thesis, and on the other hand, with economic sanctions, diplomatic blockade and political subversion, power assertion and other means to promote the things that they see as the universal values. If the universal value is popular, it will inevitably lead to the effusiveness of the extreme nationalism, and it is a serious violation of human dignity and human civilization.[47]

---

45   Zhong Zheming, Some Thoughts on Problem of "Universal Values", *Journal of Ideological & Theoretical Education*, 2009(3).
46   Wang Tingyou, "Universal Value" is a False Proposition, *Political Science Research*, 2008(6).
47   Zhen Yan, Some Cognitive Problems of "Universal Value", *Beijing Daily*, June 16, 2008.

Third, it is argued that the "universal values" theory is contrary to the historical materialism. Some scholars have stressed that advocating "universal values" is a kind of thought with strong Western Christian cultural characteristics. It is believed that there is a timeless, universal and eternal value system or institutional specification, and it is one of the main characteristics of western liberalism, and it is a typical attitude of historical idealism. At this point, we should say that democracy and other systems, ideals or values with or without "universal" character should be subjects of an in-depth research through the adoption of methodology of world outlook of dialectical materialism and historical materialism in order to draw the correct understanding and conclusions.[48] Some scholars have studied and argued that the bourgeoisie, like other exploiting classes, tend abstract discourse, and fears specific analysis. The bourgeoisie has always been practicing abstractly talking about people, humanity, freedom, equality, democracy, human rights and other good things and it also speaks for all mankind.[49] Some scholars have further emphasized that the "universal values" theorists ignore such a basic fact: freedom, democracy, equality and justice we mention is neither abstract things, nor the concepts of the West. In our country, these concepts not only have the provisions of their own ideological connotation, but also have the provisions of the socialist law. For example, the democracy we mention refers to the people's democracy of socialism, and is essentially different from the bourgeois democracy of the taking power through a multi-party system as the West publicizes.[50]

Sixthly, emphasizing the proper attitude and strategy in the face of "universal values". We will mainly propose four aspects as below:

Firstly, we should abandon the term of "universal values", and avoid a discourse which will easily cause confusion and misunderstanding. For example, we can use the concept of "basic values", "core values", "shared values" or "consensus values" to replace the concept of "universal values". This is not a meaningless quibble or a simple concept game, but an approach which claims that there are significant differences between different ways of thinking and different practice effect. Such an alternative will not conflict with the progress of civilization and the development of history, but only reduce the harm it may bring to the society.[51]

---

48   Tian Gaiwei, See the Historical Idealism behind "Universal Value", *Chinese Soul*, 2012(5).
49   Wen Ping, Analysis of "Universal Value" Identification, *Red Flag Manuscript,* 2009(1).
50   Liu Shulin, "Contraband" coated by Theory of "Universal Values", *People's Tribune*, 2013(1).
51   Ma Depu, The Complexity of Value Problem and the Misleading of the Concept of "Universal Value", *Political Science Research*, 2009(1).

Secondly, we should view the academic debate from a political level, and try to offset the harm and impact of the "universal values". All ideologies have distinct class natures and party spirits, and there is nothing wrong in judging the striking issues and difficulties in the field of ideology from the perspective of politics. It is necessary to clearly understand the weakness of promoting the "universal values". We should not regard the "universal values" as a fashionable term, and compromise with other people about their arguments. We should view the proposition and the tendency of "universal values" within the perspective of consolidating the guiding position of Marxism and doing a good job in ideological work, recognize the harm, and clear the impact.[52]

Thirdly, we should not hold a nihilistic attitude towards the "value consensus" that has been formed in the progress of human civilization and in the process of cultural exchanges, instead we should actively establish and strengthen our own discourse in the "value issue". We cannot take a dismissive and attitude of simple negation towards democracy, freedom and human rights, etc., while giving due attention and appreciation to the achievements of world civilization, and we should pursue for the concepts of freedom, democracy and human rights which are proper for the development of our nation and the country. We should maintain the position of "harmony but not sameness", and pursue the "common win" effects and raise the banner of "fairness and justice". When the status of China is rising in the world history, it should put forward its clear view on the existing shared value according to its tradition, it always must have been vigilant about the trap of the "universal values" and put forward new values from the standpoint of majority of the people in the world.[53]

Fourthly, strengthening the construction of socialist core value system. It is argued that such a big controversy caused by the "universal values" is closely related with the fact that some people do not have a clear belief. Today is an era in which the belief is in a haze but gradually becoming clear and civilized, and we must strengthen the construction of the core value system.[54] Marxism is the soul of the socialist core value system, and we should vigorously strengthen the attraction of the socialist core value system and its interaction and cohesion with the other thought trends, in order to realize the leading role of the socialist core value system. Some scholars

---

52   Eight People Talking on the "Universal Values", *Journal of Ideological & Theoretical Education*, 2008(11).

53   Xiang Lanxin, "Universal Value" or "Share Value"?, *Lianhe Zaobao*, September 3, 2008.

54   Huang Mingli, On the Question of the Universal Ethics Question–Also on the Basis of the Moral Belief from the Universal Ethics, *Journal of Nanjing Normal University* (Social Science Edition), 2007(2).

have emphasized how to construct values in China based on scientific criteria by taking Marxist theories, and historical materialism as the core system, and this is a crucial matter for current researchers and communicators of Marxism, and such a positive spirit in the ideological field will give a huge positive boost to social practice.[55]

V.4. Theoretical issues regarding the "Universal Values" thought trend

The social influence of any thought trend is related to many factors. The crucial condition depends on the corresponding level of this thought trend to social practice and people's life. Besides, such a social effect is also determined by theoretical thoroughness whether the thought trend can achieve satisfactory results when it is put into practice or not. The core element of a political thought trend is theoretical and practice property. This book will focus on the analysis on possible dilemma that the thought trend of universal value may encounter at theoretical and practical level.

V.4.1. Ambiguities in the of connotation "Universal Values" theory from the aspect of values

"Value" and "values" are two philosophical concepts, which are not equivalent. In the thought trend of universal values theory, there is a problem of equating "value" with the "values". According to the understanding of this thought trend, it actually talks about values, but not the value itself. The connotation of value is determined by the effect of the object on a subject. On this basis, value is an objective reflection on the relationship between subject and object. Therefore, value is objective and will not change according to different subjects. But such objectivity is also not absolute. The effectiveness of a certain object on subject will change. So to speak, the value that reflects the objective relationship between object and subject has the so-called "universal" meaning in a certain sense and within a certain scope. At the same time, the problem is that the "value" mentioned by the thought trend of universal value is not really value but values. Values are a kind of subjective judgment by subject on the effectiveness of object. The property of values is determined by the cognition of subject. Different subjects will generate different views about the same object. Hence, such values obtain a distinct subjectivity. If we acknowledge and affirm this, values cannot be "universal". The "universal value" equates "value" with "values", which will form an insurmountable obstacle in philosophy. The

---

55   Wang Tingyou, "Universal Value" is a False Proposition, *Political Science Research*, 2008(6).

thought trend of universal value deems democracy, freedom, equity and human right as values which are applicable everywhere and as values standard that can be applicable at any time. This identification emphasizes the generality and commonality of values, but ignores their specificity and subjectivity. Therefore, it will be inevitably questioned on academic level.

V.4.2. "Universal Values" theory does not correspond to and coincide with the dominant ideology

The structure of any social consciousness is complicated. On the whole, the consciousness structure of modern society adopts ideology as its core. In the field of ideology, the dominant ideology normally refers to a theoretical and ideological system advocated by the ruling party and recognized by most of the citizens, which is elevated to the level of national consciousness. In addition to the dominant ideology, there also non-dominant ideologies which co-exist. These non-dominant ideologies mostly exist in the form of social thought trends, the main body of which are the political thought trends. Those most influential and long-lasting social thought trends are generally the political thought trends. In most cases, there is a "quiet complicated" relationship between the dominant ideology and non-dominant ideologies. They can be in accordance or discordance. And there may exist conflicts or compromises. In respect of function, the dominant ideology always keeps an eye on non-dominant ideologies and controls them.

Historically, the dominant ideology generally considers certain social thought trends as its adversaries. However, when the dominant ideology maintains its "pressure" on a certain non-dominant ideology, it will also have a certain degree of "acceptance" or tolerance. When society is in turmoil, the dominant ideology is often attacked by non-dominant ideologies from multiple sides. In this case, the dominant ideology does not maintain the ruling power as the term implies. During peace time, the dominant ideology will obtain broad recognition in society and take the leading position in the ideological field. In such cases, the survival of non-dominant ideologies is always closely related to the dominant ideology. If the dominant ideology is "threatened", it will inevitably take measures to restrict the survival of non-dominant ideologies. Therefore, for long-lasting survival, non-dominant ideologies tend to "compromise" with the dominant ideology in some aspects.

In contemporary China, the theoretical system of socialism with Chinese characteristics assumes the role of dominant ideology, which insists on the socialist path and also adapts to actual conditions of "primary stage socialism". The thought trend of "universal value" intensively challenges the dominant ideology, which undoubtedly pushes itself into a position against the dominant ideology. The theoretical basis of this thought trend is evidently featured by the Western theological culture, implying a transnational nature of mass and cosmopolitanism as proclaimed by theology. Such a theoretical basis is not consistent with our current guiding ideology of Marxism. If we acknowledge the legitimacy and correctness of this thought trend, the materialism, Marxism and the dominant ideology will be denied undoubtedly.

At present, China is in a critical period of the Reform and Opening-up. The reform in the field of economy has stepped into a deep level, which strongly claims for a political system reform. "Freedom, democracy and equity" and other value thoughts asserted by universal values are all based on Western civilization. Universal value treats the value thinking and development mode of Western countries as the unique universal standard. This is a West-centered theory, which will not be accepted by the dominant ideology in any case and will inevitably conflict against and be opposite to socialist dominant ideology. The thought trend of "universal values" has aroused extensive attention and dispute in academic circles. However, this thought trend never docks with the dominant ideology, which will certainly influence its future development.

V.4.3. "Universal Values" theory often faces frustrations in practice

The vitality of any social thought trend is derived from its relationship with practice. Those thought trends which can both display and re-act to practice normally can display strength and a long-lasting vitality. Those thought trends which accord with and can reveal the law of social development are generally accepted by the most social members, even can become the dominant ideology in society. These core ideas of democracy, freedom, equity asserted by the thought trend of "universal values" are often disproved in practice. Since the 1990s, Western countries launched many coups and "color revolutions" in the name of publicizing the "universal democracy" and "universal freedom", as well as opposing autocracy, despotism and dictatorship. Following the Rose Revolution in November 2003 in Georgia, the Orange Revolution in December 2004 in Ukraine and the Tulip Revolution in March 2005 in Kyrgyzstan; from the end of 2010 to the early of 2011, the Jasmine Revolution triggered a series of chain reaction, causing successive changes of the regimes in Tunisia, Algeria, Egypt, Jordan, Sudan, Oman, etc. During this period, there even occurred the Afghanistan

War and Iraq War which directly resorted to arms. In these countries, the ruling regimes were overthrown successively and new regimes were established based on a "template model" derived from the Western democracy. However, the harsh reality is that none of these countries have truly achieved democracy, freedom and equity. They were all trapped in the dilemma of national secession, ethnic antagonism, seperatism and religious conflict. At present, these countries are still in a serious chaos created by economic stagnation, social turmoil, and frequent terrorist activities and suffering poor people, without any hint of beautiful prospect proclaimed by the "universal values". But, during this process, Western countries have grabbed a large amount of resources and wealth and occupied many strategic areas, obtaining excessive benefits. Faced by such reality, the assertion of the thought trend of universal values is impaired more or less, causing it lose certain level of moral appreciation and support.

V.4.4. "Universal Values" theory cannot get rid of the label of "Political Discourse"

The thought trend of universal values insists on weakening or removing ideology, which seems a non-political statement. However, in view of its actual theoretical orientation, its obvious political nature is demonstrated in its inevitable label. In fact, political nature is the basic property of all political thought trends. Such political property is basically takes the dominant ideology as its targeted object, imbued with the implications of "reform or revolution". The thought trend of universal values cannot surpass its nature of political speech. In the process of actual publicity, people normally do not understand the term "universal" underlined by this thought trend from the perspective of generality, but still believe that the term "universal" is just an "excuse" and cannot get rid of its political implications. All social thought trends are comprised of a certain social psychology and ideology. If we emphasize the aspect of ideology too much, we will neglect the factor of social psychology, making social members in greater scope lose their interests in a thought trend. Psychosocial level tends to get not interested in the political content, but the thought trend of universal values always pays much emphasis on political aspect. This will greatly reduce the integration ability of the thought trend among social members. Besides, weakening of the ideological aspect and highlighting political appeal will inevitably make people lose their sense of identity and weaken the charisma of the thought trend and generate the feeling of indifference.

V.4.5. "Universal Values" theory trapped in "Debates"

During the over 30 years of Reform and Opening-up, the "Debates between Left and Right" has become the main trend in ideological and theoretical field. Around many issues, such as the so-called "reform and anti-reform", market and plan, and state and society, the Left and Right trends insist on their own opinions, throughout the whole course of the Reform and Opening-up. When we examine the pattern of ideological pattern of China, there also exist debates about Left and Right division among many other non-dominant trends. At present, the debate on universal value in academic circle once again reflects the debates between Left and Right in the ideological field. Without a transcendence over the major debate issues between the Left and Right, there will be no chance to explain Chinese issues or integrate chaotic phenomenon in China's ideological field at a deeper level. Since the Reform and Opening-up, the cause of China's modernization has formed its own mode along a brand new road and achieved outstanding accomplishment. The superstructure has also changed greatly. However, with the constant development of economy, society interest is continuously being divided, and different interest groups have different demands as to the pattern and orientation of the social development. In the field of ideology, this is also a key cause for the surge of various thought trends. Currently, our cause of Chinese modernization is going through a crucial stage, so the society indeed needs a brand new ideological and theoretical system which can integrate all social strata and overcome the social divisions and tensions. This fundamentally requires us to get rid of the debates between Right and Left, and enhance the cohesiveness in ideological field. Such kind of ideological discourse is vital. While, the "universal values" thought trend cannot transcend this dilemma of debates between Left and Right, which means this thought trend cannot surpass the themes advocated by non-dominant ideologies 30 years ago. It has no new theoretical creation, but still a new "resurgence" of an "old issue" to some degree.

To sum up, the theory of universal values emerged with claim that it has surpasses divisions of class and ideology, but still does not break through the dilemma of ideological struggle and have indulged deeply in the debates between Left and Right. It finally returns to the old topic of ideological struggle between capitalism and socialism and finally falls into the irreconcilable discourse contradiction which are in binary opposition.

CHAPTER SIX

Between State and Society – "Civil Society" Thought Trend

Power and right has always been an important category pair throughout the trends of political thoughts in the contemporary China. Their interpretation from different aspects leads to certain different trends of political thoughts with various manifestations. After all, the core appeal of the thought of "civil society" in contemporary China is still within the discourse of proceeding from the relationship of state and society which emphasizes private sphere, highlighting "individuals" and opposing the intervention of the political power into social life. This thought trend corresponds realistically to the reality of the profound adjustment of economic relationship in contemporary China and has reflected the new demands and requirements of the members of the society from the political power and the ruling party under the newly developed social pattern.

VI.1. Origin of civil society and its evolution

Since ancient Greece, the concept of "civil society" has been evolving for over 2,500 years. In different periods, the concept has assumed different connotations. Aristotle once said: "a polis (city) is a civil group". In ancient Greece, the concept was basically equal to the civil life in the city (polis). But when it came into the Middle Ages, the dark domination by religious theology made this concept disappear for a long time. With the Renaissance, the concept obtained a political nature. Since Modern Times, with the development of Western capitalist economy, the state and society began to separate and a civil society in the modern sense was born.

VI.1.1. Civil society in the ancient Greece and Rome

The civil society can be dated back to the concept of "political society (state)" presented by Aristotle. In his book Politics, Aristotle fully generalized and expounded this concept. He indicated that "every polis we see is some kind of a social group, and all social groups are established to display certain benign actions. In their eyes, each action of human aims to make a good consequence. Since all social groups deem good actions as their purpose, we can conclude that the highest and the most extensive social group will pursue the highest and the most extensive good action. Such kind of social group is polis, namely the political association."[1] Based on this statement, we believe that civil society is a relatively broad concept set. In ancient society, the civil society was a name contrary to the savage tribe, and it mainly referred to the advancement and development of civilization.

During the era of ancient Rome, the concept of civil society and its relating theories achieved certain progress. As advocated by Cicero, a famous politician, writer and philosopher of ancient Rome: "it refers to not only a single country but also the living state in a civilized political society that has been so developed that a city emerges."[2] The Romans, like the Greeks, have confused the civil society with state, and it was something beyond their level of cognition to divide these two concepts. However, the contribution of Cicero was that, he has used three concepts to define three levels: civil society, political society and civilized society, and he distinguished state's political life from the social political life. According to his opinion, civil society can be understood based on three aspects. Firstly, civil society includes urban civilization, which comprises of urban culture, various urban activities, civilized life in urban society, and those lives driven by commercial development. Secondly, civil society includes the political civilization. In such political civilization, it is the right and paramount duty for all citizens to participate in public affairs. And each citizen has the right and duty to participate in the state affairs. The political affairs of the state are no longer under the control of those nobles standing high above the masses but becomes the affair the society and the public. The state must set up a legal system which can be recognized, understood and used by every citizen to restrict the actions of these nobles. Law system turned to be the fundamental basis used by the public to manage and restrict the state. The old violent autocratic rule should not be accepted and recognized by people. Thirdly, civil society is a community. This means that in a civil society, people are guided by the moral ideas and norms of justice and fairness, which bonded

---

1   Aristotle, *Politics*, The Commercial Press, 1996, p. 58.
2   Cicero, *De Re Publica & De Legibus*, The Commercial Press, 2011, p. 81.

people as a united and interrelated group. The society will no longer be based on loose individuals. The masses in the society start to united to form a specific political power. However, with the historical development and change of era, the ancient Greece's polis and the ancient Rome disappeared successively and finally quited the historical stage. The civil society initially presented by Aristotle gradually lost the subject for practice. But, as a kind of political culture and trend of political thoughts, the concept was handed down and lasted till today, becoming a major ideological source for the development of society.

VI.1.2. Civil society in the Middle Ages

In the Middle Ages of Europe, people's lives were strictly imprisoned by the theological system. Civil society declined and perished in this age. As Marx indicated, "the spirit of the Middle Ages can be described as the following. The hierarchy in civil society was identical to the hierarchy in the political sense, because the civil society was a political society and the organic principles in civil society were the state principles.(an overlapping of the two)"[3] Although the state politics devoured the civil society, but the sprouts of some new political and social factors had become the source of civil society theories in modernity age. Firstly, evaluating the religious theology, people always involuntarily deem the Europe in the Middle Ages as a dark era. The religious theology controlled people's thoughts, which formed a heavy chain prisoning people's minds. During this period, people were politically suppressed by the feudal despotic state and mentally controlled by religious theology. Thus, the public lost the basic right to manage the state and social affairs, and failed to control the development and fate of the state. They were even deprived of some basic political rights. However, religious theology, as a power independent of the state, played another role. Clad in the sacred cloak of religion and faith, religious theology controlled and ruled the public. Essentially, it was an independent social form and organization, playing the role of social organization through the spiritual power. Such a two-way social structure led to a division in the society. And the society and the state started to be distinguished based on the concepts of right and obligation. The power of feudal politics was mainly reflected by its control on the state, while the power of religious theology by its control on society. This further separated the society from the state, enabling religion to restrict the state by social power and giving the society some autonomous right. This reflects the restriction on state power by social force which is always highlighted by civil society.

3   *Complete Works of Karl Marx and Frederick Engels,* Vol. 3, People's Publishing House, 2002, p. 90.

Secondly, at the end of the Middle Ages, civil society was rejuvenated and developed again. By the end of the 11th Century, the development in coastal cities in Italy promoted an urban revitalization. The strength of the bourgeois (citizen) stratum, as well as the industrial-commercial stratum was enhanced. Under such circumstances, these two stratums have won the political power and struggled for freedom and equity. Civil society started to thrive in Europe. With the increasing expansion of citizens' (bourgois) struggles and the constant development of their strength, many cities which have independence and autonomy were formed in Italy. Generally, these cities established their autonomous councils which were formed as a governing bodies of these cities. Most of the members of such city councils came from the bourgois class, which further developed the civil society in the cities. As some scholars indicated, "as autonomous communes (cities and towns) emerged and bourgois (citizen) stratum thrived, Western cities and towns all got rid of feudal constraints and gained further liberty and autonomy. They set up their own governments, parliaments and laws. Besides, there also emerged trade associations and new kind of handicraft associations. By the end of the Middle Ages, urban residents had obtained full freedom to deal with their privately owned assets, marry with their beloved, leave landlords or small land plots and immigrate to cities."[4] Some scholars also said that, "the development of bourgeois and citizen stratum implied the gradual disintegration of the European feudalism, as well as the rise and development of capitalist relations of production and the rise of the bourgeoisie. Such social change and relevant contradiction was inevitably found its reflections in the ideological field. Indeed, Europe witnessed the Renaissance and Enlightenment which are deemed as the prelude and the mental preparation for bourgeois revolution. In the struggle against the dynasty and the feudal autocratic monarchy, the concept of civil society and its theories had gained attention once more.[5]

VI.1.3. Birth of civil society in modern sense[6]

The theory of civil society was greatly promoted in the modernity age of the Western society. During this period, research on civil society has prospered, through which the basic theory and value system of civil society was formed. There existed a profound historical background for the great

4   Deng Zhenglai, Civil Society and the State —Division on Academic Principle and Two Kinds of Framework, *Chinese Social Science Quarterly (Hong Kong)*, 1993(5).
5   He Zengke, *Hope of Democracy or Idol, Chinese Social Science Quarterly (Hong Kong),* 1998(22).
6   Marx has made a clear distinction between, the ancient, old civil society and modern civil society.

advancement of civil society in this period. Firstly, in this period, capitalist economy had developed significantly with the exploration of new navigation routes. Traditional social structure started to break up and new social classes and strata came into being. These new modern classes and strata accelerated the division of society by creating the basic condition for the formation and development of civil society.

Secondly, the operation of market economy laid the conceptual foundation for the development of civil society. In its early stage, capitalist economy was completely governed by market. There formed a system of values, such as freedom, equity and voluntariness, which were the products of self-discipline in economic operation. Such economic base of self-operation and self-management corresponded to a social mode: civil society. Affected by market economy, the independence awareness, competitiveness awareness and especially civil consciousness were shaped. Finally, the development of market economy broke down the original social subject, represented by social groups, village groups and ethnic groups, and shaped a new social subject represented by the individual. This new social subject formed the subject of civil society, which laid basic social foundation for the development of civil society.

The civil society in modern sense corresponds to state power. As for the thought of civil society in modern sense, some scholars have concluded that, "its connotations show the prominent hint of ancient Greece and Rome, or in other words, it has not exceeded the meaning given by Aristotle and Cicero. It shows three main features. Firstly, civil society is deemed as a state of civilized, progressive and moral societal life. Secondly, it highlights the nature as a political society, believing that the main characteristic of civil society is that it contains some political civilization elements, such as government and law. This kind of political state does not oppose the civil society, but the human's natural state or sublation of the savage tribal life. Thirdly, the political society mentioned above is a civil society comprised of men being the members of a state, and so it is a political ethical society where every citizen can equally participate."[7]

Hobbes presented his theory of civil society under a certain premise. He believed that human first lived in a society which has been chaotic and lacked order. In such circumstances, the society was indulged in war and violence. Such state was generated because human as natural person all tried to defend his own rights and suppress others to satisfy his rights. In this state, "worst of all, people were constantly trapped in the fear and

---

7   He Zengke, The Historical Evolution of the Concept of Civil Society, *Social Sciences in China*, 1994(5).

danger of violence and death, and they lived lonely, poorly, lowly, cruelly and shortly."[8] Based on the understanding regarding such a cruel society, people had began to make a profound reflection on this chaos and decided not to live like this. They signed a contract and formed the civil society. This civil society can successfully avoid from the interruption in human social civilization and prevent being caught again in disordered living environment. However, such an approach on the formation of the civil society actually overlaps with political state in respect of its essence. Hobbes did not demonstrate political state, and just made explanation from the perspective of civil society.

There is a certain similarity between Locke's thought of "civil society" and Hobbes'. Locke assumed that the sole right to defend in the state of nature was not enough, so people established a civil society to resolve conflicts in a civil way with help from government in a state of society. Locke addresses the natural instincts of people, or the state of nature, in order to define political power. Locke ever wrote: "Wherever, therefore, any number of men so unite into one society as to quit every one his executive power of the law of Nature, and to resign it to the public, there and there only is a political or civil society". Locke concludes by noting that all people are in a state of nature until a special compact or agreement between them makes them members of a political society. Quite evidently, in Locke's opinion, the political state is the civil society, or, the civil society is the organ of power of the political state. However, different from previous philosophers, Locke indicated: "Civil society is a kind of human consent form existing antecedent to or outside of the state." Society exists anterior to the state, and this impliedly reflects Locke's awareness regarding the distinction between political field and non-political field. Although in his philosophical writings and theories, Locke did not separate state and society, and the society he discussed already existed anterior to state, he recognized the difference between society and state, implicitly offered a new cognition to society and state, thereby opening a new stage in the study of the two specific concepts of state and society, which lays ideological and theoretical basis for the beginning and development of civil society thought in the modern times.

Hegel is one of the greatest thinkers in modern Europe with one of the biggest contributions in the exploration civil society concept, a third territory independent from the state and family. He truly separated the state from the society and systematically made demonstrations for the first time taking the civil society as an independent territory. In Hegel's opinion, the formation of bourgeois stratum was the result of economic development,

---

8   Hobbes, *Leviathan,* The Commercial Press, 1985, p. 96.

which does not append to the past old state but a social organizational form opposed to the state. The citizen stratum is the sum of economic relations which was generated from the development of capitalist exchange relations (commerce). There are meticulous elucidations on the civil society concept in Hegel's master philosophical work "Elements of the Philosophy of Right". He had argued that the civil society is comprised of three levels: "Civil society is an association of members as self-suffcent individuals (Ger. *Einzelner*) in what is therefore a formal universality occasioned by their needs and by the legal constitution as a means of security for persons and property, and by an external order for their particular and common interests."[9] If we explain: first, is the demand an intermediate and individual contentment by individual labor, and the satisfaction of all other persons' labor and needs, which is the need system; Secondly, the freedom included in such system is protected by the legal constitution which secures persons and property; third, is the external order which cares for—the contingency left over from such two systems—their particular and common interests via the state's police power plus professional associations and trade guilds.

VI.1.4. Marx's thoughts on "civil society"

As the most important thinker of the millennium, Marx did not use the term civil society directly. Instead, he used the concept of civil society (Bürgergesellschaft) to elaborate his thoughts on the issue of civil society. And Marx's thoughts were mainly elaborated from the critical perspective. Through the study of the Hegelian thoughts he excavated and inherited its reasonable (rational) element and criticized and superseded (Ger. *Aufheben*) its unreasonable element. Some scholars have pointed out: "The main characteristic of Marx's civil society theory: on the one hand, it has inherited and deepened the basic stipulations of Hegel's civil society, on the other hand, reversed the inverted relationship between the state and civil society within the Hegelian thought."[10]

Firstly, Marx inherited and developed the basic stipulations of (Bürgergesellschaft) civil (citizen) society in the Hegelian thought. Marx's study on civil (citizen) society was carried out at the height of dialectical materialism and historical materialism and from the angle of historical movement, thus avoided to fall into Hegel's pre-determined theoretical aim. Marx thought that the bourgois (citizen) society is the inevitable process of historical development and an inevitable result engendered by human

---

9   G.W.F. Hegel, Elements of the Philosophy of Right, § 157.
10   Yu Keping. Socialist Civil Society: A New Research Subject, *Social Sciences Journal of Tianjin*, 1993(4).

practical activities. Marx has argued that the civil society which he regarded as a phenomenon emerging at a specific development stage of the history, which was caused by the development of men's own social practice, instead of being a product of men's subjective consciousness. For Marx, the civil society would ultimately wither away and be overthrown along with the social and historical development. Furthermore, Marx grasped the civil society from the angle of "the relationship of material intercourse". "The relations of material intercourse" are in essence "the relationship of economical intercourse". Only from this perspective, can we grasp and analyze the civil society, and thus in this way can we grasp the relationship of man with man in the civil society more thoroughly, and more correctly, which does not only include the human "relationships of immediate demand (needs)", but also includes the human "relationship of mediated demand (needs)". Only in this way can the civil society be explained comprehensively, instead of treating it simply as being determined and guided by social and economic relationships.

Secondly, Marx rejected and criticized Hegel's notion of civil society and carried out the reversal of the relationship between the state and society. Hegel thought that the development of the state determined the development of the family and society and that the state was the foundation of society. Proceeding from the basic tenets of materialism, Marx thought that the development of state is determined by that of the society, and this reversal of the relationship has led to the formation of Marx's outlook on the civil society who could now further develop his investigation from a brand-new perspective. Only from this perspective can we truly understand what the civil society is based on which Marx established his basic conception of civil society. Marx once said: "the family and civil society make themselves into state. They are the driving force. According to Hegel, however, they are done by the real idea; it's not the course of their own life that joins them together to comprise the state, but the life of the idea which has distinguished them from itself. They are moreover [the] finiteness of this idea; they owe their existence to a spirit [Geist] other than their own; they are determinations established by a third party, not self-determinations; for that very reason they are also determined as 'finiteness', as the proper finiteness of the 'real idea'. The purpose of their existence [Dasein] is not this existence itself; instead the idea divests itself of these its presuppositions 'in order to rise above its ideality and become infinite real mind for itself'. This is to say that the political state cannot exist without the natural basis of the family and the artificial basis of civil society; they are a condition sine qua non,for it."[11] Marx thinks that with the constant development of productive forces, the relations of production also undergo various changes. When the development of the economic relationship reached a certain phase, various kinds of organizations of social life would come into being on the base of the commodity-economical life. These organizations of social life are the products of economic development, which are controlled and influenced by the relations of economic intercourse, being independent from the state policy, not dependent or attached to it. According to Marx's theory of civil society, the civil society could not exist or occur in every society, for it was the product of the development of social productive forces and could only exists in relatively developed commodity economies. In addition, Marx has argued that the stage of development which corresponds to civil society is the capitalism stage. Along with the unceasing development of human society and abundance of means of material subsistence, thus along with the increase of the social production's ability to satisfy people's needs and the constant improvement of the relationship between man and man, but in the future this edifice of civil society would collapse and be consigned into the "dustbin" of history.

To put it in a nutshell, through brief and simple analysis above, we can see that the concept of civil society itself is a constantly developing theoretical system. With the development of history and change of times, the content and category of civil society is also being readjusted and encounters changes. From the course of the development of civil society, we can see that it had primarily emerged as a distinction from the savage tribe, followed by the division of state and society after which it became an independent sphere until the modern civil society began to withdraw further from economic relations and became a unique ensemble of social relations. In this process, although there is disagreement and dispute on various theories of "civil society" among scholars, it is generally agreed that the civil society is the product of economic development and its emergence and development is closely bound up with the economic development. The civil society is an ensemble of organizational relations distinguished from the state, which controls a large amount of resources that drifted away from the control of state. The prominent function of civil society lies in dealing with the contradiction between the interests of the state and private interests and is an important mechanism to coordinate the public interest relations.

---

11   *Complete Works of Marx and Engels,* Vol.3, People's Publishing House, 2002, p. 11.

VI.2. Contemporary Western "civil society" theory

Civil society of the western mainstream (bourgeoisie) ideology (contemporary sense) refers to the sum of all civil organizations and civil relations excluding the government and market, which includes non-governmental organizations (NGOs), voluntary associations of citizens (NPOs), communities organizations, interest groups and independent movements/activities organized by citizens. This understanding constitutes a major adjustment to the relationship between the state and the society in western countries after they were hit by the welfare state crisis of the late 1970s. In the contemporary times "civil society" has been endowed with new content and new features. But we must notice that this theory of civil society theory is far from perfect and still contains certain theoretical flaws.

VI.2.1. Connotation of contemporary Western "civil society"

The contemporary Western "civil society" theory is a concept which emphasizes independence, autonomy and pluralism, being closely related with bourgeois freedom of human rights, equality and rule of law, which is in essence the theoretical abstraction of the theoretical thought of western liberalism. The contemporary western theory of "civil society" has experienced two high tides. The first one occurred represented by Antonio Gramsci, an Italian Marxist theorist. The second one occurred from 1980s up to today, which is represented by the German scholar Jürgen Habermas and the American scholar Jean L. Cohen and others.

Gramsci thought that with deepening of the development of the capitalist market economy in the 20th Century numerous independent, autonomous social associations and organizations had emerged, which had a huge impact and dominance in the society and the role of such social associations and organizations received the attention of the state. In the process of its development, the state power had always been striving to draw these organizations into its sphere of influence and make them obey its summons by its ideological control, thus let them serve the state power. Gramsci has keenly realized (seen) this phenomenon of the swallowed civil society and engaged himself in profound exposition and critique of this phenomena. Gramsci thought that the civil society was not a form of economic organization, but belonged to the category field of superstructure. But for Gramsci, a superstructure of a state could not be merely regarded as belonging to the political field, but it should be divided up. (Thus Gramsci produces two superstructures). On the one hand, there is one superstructure which exists belonging to the "political" superstructure of the state. On the other hand, there is another superstructure which belongs to the "social" superstructure of the civil society. Thereby, the civil society separated from the category of state was turned to an independent domain. Gramsci thought that state's rule over the society was based on violence, while the rule of the civil society over the society was based on the common will. Gramsci once wrote: "What we can do, for the moment, is to fix two major super structural 'levels': the one that can be called 'civil society', that is the ensemble of organisms commonly called 'private', and that of 'political society' or 'the State'. These two levels correspond on the one hand to the function of 'hegemony' which the dominant group exercises throughout the society and on the other hand to that of 'direct domination' or command exercised through the State and 'judicial' government. The functions in question are precisely organizational and connective."[12] With respect to the significance of the state, the civil society is the ensemble of private relations, but also the civil society is the sum of cultural relations. Since the civil society is a united body, civil society is built on the foundation of "common will" and influenced by customs and cultural elements; it should be built on a cultural guidance.

Habermas has argued that with the failure of welfare state system in the western society, the collapse of socialist countries in Eastern Europe and the disintegration and demise of the Soviet Union since 1980s, the modern society and state faced a great shock and turbulence. Many thinkers began a new round of reflection and investigation on state and society and the question of how to build a rational social order turned to be a theoretical hot spot. Habermas' thoughts on the theory of civil society are conducted along the thinking path followed by Gramsci, but there is a radical difference between their theoretical positions. Habermas thought that the generation and development of civil society is inseparably connected with the development of capitalist market economy and that the capitalist market economy has brought forth the civil society. The civil society is a brand new "private sphere" opposed to the state and this brand new private sphere contains two layers of conceptual meaning. The first one refers to an economic relation that evolves objectively such as capital market and economic society. The second one refers to non-official, non-governmental autonomous associations, social organizations, church, etc. spontaneously formed in the economic development process. Habermas' theory on civil society is founded on the reflection and critique of the capitalist system and tries to make the civil society survive and develop under the capitalist system, maintain its independence and play its role through a legal way.

---

12 Antonio Gramsci, Selections from the Prison Notebooks. Beijing: *China Social Sciences Press*, 2000, p 71.

VI.2.2. Features of contemporary Western "civil society"

Each theory has its own feature. The theory of "civil society" conceived as a domain independent from state and family has inevitably its own feature too. Its features are specifically shown in the following aspects:

Firstly, it is based on the market economy. Although the academic circles have differences or even disputes about the theory of civil society, it is generally agreed to conceive market economy as the basic feature of civil society. According to the basic theory of civil society, the civil society pursues the idea of modernized consciousness of individual freedom and equality and these basic spiritual thoughts can only be realized under the condition of market economy. From the sprout of the capitalist economic development to the universal establishment of the system of market economy in the world, this economic system has accelerated the operation of society, broke the past net of social relations of blood ties and regions and also awakened the idea of interest that was dead asleep in people's mind. Under this economic system, setting up the modern social contract becomes the necessary condition to maintain it. By signing a variety of market rules, the market economy can operate freely, without the interference of the state power. The higher the degree of the market economy, the stronger is the repulsive force against the interference of the state power. The bourgeoisie adhered to and developed the laws of the development of market economy and overthrew the rule of feudal despotism, thus became the ruling class of the state. And it was in the social model of market economy that the civil society was built up. Therefore, without the buildup and development of market economy, there would be no civil society in the modern sense.

Secondly, the feature of the "civil society" is the emphasis of the political participation of the citizens and putting restraints upon the state power. Civil society, as the word literally suggests, inevitably aims to enable that the citizens hold an important status in the society and enable them to have positive and active effect in the society. The civil society thought emphasizes the protection of citizens' individual rights, individual freedoms and equality. The realization and maintenance of citizens' individual rights requires the role of the state, but if the state's power is not supervised, restricted and controlled, the state power will likely get out of control resulting in violations and infringement of the rights of the citizens. Thus, an important feature of the civil society is the active participation of the citizens in political affairs of the state, which will also enable them to supervise the state to avoid state power become unrestricted. In the Western society, it is assumed that in order to restrain the state's power, it is necessary to arrange and establish the separation of the three powers of the state, so that these three powers would mutually restrain, check and supervise one another. But the practice proves that the expected positive effect delivered by the separation of the three powers of the state (legislation, execution, judiciary) is relatively limited, and often the idealized effect cannot be achieved, in practice. On the other hand, as the market economy continues to develop, numerous institutions and organizations bearing social characteristics have emerged, which can participate in the public (Ger. *öffentlich*) and political affairs of the state to a certain extent, which enable the citizens' supervising and restraining the state power.

Thirdly, the feature of the "civil society" is that the equal contract relations constitute the inner connection among the members of the society. The social associations active in the civil society breathe an existence of relative independence and autonomy. Each social association has its own rights and duties. Any social association may interfere in another and make demands from another. The principle relationships among the citizens is equity, it should be a relation based on equality and autonomy. Namely, the relationship among the citizens is neither characterized as the one between superior and the subordinate nor as the one of overlapping coherence (harmony). Instead freedom and equity should prevail. The reason why their relationship should be characterized by relativity is that, each citizen when freely exercising his or her own particular freedom (right) should not interfere or infringe others' freedoms. Briefly, these two above relationship forms constitute the two basic relationship forms of the civil society, within which they coordinate their relations with one another.

The fourth feature, acknowledges the non-governmental organizations as the core actors of the operation in the civil society. Non-governmental organizations are also called as the non-profit organizations, or the "third party" or the civil organization. They exist and operate in an autonomous, voluntary and independent mode. The virtue of these features of their operation mode, determine that they are acknowledged as the core actors civil society. On the one hand, the existence of these non-governmental organizations, facilitates and promotes citizens' participation in political activities and they also enable the citizens' participation in the management of state affairs, thus they offer them easier access to participate in public affairs. On the other hand, while they promote citizens' participation in the management of public affairs, the non-governmental organizations can also promote the feelings of individual responsibility, duty and commitment among the citizens, foster mutual understanding among citizens, and consequently foster the further development of the civil society.

The fifth feature of the civil society is that it advocates a cooperative and tolerant social idea. Within the civil society, since the rights of the private sphere are to be secured, a plural value pursuit is implemented. On this basis a wide range of interest groups evolve, inevitably reflected in numerous and complicated thoughts and doctrines of them. In this case, the orderly operation of the civil society requires a conduct and a behavioral spirit which is tolerant and cooperative which coordinate their interrelations through self-coordinated concessions to each other. Thus, by the virtues of self-coordinated mutual understanding and tolerance, the citizens can achieve, proper coordination of relations among themselves and proper decision-making related to public affairs, thus the situation in which state interference and intervention is necessitated to solve these issues will be sublated. Consequently, the spirit of tolerance and cooperation is one essential requirement of the civil society.

The sixth feature of the civil society is the principle of rule of law. The civil society is the product of market economy, the basic condition for the operation of the market economy is to abide by the principle of the rule of law. The rule of law principle is the highest principle within the civil society, a ruler or a person no matter what superior status or no matter what abundant powers he or she enjoys should act within the established laws, the principle which ensures that the subjects of the civil society can solve their internal affairs without the interference or interruption of external factors, thus the rule of law principle facilitates benign and orderly operation of the civil society.

VI.2.3. Flaws of the contemporary Western "civil society" theory

Certainly, the establishment and development of any theory is bound to pursue a certain value target or philosophical theory as guidance, which is also true for the contemporary western civil society theory. As one important theory developed in the Western world, the civil society theory pursues prominent Western values such as individualism, pluralism and other value propositions, those of which contain certain obvious flaws within themselves. Below we will examine certain aspects of these flaws:

First, is the vulgarization of individualism value. We should acknowledge that the modern civil society theory of the West finds its roots in the struggle and opposition against the feudal despotic system. Western ideologists in order to oppose the rule and the violence of the despotic and authoritarian states, which infringed and trampled upon citizens' basic human rights, freedoms—have developed the civil society theory as the powerful ideological weapon to serve this end. On the one hand, they have advocated the development of the civil society, elaborated on the irrational character of the feudal despotic rule, thus tried hard to publicize critical revolutionary thoughts in this direction. However, the proposed value concept of this civil society is liberal individualism, which particularly emphasizes the subjectivity of the individual. This guiding value holds the view that all the political, economic, cultural, and social organizations (including society) are comprised of individuals, and stresses individuality and particularity; consequently these associated organizations are unions of these independent individuals. This so-called individualist value principle, advocated by liberalism aims to illustrate, on the one hand, the legitimacy and rationality of individual's pursuit of self-interest, on the other hand, that the civil society is both the association of individual interests and the sphere of market economy within which individuals can seek to maximize their own material interests, and that only in this way would the common interests of the society be boosted. This above theoretical content tends to vulgarize the concept of civil society, which regards it as a sphere within which the competition for maximum interests is pursued. In addition, along with the continuous development of the economic society, the liberalism enjoyed great popularity when the world and its relatively despotic system appeared as a decline. Consequently under the guidance of liberal ideology, more and more people increasingly began to become aware of the importance of the realization of their self-interests, which has led to the vigorous emergence of various numerous political parties, associations and social groups that sought to achieve citizens' interests. But once these civil society associations develop and achieve certain degree of progress they will inevitably depart from the original individualistic value principle that was advocated when they had emerged. The individualistic value principle of liberalism stressed that each and all should pursue for self-interests and that these interests are imbued with certain unique particularity. But instead, civil society associations are established and develop according to the basic principle of basic democracy and once they develop and achieve certain degree of progress they will inevitably form a rigorous value/norm system that seeks for the interests of the entire association. By then and in this case the liberal civil society theory, which advocates for individual self-interests, will decline and awareness of collective/group interests will develop. And since the will and the strength of the individual is unable to change the behavior and position of social group, ergo the validity of individualism value advocated by the western civil society theory, is a sheer false fantasy.

Second, is the contradictions embodied in the value of pluralism. The individualistic value principle of the Western civil society theory is accompanied by that of the pluralism value which advocates that the civil society is a society which embodies the development of multiple values. Thus the pursuit of pluralism value is another core value of the Western civil society theory. This pluralism value of the Western civil society theory has two-fold or two-layered meaning. On the one hand, the value of pluralism principle emphasizes each and every individual's ideas and faith, and also his/her right to pursue this faith, ergo numerous different social organizations and associations representing these individuals should freely and autonomously exist and develop. On the other hand, within the civil society, these associations should be self-functioning and all these value systems should be equally realized. And various social organizations that are spontaneously and independently established by the citizens, enable the sharing of the social functions to every corner of society. The state should not interfere and criticize such spontaneous societal role. However, if we evaluate realistically this pluralism value of the civil society theory, often we observe that it cannot be realized in most situations and becomes a kind of wishful thinking. The strength of the different citizen associations representing those various interest groups established in such plural society are asymmetrical and uneven, which means that the weaker associations will find it difficult to defend themselves against the stronger ones, ergo in that case inevitably the interests of the weaker one will be sacrificed without hesitation. In that situation when the interests of different associations collide, inevitably the interest of the weaker party would be subordinated to the other. Such pluralism value, in its essence, serves to conceal the reality of asymmetrical social development between various interest groups. In addition, the pluralism value of the Western civil society emphasizes social pluralism and equality, but due to the influences of various factors on the social individuals, this equality often cannot take effect and cannot be realized.

Third, the malpractice of the market value. The civil society is a result and product of the development of the market economy. In the theory of civil society, the theory and viewpoint of market value is widely accepted and affirmed. However, this viewpoint of market value is itself problematic. Firstly, the development of free and open markets intensifies the inequalities in the market and social development. Social advancement degree will be high where market economic development level is high. This trend will maintain itself for a long time and affect the economically underdeveloped regional economy. The free market economy unceasingly intensifies the imbalances in the economic development of different regions. In the society, the gap between the rich and the poor also keeps widening unceasingly, making the social impoverished social strata be impoverished for a long time, with their self-interests hardly maintained and satisfied. Secondly, according to the theory of civil society, it emphasizes a kind of freedom and spontaneity, and rejects and resists the state's interference in the market and the civil field. However, the economic foundation established by civil society is a free economy. The development of this kind of economy has the malpractice of market nature, such as the nature of spontaneity, lagging behind, blindness, and avoiding state intervention is not feasible. Thirdly, the market economy is competitive. Because of this competitive nature, people often abandon the interests of others for their own interests. In many cases, the interests of others, the interests of the collective, and even the interests of the state are discarded. Because of this competition and contest of mutual interests, there is no effective communication between groups. This process of competition will inevitably lead to the irrationality of resource allocation, leading to a contradiction unable to be coordinated.

VI.3. The "civil society" in contemporary China

During the late 1980s, along with the profound changes in the socio-economic structure of the world, the concept of "civil society" has attracted substantial attention and caused a mainstream support, on the global scale. During the 1990s, scholarly studies in China related to the "civil society" have seen a significant boom.

VI.3.1. Scale and progress of civil society studies

Currently, comprehensive database of social sciences and humanities researches, the well known research web facility, the China National Knowledge Infrastructure (www.cnki.com) has become an important source for those who would search scientific information and knowledge through periodicals. Articles from academic journals published in China can be reviewed or downloaded from this web portal, and all academic journals of China are included in it. Below, in order to give the reader an idea on the scale of "civil society "studies we will use certain data, we have collected from the China National Knowledge Infrastructure web site. Though this data cannot fully reveal the real scale and is incomplete, the data results we get from the analysis of this source can reflect the basic situation of the research to some extent. We did first search in the "titles" field of the web facility, using the term "civil society" and "titles" catch words and found that 2,256 articles were published in the encompassing the period of January 1, 1982 to May 1, 2013. We did a second search in the "theme "field, again on the term "civil society" and "theme" catch words and found 9,623 articles in the period between January 1, 1982 and May 1, 2013. We did a third search in the "keyword" field, this time using the catch words "civil society" and "keyword" we have found that 12,701 articles were published in the period between January 1, 1982 and May 1, 2013.13

In China, studies that focus on the issue of "civil society" have only begun in the last 20 years. As for those articles bearing the term "civil society" in the article title, the yearly distribution of such articles is as follows: In the year 2013 a total of 69 such article was published, similarly 253 in 2012, 332 articles in 2011, 315 in 2010; 300in 2009; 273 in 2008, 207 in 2007,167 articles in 2006, 111 in 2005, 87 in 2004, 55 in 2003, 38 in 2002, 9 in 2001,11 in 2000; 5 in 1999, 5 in 1998, 5 in 1997, 3 articles in 1996, 1 in 1994,1 in 1993,1 in 1992, 1 in 1989, 1 in 1988, 1 in 1982.

In addition, when we made a search in the China National Knowledge Infrastructure among those diverse study articles—theses or dissertations—including the term "civil society" in their titles, we have seen that the first article including a thesis has appeared in 2004. The number of such theses which include the term "civil society" in their titles, and their distribution according to years is as follows: In 2004, 6 theses, 7 theses in 2005, 16 theses in 2006, 20 theses in 2007, 15 theses in 2008, 16 theses in 2009, 31 theses in 2010, 41 theses in 2012, 19 theses in 2013.14

Apparently, from 2004 to 2013, we can see an obvious increase in their numbers. Here we should note that the important article "Building a Civil Society in China" co-authored by Deng Zhenglai and Jing Yuejin gave an important impulse for further researches related to the "civil society."15

Stages of "civil society" studies in China:

Some scholars have classified the "civil society" studies in China into two phases: the first stage includes the period from the late-1992 to the end of the 20th Century, and the second stage includes the period from the beginning of the 21st Century, till today.16

On the other hand, some scholars have classified the stages of the "civil society" studies into three phases: The first stage includes the period from the late 1992 to the end of the 20th Century, and this period is evaluated

---

13   CNKI-China National Knowledge Infrastructure; http://epub.cnki.net/kns/brief/default_result.aspx.
14   Ibid.
15   Ibid.
16   Yu Jianxing and Zhou Jun. *New Progress on China*, China Civil Society Studies, *Journal of Marxism & Reality*, 2006(3).

as the initial stage of studies related to civil society ; the second stage has started together with the turn of the new century, and covers the period till the year 2006, the year in which an important decision was promulgated, when the 6th Plenary Session of the 16th Central Committee of the CPC had convened, and this second stage is evaluated as the development stage of the studies; the third stage starts with the year 2006 and includes the period till today; and this stage is considered as the stage of deepening of these studies.[17]

Generally, many scholars agree on the first classification of two stages, and evaluate the stages as follows: the first stage began along with the reforms of China related to political, economic and social fields of the society. In the beginning of this stage, academic community has started with the preliminary research on the elucidation of the concept of "civil society". Also, in these stage considerable research efforts by the research community has focused on the Marxist classics which has discussed and elaborated on the issue and related thinkers such as Hegel, Gramsci, Bernstein and others. The studies in these periods have also introduced and debated the basic theories on civil society prevalent in the West, debated whether there is a civil society in China, and discussed the problem of how to construct civil society in China. Another issue debated was the relations between the civil society and socialist modernization.[18]

The civil society debate has also attracted great attention of the Chinese intellectuals and public. Some scholars have evaluated that, at this first stage, the initial debates on civil society among Chinese intellectuals, have revolved around the process and road of modernization and advancement of modernization and there has emerged a certain polarization between those arguing for the "exoticism" of the civil society concept (related to the Chinese society) and those who argued for the benefits of its introduction. The results of the debates and researches of this period includes two aspects : first, exploring how China's civil society could be developed and established, and the main focus of this exploration and debate has revolved on the characteristics and merits of the Western civil society and the issue of its possible transplantation in China.[19]

---

17   Li Yihuang, The Studies and Comments on Civil Society in Contemporary China, *Journal of Beijing Administrative College*, 2004(2).

18   Kuai Zhengming, The Studies and Comments on Chinese Civil Society after the Reform and Opening-up. *Journal of Gansu Theoretical Research*, 2008(4).

19   Zhou Guowen, "Civil Society": Its Concept, History, Studies and Comments, *Journal of Philosophical Trends*, 2006(3).

In evaluating the second phase, many scholars have argued that this stage was strongly driven by the effects of China's reforms in the various fields of social life. In this stage, when the Reform and Opening-up of China further deepened, also the findings and the discussion of the previous period were deepened. The wave of globalization and China's engagement with the globalization process has swept over almost every field of the Chinese society.[20] Compared with the previous phase, the research on civil society in this phase has showed significant new features: While the concept of civil society was still being discussed and pursued as one ideal paradigm, the attention of the debates and researches has shifted more and more on the civil society theories of the Western left-wing. Some scholars have tried to transcend the simple opposition of the nationalism and liberalism and have sought to construct a viable model or concept of "socialist civil society."

At the same time, there searches on civil society by the political sociology branch of the academy has shown remarkable progress and a large number of empirical research fruits were created, causing an important social impact. With these findings and debates the concepts of NGOs, the concept of the third sector and so on has spread beyond academia and reached the ordinary masses.[21]

VI.3.2. Does China have "civil society"?

Is China's "civil society" being formed? When this question came to the fore with introduction the civil society theories into China, the academia launched a large-scale discussion.

1. The thinking that there is no "civil society" in China

Some have argued that there does not exist a civil society in in China. And some scholars have argued that the reality of the situation in mainland China at the moment is that the space and the strength of the "private sphere" (private sphere) which can restrain political authority is of course grown larger compared to previous epochs; but they assert that yet the "public sphere" did not develop out of this space of "private sphere". Therefore they came to conclude that the "half-baked or the pseudo-civil society" will have a hard and longer time before it will evolve into a "full-fledged civil society", similarly the development of the advanced rule of law system out of this "private sphere" will not be so easy, the same applies

---

20   Ma Xiheng, "On the Formation and Path Analysis of China Civil Society", *Journal of Legal System and Society*, 2013(1).
21   Zhou Jun, "New Progress in China's Civil Society Studies, *Marxism and Reality* (bi-monthly), 2006(3).

for a healthy formation of a modern civil society which could emerge out of the development of the "public sector".

They have argued that the "half-baked civil society or the pseudo civil society" allows bribery, corruption, and promotes the understanding of "entering through the back door". Almost all solutions to matters are sought by depending to personal or quasi-personal relationships. And such half-baked civil society is the hotbed for the development of various kind of "interest based" gangs, "interest based" local forces and other "private" organizations.[22]

Some scholars have investigated the civil society based on tha facts of the Chinese history. They have arrived three conclusions. First, in Chinese history, there existed no real citizen stratum. Secondly, Chinese grand unification based on intensive centralization of power was a powerful obstacle for the development of the civil society. Thirdly, China has been an agricultural country, lacking of basic condition to form a civil society.[23] In such history and culture, China would never have or foster its own civil society.

From the perspective of the Chinese people's awareness, some scholars have argued that citizenship awareness will be the product of introduction of modern constitutionalism. Such awareness has two implications. When the public faces the power operation of government, it is reflected as the recognition and supervision by the public on the public nature of the power. When the public faces public domain, it is reflected as conscious safeguard of an active participation in public interest. Therefore, citizen awareness has a public nature, instead of a private nature at the beginning. It is the product which does not emerge until power has turned into public goods and until there emerges the public domain between state affairs and private affairs. Before power turns into a public good, all consciousness of the public can only be deemed as a collection of private awareness. In China, the state of such a private collection has a natural name of "ordinary people". Ordinary people are an aggregation of multiple blood relationship and family names, reflecting the remnant ideas of patriarchal natural economy. In fact, it is too far away from the concept of citizen.[24]

Some other scholars have argued that, in the traditional society, the public did not fully enjoy the right as master and established full trust on rule. After the establishment of New China, the awareness of the people "being master of all the state affairs" was lifted up gradually. But the long-lasting planned economy has made people lack initiative and creativity, as well as

22   Tian Hua, "Theory of Civil Society", "Democracy and Science", 2004(1).
23   Xia Weizhong, Civil Society: Dream of China Hard to Come True in Recent Times, *Chinese Social Science Quarterly (Hong Kong)*, 1993(4).
24   Zhu Xueqin, *The Revolution in the Study*, Changchun Publishing House, 1992.

the activity and initiative to join social management. Government acted like the patriarch of a big family who kept everything under his own control. This has led to the dependent mentality and passive psychology among the masses. Without a perfect legal system, civil right would never be guaranteed and so the public will not actively undertake their obligation. Such thousand-year old tradition still affects us because there is the soil for its survival.[25] With such public awareness, there is no chance to have or form a civil society.

From the perspective of Chinese social organization, many scholars indicate that the reason why a civil society cannot be formed in today's China is that some leaders in government and the Party, restricted by traditional thinking, are reluctant to or dare not to encourage the development of the civil association. These leaders do not show enough respect for the constitutional right of citizen's freedom of association. The growth of our civil organization is still handicapped, unnecessarily. So far, as many as 800 million farmers fail to form their own organization, and the migrant workers cannot guard their rights with the assistance of their own organizations. It is reported that, as a result of the quite harsh requirements by the government, 90% of the non-governmental environmental organizations in China have not obtained any legal status and have had difficulties to carry out activities. By now, China has not issued any law of association to guarantee the freedom of association. Only the State Council enacted the Association Management Regulations (an administrative regulation) for administrative management. This cannot meet the requirements to build civil society.[26]

Some scholars have argued that, although a special agent stratum, which is controlled by intellectual groups and on behalf of citizen interest, has been formed in China, these intellectual groups generally exclude the public and make the public depend on their protection. In view of the supervision to be imposed by civil society upon on the state (like the ideal design suggested by Habermas and Dahrendorf), China has not formed a civil society. Civil society requires a dual autonomy: one autonomy independent of the state and the other autonomy independent of traditional structures, such as clan, organization or family. If this is an indicator of the civil society, China still has a long way to go.[27]

25   Shan Aihong, *The Rising of Chinese Civil Society and the Cultivation of Citizen Consciousness, Studies on the Socialism with Chinese Characteristics*, 2004(6).
26   Guo Daohui, *Citizenship and Civil Society, Chinese Journal of Law*, 2006(1).
27   Wu Zhicheng, Chinese Civil Society: Present and Future-Academic Dialogue with Famous A German Expert on Chinese Issues Professor Thomas Heberer, *Marxism & Reality*, 2006(3).

2. Some people believe that there has emerged a civil society in China

Some scholars have argued that there has formed a civil society in current China. On the one hand, Chinese society has shown the general characteristics of a civil society. This civil society is relatively independent from the state and government and its main body comprises of non-government and non-profit civil organizations. It is an inevitable product of market economy and reflects inevitable demand of democratic politics. This civil society runs under the different rules of the government system and the market system, and it makes a great effect on the sound development of market economy and the advancement of democratic politics. On the other hand, such civil society has its own distinct features, just like Chinese market economy and democratic politics.[28]

Among academic community, there are scholars who researched the causes in the formation of civil society from such many perspectives as the development of market economy, reform of political system, social change and historical culture to demonstrate the existence of a real civil society in China.

From the perspective of market economy, some scholars have argued that market economy has speeded up the disintegration of traditional uniform and holistic society, and pushed the separation of the state and society, and promoted the division of social stratum, which provides the precondition for the formation and development of civil society. Market economy also creates a stage for the operation of contract and the available ground for the growth of the contract culture. It activates people's desires for material benefits and provides a vast space and equal opportunity for individuals and groups to achieve their own material benefits. And it also shapes individuals and groups with the consciousness of independence, equity, competitiveness, openness and civility, and therefore gradually forms and increasingly enhances the independent character of civil society. Market economy transforms people from group subjects into individual subjects and forges the subject of civil society.[29] Therefore, the development of market economy will stimulate the conscious emergence and growth of the civil society in China. So, there actually exists a civil society in China.

From the perspective of politics, some scholars have argued that the scope of the control by the state on society is narrowing. In respect of daily life, literature and arts, scientific research and so on, the direct control and

---

28   Yu Keping, Some Thoughts on Improving the System Environment of Civil Society in China, *Contemporary World & Socialism* (Bimonthly), 2006(1).

29   Wu Junbin, Discussion and Analysis on the Basic Dimension of Contemporary Chinese Civil Society Construction, *Journal of Central South University*, 2003(1).

intervention by the government are gradually decreasing. In those fields which are still controlled by government, the controlling mode is changing and controlling force is declining. In many aspects of management, the government focuses on the principle guidance and emphasizes its function of serving. The government's control is becoming more normalized and more routine. A series of complete regulations and rules have been enacted. People have begun to concern the justice and significance of the procedure itself, and the role of the legal system has enhanced.[30] Chinese government is turning into a service-oriented, power-separated and limited government, which objectively creates the proper political conditions for civil society.

Besides, some scholars also indicate that the initial driver for the existence and development of civil society in China lays on the change in the ruling policy by the CPC. Some policies have laid elementary foundation for the development of civil society, such as taking economic construction as the central task, carrying forward socialist democracy and improving socialist legal system.[31]

From the perspective of society, some scholars have argued that the Chinese society became an independent fountain to provide resource and opportunity. Throughout the over 30 years Reform and Opening-up policy, society has played an increasingly significant role in the resource allocation, and it also has gradually achieved more opportunities. The provision and exchange of these resources and opportunities were realized mainly by the market. In today's society, there has emerged freely flowing resources and free spaces. Such independence provides the ground to foster new elements in the social structure.[32]

From the perspective of the change of the relationship between the state and the society, some scholars have argued that the state has gradually separated from social life. In the rural areas, the state has delegated the right of production and operation to farmers and no longer undertakes rural production and operation. Individual farmers, their families and village communities have obtained autonomy and decision-making power in rural production. In urban area, the state has opened up the market and permitted individual and private economy to exist and develop in the areas of service, industry, finance and so on. The trend of small government and big

---

30   Li Jin, The Concept Demarcation of Civil Society and the Reconstruction of Chinese Modern Social Structure, *The Journal of CPC Yunnan Provincial Committee School*, 2008(2).

31   Zhang Qi, Towards Harmony: Exploration and Analysis of Civil Society in Contemporary China, *Journal of Peking University*, 2005(4).

32   Li Jin, The Concept Demarcation of Civil Society and the Reconstruction of Chinese Modern Social Structure, *The Journal of CPC Yunnan Provincial Committee School*, 2008(2).

society started to form. During the reform of the state-owned economy, the government gradually has delegated its control power partially to the enterprise and the society. Meanwhile, the government's power in the political and cultural fields was also been transferred the society. Governmental affairs have become more and more transparent, and supervision by the society was enhanced. The new recruits for official government posts is wider opened for ordinary people. The cultural field also shows a trend of diversification. All these developments reflect a socialization tendency regarding the state power.[33] All these changes make civil society turn to be an objective existence in China.

As indicated by some other scholars, since the 1990s, government got over the omnipotent image of managing and running society and started to change its functioning. It launched the reform in social security system, and transformed itself from a service provider to an authorizer. Accordingly, a bunch of self-serviced and self-managed civil organizations were fostered, such as cultural and sports associations, trade associations, volunteer organizations and community type of organizations. By the year of 1997, the number of associations on county has reached to over 180,000; the number of national level associations reached up to 1,848; the number of civil organizations on the county level was estimated about reach to 3 millions. In addition to associations, the number of private non-corporate entities hit over 700,000 by 1998.[34] The cultivation and development of these civil organizations constitute the main body of civil society.

From the perspective of civil awareness, some scholars have argued that citizens have been aware of that the essence of democracy depends on democratic rights, not the gift of democracy (state). Without democratic rights, citizens will not possess the freedom and equity of democracy. Besides, citizens have gradually gained more opportunities to engage in social management, such as political affairs and social governance, including voting rights, autonomous management and negotiation rights. Moreover, community life, social security and public management related to civil citizen life has greatly enhanced. During this process, citizens have constantly improved their legal/law consciousness and cultural level. The learning and education has become a life-long pursuit for citizens. Many citizens are consciously making use of media to express their demands, their desires and critique.[35]

---

33   Jiang Yong, The History and Present of the Concept of Civil Society, *Journal of Ocean University of China (Social Sciences)*, 2003(6).
34   Yu Keping, Wang Ying, The Rise of Civil Society and the Good Governance of the Government, *China Reform*, 2001(6).
35   Jiang Yong, The History and Present of the Concept of Civil Society, *Journal of Ocean University of China (Social Sciences)*, 2003(6).

Besides, in view of the Internet, some scholars also indicate that the mode of Internet puts the growth of Chinese civil society under the macro background of globalization. By breaking up power and authority and claiming for individual right, the Internet not only overcomes the restriction by traditional social relational state and ideological public opinion, but also activates and strengthens social members' consciousness about being subjects and having rights. The virtual space created by the Internet has provided a fertile soil for the sprouting of the spirit of civil society and citizenship consciousness by creating a brand new platform and broad spiritual space to build a Chinese civil society.[36]

VI.3.3. Does China need to establish a civil society?

Upon the establishment of civil society in China, the academic circle has much in dispute. Some scholars hold a pessimistic and questioning attitude on the construction of civil society in China. They have argued that it is difficult for China to construct a civil society and such society will not become an "effective means" to govern China, while other scholars keep a positive attitude on this issue. They explore and investigate the necessity to construct a civil society in China based on positive expectation of its role.

1. Those who insist that it is difficult and not necessary for China to construct a civil society

Some scholars believe that it is quite impossible to foster a civil society in China. Firstly, it is very difficult for Chinese people to advance their civil citizen consciousness. Or in other words, if it will take too much time (e.g. five centuries) to advance Chinese consciousness, the actual feasibility of such possibility is actually close to zero. Secondly, Chinese people have historically repelled "rationalist culture". For example, the cultural spirit of the Cultural Revolution (1966-76) was just similar to the asceticism age in the Western Christianity, which had been the spiritual basis for a civil society, but a nightmare for present Chinese people.[37]

Some scholars indicate that even if China is able to construct a civil society theoretically, it is also difficult to realize it in practice. Some scholars argue that the concept of civil society is derived from Europe not from the Orient. So it cannot be achieved in China in a short time. There are three reasons. Firstly, the strong tradition of anti-civil society accumulated

36   Zeng Shengcong, The Modernization of China and the Development of Civil Society, *Chongqing Social Sciences*, 2005(2).

37   Xie Xialing, Discussion on the Possibility of Developing Civil Society in China, *Social Sciences Weekly*, September 2, 1993.

in Chinese history will exert and continue to maintain its great influence. Secondly, the base for "grand unification" centralization, whose power is beyond people's imagination, is so solid and firm. Thirdly, it is hard to solve the rural issue and the irrational urban-rural relationship.[38]

Some scholars have argued that there only existed a folk society before modern China. And although traditional folk society had an autonomy to a degree, a real civil society has not appeared. Since the mid-19th Century, civil society in modern China gradually emerged from the womb of the traditional social structure, which was driven by the development of industry, commerce, and civilized tolerance in modern times, as well as social reforms in the modern era (19th Century). However, the development of Chinese civil society was hindered in three aspects. Firstly, before the modern times, despotism had made it unable to grow a civil society naturally. Secondly, when despotism was dissolved, the malformation in the field of social self-organizations and the weakening of regime made it much difficult to develop civil society. Third, when state-oriented departmentalism rose, even "weakened regime" constantly encroached on civil society.[39]

While some other scholars insist that civil society is an absolutely imported idea. They have argued that it may be utterly not applicable to introduce the idea of civil society formed in western context into China. On one hand, the citizen stratum in Europe was generated through Roman Law, Enlightenment, French Revolution and many other events. On the other hand, civil society requires the transformation from clan or family interest to individual social interest and the process of education as a premise, which can arouse the duty understanding of free citizens and common duties were generated. Therefore, although contemporary China has encountered social divisions (stratums), re-adjusted interest relations in the society and the re-constructed the forms of interest representation, civil society construction of China still has a long way to go, as it requires the change of citizen structure and their thinking mode. In today's China, it is quite difficult to construct a civil society.[40]

Some scholars had a questioning attitude when they made a holistic comprehension and investigation on the civil society. In the book *Disillusioned by Civil Society*, the author Wang Shaoguang indicated: "it is an absolutely false hypothesis if we treat civil society as a whole without any class difference

---

38   Xia Weizhong, Civil Society: Dream of China Hard to Come True in Recent Times, *Chinese Social Science Quarterly (Hong Kong)*, 1993(4).

39   Xiao Gongqin, The Three Obstacles of Civil Society and China's Modernization, *Social Sciences Weekly*, September 2, 1993.

40   Thomas Heberer, Norah Sausmikat, Is the Western Idea of Civil Society Appropriate for China, *Journal of Nankai University*, 2005(2).

where various associations compete on a completely equal base." "Any wise man will know that a realistic civil society is definitely neither a homogeneous entity nor a pastoral paradise". On the contrary, "in a civil society, there both exists slums and garden villas, tear and blood, sword and fire. It is either ignorance or cheating to describe it as a place full of peace and tranquility." By investigating on civil society, the author indicates that, "among family, market and the state, there also exist other organizational forms other than "good" organizations", such as the Mafia in Italy, the Triad in Hong Kong, China, the Aum Shinrikyo in Japan, the Ku Klux Klan in USA, and the al-Qaeda of Bin Laden. All these are non-governmental organizations. And I can give thousands of other examples." Besides, the author also indicates that "almost every civil society mainly depends on commercial income, government funding or foreign donation." Such economic dependence results in that "civil societies of all countries are not completely independent. Moreover, as long as they are not economically independent, they cannot eliminate foreign influence, and hence cannot decide their activities agenda freely." At last, the author concludes that civil society is not the only road to develop democracy in China. "It is generally believed that, in the developed Western capitalist countries, the enthusiasm of the public to participate in associations is relatively high, but the facts are different. The level of participation of the public in Sweden, Netherlands, Iceland, US is high, while that in the UK and Spain is low, comparable to Russia. The public in some developing counties may also actively join associations, such as Tanzania, Uganda, Zimbabwe and Bangladesh. As shown by the actual facts and distribution map, the pubic in many democratic countries show less enthusiasm about participating in associations compared with the public in those less democratic counties. This indirectly challenges the dominant opinion about the relationship between civil society and democracy, namely, the idea of that the more developed a civil society is, the more possible democracy will emerge."[41]

2. Some have argued that China is able to construct a civil society, which will play a positive role in China

As for the role played by civil society in China, scholars have made discussions from different perspectives as given below:

Firstly, civil society is good for the development of a market economy. Some scholars have argued that civil society can create sound social environment for the development of a market economy; the emergence of civil society can lay foundation for the orderly and rational operation of market economy; organizations in civil society have great employment potential

---

41   Wang Shaoguang, "Civil Society" Disenchantment, *Green Leaf*, 2009(7).

and are indispensable to solve the employment problem; civil society can play a role of regulating industrial activities and stabilizing economic order; and civil society can also function as a major force to push ahead economic reform and development.

Some other scholars have emphasized that the civil society organizations can actively participate in the decision-making of various economic reforms and give suggestions for economic developments and economic policy. This will activate the initiative and innovative spirit of people to enter market. It will not only hinder stagnation in the national economy of the country, but will also contribute to the prosperity and healthy development of economic life.[42]

Civil society can promote democratic governance. Some scholars have argued that, the rise of civil society creates an organizational base for a grassroots democracy, especially the autonomy of the society. The rising civil organizations can build an important bridge through which the government can communicate with the citizens. A group of civil organizations and associations which have grown since the 1980s became the key factor to influence government's decision-making and the great driving force for pushing forward government reform. Civil organizations have actively devoted themselves to public welfare work, which improves the image of government and enhance the political identification among the citizens. Although it is a governmental duty to develop public welfare, it is may be unsuitable for the government to organize and implement certain public welfare services so as to produce an optimal effect. In this respect, civil organizations play an irreplaceable role. Besides, civil organizations can effectively restrict and supervise the government activities.[43]

Civil society can promote the change in governance functions. Some scholars indicate that, civil organizations became the force to affect government decision-making and drive government reform. As a result of the profession and diversity of the civil organizations, they cannot only share the function in public service by contributing to the establishment of an efficient, responsible and law-based government, but also begin to take up the role of government adviser by providing consultancy and advising for government decision-making and pushing forward the democratization of government decision-making.[44]

---

42   Wu Junbin, Discussion and Analysis on the Basic Dimension of Contemporary Chinese Civil Society Construction, *Journal of Central South University*, 2003(1).
43   Yu Keping, Some Problems in the Study of Chinese Civil Society, *Journal of the Party School of the Central Committee of the CPC*, 2007(6).
44   Lan Hua, The Development of Civil Society and the Construction of Service Oriented

Civil society can improve the quality of public service. Some scholars have suggested that the experience of all countries in the reform of public service shows that the government can transfer a part of its authority to civil organizations and allow them to undertake partial administrative management functions with the development and improvement of the social management system. Besides, government can hand over some public service functions to civil organizations. For example, in the field of public education, health care, infrastructure construction, utilities, environmental protection, security and joint defense, government may allow qualified civil organizations to subcontract or bear alone partial public service through competition. This will not only relieve the burden of government, but also significantly reduce the cost of public service and improve its quality.[45]

Civil society can promote social harmony and maintain social stability. Some scholars insist that organizations in civil society can provide various public welfare services, so as to send care and help for social vulnerable groups which are eager for various services but barely obtain assistance. To some extent, this can redistribute social resource, effectively solve social contradictions, maintain and promote social fairness and justice. Organizations in civil society can cultivate citizens through the spirit of cooperation, unity and democracy so as to regulate citizen behavior. This is essential for building a harmonious society with stability and harmony.[46]

Some scholars have suggested that civil society can be used as a new perspective to achieve China's socialist modernization. Generally, the middle strata are always the most important social force to keep society stable in any society. The formation of civil society breaks the original social structure and constructs a powerful middle stratum, which is a strong power source on civilian level and can promote social stability. Democratic politics, civil society and modernization of economy can be included into our goal of establishing a systematic concept of modernization, which can correct the deficiencies of one-sided development during socialist modernization and thus avoid a deformed social development.[47]

Government in China–Governance Theory Perspective, *Journal of Shandong University*, 2005(2).

45   Yu Keping, Some Problems in the Study of Chinese Civil Society, *Journal of the Party School of the Central Committee of the CPC*, 2007(6).

46   Yang Yueru, The Function of Civil Society Organizations in Building a Harmonious Society, *Seek Truth from Facts*, 2005(2).

47   Han Keqing, Civil Society and the Modernization of China, *Jiangsu Social Sciences*, 2001(6).

VI.3.4. How to construct Chinese civil society

The academic community has also discussed how to build civil society in China.

1. The stages for the establishment of civil society in China

There are three opinions about the development stage of civil society in China. The first opinion is that civil society will be established in two stages. In the first stage, the civil society will gradually form. During this stage, the state and civil society will make efforts together. The state will drive a top-down reform, accelerate the change in government functions and actively and gradually withdraw from those social and economic fields which it should not intervene. Social members will make full use of the advantage and opportunity of such reform to consciously and rationally promote the establishment of a civil society from top to bottom. In this stage, activities mainly concentrate on and are reflected in the economic field. In the second stage, civil society will enter its maturity. During this stage, social members will continue to develop and improve themselves. Meanwhile, they will enter a "public domain", where they will participate in and affect government decision-making and form a positive interactive relationship with the state.[48]

The second opinion is reflected by a theory of three-stage drive. The first stage is driven by government policy. In this stage, civil society in China still remains to be in a growing period, needs to accumulate energy and has not obtained an independent and autonomous status. It is impossible for it to supervise the state. The second stage is driven by the system. During this period, civil society will become stronger. This drive by the system will naturally lead to a duality between the state and society, the government and the citizens, so as to more durably and powerfully promote the growth and expansion of a civil society in China based on the continuous influence of drive by government policy. The third stage is driven by the market, wherein civil society will step into its mature period. As China's societal modernization process advances into this stage, the structural relationship between civil society and the state will encounter a major transformation. Civil society and the state, citizens and the government will integrate in a mutual relation at a higher level.[49]

---

48   Yu Keping, *The Emerging of Civil Society and Its Significance to Governance in Reform China, Chinese Social Science Quarterly (Hong Kong)*, 1999.
49   Shi Xuehua, Modernization and Chinese Civil Society, *Chinese Social Science Quarterly (Hong Kong)*, 1994.

The third opinion has been proposed as the theory of four-stage development. The first stage is the cultivation stage. Since 1978, China conducted a series of reforms regarding its political and economic systems. In respect of political system reform, China separated its government from the enterprises, also its state administrative body from the public institutions, its government organs from the social organization so as to realize the target pattern of small government and big society. In the field of economy, the introduction of market economy enabled China to allocate resources by the market, rather than plan mechanism. The retreat of political power and the expansion of powers of economic actors have provided a systematic space and laid the economic base for the development of the third sector. The second stage is the construction stage, also called as a government-leading stage. In this stage, government will conduct multiple reforms to shift some functions of official departments to business associations and to establishing some associations which will undertake some official administrative functions. During this stage, government promotes the establishment of the third sector from top to bottom so as to construct civil society in China. Citizens will make full use of advantage and opportunity of such reform to consciously and rationally advance the establishment of a civil society from bottom to top. The third stage is a development and maturation stage. In this stage, through participation in various activities by social association, citizens will enhance their consciousness of rights, improve the ability of participating in and discussing state affairs, and foster the capacity of self-management, self-constraint and self-service. They will be required to enter into public domain to express their opinions and restrict arbitrary behavior of government. The fourth stage is a maturity stage. In this stage, the state, the market and the society will be apart from one another and reach a relative balance. They will also mutually complement each other and realize a collaborative development by forming an independent civil society indeed.[50]

2. Specific propositions about the establishment of civil society in China

One proposition emphasizes the improvement of market economy. At present, most of the academic circles affirm that the market economy breeds a modern civil society. The contract spirit, freedom mechanism, idea of law-based governance constitute the key pillars of the civil society. Hence, this proposition argues that we must perfect our market economy so as to establish civil society.

---

50   Yang Linhong, Zhai Xiuhong, On the Necessity of Existence of Civil Society and Construction Path, *Journal of Yunnan University (Humanities and Social Sciences)*, 2003(1).

Some scholars have argued that the establishment of civil society requires improving the market economy and accelerating its construction, so as to enhance the base of civil society and provide the material guarantees for the freedom, rights and equity of citizens.[51]

Some scholars insist that, in order to establish a perfect civil society, we must greatly promote a modern market economy and build a relatively mature market economic system based on free contract relations and equity, so as to promote the rapid growth and the gradual maturation of the civil society within the rapid development of economy and society.[52]

Some other scholars have argued that, when market is being improved, we should pay attention to their smooth internal relation. We must actively advance and reform property relations and economic and cultural activities in order to develop in the folk, and set up social, economic and cultural relations which have been de-statized and de-politicized. For example, we need to dispose of various outdated ideas on property and establish a social possession relationship. Even state-owned enterprises should adhere to the principles of market participation and fair competition.[53]

Another proposition is to highlight the propulsive role of the state. It is a popular idea in academic circles that Chinese civil society will not rise up on a completely spontaneous base. The formation of civil society in China depends on people's conscious activities, thus the state will play a key role.

Some scholars have suggested that, during the construction of civil society, the state (government) should play an active role rather than a passive one. The mode of late exogenous type of modernization that was followed in China and its very nature determines that Chinese modernization will not occur at the level of society, but will first occur at the level of the state; namely, the modernization will be compulsively started by the state through political power. This means that the state's political driving force will become a necessity, which will last for a long time during the construction of civil society. The propulsive force of the state will be needed for the dual division between the state and society and the establishment of a modern civil society. Such pushing force is a more modern and conscious force in respect of its direction, strength and action mode.[54]

---

51   Xie Weiyan, Constitutionalism and Civil Society, *Journal of Sichuan Normal University (Social Science Edition)*, 2002(6).
52   Shi Xuehua, Construction of Chinese Civil Society with Mature Rules, *Study Monthly*, 2005(8).
53   Jia Dongqiao, Civil Society: The Social Basis of Establishing Market Economy System, *Social Science Research*, 1994(6).
54   Ibid.

Some scholars insist that the development of civil society in China can be deemed as a part of global associational revolution. During such development, government will take the initiative to reform and release partial function and power under the influence of Western ideas and the background of the emergence of a risk in the system of omnipotent state. Unlike the process of the rise of the Western noble bourgeoisie and power division by class conflict, voluntary power release by government plays a leading role. In such development, a government-led mode will occupy an important position.[55]

Some scholars have emphasized the propulsive role of the state from the perspective of government response. They have argued that, with the advancement of political democratization, our government will pay more and more attention on responding to policy participation by the civil society. The response by government will mainly adopt three modes: suggestion-response, guidance-response and rights safeguarding-response. During policy making, government sometimes needs to maintain a certain policy autonomy, and should dare to and be good at educating the masses and correcting wrong opinions in the masses.[56]

In view of political reform of the state, some scholars insist that, in order to build civil society, we must first reform political relations and change the power distribution system operating between the center and the local. Secondly, we should adjust government structure and transform regulation mode and management means, realizing the change from the imperative regulation mode to a persuasive regulation mode, from the passive management mode to an interactive management mode, and from the micro-interference management mode to a macro-regulatory management mode. Finally, we must clarify the relationship between the Party and the government and improve the status of grassroots democracy.[57]

The third proposition emphasizes that we must improve legal system and implement law-based governance. It argues that civil society is established by a universal contract spirit, which can guarantee its benign operation. Hence, during the construction of civil society in China, it is essential to improve legal system and implement law-based governance.

Some scholars have underlined that duality of civil society and political state is the base and boundary for law-based operation. Laws will be

55   Jia Xijin, Three Paths to the Growth of Chinese Civil Society, *Chinese Public Administration,* 2003(3).

56   Sun Fafeng, Government Response: Key Link to Play the Policy Influence of Civil Society in China, *Guangxi Social Sciences*, 2010(5).

57   Guo Dingping, The Development of Civil Society and the Political Transition in China, *Social Sciences*, 1994(12).

developed during an interactive development and a dual contradiction between civil society and political state, as well as during a process of conflict and coordination between general interest and special interest. At the
same time, the pluralistic rights of civil society can effectively dissolve
state power and suppress the arbitrary tendency of public power. The diversified and autonomous development of citizen organizations generates
a division of roles and a power which will balance the state power. The
conflict, interaction and integration of multi-level interests in civil society
derive out rational rule and rational order. The citizen's civil consciousness
with freedom and rational spirit constitutes the non-institutional element of
law-based governance. To step into a real law-based society, China must
restructure the relationship between the state and civil society and set up a
pluralistic rights basis, public authority and benign law-based atmosphere.[58]

Some scholars insist that we should accelerate the formation of a contrac-
tual society so as to integrate scattered individuals into the common contract and protect the independence and voluntary union of people and their
organizations. We must guarantee the joint force of civil society and keep it
from damage. In this respect, especially, we must improve and strengthen
the law system for the societal contract so as to effectively and orderly
regulate various relations in the state and society by the authority of law.[59]

Besides, some other scholars have argued that the establishment of civil
society requires the improvement of the law system, especially the system
of citizen rights and duties, so as to make citizens an independent subjects in
the legal sense. On the one hand, we must further improve the system of basic citizen rights and duties stipulated in the constitution; on the other hand,
we must enact civil code, property law and other relevant laws as soon as
possible to perfect our system of private law system. Meanwhile, we should
enhance the protection of citizen rights, transforming these rights on paper,
to real, actual rights. We must practically guarantee the citizen's freedom of
association and strive to develop associations and other intermediary organizations which are independent from the government and other authorities,
so as to gradually form a force that can contend with public power. We must
establish a constitutional complaint system to protect citizen rights in practice. Finally, we should safeguard the basic rights of citizens and prevent
public power from infringing citizen rights, arbitrarily.[60]

58   Ma Changshan, Civil Society and Political State: Basis and Limits of the Rule of Law,
Chinese Journal of Law, 2002(3).
59   Jia Dongqiao, *Civil Society*: The Social Basis of Establishing Market Economy System,
Social Science Research, 1994(6).
60   Xie Weiyan, Constitutionalism and Civil Society, *Journal of Sichuan Normal
University*, 2002(6).

Moreover, this will mean to emphasize the cultivation and the establishment of a civic culture and a civil consciousness. Construction of a mature civil society positively cannot be separated from the cultivation of a civil consciousness. Due to the influence of history and reality, the civil consciousness of people in China is still not mature and not sound, thus the construction of "civil society" needs to cultivate a civic culture and shape a civil consciousness.

There are some scholars who believe that the essence of civil society is a kind of cultural mechanism, hence the construction of civil society culture should be attached with attention, make the spiritual information of civil society permeate into social traditions and habits to create a new modern culture and a traditional gene possessing national spirit, so as to improve the vigor and the ability of resistance to the weakness of civil society. At the same time, it is also necessary to cultivate active civil consciousness, civic idea and civic competence of social members with cultural education and other means to urge the universal generation of an independent and equal personality in society.[61]

There are some scholars who believe that cultivating a civil society requires to cultivate a rational citizen culture. "Culture is the mother of the system". Consequently, we cannot only think highly of system construction (moreover, the current system construction is referred to a transplantation of the Western system usually), while ignoring the cultural construction. There are two problems needed to be aware of here: one is that traditional culture has to be updated to realize its modernization, and the second is that the cultural basis of the system has to be expounded. This requires us to keep the value significance of the system consistent with its cultural meaning during constructing the system.[62]

There are scholars who believe that the cultivation of a civic culture and shaping a civil consciousness has to be started from the political and cultural aspects. They believe that: first, consciousness political subject should be established.. Individuals should evade their dependence and passive psychology, overcome their political indifference psychology, and possess an independent individual political consciousness, and change to active and positive subjects from being passive and negative objects in the social political life. Secondly, strengthen their consciousness of political participation. The degree of citizen's political participation reflects the development

61   Jia Dongqiao, Civil Society: The Social Basis of Establishing Market Economy System, *Social Science Research*, 1994(6).
62   Xie Weiyan, Constitutionalism and Civil Society, *Journal of Sichuan Normal University*, 2002(6).

of a civil society, as well as the level of democratization of the social of the society. Thirdly, cultivate consciousness of political supervision. Without the supervision and restraint on power and without avoiding the corruption of power, there will be no healthy environment for the development of a civil society, or political stage for citizens' playing their roles as subjects. The cultivation of consciousness of political supervision is the inherent meaning of civic culture topic. Fourth, establish political rule consciousness. Overcome the thinking pattern of the rule of people which has existed for thousands of years, realize the legalization and institutionalization of the state's political life, and promote an orderly and a rational political participation of the citizens.[63]

There are some scholars who believe that during the process of cultivating Chinese civil society culture, some universal values of international civil society or global civil society should be put efforts to pay attention to absorb at the same time when maintaining the relative independence of the traditional value orientation of Chinese civil society. That blends the accepted freedom, equality, universal love and other values of the international civil society or the global civil society (under construction) into the value system of Chinese civil society organically while continue maintaining and developing the value of communism, socialism and collectivism. It is necessary to discard both the extreme individualism of the West and the liberalism of anarchism while respecting human rights.[64]

Some scholars have also argued that the contemporary modern civil consciousness should include five aspects, namely the consciousness of responsibility, duty, kindness consciousness, self-discipline consciousness, tolerance consciousness, and competition consciousness, whereas the cultivation of civic culture and shaping of spirit have to be started from.[65]

Fifthly, emphasizing to promote the development of "non-governmental organizations" vigorously. The "non-governmental organization" or "the third party" is an important component of civil society; there are also scholars who believe that it is the subject of civil society.[66] However, from the view of actual situation, "non-governmental organizations" in China still

63   Wu Junbin, Discussion and Analysis on the Basic Dimension of Contemporary Chinese Civil Society Construction, *Journal of Central South University (Social Science Edition)*, 2013(1).
64   Shi Xuehua, Construction of Chinese Civil Society with Mature Rules, *Study Monthly*, 2005(8).
65   Shan Aihong, The Rising of Chinese Civil Society and the Cultivation of Citizen Consciousness, *Studies on the Socialism with Chinese Characteristics*, 2004(6).
66   Yu Keping, Some Problems in the Study of Chinese Civil Society, *Journal of the Party School of the Central Committee of the CPC*, 2007(6).

have development to reach a mature level problems. The construction of contemporary China's "civil society" has to vigorously promote the development of "non-governmental organizations". Some scholars have argued that the masses' self-governing organizations and self-governing social groups are the intermediaries of the establishment of a civil society, which constitute the "safety valve" full of flexibility and protectiveness among the three, i.e. the state, society and individuals by protecting the basically balanced ecology of the civil society.[67]

There are also some scholars who believe that in order to promote the development of non-governmental organizations vigorously, we should start from the system of "non-governmental organizations". In their opinion, each non-governmental organization has to formulate a strict internal management system, and everyone should be equal before laws and regulations, standardize behaviors of the citizens and maintain a benign order, and establish a strict government accountability mechanism and severely punish misconducts. Each organization will improve the capacity of self-governance, define its own goal and mission, and be active in accepting petitions and supervision from the whole society. In the first place, our government should establish a procedural law and system regulating non-governmental organizations. In the second place, construct unity and systematization for numerous regulations, rules, by-laws, measures, opinions, etc. involving in non-government management, and make these systems play the incentive effect for normalizing and encouraging non-governmental organizations development in actual practices.[68]

Some scholars also believe that the construction of civil society in China should pay attention to the importance of talent construction, establish reasonable talent mechanism, attract high quality talents to participate in organization construction, make active policies, and encourage all quarters of society to provide support for development of non-governmental organizations. The government should increase the support efforts to non-governmental organizations on funds and taxes. The government should provide more preferential treatment on taxes to public utilities and non-governmental organizations, and it can also provide financial aids to the non-governmental organizations engaging in public welfare undertakings by direct financial appropriation, as well as award contracts of some governmental public services to non-governmental organizations with better qualifications in form of government bidding, making non-governmental

67   Jia Dongqiao, Civil Society: The Social Basis of Establishing Market Economy System, *Social Science Research,* 1994(6).

68   Ma Xiheng, On the Formation and Path Analysis of China Civil Society, *Journal of Legal System and Society*, 2013(1).

organizations obtain necessary financial support during the process of providing public service which helps the government.[69]

VI.4. Theoretical Problems of "Civil Society" in China

Since the civil society thought trend was introduced into China, different scholars have conducted different concepts of "civil society" from different angles or standpoints, and the starting point of some scholars who have carried heated debates on the issue of "civil society" aim to promote a better social development and society construction in China, and beneficial views and opinions have been put forward. Some scholars connected the concept of "civil society" with the protection of the interests of specific social groups, for the independence of the judicial system, the process of democratization, the freedom to establish social organizations and associations, the freedom of media and freedom of expression and public opinion, which are meaningful. For instance, at the beginning of 1990s, someone claimed that: "Based on the reality of China's Reform and Opening-up and historical experiences and lessons, it has become necessary to build the theory of Chinese civil society."[70] In general, the rise and development of the "civil society" thought trend are in accord with the development of China's socio-economic systems. Additionally, looking from the angle of theoretical debates and specifically reviewing the research status of domestic academic circles, this book holds that the researches on the civil society still have some aspects which need to be perfected:

Firstly, the theoretical consciousness need to be further enhanced. Some individuals researched upon "civil society" are neither exploring the preciseness of concepts, nor studying whether the assumptions behind theory come into existence or not. They just copy blindly, and then serve for expressing political appeals, lacking of any theoretical consciousness and confidence. The concept of "civil society" is not a scientific and rigorous concept. Many people ever used this concept, such as Hobbes, Rousseau, Locke, Hegel, Marx, Tocqueville, and Gramsci, while the understandings of them are not totally identical. This concept has different contents under different historical periods in the West. It is generally acknowledged that "civil society" refers to an autonomous political community or a city state rather than a savage tribe; so, the meaning is close to the meaning of

---

69 Ibid.
70 Deng Zhenglai, Jing Yuejin, Constructing Civil Society in China, First issue, *Chinese Social Sciences Quarterly*, Hong Kong, November (1992).

political society and state. By modern era, "civil society" turns to an ideological weapon of bourgeois in earlier period arguing against the thought of the feudal autocratic monarchical divine, emphasizing balancing and confrontation to state. By the contemporary age, "civil society" mainly refers to summation of all the non-governmental organizations and civil relations other than government and market, including NGOs, citizens' voluntary associations, communities, associations, interest groups and movements organized by citizens, spontaneously. In late 1980s, along with the profound changes in the social and economic structure of the countries around the world, the concept of "civil society" has become vogue all over the world. The Western countries also regard the development and cultivation of civil society organizations as a powerful weapon for promoting a Western-style democracy and realizing "good governance", and promote it to the Third World countries and the socialist countries with all force. After bearing such an important function, the political nature of "civil society" is more vivid. For some scholars, the core idea during research and discussion is to dock "civil society" and "universal value", and take over the appeal of balancing and confrontation to state, and associate such concept with special social group benefit protection, independence of the judicial system, process of democratization, freedom of establishing social organizations and associations, and freedom of media and public opinion. Such theoretical appeal is based on three theoretical assumptions; the first one regards civil society as a whole and denies the differences in it; the second one regards civil society as a piece of pure land, opposite to the evil state, the civil society is the one doing all the good things, while states commit terrible crimes continuously; the third emphasizes that there is a natural relation of opposition between civil society organizations and the governments. On the basis of these assumptions, the role of civil society infinitely and exaggerate the transmission role of civil society to the "universal value" are affirmed. These assumptions carry on the gene of Western liberalism, becoming "native place" "gestating" autonomy, autonomy, pluralism and docking human rights, freedom, equality and the rule of law in theoretical discussion. It is unimaginable that this is not a performance lacking of theoretical imagination and theoretical confidence to a certain extent.

Secondly, the cognition on the issue of state and social relations needs to be deepened. Dealing with the relation between state and social relation is a major topic for "civil society" doctrine. The question of the relationship between state and society appeared in the Western societies at first. Does China also have the question of the relationship between state and society? The answer is yes. Before the implementation of Reform and Opening-up, China has implemented a highly centralized and unified planned economic system and a corresponding societal management system. Under such system, various social resources are highly concentrated in the hand of government with a high concentration of social management, the social production and life possess a higher degree of homogeneity. Since the implementation of Reform and Opening-up, the majority of Chinese people have become citizens with high degree of autonomy compared to a citizen belonging to a nation-wide unitary, uniform social management system, in the past they were part of this kind of social management system (danwei, work units). After this change, many people, developed a feeling that they were forced to be "lonely" or "out of the system."

According to the opinion of common people, a significant minority of citizens have become "social citizen" from "citizen of the state". Such a huge change in the relation of inside-outside of the system and such structural relation to a certain degree reflects the "separation" of "state" and "society". The separation of state and society in contemporary China, to a certain degree, is a historical necessity, result of the progress of the China's social development, which has to be paid highly attention and treated carefully. The issue of dealing with the relationship between state and society under conditions of socialism with Chinese characteristics is a basic issue for the construction of socialist society with Chinese characteristics.

On the issue of how to understand and treat the relation of state and society in contemporary China, it is mainly based on the experience of Western societal development. The theory of "civil society" desires to weaken and restrain the state power of capitalism or capitalist class as well as the oppression and regulation of the ruling classes on the masses of the people through developing "social power" in capitalist society, and hopes to make the masses obtain more freedom and rights through autonomy of society, which gives no cause for much criticism. Yet when understanding and dealing with the relationship between state and society on Chinese scene, the actual situation in China should be paid more attention.

There is fundamental difference between the western society and Chinese society. China is a socialist country. In essence of state system, the socialist system practiced in China takes people as the masters of state affairs, and aims at guaranteeing and expanding people's rights and freedoms as its founding purpose. The state's political rule and social governance system of China are not ruling or dictatorship means tools mastered by capital or any other power group, but the means in the service of the broadest masses of the people, for their realizing the socialist modernization, and a sharp weapon to realize the national rejuvenation. As a result, we cannot

not assume a fundamental opposition between state and society in China, and it is inadequate to confuse the relationship between state and society of China into the Western discourse system and artificially – evaluate the "state" as an "inevitable evil", and unconditionally treating the "society" as the sphere of "goodness".

Today, the development stage where Chinese society stays is different from that of the Western societies, and the modes and methods adopted for realization of development and modernization of China are different from that of the West, especially those developed countries with early development time and high development degree. China realized industrialization and modernization through national independence and people's liberation revolution, as well as an independent development under a historical background that capitalist world system has formed, and China walks to the rejuvenation of the nation by struggling to free itself from the constraint of unreasonable, unequal and immoral world economy and political order led by the West. The development and modernization achievement of China are obtained through fight of plain living and hard struggle, as well as a collective wisdom and efforts under mobilization and organization led by CPC and the people's political power. The market economy in China is socialist market economy, and the politics in China is socialist democratic politics with Chinese characteristics, this is the most foundational thing, the biggest characteristic, namely unified planning and leadership, other than a heap of loose sand or everyone acts in their own way; it is not a spontaneous development, but a strategic development. This is the reason of regime for China obtaining great achievements that attract world's attention, which is the foundation of China's success, as well as the biggest interests and hope of Chinese people.

Thirdly, there is an obvious deviation in the understanding of Marx's conception of "civil society". Marx's civil society thought has a specific background and an explicit goal orientation. However, in some researches, Marx's "civil society" thought is used to demonstrate cultivation and development of the "civil society" in China. There are scholars who have argued that: "The researches made regarding Marx's civil society concept are not accepted and grasped so comprehensively that it can further become a kind of important conceptual basis for good governance, so that it can further form an important constituent part of Chinese socialist political civilization."[71] Similar claims quote the discourse of Marx, about bourgois civil society, and have argued that construction of a socialist civil citizen society will be a regression and contradicts Marx's civil society thought. Such

---

71   Yu Keping, *Democracy and and Rule of Law*, Peking University Press,2006, p. 127.

understanding blurs the real connotation of Marx's civil society thought, which fails to see the essence of Marx's concept of civil society and its aim.

Firstly, the mature "civil society" discussed by Marx and Engels is a capitalist society with capitalist mode of production established. Marx and Engels ever used the concept of "civil society" in many works, such as *Critique of Hegel's Philosophy of Right*, *Holy Family*, *German Ideology*, *Preface to the Critique of Political Economy*, *The First Draft of the Civil War in France*, *History about the Communist League* which all refer to the concept of "civil society". The "civil society" of Marx and Engels has two meanings. One is that citizen society is the result of a modern bourgeois political revolutions, and its foundation is the private ownership, which is equivalent to the formation of the capitalist society. "Now, the bourgeoisie took possession of the productive forces it had developed under feudalism. All the old economic forms, the corresponding civil relations, the political state which was the official expression of the old civil society, were smashed."[72] Therefore, "the real civil society could only be developed with the bourgeois class"[73], which is a "'civil society'[74] towards maturity with big pace of 18th Century" and "developed the civil society."[75] In fact, such a civil society was the bourgois society. While the so-called process of the separation of the civil society and political state was the process, wherein the emerging bourgeoisie contested for economic and political survival space against the feudal monarchy, and as a matter of fact, the capitalist society has developed along with a maturing civil society.

The other meaning of Marx was to regard civil society in sense of an economic relation. Marx and Engels ever said in German Ideology that: "The form of intercourse determined by the existing productive forces at all previous historical stages, and in its turn determining these, is civil society".[76] The Preface to the Critique of Political Economy calls "the sum of relations of material life" as "civil society". The reason for such discussion of civil society by emphasizing the relations of production or relation of communication (Verkehr) is related with the formation of new view of history – historical materialism, directly. Marx has opposed to the idealists who interpret the development of human society through the "absolute spirit"

---

72 *Selected Works of Karl Marx and Frederick Engels*, Vol. 1, People's Publishing House, 1995, p. 152.
73 Ibid, p. 130.
74 *Selected Works of Karl Marx and Frederick Engels*, Vol. 2, People's Publishing House, 1995, p. 1.
75 *Complete Works of Lenin*, Vol. 55, People's Publishing House, 1990, p. 101.
76 *Selected Works of Karl Marx and Frederick Engels,* Vol. 1, People's Publishing House, 1995, p. 87.

and considered this as a reversed view of history. In order to implement his thorough materialist view of history, Marx made an in-depth analysis on "sum of material relations of production" as the foundation of the bourgeois society, namely "civil society" as a breakthrough point to emphasize that "civil society is the real cradle and the real stage of all history"[77], "the foundation constituting the state of all eras as well as the foundation of any concept of superstructure"[78] against historical idealism view which tried to explain everything with "absolute spirit". Marx has reduced civil society into economic relations, merely to explain that this view of history is different from the idealist view of history, Marx did not search for some category which would be valid in every era, but has always based himself on the process real historical development, and he didn't attempt to explain social practice from concepts, but aimed to explain various ideologies starting from real material practice,[79] meanwhile, the "bourgeois society" in the aspect of political sense and from the aspect rule of law was exactly the society which adopted the capitalist mode of production.

Secondly, it is a serious misunderstanding of Marx's civil society concept to explain the construction of "socialist civil society" in China and advocating "fights against" the state with Marx's civil society concept. The so-called research achievements to "socialist citizen (civil) society" in academic circles are basically to construct a society based on private ownership through developing and expanding individualistic values, and fighting against the existing state relation on politics. Such society is inconsistent with Marx's civil society concept.

The discourse regarding civil society by Marx and Engels was expounded with their new view of history, and aimed to "positively sublate (Ger. *Aufheben*) the private ownership system" and the "emancipation of mankind or man" has been their ultimate goal all the time. This is fully reflected in their discussion on the relationship between the civil society and the state. The civil society, as the synonym of bourgeois society, has discarded the feudal monarchic state, while the state is the domain wherein class interests are demonstrated, and the formation of a civil society based on private ownership has been favorable for the collapse of the state representing feudal monarchy and the authority of the church. The state which is based on a civil society is also a product of class struggle, and under the conditions of modern civil society, men will still follow one-sided and alienated

---

77   *Selected Works of Karl Marx and Frederick Engels,* Vol. 1, People's Publishing House, 1995, p. 8.
78   Ibid, p. 131.
79   *Collected Works of Karl Marx and Frederick Engels,* Vol. 1, People's Publishing House, 2009, p.54.

life, which also needs to be sublated. In consequence, the proletariat "will overthrow the state"[80], "the working class will create the free association of men, association of free producers by eliminating class and class antagonism to substitute the civil society; and the state will not exist anymore in its original meaning."[81] Such "a free association of men union body eliminating class and class antagonisms" "we shall have an association in which free development of each is the condition for free development of all."[82]

Thirdly, the correct understanding of Marx's civil society concept should start from the viewpoint of historical materialism, and understand the civil society discussed by Marx with the viewpoint of practice and development of Marx. Some scholars to a certain extent have a misunderstanding about this conception of Marx and Engels. What needs to be pointed out is that advocating fights against the state by establishing the so-called "socialist civil society" faces a logical contradiction which cannot be solved to some extent.

Firstly, China is a socialist state governed by people's democratic dictatorship with a long past of a despotic state, full of feudal colors. If we admit that China is a socialist state of the people's democratic dictatorship, then it makes no sense to fight against state by leaning to the civil society. Secondly, through the Reform and Opening-up policy, is China trying to perfect the socialist system or change the socialist system; is it trying to carry out a thorough privatization, or to maintain the basic economic system with public ownership as the main pillar, and common development of various different economic sectors with different ownership forms developing side by side. If the basic economic system of socialism is admitted, then it also makes no sense to establish a civil society with a complete "private domain". Accordingly, the civil society concept of Marx must be understood and mastered comprehensively and correctly. This requires us to pay further attention to the reality to achieve perfection of this concept with deeper studies of it.

---

80   *Selected Works of Karl Marx and Frederick Engels,* Vol. 1, People's Publishing House, 1995, p. 121.
81   Ibid. p. 194.
82   *Selected Works of Karl Marx and Frederick Engels,* Vol. 1, People's Publishing House, 1995, p. 294.

CHAPTER SEVEN

Echo of "New Collectivism" – Nationalism Thought Trend

The nationalism thought trend is one of the quite prominent political thought trends in contemporary China's ideological field. Some scholars have pointed out that: "As long as the divisions of state, nation and race still exist on earth, nationalism will have value of existence, and it will be impossible for human rights to exist completely divorced from ethnic/national rights."[1] There are even scholars who make such a judgment: "Seen from the political aspect, the sources of nationalism are already an important component part in the political ideas of the leading strata in the new period."[2]

The theoretical imagination of nationalism is rather aimed against the liberalism in the national development and ideological field. It emphasizes an even and neat uniformity of collective memory, collective strength, and collective consciousness, as well as the synthesis of concepts so as to realize a completely new reunification at the spiritual level and achieve the great rejuvenation of the nation. The mass psychological basis of nationalism thought trend is more extensive than that of other thought trends, closely related with the mainstream and non-mainstream ideologies. Correctly grasping the development trend, actual manifestation, basis appeal, theoretical basis, etc. that the nationalism thought trend has is conducive to profoundly grasp the basic shape and state of political thought trends in contemporary China.

---

1 Wang Xiaodong, *Nationalism and Democratism*, recorded in: *Intellectual's Standpoint: Nationalism and Destiny of China during Transformation Period*, The Time Literature and Art Press, 2000, p. 93.

2 Xiao Gongqin, *Nationalism and the Ideology during Chinese Transition Period*, recorded in: *Intellectual's Standpoint: Nationalism and Destiny of China during Transformation Period*, The Time Literature and Art Press, 2000, p. 447.

VII.1. What is nationalism?

The rise of any social thought trend is never groundless. "The emergence of nationalism thought trend is certainly linked with the fundamental needs of a country, it is not shaped according to the will of individuals."[3] There are two basic premises for formation of any social thought trend, one is changes of actual social life practice, and the other is social psychological and theoretical origin. Just like material production, the human spiritual production has the characteristics of inter-generational accumulation. Any new thought, new concept and new theory have their origin of historical germination. The core concept of a social thought trend is even more so, often being an old discourse system which obtains new expression under new historical conditions. Therefore, without understanding the theoretical expression and actual manifestation of the core concept like nation, nation-state, nationalism and national separatism, it is very difficult to properly grasp the nationalism thought trend in contemporary China. The understanding of these issues is the premise for dissecting the nationalism thought trend in contemporary China, and is conducive to determine the theoretical coordinates of the core concepts of the nationalism thought trend among many complicated nationalism theories in contemporary China.

VII.1.1. Nationality and nationalism

Theoretical indicators of nationality and nationalism are all different and numerous. The research of academic circles in China about nationalism, especially theory and practice of nationalism in contemporary China are still not enough, while relevant foreign research achievements are more abundant.[4] Their arguments, methods and conclusions are all helpful for us to make a deep analysis on the nationalism thought trend. Of course, there are also some shortcomings in such researches, which are mainly sinking too much into discussion of concepts, instead of starting from the angle of practical activity, lack of a dynamic grasp of the actual movement of nationalism, especially treating the nationalism of the Third World by applying the

3   Wang Hui, Zhang Tianwei, *Culture Critical Theory and the Issue of Contemporary Chinese Nationalism*, Recorded in *Intellectual Standpoint: Nationalism and Destiny of China during Transformation Period*, The Time Literature and Art Press (2000), p. 400.

4   As for the research on nationalism overseas, the English works is massive only in the respect of method, scale, depth and quantity. In the recent two decades, the accomplishments of the research include *Nations Before Nationalism* by J. A. Armstrong (1982), *Nationalism and the State* by John Breuilly (1982), *Nations and Nationalism* by Ernest Gellner (1983), *Social Preconditions of National Revival in Europe* by Miroslav Hroch (1985), *The Ethnic Origins of Nations* by Anthony Smith (1986), *Nationalism Thought and the Colonial World* by P. Chatterjee (1986), and *Nations and Nationalism after 1788* by Eric Hobsbawm (1990), all of which pushed the research on nationalism to a higher level.

general theory of Western nationalism dogmatically, and equating national-ism of the Third World to the nationalism of Western developed countries. It is apparent that there are differences between the nationalist appeals of the Third World, especially of the oppressed nations and the mainstream theory of Western nationalism. Besides, some researches fail to conduct theoretical distinctions between nationality and nationalism from the stand-point, viewpoint and method of Marxism. This book will analyze and sum-marize the concepts of nation and nationalism from the angle of Marxism.

What is nation? Nation refers to a stable community formed by people in history possessing a common language, common territory, and economic life, as well as showing common psychological quality based on a common culture. Fundamentally speaking, the development of a nation is restricted by the production relations and the social system. Nation is a historical category, which has the process of generation, development and demise. At the final period of the primitive society and along with development of men's productive forces, commodity exchange, private ownership and class differentiation emerged, which made the clans which take the original bloodline as foundation and bond disintegrate, and the nation and the state gradually took shape based on tribes and tribal alliances. The modern na-tion is a community form composed along with the emergence of capital-ism. The elimination of the feudal segmentation, strengthening of economic ties among regions and the formation of the national market have provided the economic base for the emergence of the modern nation.

In the class society which based on the private ownership of means of production, each nation is split into two basic opposing classes. The oppres-sion of the dominating nation upon other nations we see in history is, in the final analysis, the exploitation and oppression of the vast working people of other nationalities by the exploiting classes in the dominant nation. In the era of imperialism, national oppression has become a universal phenom-enon, and the struggle of the oppressed nations for national liberation has become an important content of the international proletarian revolutionary movement. In the fairly distant future, when the victory of socialism in the whole world, after a long term economic and cultural development, the national differences will gradually disappear, all nations in the world will gradually form a common whole, i.e., the communist era in the world.

Seen from its essence, nationalism is the principle, guideline and policy for bourgeois and petty bourgeoisie classes dealing with national issues and relations among nations. By viewing nationalism historically and con-cretely, we can find that it has three manifestation forms different from each other. The first is the nationalism at the very beginning of capitalism.

This nationalism was a sharp weapon for bourgeois and petty bourgeoisie to fight feudalism which hindered the development of the society, and this nationalism had a progressive effect in history. The second is the nationalism in the outward expansion period of the bourgeoisie. At this time, the bourgeoisie, not completely satisfied with the occupation of the domestic market, desired to grab raw materials and dump its products worldwide. When the bourgeoisie re-asserted nationalism now, it only meant bullying and oppressing the weak and small nations, inciting the national sentiments of the people in the country, and even grabbing colonies by war and fight and plundering overseas markets. The process of capitalism developing into the stage of imperialism was exactly the process by which bourgeois nationalism changed from progressive to reactionary.

The third manifestation form of nationalism is the nationalism of oppressed peoples of the world against imperialism and feudalism. Let us illustrate Sun Yat-sen's nationalism as an example. Sun Yat-sen proposed and summarized the program of the Chinese bourgeois democratic revolution with the slogan of "Three Principles of the People", namely nationalism, democracy and the people's livelihood, among which the nationalism policy was the main pillar. The revolution of 1911 led by Sun Yat-sen was a struggle of the national bourgeoisie against feudalism in the early period of Chinese capitalism, whose goal was to establish a bourgeois republic. Looking from this point, the nationalism of Sun Yat-sen was not identical but was close to the aforementioned first kind of nationalism but not the second kind absolutely. Such difference was determined by the nature of Chinese society and the nature of the revolution. When the bourgeoisie in Western Europe struggled to establish the nation-state, its spearhead was pointed at the feudalism, while the bourgeoisie in China was rising, the capitalism of Europe had developed into the stage of imperialism, which was looking for colonies all over the world; therefore, the nationalism of Sun Yat-sen had the content both against feudal ruling and external aggression from the beginning, and this is an important characteristic of the third kind of nationalism. Due to such nationalism possessing a revolutionary nature and progressiveness, not only the bourgeoisie fight for such kind of nationalism, in order to overthrow imperialism and feudalism, as well as to strive for national independence and liberation, but also workers and peasants accepted such nationalism in a certain historical period.

Certainly, the nationalism of Sun Yat-sen can be divided into two stages, the early and the late. Although the "Three People's Principles" in the early stage contained ideological contents against imperialism and feudalism, it wasn't a complete program against imperialism and feudalism, therefore, in China it is called "the old Three People's Principles". Afterwards, under the influence of victory of the October socialist revolution in Russia and with the help of the CPC, Sun Yat-sen determined the three policies of alliance with Russia and the Soviet Union, alliance with the Communist Party and advocated helping farmers and workers, and re-formulated the Three People's Principles in Declaration of the First National Congress of the Kuomintang of China in 1924, and this is the new Three People's Principles. This new Three People's Principles has same and different phrases with the struggle program of CPC at that time in which the new democracy was claimed Mao Zedong made a very thorough analysis about this in On the New Democracy. Regarding nationalism, Sun Yat-sen turned from the original "Expel the Manchus for restoration of China", namely to overthrow the feudal system of the Qing Dynasty and establish a bourgeois republic, and proposed the idea of opposing imperialism, and the idea that Chinese nation would seek for self-liberation, and that all nations in the country should be equal. In the Prime Minister's Will, he had proposed more explicitly: "Arouse the public and unite the with those nations which treat our Chinese nations equally in the world, unite them to struggle together." Just because of this proposition, the CPC members employed the policy to cooperate with Sun Yat-sen and his party naturally, which was very necessary for national independence and liberation of the people, and which was in conformity with the interests of the proletariat and the broad masses of working people in China. But later, those shameless figures who betrayed the legacy of Sun Yat-sen have undermined the cooperation between the CPC and the KMT.

The viewpoints and principles about national issues of the proletariat and its political party are based on the world view of dialectical materialism and historical materialism, and in consequence, they are different from the bourgeois nationalism, especially its second kind of expression form. It requires that everything should be started from the common fundamental interests of the people of the country, and from the fundamental interests of the people of all nations in the world, namely all mankind at the same time. The proletariat does not exploit anyone, and would struggle for the pursuit of a social system in which there cannot be existed any exploitation from anyone to people; accordingly, it opposes the oppression of any nation by any other nation: not only oppose to any national oppression to their own nations from a foreign nation, but also oppose the oppression of their own people to any other nation resolutely, and claim that all the nations (no matter big or small, strong or weak) should be equal completely, internationally and in domestic. Exactly, due this point, the Chinese Communists have found common ground for the joint struggle with the new "Three People's Principles" of Sun Yat-sen.

VII.1.2. Contemporary national separatism

From the view of the specific manifestation of nationalism, the national separatism is also one of the expressions of nationalism. It is quite necessary to analyze the contemporary national separatism. This is because the contemporary national separatism shows a remarkable performance in the current epoch, which exists objectively. During our process of completing the process of building a moderately prosperous society in all aspects, a high degree of vigilance to national separatism need to be maintained; the research point of view to contemporary nationalism thoughts and analysis to national separatism of this book claims important aspects for understanding of contemporary nationalism thought trend in China. When facing contemporary nationalism thought trend, people will be interested to the relation of it with national separatism. Among the discussion on contemporary nationalism thought trend, there is one kind of understanding which believes that nationalism is a "double-edged sword", which is easy to cause the separation of nationalities. Analyzing national separatism from levels of practice and theory and making a contrast of it with contemporary nationalism thought trend will be helpful for understanding contemporary nationalism thought trend more objectively and deeply. What is national separatism? There are scholars who believe that all those "generally speaking those thought trends and actions that tend and aim to break an established nation-state or a historically formed national community, should be called as national separatism or national secessionism generally."[5] This book agrees with such definition of national separatism. Eventually, the contemporary national separatism is the demonstration of ethnic separatism in the current epoch.

First, the contemporary national separatism is changing the political map of the world. The national separatism which was first demonstrated in the former Soviet Union, Yugoslavia, Czechoslovakia and other multi-national federal states have emerged internal national separatist movements one after another in present age intensively, and the formerly aligned republics have gained their full sovereignty and independence from the former federal system in succession, including both violent separation and peaceful separation. Under the influence of such national separatist wave which first occurred in former Soviet Union and socialist countries of Eastern Europe, not only in the Middle East, Africa, South Asia and the Asia Pacific region appeared similar national separatist or ethnic nationalism trends, even in Western Europe and North America regions are faced with such national movements in Northern Ireland, Corsica, Basque, Quebec and Hawaii and

---

5   Luo Fuhui as chief editor, *Theses on Chinese Nationalism Thought Trend*, Central China Normal University Press, 1996, p. 19.

in other places, which have caused several striking issues of national conflicts. Thus, from the Balkans to the East, across the West Asia and the Caucasus region and reached the Central Asia region which are the main regions of contemporary national conflicts.

Second, when we discuss the driving causes of national separatism. The reason why contemporary national separatism is remarkably active has its profound historical and realistic reasons, as given in the following.

First, it is rooted in the impact of the end of the Cold War era, and the original interest pattern which was formed in this Cold War era. After the end of the World War II, the world has formed an international political configuration which mainly featured a confrontation between the Soviet and the United States, which was designed by 3 major world powers, in the city of Yalta and called as the Yalta System. The East and the West were in the "Cold War". This pattern has made national conflicts in socialist countries and Western countries remain in a secondary position, and they were even concealed. The status of national issues in the larger Third World could not be independent from the constraints of this pattern. As a Japanese scholar has written: "The world system established by Cold War pattern strengthens the tensions in the world and also plays the role of maintaining international order, as a matter of fact, this pattern has also restrained and suppressed the national issues in the world. In order to avoid fundamental conflicts, these two opposing camps have stealthily suppressed the local interest conflicts in small countries. Once this world pattern disintegrated, not only the Soviet Union, even the seemingly victorious Western Alliance countries will also lose their control in their influence regions, and will not be able those nations demanding to express their own claims."[6] With the end of the "Cold War", the drastic changes in Eastern Europe and the disintegration of Soviet Union, the national conflicts concealed by the Soviet Union and Eastern European socialist countries for a long time burst out all of a sudden. The Third World countries also adjusted their international status one after another, and explored own new positions in the international environment, with great turbulence, and put safeguarding their national in more prominent position, which has made the phenomena regarding territorial division and national separation, an important demonstration of interest struggle, which is generally defined as national separatism.

Second, the intervention of the Western developed countries, as one important cause. The intervention and interference in the internal affairs of other countries by using national issues by the Western countries are the

<hr/>

6   Fumio Uda, *Some Considerations on "National Problems"*, selected and translated by Zhang Ying, *Collection of Ethnological Rendition*, 1994(1).

new means of Western expansion of nationalism for the purpose of striving for interests of their own states and nations in contemporary times. Analyzing the international pattern after the Cold War, there are shadows of great power hegemony behind every national separatist event. The Western countries headed by the United States took the end of "Cold War" as an opportunity, trying to re-lead the new international political order. Under the banner of "human rights" and "humanitarianism", they interfered in the internal affairs of other countries on the grounds of national issues corruptly. Such approach provides a powerful protection for national separatist forces watching for a chance to engage in various separatist activities, fueling the arrogance of the separatists. The national separatist forces of various countries also pin their hope on the intervention of the Western countries, seeking international support and intervention to achieve their ultimate goal of national separation.

The Western countries led by the United States based on their strategic goal of promoting "peaceful evolution"[7], in the Soviet Union and Eastern European socialist countries, have manipulated the wave of "political pluralism" and "democratization"; they have spared no effort to penetrate into their ideological spheres and also encouraged the national separatist forces in these countries. For example, when the three Baltic States set off a national separation (independence) movement, the United States and other Western countries formally recognized them diplomatically despite the strong protest from the Soviet Union. In a series of national separatist activities in the former Yugoslavia, the role played by the Western countries was more prominent, such as secret instigation and planning, open solidarity with separatism, first recognition, and military intervention, which has led to today's divided situation of the Federal Yugoslavia eventually.

Third, it comes to the consequences of colonialism. "The Third World countries have been under the domination of the Western colonial (old) imperialism for a long time, the division of their state borders are artificial and random result of interest fights and interest concessions among the Western colonialist powers, and there is not any consideration of the complicated factors, such as the nature of the nation. Furthermore, on the eve of independence in these countries, the colonial empires implemented the so-called policy of "divide and rule", tried every possible means to create and expand the Third World political, economic, territorial, cultural and other aspects of the gap and inequality, and sow seeds for the national

---

7   Peaceful evolution in the Chinese political context refers efforts to replace socialism by capitalism targeting a socialist country.

contradictions in the Third World."[8] The colonialism, hegemony and power politics in modern international relations are exactly the profound historical roots of the national issues of the world today. Some scholars have made more in-depth analyses. In the process of the construction of the world colonialism system, the Western colonial power took the racial, national and religious policies of "divide and rule", "play off one power against another", etc. to pass on contradictions and alienations on the basis of brutal conquest, killing and raging, and divide territory or region of national minorities of some countries arbitrarily in the struggles between the interests of the colonial forces. Even to the extent that when being forced to withdraw from the colonies, they would leave many troubles including national issues by way of the territorial dismemberment and partition of independent countries.[9] Exactly the colonial conquest and imperial ruling of Western colonialism for up to 400 years of history laid the hidden dangers of national separatism all over the world, causing difficulties and troubles for many countries in today's world to deal with and solve the national problem.

Fourth, it comes to national policy mistakes. The deviation and error of the nation-state on national policy is an important inducement of national separatism. The national policies are the principles and the measures for domestic value and benefit distribution of various nations in a country, an unfair attitude at any level, such as politics, economy and culture, may lead to a national separatism mood.[10]

Politically, the majority nations of some countries pursue great nationalism by oppressing and discriminating against national minorities; some countries deprive national minorities from the political rights and block their participation in politics, and only offer nominal autonomy for the minority nationalities, but restrict them in many aspects, which makes it easy to cause a separatist tendency. The governments of some countries disregard the objective reality and reject to recognize the existence of some minorities; and some countries ignore the long term existence of national issues, neglecting to accept the domestic national conflicts that are developing rampantly.

Economically, some governments only narrowly consider extracting and utilizing the natural resources of the minority nationality regions, regardless of the coordinated development of the local economy, leading to abnormal

---

8   Compiled by China Institute of Contemporary International Relations: *Third World in the 1990s*, Current Affairs Press, 1992, p. 172.
9   Wang Hongyan, *Analysis on Ethnic Separatism at the End of the 20th Century, Journal of Liaoning Teachers College,* 2003(10).
10   Ibid.

industrial structure and serious pollution of the ecological environment in minority regions; some countries do not pay attention to coordinate the balanced development of the national economy, or unfair distribution of realistic interests due to the regulatory mechanism, resulting in appearance or aggravation of unbalanced development state of national economy, which may lead to a demand for separation in the poor regions, or nationalities in the rich regions seek for independence, such as Catalans in Spain. Such cases do exist: "Some national minorities living in the more economically developed areas have the desire to seek for improvement of a corresponding political status, and for this purpose, they are unwilling to bear the obligation of economic assistance to backward areas and wish to avoid the common burden and seek for independence."[11]

VII.1.3. "National self-determination" and the theory of "one nation, one state"

"National self-determination" and "One nation, one state" theories are often regarded as the theoretical cornerstone of the contemporary national separatism thought trend. It is necessary to have a profound understanding of national separatism by analyzing it deeply. The national separatists and some Western personages who have ulterior motives often cite the national self-determination principle to defend their behaviors. For example, the Armenian social sciences professor Levon Ter-Petrosyan who has held the first presidency of the newly independent Armenia once preached: "The national self-determination right is absolute and once a nation determines to grasp its own destiny, there is no one who can reverse this course."[12]

Firstly, "national self-determination" exists as a strategy during the formation of a national state. In the American War of Independence in the 18th Century, the leaders of this war have applied the slogans such as nation, independent state sovereignty against the British colonialists inspired by the European Enlightenment thinkers' theories of "social contract" and "man's natural rights" in order to defend the rationality and legality of the colonial people fighting for national independence and freedom. They have pointed out in the Declaration of Independence in 1776 that a nation must relieve the unequal relations with another nation in order to obtain the independent and equal status given by the "natural law" and "natural gods" in the

---

11   Compiled by China Institute of Contemporary International Relations: *Third World in the 1990s*, Current Affairs Press, 1992, p. 173.

12   Valery Tishkov, *Discussion on Crisis in the Ethnology of the Soviet Union, Collection of Ethnological Rendition*, 1994(3).

world.[13] "National self-determination" was only limited to national states when it generated during the French Revolution, so it was not applicable to multi-national states at all.

Secondly, the "self-determination of nations" has existed as the strategy to "fight against imperialism and colonialism". Yu Jianhua has made an in-depth study on such question. In the mid-19th Century, after the intensive study on the Ireland issue, Marx and Engels have started to realize that it is under the premise of maintaining its colonial rule that the capitalist states maintain their native class governing, it is difficult to liberate themselves for the working class in capitalist countries if the colony is not liberated; to realize the democratic change in international society and the international unity among the labor movements must first realize the national self-determination. During the 20th Century, especially the periods of the First World War and the October Revolution, Lenin has made contributions and systematic injunctions on the national self-determination theory in a series of works such as Discussion on the Right of National Self-determination, Socialist Revolution and Right to National Self-determination based on the problems of world's oppressed nations, colonies, semi-colonies and the keen-edged realistic conditions of the national conflicts in Tsarist Russia at that time. He has made a vivid description that the law's stipulating the freedom of divorce is not equal to encourage people to divorce as a meta-phor to indicate establishing the principle of the national self-determination right is not equal to support the national separatism. He has put it through which the implementation of national self-determination must make specific analysis on specific problems and the application of it must be based on the specific historical conditions of nations and states.[14] He has also admitted that the Brest-Litovsk Peace Treaty signed on March 3, 1918 did not respect Poland's national self-determination which is necessary for the subsistence of the newly born Soviet regime as he thought. There is no doubt that the national self-determination right exists as a powerful weapon for fighting against imperialism and colonialism in Lenin's eyes.

There is a specific provision in Clause 2, Article 1 of Charter of the United Nations in 1945: "To develop friendly relations among nations based on re-spect for the principle of equal rights and self-determination of peoples, and to take other appropriate measures to strengthen universal peace."[15]

---

13   Zhou Yiliang, Wu Yujin as chief editors, *Selected Compilation of Materials on Global History* (Modern Part, First Half Volume), The Commercial Press, 1972, p. 93.

14   Yu Jianhua, *Analysis on the Background and Theory of Global Ethnic Separatist Movement World Nationalities,* 1999(6).

15   *United Nations Charter*, Approved by the 15th UN General Assembly and took effect on October 24, 1945.

In 1952, the United Nations has adopted Resolution The Right of the People and Nations to Self-determination again by emphasizing the realization of universal human rights can be guaranteed only based on giving colonies the self-determination rights. In the Declaration of Giving the Colonial Countries and People Independence adopted by the United Nations in 1960, the applicable objects with the right of national self-determination designated are the nations of dependent countries in colonies "conquered, ruled and exploited by the foreign countries", and it definitely announced: "Rapidly and unconditionally terminate the colonialism in all forms and performances"; "all people have the right of self-determination, based on which they can freely determine their political status and develop their economy, society and culture".[16] In the over 30 years after the war, the concept of de-colonization became the true meaning of the national self-determination principle.

In fact, a series of international documents such as the Charter of the United Nations all emphasize that the applicable subjects of the self-determination right are the colonial people in various forms under the occupation or ruling of the Western colonial powers since the modern times for the purpose of urging the colonial suzerain to rapidly and unconditionally terminate the colonialism in all forms as soon as possible and not to hinder the self-determination of the oppressed nations by force or by other repressive means or additional conditions. In addition, the right of national self-determination as a principle of international relations belongs to the International Law category with its suffering subject only as the subject of international law. Therefore, the right of national self-determination is not given to all specific minority nationalities in a country, and it is not the principle and policy used to treat the domestic national relations. "The definition of the right of self-determination is not applicable to a state with independent sovereignty or part of the people in a state, which is necessary for the integrity of a state."[17]

Moreover, recently "national self-determination" has become the major pretext for developed countries to claim the theory that "human rights override sovereignty". From the beginning, "national self-determination" has not been a commonly agreed criterion which is universally applicable but the result of conflicts among the major states as the interest subjects in history. After the World War I, the US President Wilson has published the "Fourteen Points" declaration, put forward the concept of "right of national self-determination" and asserted that the national self-determination should

---

16   Compiled by UN News Service: *UN Manual*, The Commercial Press (1973), p. 483.

17   Guan Jianqiang, *It is Appropriate for China to Preserve* International Covenant on the Civil and Political Rights and Adjust Domestic Laws Accordingly, Journal of *Law Science,* 1999(4).

be the basis for re-partition of the territories of the "defeated nations" such as Germany, Austro-Hungary, Ottoman Empire and Bulgaria. However, in the Paris Peace Conference in 1919, the concept of "right of national self-determination" raised by the US president Wilson was not implemented due to the partial reason that the defeated nations have accused the victorious nations for not respecting the right of national self-determination, proposed the evidences of Ireland issue in Britain and the black people issue in the US. The United States Secretary of State had also acknowledged that if "the right of national self-determination" was truly implemented, the US and Canada would no longer exist, as multi-nation states . After the 1941 "Atlantic Charter" was signed, Churchill had hurriedly and enthusiastically, in his address to the Member of Parliament, that the right of national self-determination agreed and affirmed in the "Atlantic Charter" would not be applied to India and other British colonies, but would only cover the territories occupied by Germany and other fascist countries.[18]

For the first 20 years of the United Nations, the Western countries have always ignored the Chapter I Article II in the Charter of the United Nations by considering it only as a general principle and have argued that it cannot be used to support the anti-colonialism. However with the irreversible development of people's independence and liberation trends in colonies, the international relations theorists and diplomats in Western countries have changed from the defensive policies to offensive ones, they would not weaken or deny the right of national self-determination anymore but give a new meaning to the "self-determination right". Their most important new theory is to make a distinction between the "external self-determination" and the "internal self-determination". The former refers to anti-colonialism and the latter refers to the right based on which the people of all nations can select and change their own political, economic and cultural systems. The declaration passed on the "Conference on Security and Co-operation in Europe" in 1975 has further defined the "internal self-determination" referring to respect human rights and democratic voting rights. Since then, the concept of "human rights" has been linked to "state sovereignty" via the "internal national self-determination". Since the national self-determination is an approach to establish the state sovereignty, while the human rights are the core of "internal self-determination", then the conception of "human rights override sovereignty" seems well-reasoned as a result. It is thought-provoking that the Western new theory of "internal national self-determination" did transform its passive situation in the United Nations,

18   Cui Zhiyuan, National Self-Determination Right, Human Rights and Sovereignty–An Analysis Based on the Breakup of Yugoslavia, *Strategy and Management*, 1999(8).

and vast developing countries seem to suffer from "mutism" for a short while.[19] Against fraudulent political rivals, the developing countries appeared powerless.

"One nation, one state" or "integration of state and nation" theory is also closely linked with the formation of Western European nation states with their specific historical background and practical conditions. Since the 12th Century, the productive forces of Western Europe have greatly developed with the enlargement of the economic scope, which promoted the people of all nations to start an accelerated internal unity process whose political performance is that people with the same or similar cultures have united as never before. Western Europe has entered a period of transformation from the feudal decentralized "subjects kingdom" to a unified "state composed based on a nation."[20] During such period, people with the same or similar languages and cultures have strengthened their common destiny consciousness and formed the inter-nation political relations by taking the principal kingdoms as the cohesive core. Since the 16th Century, Western Europe has completely started to enter the age of the "nation-state". Its political territory is constantly adjusted with the modern "nation-state" pattern which was basically established via the mutual conflicts and compromises, the status and territory of various "nation-states" are mutually recognized. In the 19th Century, the European bourgeoisie thinkers have widely believed that the nation-state is the best state form. Every European civilized ethnic entity (people) should have the self-determination right and should realize national independence and unity with free choice, free merging and unification methods and establish their national sovereign states. In those days, the European nationalism movement has advocated the nation state with a "classic pattern" as "one nation and one state". "Nation-state" phenomenon is theorized and sanctified. In the late 1950s, researchers of nationalism ideology history have summarized the classical theory related to the relationship between the nation and the state—"integration of state and nation" theory based on the Western European intuitive experience which is seen as the summary of the "nation-state" phenomenon, such theory said: the inconsistent national commitment and the commitment to the state are the keys of the contemporary national problem, the fierce violence and conflict among nations can be avoided only when the commitment to the state meets the national commitment with the formula of "one nation, one state" for short.

---

19   Cui Zhiyuan, National Self-Determination Right, Human Rights and Sovereignty: An Analysis Based on the Breakup of Yugoslavia, *Strategy and Management*, 1999(8).
20   Yaroslav Krejci and Vítezslav Velimsky: *Ethnic and Political Nations in Europe*, 1981, Shanghai People Press.

The "nation-state" theory has paved the way for the development of Western Europe's capitalism and industrialization and laid a foundation for the establishment of colonization. However, some districts formed some modern sovereign states with vast territories and numerous nations, rather than small countries with small population after the victory of non-colonization movements. After Europeans have understood the collapse of the colonization, the suzerains seem like small countries with small population on the contrary, which were at a disadvantage in the face of law of competition. They have suddenly come to realize the truth and the European Union idea has come into being since then. "Considering the rigorous regional cooperation situation which has occurred in Western Europe, North America and Southeast Asia, it seems that it is not impossible for the most of the former-Soviet nations to unite again without use of, with free will or respective coincidence of interest needs, unless in the future, there will appear a more reasonable organization exceeding the state."[21]

When the "nation state" theory underwent a change in Western Europe, the national separatist movements in some places started to surge, and it seems that the "integration of state and nation" played a role. However, the "one nation, one state" is only an ideal pattern generated in the specific historical environment of Western Europe without having any universality by itself. There were disputes among the minorities and national discord even in the ancient nation states in Europe such as Britain, France and Spain. The conceptions of nation and nation-state supplement each other, which are nothing but the development pattern of Western European capitalist countries, and the states and nations in East Europe, Asia and the whole world which mostly consists of multinational states are not in synchronization. The principle of "one nation, one state" is not applicable to the whole world, and it only becomes the excuse for national separatism in contemporary world.

In fact, "the universal law for all previous 'nation-state' movements and the process of state establishment around the world in modern times is starting from the 'nation-state' idea (of a single ethnic body) and ending up with the multinational state reality".[22] Because the national communities in history have huge stability with the constant process of national absorption, disintegration, aggregation and spreading, a few nation states have the single nation structure in modern times, especially in the world today. As a matter of fact, if the single nation state is determined based on the

---

21   Luo Fuhui as chief editor, Theses on Chinese Nationalistic Thoughts, *Central China Normal University Press*, 1996, p. 21.
22   Zhu Lun: *Discussion on National and Multinational State, World Nationalities,* 1997(3).

standard of "over 90% of the population belongs to the same nation", there are only less than 10% of the states belonging to such type among nearly 200 states at present.[23] Even in the "single nation states" (such as Japan and Mongolia) as generally considered by people or those (such as Turkey and Bulgaria) which self-proclaim to be "single nation states" in their establishment process, there are some native minorities or foreign immigrant groups in these countries, in different percentages. Especially under the action of current global integration trend, politics, economy and cultures of different nations are integrated at different levels, and the mutual contact and connection are increasingly frequent, even the single nation state also appears the heterogeneity of social groups due to the increasing immigrants. On such occasions, "if establishing 'nation-state' is thought as a rational appeal in line with the historical trend, it would inevitably cause two 'movements' with the same nature but different patterns of manifestation worldwide: the 'national purification movement' caused in some states with single nation composition, expelling the 'outsiders' out of the state; and the 'national separation movement' in states with a complex national composition, nearly each nation and even the constituent part of some nations require to establish their own states. Thus there will not be more dependent on each other worldwide. However, such choice is obviously objected by almost all nation-states".[24] As we can see from actual conditions of the states built through the nationalist separatism, establishing a new nation-state by the national separation would not necessarily and truly solve the national issue as they think. After some native minorities have established their own independent sovereign states via the separatist movement, the internally original majority nations and other minorities require another separation inside the newly independent state in succession based on the "integration of state and nation" theory, the demands for national separation seem to demonstrate an "atomic fission-like" situation.

Therefore, the "integration of state and nation" theory is quite idealistic for the theoretical summary on Western European "nation-state" phenomenon in the Romantism Age; it is neither the perpetual and absolute truth nor an axiom which can be put into practice anytime and anywhere, and even not a sacred doctrine applicable for all nations. Some national separatists' attachment on the "integration of state and nation" theory only means an earnest hope for a real separation of territory rather than having so much theoretical interests.

---

23 Anthony D. Smith, *Nation Sate*, *The Blackwell Encyclopedia of Political Science*, China University of Political Science and Law Press, 1992, p. 490.
24 Hao Shiyuan, The Development and Decline of National Issue in the 20th Century and its Effect on the New Century, *World Nationalities*, 2000(1).

VII.1.4. Theoretical thoughts in the analysis of national issues

There are two theoretical thoughts about the research and analysis of theoretical problems related to nation, nation-state and nationalism.

The first is the Marxist analysis method. As Marx and Engels once definitely pointed out: "The production mode of material life restricts the process of the overall social life, political life and spiritual life."[25] That is to say, the conditions of the national relation depend on a certain production mode of social material goods and a certain development status of the social productive forces. The formation and development of national community as well as the national difference are radically determined by certain development status of social productive forces; the national contact, national relation status as well as the emergence, existence and development of national contradictions ultimately depend on the certain development status of social productive forces. If there is a most essential opinion on the national contradictions in Marxism, which argues that in fact, fundamentally, it is the class conflicts that are behind the national conflicts, and that the emergence, existence and development of national contradictions ultimately depend on a certain level of development of social productive forces.

There are scholars who have argued: "The contemporary national liberation movement, which was promoted by colonial and semi-colonial nationalisms— as the historical form—has its main theoretical source in Marxism. The worldwide Marxist-socialist revolutionary movement has become a motive force for anti-colonialism and building national-states because Marxism has provided great ideas and inspiration which has challenged world's current political and economic order, centered narrow 'capital' interests in contemporary times. Thus, Marxism has provided a new historical prospect for the colonial and semi-colonial peoples to establish their own nationalisms and nation-states. Up to today, the nationalism was only a legend based on the practice of modern states located in Western Europe and the surrounding regions and was just extended to the continent of America, wherein nationalist social thought trends and movements were formed.

While Marxism has placed and extended nationalism to the landscape of the whole world—to realize the ideal of worldwide revolution by and for humankind. According to this idea, the world nationalities are divided

---

25 *Selected Works of Karl Marx and Frederick Engels,* Vol. 2 People's Publishing House, 1995, p. 32.

by the world revolution theory of Marxism as: one part of oppressing and exploiting nationalities, the other part of oppressed and exploited nationalities, and the national contradiction has become the class contradiction at the bottom; the oppression and exploitation among nationalities worldwide are the relationship of international capital to wage labor. The contradictions between different nationalities, different regions and different classes inside a country ultimately depend on such a basic fact of global capitalist rule. As a result, global proletariat and the oppressed people and nationalities should get united to jointly oppose imperialism. The anti-imperialist national revolution in the colonies and semi-colonies is not only a historical prospect to promote their national liberation, but also an organic component of world revolution."[26] Here it definitely describes the nationalism principle prescribed in the Marxist view.

As Marx and Engels wrote: "The modern large-scale industry universally destroys the national fences in such centralized force, and gradually eliminates the production and social relations as well as the nations' local features with national character."[27] This phrase expressed that their thought of the national intercommunity increased as the modern industry and market economy developed. For another example, Lenin once said: "There is only one solution to the national problem (insofar as it can, in general, be solved in the capitalist world, the world of profit, squabbling and exploitation), and that solution is consistent democracy."[28] Such principle is also applicable to our analysis on nationalism.

The second trend in the nationalism research literature describes the emergence and development of nationalism under the "modernity" view successively. It is particularly unique to explain the issues of nation and nationalism with the modernity/modernization view. The so-called "modernity" originated from Western academic discourse is often mentioned currently in Chinese academy. The explanation mode of "modernity" thinks that the modern world history is the history of modernization, and the nationalism has emerged, developed and evolved in the modern historical frame of the world. The modernity is not mystical term, it is rather the relatively stable ideological pattern above the economic base which has served the hundreds years of capitalist development, the solidifying capitalist spirit, the culture accumulation during the economic development and the specific quality and pattern of social survival in brief.

---

26   Xu Xun: *Nationalism*, China Social Sciences Press, 1998, p. 83.
27   *Complete Works of Karl Marx and Frederick Engels,* Vol. 7, People's Publishing House, 1959, p. 503.
28   *Complete Works of Lenin,* Vol. 24, People's Publishing House, 1990, p. 123.

Our understanding of "modernization" is to build a prosperous, democratic and civilized socialist country. In terms of Western conception of universalism, modernization means becoming a bourgeois society. The modern society is a human organization structure based on modernization and marked with modernity. "Modernity is indeed the basic feature of the modern nation-state."[29] Within the view of Marxist historical materialism, the so-called modernization and modernity are actually involved in the relationships between the human and the nature or between the men and the humanized nature both economically and from the perspective of an aesthetic appreciation and culture. In our view, the "modernity" issue needs a philosophical and detailed analysis based on the relationship between men and the nature. In accordance with the "modernity" theory, Chinese "modernity" has gone through five major shifts. Since 1840, technology-oriented ("learning from foreigners in order to contain their invasion"), regime-oriented (reform movement strategy), science-oriented ("scientific" "enlightenment" should be the prerequisite), sovereignty-oriented (recovering own sovereignty) and culture-oriented (cultural introspection trend of 1980s). However above five roads failed to return China to the center of the world history arena and failed to "re-establish the center in reference to Western discourse."[30]

When studying the nationalism issue, should Marxism standpoints, viewpoints and methods be replaced by the "modernity" explanation mode? The answer is no. The analytic method of Marxist political economy and the scientific spirit of Marxism cannot limit itself with understanding the issue of nationalism issue but also can explain the modernity. The Western nationalism theory emphasizes only the modernity issue, this is mainly because it avoids the capitalism question in the study of nationalism issue, which seems to try to draw a clear distinction with Marxism which have the most profound analysis on the essence of capitalism. However this is just a self-deception. Generally, the modernity is the capitalist modernization and nationalism develops along with the development of capitalism. In this way, its attempt to avoid Marxism is impossible.

Nevertheless, a correct understanding of the modernity is beneficial to grasp the historical course and different forms of the emergence and development of nations and nationalism. The nation-state and nationalism issues have already existed long before the emergence of Marxism with the basic reason of profound changes in the social production mode. The factor of capitalism comes into being and grows up, and then the nationalism theory and

29   Eric J. Hobsbawm: *Nation and Nationalism*, Shanghai People Press, 2000, p. 17.
30   Zhang Fa, Zhang Yiwu, Wang Yichuan, From Modernity to Chineseness: Research on a New Episteme, *Literature and Art Forum*, 1994(2).

practice come forth. It is acceptable to generalize the different explanations of time features with "modernity" and "modernization". The "modernity" can be used to explain the relationship between the nationalism and the time. At first, the nationalism stresses the class and stratum cooperation, paying more attention to the boundaries among the nation-states instead of that among different interest groups not inside the nation. If we fully explain the nationalism theory and practice as the representation of class contradictions, it would not be in line with the historical reality, so we should avoid simplification. When the capitalism develops and expands to the current "globalization" phase, the nationalism theory and practice also have a huge differentiation. The contradictions between the East and the West, between the developed countries and the backward countries and between the capitalism and the socialism have provided an enough space for Marxist interpretation on the nationalism. Moreover, the nationalism itself of some states in some forms is based on Marxism, which is an introspection and critique to the modernity.

The modernity marks massive changes in human history. In terms of social structure, the first is the formation of "modern states", "the emerging modern states established based on strong nationalism affection are a logical historical reflection of the industrial revolution"[31]. The concept of "pre-modern" in modern discourse system claims that there existed state in the traditional society, but its social, cultural and legal bases were totally different from modern states. In the historical process formed by modern states, the worldly national conception replaced the theocratic national conception and the legal system replaced the church hierarchy. In China, the modern state and its corresponding political and social systems replaced the Confucian ethical order.

The modern states were established based on "nations", and the nationalism was the historic force in the establishment of the modern states, which is the general relationship of such historical phenomenon among "nation", "nationalism" and modern nation states. The modernization course is not the history of a certain state but a worldwide historical movement. As a result, nationalism is not an isolate phenomenon in a couple of states but the "medium" or mode of connecting the relations among modern states. Therefore, the modernity theory can be seen as a uniform systematical theoretical frame to understand the histories of various states on the nationalism emergence and development. One of the maladies for the modernity is easily leading to universalism as such, there is only a West and the western modernization in the world, which easily results in the disappearance of diversity of world's human society development. The nationalism outside the West is just simply

---

31   Theodore Couloumbis et al., *Power and Justice*, Huaixa Publishing House, 1990, p. 71.

evaluated as breaking such univeralism. In this sense, it can be said that there are two forms of nationalism: modernist nationalism and anti-modernist nationalism which opposes "universality". For example, the nationalism since the modern era of China, especially in Sun Yat-sen's new Three Principles of the People had the idea of longing for the realization of development and always revolted against the earlier Western rule and oppression order; such revolt was not only reflected in politics and economy, but also in ideology and culture. The human is in a time in which the capitalism has a great development level. There is nothing about post-modernism but only the prospect dominated by capitalist modernity for Chinese people's living environment, while the formation of nationalism thought trends are just anti-modernistic manifestations in ideological and cultural spheres.

VII.2. Realistic presentation and theoretical expression of nationalism trend of thought in contemporary China

The contemporary nationalism trend of thought referred in this book covers the time period "the contemporary era" which is the new period of the whole Reform and Opening-up era. This is because the differences between China and the world, especially the developed countries in many aspects make the general public much enthusiastic about how ethnic peoples in China speed up to catch and realize the great national rejuvenation. The national awareness and state awareness as the "keywords" for the nationalism of all kinds, has taken up very important place in the public and intellectuals' behavior and discourse expression by becoming the social thought trend with both social mentalities and ideological concepts. The nationalism thought trend has stepped on the stage of thoughts, culture and ideology among worships and critiques. The favoring voices said: "The proponents of nationalism in contemporary China try to struggle and find a solution to the long-range objective of enabling China become a superpower", "now it still cannot be affirmed whether contemporary discourse of nationalism can become a mainstream ideology in China's realm of thought in the future, but the possibility of its vigorous surge is considerable and possible."[32] An opposed view said, "the contemporary discourse of nationalism is "a mark of people's desire to get rich immediately."[33]

---

32   Wang Xiaodong, Going ahead of the Mainstream Thoughts in China–A Review and Outlook on Contemporary Chinese Nationalism, *China and World Affairs,* 2005(1).
33   Xu Jilin, *Anti-Westernism and Nationalism*, Recorded in *Intellectual Standpoint: Nationalism and Destiny of China during Transformation Period*, The Time Literature and Art Press, 2000, p. 422.

The nationalism thought trend enjoys a quite broad social psychological basis. It derives from the evolution of state consciousness from the internal logic developed from the nationalism thought trend in contemporary China. During this period, the speeches of some figures in certain events are becoming the realistic presentation of fully embodying the national consciousness and acting on the contemporary nationalism thought trend. The ideology of core figures and the relevant awareness of the public basically are matching up with two basic subjects of a thought trend. The ideology of these events and figures is the basic element of nationalism thought trend.

VII.2.1. Emergence of national consciousness

The political awareness and national consciousness of different social groups are generally established on their self-examination in regard to the relationships between the individuals, the state and the society, as well as the self-examination on the national identity or nation's historical path and also includes realistic choices. At the beginning of Reform and Opening-up, the social and political awareness was full of critiques on the past national history and there were hopes and fears about the West due to the impacts of Reform and Opening-up. In general, the characteristics of the public national ideology and emotion in such period are mainly in two aspects: the patriotic tradition remains to be maintained but the point of view regarding the relationship between the nation state and individuals has gradually transformed from the state-oriented view to an individual-based view.

In the early period of Reform and Opening-up, while China pursued to get rid of the influence of "left" thought trend prevalent for a long time in the recent past, the western humanitarianism thought was widely accepted by public, especially among the youth, and they were delicate on the issues of individual liberties and have demanded self-development and self-realization, and consequently, arrogantly proposed a new type of state and nationalism concepts which was quite divergent from the traditional nationalism thought of China. As the commodity economy was promoted and had developed in this era, people have paid attention to and participate in the reform with great patriotic enthusiasm with a hope for turning the state into a thriving and powerful state; when the requirement and participation suffer a setback, the patriotic enthusiasm has declined. The high material civilization in Western developed countries in people's eyes is in a sharp contrast to the relatively backward Chinese economy, resulting in the formation of a national inferiority feeling.

In the late 1980s, there are some discussions about the vicissitude and honor on nation and state including the argument of learning from Western capitalism and criticizing the socialism. Driven by the strong nation crisis perception, the awareness of unexpected development and the sense of times mission, the patriotic awareness is often expressed by radical mood or further evolves and changes into the radicalism thought trend with critical and theoretical properties. The radicalism in this period expresses a deviation from the modern state and national consciousness until the ancient Chinese civilization and socialist system under special conditions. Various radicalism viewpoints criticize the traditional national culture or traditional system, even the socialist system with an extremist individualist narrative.

Broadly speaking, the national consciousness in this period is the entity of affirming the "positive" performance of the nation and negating the "reverse" performance. During such period, the profound experience of the national consciousness is widely reflected on a large number of young people who display the critique and yearning on the past and the future in great passion and try to rethink the relationship between the individuals and the society as well as the individuals and the state in the new period. People's value evaluation criterion started to be converted from the past society and group to the combination of society and individual, even to another extreme end—arrogation. These discussions contain doubts and negation on traditional view of life, the negation on traditional relationship between the individuals and the state, and contain the affirmation of individual values above the society and the state. In the later period of 1980s, the "cultural craze" which was widely popular in Chinese thought cultural circles and influential in the public, especially among the young students and young intellectuals, has opened another phase of evolution in regard to national consciousness with a radical qualitative change if compared to the trend of self-examination on national culture and national history. It is highlighted in the nearly trenchant critique on the nation's history and culture, which even requires a "total westernization" to seek the nation development prospect. The thought trend criticized as "national nihilism", even a "reverse racism" at that time and afterwards has risen in late 1980s with wide influences. The formation of River Elegy is an important mark, which limits the insight of Chinese history and culture as well as the discussion on modernized road only to the longitudinal development vein of Chinese history, only to the self-examination on Chinese realistic politics and systems. There is no doubt that such discussion horizon on the historical development is too narrow in the economic globalization era by lacking of the horizon of global economy and political integrity. Using a specious "frame" to suit Chinese history and reality is an absurdity hard to avoid. Such trend of self-examination and critique is easily leading to thorough negation of the self and total westernization for pointing to and with individual emotional feature.

VII.2.2. Growth of nationalism thought trend

At the beginning of 1990s, the international environment facing China had undergone great changes. China suffered from a series of impacts from the West: the Western major countries which collaborated to impose certain economic sanctions upon China; the leaders of the student strike who had defected abroad and cooperated with the Western anti-China forces have boosted the offensive public voice targeting China; the United States Congress proposed to dispatch an "ambassador" to Tibet and allowed Dalai Lama to visit the US but hindered China's participation in the WTO and blocked China's hosting of the Olympic Games; there also repeatedly experienced Japanese senior governmental officials' efforts for whitewashing their aggressive war history and attempts for modifying Japan's history textbooks; the Japanese Prime Minister made a formal publicly open visit to the "Yasukuni Shrine" and the Japanese right-wing forces provoked the issue of "Diaoyu Island". Chinese people going through the Reform and Opening-up started to find both the aggressive side of the Western countries implementing the "Peaceful evolution" in China and the rigorous side of global clarion. The changes of the international political ecology have a larger influence on Chinese political psychology.

In this way, some people have started to criticize the worship of Westernization in terms of a realistic capitalist globalization critique which has led to the initial formation of nationalism ideology. And gradually this nationalism ideology, began to embody the combination of nationalist social psychology and a theoretical expression, which more and more became evident. In the early days the theoretical expression of the nationalism thought trend embodied a self-examination of the precious "positive" national consciousness and doubted about the self-examination on the so-called "negative" one which was represented by the River Elegy, which remarked the divergence of how Chinese intellectuals evaluated the China's national fate in those early days (early 1990s); here at this point of time, we see an obvious change of the self-examination theme, among the leaders of this nationalism thought trends. Such theme of nationalism thought trends in 1990s was the self-examination on the so-called "negative" "national nihilism" of the 1980s. On a certain social basis, such new nationalist thought trends were advocated by minority scholars and intellectuals who differed regarding their aspirations and also regarding their interest relation (status) in comparison with the mainstream "intellectual elites" of the 1980s, we can say that these nationalist thought trends was relatively weak, but had bright prospects in the trend thoughts pattern of the1990s.

Since the 21ˢᵗ Century, the Chinese nationalism thought trends have shown new features, which further upsurge in 2008 in terms of the Tibet issue, Wenchuan Earthquake and the Beijing Olympic Games. The world pays attention to the rise of such nationalist sentiment based on national recognition generated from the "Tibetan independence" and "Taiwan independence" splitting activities, and the Wenchuan Earthquake has manifested the spirit of patriotism in the rational nationalism, and the organization of the Olympic Games has also awakened Chinese people's persistent "Dream of building a powerful country". Especially after the 18ᵗʰ National Congress of the CPC, the proposition of "The Chinese Dream", call for the realization of the great rejuvenation of the fChinese nation has brought the rising passion of Chinese nationalism into a new historical development phase.

VII.2.3. Theoretical debates in the ideal-conceptual level

At the beginning of the 1990s, a long article titled "Only Socialism Can Develop China" undersigned by Wen Di, an overseas Chinese author has raised comprehensive doubts on the ideological trend of so-called "intellectual elitism". At the same time, in December 1990, a native scholar He Xin has published a series of articles criticizing Westernization and national nihilism, which paved the way for of re-self-examination on the self-examination of 1980s, as a result. A renown Taiwanese writer Chen Yingzhen has then published the article titled, Look for a Lost View—Reading He Xin's Global Economic Situation and China's Economic Issues,[34] which was an accurate interpretation on He Xin's opinions. The text sharply denounced the "torment" of "imperialism" and "neo-colonialism" in Asia and China, and criticized that the mainland Chinese intellectual circles have lost the historical sense of direction at the time, lost the standpoint objectively belonging to the Third World, lost the correct understanding of the national interest relations between the West and China as a Third World country and lost the "global vision" of Chinese and national interests in the objective knowledge from the existing order of the contemporary world economy and politics to some degree.

These two important discourses have opened the prelude of nationalism thought trend from a brand new view. Meanwhile, the "re-evaluation of China's modernization" and the post-colonial cultural critique as well as the so-called "radical school" further theoretically manifests the theoretical

---

34   Chen Yingzhen, Seek for a Lost Vision, (Taipei) *Channel Comments*, 1991(2).

expression of nationalism thought trends in the ideology level. The symposium on the "re-evaluation of China's modernization" focuses on these two issues of Chinese society's structural contradictions and China's road to modernization during the process of globalization, which deeply makes a wide and intensive discussion on the road to modernization in contemporary China and combines the struggle for Chinese national interests with national cultural strategy in contemporary world's structure. But modernization has always occupied a well-defined correct position in the context of China's recent times, as a common consensus, its meaning and source as well as its social connotations, and it so established that it cannot be degraded. The discussion on the "re-evaluation of China's modernization" has reminded the Chinese academic circles of that the modernization is a specific social process with particular source, route and direction, but not merely a universal value for the first time. It is the first structural analysis on the modernization concept, restoring the "modernization" from the suspension in value into such a status available for economic and political analysis. Afterwards, another "powerful anti-westernization thought trend which gradually incubate and subsequently break out for the first time"[35], among which the more influential one at home and abroad is the postcolonial cultural critique that complements the "re-evaluation of modernization" in the economic and political analysis level with each other.

The self-examination on the "modernity" is the starting point of the postmodernism. When Chinese intellectual circles have started to re-evaluate the "modernization" itself as the development goal, they have echoed some ideological aspects of western postmodernism. Especially China, as a developing "backward" country and a Third World country at the margins of the world's capitalist system, has inevitably described its modernization goals in a post-colonialist manner during the self-examination of Chinese modernization. The logic of self-examination of Chinese "modernity" course has mainly taken the form of cultural critique.

After the reassessment of various marginal discourses in China, the up-to-date theory in the west has provided Chinese a starting point in turn making them review themselves"[36], and looking for the lost third-world vision. In the early 1990s, some young scholars have shaped their own systematic ideas. Facing the decade of large-scale cultural expansion, they thought the cultural expansion is not a process with the equal dialogue among various

---

35   Xu Jilin, *The Dilemma of Cultural Identity: The Trend of Anti-Westernization Thoughts in Intellectual Community of China in the 1990s*, recorded in: *Seek for Meaning*, Shanghai Joint Publishing, 1997, p. 286.
36   Chen Xiaoming, Dai Jinhua, Zhang Yiwu and Zhu Wei, *Orientalism and Post-Colonialism*, Journal of *Bell Mountain (Zhongshan (Mount Zhongshan)*, 1994(1).

cultures of the world, "the motive power of the cultural expansion is originated from the economic practice promoted by the modern industrial civilization. Therefore, it seems that the multinational cultural interpenetration
will not attain the character of equal dialogues among various cultures.
Those economically leading developed countries are likely to be at a superior cultural position. While the developing countries (or the Third World
countries) consciously recognize the supremacy of the developed capitalist
economy, they also unconsciously agree with its culture hegemony."[37]

The re-self-examination on the Chinese culture characterized by the
re-evaluation of the modernization and the post-colonial cultural critique
which obtained academic inspiration from the non-mainstream ideology of
the developed West, and anti-globalization and anti-capitalism thoughts of
the Third World. In the globalization context, the Chinese thought trends
are all have an international background and the international ideological
resource nutrition. The "radical school" in the development economics of
the Western and the Third World countries just provides with the main ideological material of new thought trends. In the Western development economics, the left-wing economists stand in the civilian position and have the
Third World vision are called as the "radical school". At the moment, there
are some Chinese young scholars who likely possess the features of the
"radical school". One of the features of these people is that they mostly live
in abroad, and some even have entered the Western academic circles but objecting to the Western-type modernization pattern in an explicit or implied
manner, and rediscovered and approved some Chinese traditional values.
Of course, they did not conduct a simple and non-specific culture discussion like in the "cultural craze" phase before but took advantage of the train
on Western economics in which they have accepted to make an empirical
discourse in terms of the economic history for Chinese social development.
Of which the most representative ones are Gan Yang and Cui Zhiyuan and
their Re-evaluation on the role of Chinese "social change" in rural industry
as well as the study and discourse on the Re-evaluation of some Chinese
social economy and politics systems before or after the reform is based on
the "new evolutionism", "analytical Marxism" and "critical legal studies".

The radical school argues that there are deep-seated dilemmas in Chinese
"modernization" road and "modernity" goal and China has attempted to
seek roads to overcome this dilemma. Their explorations represent that the
intellectuals are broadening their understanding horizon on Chinese historical road in contemporary China. Maybe they have this or that defect and
problem on the understanding of practical issues, and the true value of their

---

37 Ibid.

thoughts may not be within a specific issue field but these are the efforts and achievements of advanced Chinese young people to overcome the serious restraint from the Western discourse on Chinese thought circles.

VII.2.4. Actual appearance of nationalism at the popular psychological level

The popular psychology level of nationalism thought trends undertakes more positive expressions of the national consciousness with the core of an intense patriotic feelings regarding the relations between China and the world, which has attracted an extensive attention at home and abroad and there are voices one after another that the "nationalism is strongly rising in China". Although these display that the so-called Chinese nationalism has nearly and completely contrary expression with critiques and applauses from different aspects, it is consistent at the point where these facts subordinated to the social thought trend psychology level are confirmed. Several incidents are generally regarded as the remarking psychological-level expressions of nationalism thought trends. It is exactly the large-scale reader investigation of "China Youth's Worldview" and the bestseller China Can Say No. In addition, the protest activities of large masses in many ways caused by the damages to Chinese nation's interests and by the hurt on Chinese people' feelings from a part of Western countries' hegemonic misdeed are also widely regarded as the inevitable components of the actual presentation of nationalism thought trends.

Since the 1990s, the large-scale surveys carried out continuously in response to the political socialization issue of the youth in contemporary China in which especially their national consciousness have reflected, to some degree, the objective and rational side of the national consciousness and national sentiments of the public in China, then especially the youth, which is thought as the depiction of the true national consciousness state in Chinese public, especially the youth, and often cited by the public figures studying the nationalism thought trends in contemporary China for the explanation on the existence of Chinese nationalism. Chinese youth's opinions regarding the US displayed in the survey findings became the focus fixing on people's eyes. The survey results have displayed that the US ranks the first among the countries unfavorable for Chinese youth, accounting for 57.2% that is 25.1% higher than Japan (accounting for 22.1%) which has launched the war of aggression against China and caused extremely huge damages to Chinese people. The proportion of people deeming the US as the most unfriendly country to China is as high as 87.1%.[38] The survey has shown that the cognition and feeling of the group of young people, which enjoy a higher level of political socialization, regarding the world and foreign countries, demonstrates a remarkable change compared with the mainstream consciousness of the same group, 10 years ago. The survey has demonstrated that and a positive kind of national consciousness has taken root among this group.

The book "China Can Say No" has been evaluated as "reflected the national sentiments among the Chinese people." In his book the author has described the transformation of his thoughts from worshipping of the US to anti-Americanism. He has argued that saying "No" to the West should first start from saying "No" to oneself. It is rather a self-examination regarding the thoughts of some domestic public figures, than a demonstration of feelings targeting the foreign West. However, such book was a popular bestseller written by an "amateur writer" and has cause a great social sensation, which was exactly a cultural incident. Afterwards we can see that the China youth, especially those elites with the generalization and expression capacities, have paid an increasing attention on the national interest, national culture development strategy and relevant theories and strategies in contemporary China. There are scholars commenting afterwards that, China Can Say No, "It is remarkable yet for the social thought trends of and ought to say that the formation is not by accident but a new wave of expression of the potential anti-West sentiments in Chinese society"[39], which also evidences China Can Say No is one of the iconic events of the nationalism thought trends at that time. There is another study arguing that the nationalism indeed strives for a sovereign and independent discourse power and make people practically feel their power, which is the mark for the publication of such book. This study stresses that the book "Truth Behind Demonizing China"[40] published in the same year and the "Chinese Path in the Shadow of Globalization" published in 1999 both came into being in the form of such nationalism, the above three constitute the trilogy of the expression of the nationalism thought trends in the intellectual circles, "their publications should not only be deemed as the emergence of nationalism as an independent academic standpoint in academic stand, but also be regarded as the expression of common people' intensive nationalist sentiment in public discourse fields."[41]

---

38   *China Youth Daily World View Reader Survey Statistical Report, China Youth Daily,* July 14, 1995.
39   Xu Jilin, *Anti-Westernism and Nationalism, Recorded in Intellectual Standpoint–Nationalism and Destiny of China during Transformation Period,* The Time Literature and Art Press, 2000, p. 420.
40   *Behind a Demonized China,* China Social Sciences Press, 1996.
41   Ren Bingqiang, *The Re-Rise of Nationalism in China: Its Cause, Characteristics and Effect, Academia Bimestris,* 2004(1).

In addition, the Galaxy incident, the US's obstruction attempt against China's bid to host the 2000 Olympic Games and the allowance of Li Denghui's visit to USA, the bombing of Chinese embassy in Yugoslavia by US airstrikes and the China-US Aircraft Collision Incident of April 2001, etc., all show the US and the Western hegemonism and arrogance without doubt. However, all the above have caused a general disgust of a large number of young people towards the US and the Western interference in the domestic affairs of China. The historical issues, textbooks issue, visiting to the Yasukuni, the Diaoyu Islands dispute and Taiwan Issue between the Japan and China have caused the relations to a historical fall since 2002, and the Japanese proposition of "participating in the United Nations" in 2005 has greatly angered the Chinese youth. There occurred large-scale demonstrations nationwide, the netizens have been even more active and gathered that tens of thousands of signatures via web, against Japan's becoming the permanent member of the United Nations Security Council. Therefore, someone put forward that "Internet Nationalism" has emerged and formed in China. An investigator analyzes that, "The gradual popularization of network has provided another important stage for the nationalism. There are various comments on nationalism around the virtual network including both the rational nationalists asking for focusing on national interests in the international relations and the national expansionists announcing wars; as well as not only the cultural nationalists emphasizing the traditions but also the radicals condemning the social inequality and attempting to build an extreme equality. Their common ground lies in a strong anti-US sentiment and a deep concern on the national interest with the apprehensiveness and sense of mission and concern for the fate of the Chinese nation."[42]

In response to the demonstrations by college students and the masses filled with indignation nationwide caused by the attack to China's embassy stationed in Yugoslavia from NATO led by the US, the scholar Cao Jinqing has summarized as follows: "Most of the sentimental reactions by the Chinese people to such an incident is rather consistent: shocked, rage with intensive protest, which is the most obvious in the cluster of sensitive college students with a quite expressive ability in everywhere. Why do the scattered, specific and strange Chinese everywhere have the quite consistent sentiment reaction directly to the same incident? That's because such people all regard themselves as 'Chinese', a member of the national community with the common fate, who all believe that US's flagrant violation of the international convention and bombing the Chinese embassy in Yugoslavia are provocations against the China government and has even

---

42   Ibid.

humiliated the whole Chinese people. Such feeling as spontaneously com-bining oneself with all the compatriots and sharing the same fate is the nationalist sentiment."[43] Such conclusion is the rather typical generaliza-tion of positioning the general public's patriotic action and patriotism as the nationalist sentiment among the numerous study results of the nationalism thought trends in contemporary China.

There are also some commentators who equate such appearances and acts of nationalism thought trends to anti-West sentiments and argue that the Chinese anti-Westernism in 1990s encountered three development stages: the first is He Xin's anti-Western utterances in 1990s; the second was the anti-Western thought trends emerged in intellectual circles since 1994, such as the postcolonial cultural critique of Zhang Yiwu and Chen Xiaoming, the institutional innovation of Gan Yang and Cui Zhiyuan as well as Sheng Hong's cultural comparative theory; the third is represented by China Can Say No.[44] It indirectly indicates that the actual presentation and theoretical expression of nationalism thought trends are closely related to the "Western" reference system.

With the development and change of the political and economic situations at home and abroad since the 21th Century, Chinese nationalism has dem-onstrated a new development trend with the new performance platform of newly-emerged modern media such as the Internet and mobile phones; and the content is gradually involved in many fields such as the politics, econ-omy, society, culture, education, sports, military affairs, diplomacy and life with means of expression increasingly diversified.[45] The platforms for the general public's expression of national sentiments are not merely limited to such traditional media as newspapers, radio and TV but are relying more on the modern media like the Internet and mobile phones. The Internet which is called as "the fourth media" has quickly become the most important means for the general public to express their voices for its high degree of timeli-ness and degree of freedom as well as the most important platform for the masses to fully express their nationalist sentiments and patriotism. In 2003, the main incidents related to the network are: some websites advocating na-tionalism have organized Diaoyu Island Protection activity of landing on the island; and several websites have initiated the 100,000 network signature col-lection campaign against the Beijing-Shanghai high-speed railway; protest

43   Cao Jinqing, Chen Baoping, *Seven Questions on China*, Shanghai Scientific and Technological Education Press, 2002, pp. 105-106.
44   Xu Jilin, *Behind the Huge and Empty Mark*, recorded in: *Another Kind of Enlightenment*, Flower City Publishing House, 1999, p. 212.
45   Bao Changyong, *New Tendency in Chinese Trend of Nationalism Since the 21st Century and its Impact on Socialism with Chinese Characteristics*, Henan Social Sciences, 2009(6).

on the Japanese right-wing activists landing on the Diaoyu Island; burning Japanese flags outside the Japanese embassy stationed in China and so on. Therefore, the year of 2013 was an important juncture in the fermentation of "Chinese Internet Nationalism". With the popularization of modern communication means and intelligent mobile phones with the new functions as WeChat, Fetion and microblogs which can also transmit excellent photos and essays, they have become another quite rapid and easy means for the people to express their nationalist sentiments and patriotic enthusiasm. After the formation of Tibet "3/14" incident and "Olympic torch relay incident" in 2008, most of the nationalist sentiments and patriotic enthusiasm has spread via short messages and Fetion. In terms of the content, the nationalist sentiment upsurged more and there were incidents reflecting Chinese nationalism happened in many fields such as politics, economy, society, culture, education, sports, military affairs, diplomacy and life. For example, the Tibet "3/14" incident and "Olympic torch relay incident" in political field; the incidents of US Carlyle Group's acquisition of Chinese company XCMG and French Danone's acquisition of Wahaha in the economic field; the Carrefour incident in the social field; the "Dragon Boat Festival Application for World Heritage" in the cultural field; the Northwest University incident and Zhejiang University incident in the educational field; the Chire Koyama and Tang Na incident in the sports field; the China-US Aircraft Collision Incident and China-US Spy Case Event in the military affairs field; the incident of Zhao Wei Putting on the Ensign and Sharon Stone Event in the life field. With the rapid growth of its comprehensive national power, China has surpassed Japan by becoming the second largest economy worldwide and the nationalism became one of the most active and widely spread thought trends especially since 2012. In the investigation and assessment for the most remarkable Top 10 thought trends in 2012 at home and abroad organized by the People's Tribune Magazine, the nationalism ranked the first.[46] These agitated nationalism thought trends include the South China Territorial Waters dispute and China-Japan Diaoyu Island dispute and the re-examination on Chinese road in society as well as the passion for Chinese culture evoked by Mo Yan's being honored by Nobel Prize in literature. Especially the China-Japan Diaoyu Island dispute has evoked the domestic patriotic youth's nationalist sentiments and their extreme emotions of more inclining to hate Japan, such as boycotting the Japanese goods, burning or pounding Japanese branded cars and carrying out personal attacks. Such national sentiments long for a strong China and aim to wipe out the national humiliation which began since the (1894-1895) Sino-Japanese naval battle to the Japanese War of Aggression against China (1931-45).

46 People's Tribune "Special Planning" Group, 2012, Chinese and Foreign Top Ten Trends of Thoughts, People's Tribune, 2013(1) (Book Two).

VII.3. Causes for the generation of nationalism trend of thought in contemporary China

Any social thought trend nurtures its origin and source from a certain social existence. Normally, the social and historical conditions for the formation of social thought trends can be divided into economic, political, ideological and cultural conditions. The economic conditions based on which social thought trends may occur refer to the level of productive forces , the nature of the relations of production and economic system, as well as people's daily material life status at certain social stage. The level of productive forces is the most fundamental and crucial factor, but its crucial role is not direct but achieved indirectly and circuitously by a series of intermediaries. The dynamic adjustment of relationship between productive forces and the relations of production makes great effect on the formation and development of social thought trends. It is said that "the production mode of material life restricts the process of the whole social, political and spiritual life"[47]. During the period when social thought trends behave most actively, the relations of production normally need to be adjusted to meet the demand of productive forces development. For example, the contradiction between capitalist private ownership system and socialized mass production hindered the development of productive forces, which fostered the utopian socialism. When China was under the yoke of imperialism, feudalism and bureaucratic capitalism, the level of productive foces were extremely low, and various thought trends surged simultaneously. During the Reform and Opening-up, through proper adjustments of the relations of production, the structure of ownership was significantly changed and many social thought trends have responded energetically. So we can find a law by which social thought trends will perform much actively when there is diversified ownership in a society. Besides, political and cultural conditions also play an important role in the formation of thought trends.

These conditions may vary in regard to different social thought trends. As for the trend of nationalism, the main social condition of its formation is the change of domestic life practice and the relationship between China and the world, which has a double nature of economy and politics. Over one hundred years, in the struggle against imperialism and feudalism and for national independence and liberation, Chinese nation has formed the theory and practice of nationalism, which has provided the key ideological and cultural condition for the nationalism thought trend in modern China.

---

47 *Selected Works of Karl Marx and Frederick Engels,* Vol. 2, People's Publishing House, 1995, p. 32.

VII.3.1. Historical memory of nationalism

Generally, nationalism is a product which has the connotations of modernity in Western context, and it is generally considered as a theory rising in Europe at the early 19th Century. Before modern times, the ancient Chinese nation had no nationalism in modern sense, but this does not mean that Chinese nation did not have a certain identity consciousness and a sense of belonging. During the union of various nations and the final formation of the pattern in which ethnic minorities dwell among Han ethnicity but they also live in a compact community, various connections in respect of history, myth, religion, literature and arts, politics and certain level of economy created a profound psychological heritage in people's mind. The ancient concept of Chinese nation has lasted for a long time.

The historical experience and severe humiliations and frustrations in The recent centuries accumulated an inferior complex in the deep minds of Chinese people, which has shaped the dream of a powerful nation. Chinese people long to relieve the national humiliation which has lasted over a century and live up to the expectation of their ancestors and later generations."[48] Since the modern times, China has encountered unprecedented radical changes that was never seen in past thousands of years. The domestic crisis and the foreign invasion had strongly hastened the birth of a sovereignty consciousness. It can be said that the awareness for longing a rejuvenated nation among the Chinese people was gradually formed with the emergence of the national independence feelings and the growth of the sovereignty consciousness. As early as 1860s to 1870s, a generation of forerunners had clearly put forward the issue of safeguarding national independence and sovereignty.

Those Reformists at the late Qing Dynasty and some abroad students first introduced the term "nationalism" into China. Liang Qichao quoted this term in his article. At the late Qing Dynasty, both Reformists and Revolutionaries held the flag of nationalism and closely combined nationalism with the resolution of Chinese realistic political issues. Nationalism constituted the major part of Sun Yat-sen's Three Principles of the People. In the first half of the 20th Century, nationalism made a significant effect on the intellectual, cultural and political circles in China. The enhancement of sovereignty consciousness promoted the upsurge of Anti-Russia Movement, Anti-France Movement, Reject the US Goods, Mine Protection

---

48   Xiao Gongqin, *Nationalism and the Ideology during Chinese Transition Period*, Recorded in *Intellectual Standpoint–Nationalism and Destiny of China during Transformation Period*, The Time Literature and Art Press, 2000, p. 446.

Movement and Railway Protection Movement and so on. The enhancement of civil rights consciousness advanced the unfolding of Constitutional Movement and Revolutionary Movement. As a result of all these movements, Chinese people finally overthrew the rule of autocratic monarchy of the Qing Dynasty which had caused national humiliation and betrayed its sovereignty, and finally cheered the birth of Republic of China, which later failed to solve the issues and failed to change the fate of the nation, i.e, the domestic and external frustrations and the national crisis. Chinese communists have integrated Marxism with the basic appeal of national goals and patriotism. They have successfully solved the sovereignty and unity issues of Chinese the nation by using the fundamental resolution of toppling the Three Great Mountains, imperialism, feudalism and bureaucratic capitalism.

In the past century, all reforms and progress in China converged into the demand and longing of national revival and rejuvenation, showing the one-hundred-year theme of striving for the prosperity and independence of the national state. Many people agreed with such a judgment, "whatever the difference in cultural orientation or whatever the direction it goes, such as the choice of Western value system or Chinese traditional value system after the May Fourth Movement, there was no real dispute upon the sovereignty or development of national state, which have always been a common goal."[49] The cultural memory of a nation is a component part of national consciousness, also a key foundation for maintaining and developing national consciousness and the national spirit. In modern history, Chinese nation stayed poor and weak and was defeated almost in all wars, forced into the edge of national extinction. However, even at the most dangerous moment of Chinese nation, Chinese people never lost their confidence on their nation, never despaired or gave up. After years of Cultural Revolution, we readjusted the fundamental policy of the state and Chinese people started to strive for the grand revival of Chinese nation. As time goes, the rise of Chinese nation shocked the world. Some forces accelerated their suppression acts and slanders on Chinese development. Thus, the historical memory of national consciousness buried deeply in the hearts of Chinese people was aroused naturally and expressed by multiple events. These events contained many patriotic acts of the public and theoretical breaks, which were weaved together to form a symphony of the nationalism trend in contemporary China.

---

49   Wang Hui, Zhang Tianwei, *Culture Critical Theory and the Issue of Contemporary Chinese Nationalism*, Recorded in *Intellectual Standpoint: Nationalism and Destiny of China during Transformation Period*, The Time Literature and Art Press, 2000, p. 397.

VII.3.2. New changes in the life practice of the society

In their constant material production activities and the resulting social relations, men continuously and initiatively develop their cognition on the existing world by their practice, and form an ideological system to learn and understand the world and utilize such experience system to change the world. The constant change of social life practice alter people's thinking mode and experience system. Also, the formation of the nationalism thought trend could not overcome the restrictions imposed by the era in which it emerged. The fruitful practice of the socialism with Chinese characteristics (such as the Reform and Opening-up) created another foundation for the growth of the trend of nationalism in contemporary China.

The 3rd Plenary Session of the 11th Central Committee of the CPC in 1978 established such a fundamental national policy that China should take economic development as its central task, which also proposed Four Cardinal Principles and the Reform and Opening-up. During this period, new and old systems and ideas, and even every aspect of social life showed constant intersections, conflicts and vibrations. New and old forces crossed and domestic and foreign ideas collided. The society presented an unprecedented image full of vitality and mess, which constituted a colorful era panorama in the march to modernization. The profound change in economic life drove the deep change in the field of social life. Various ideological systems surged across the whole China. From a new perspective, these systems shown a profound change in the field of social life by reflecting the extraordinary century that Chinese people had passed and all aspects of the five-thousand-year civilization of Chinese nation, and measured the brand new world in a new view.

As a powerful social thought trend, the nationalism puts the word China into its discourse and discusses the world by reassessment and critique. Its formation was based on the following facts:

Through the economic reform process, China has stepped into path which has to prosperity, but is encountering some specific difficulties with the deepening of the reform process. Against the current domestic and international conditions, China is indeed faced by both opportunities and challenges. As time goes, the challenge will become more and more specific and prominent. In front of external pressure, China needs to integrate by solving its internal conflicts and contradictions. And the internal conflict is reflected mainly in the division of interests. Interest division leads to a difference or even contrary political demands. As China is under severe external pressures, and when different interests collide domestically, various political thoughts try to advocate common national interests, and they require to reach a consensus, as known generally cohesion is the pursuit of all types of nationalisms.

The advance of the socialization of domestic politics can also contribute to the formation of the context where nationalism resorts to the masses. Since the Reform and Opening-up, the economic development of China has seen rapid growth, creating favorable environment and favorable material conditions for political socialization. The development of the relations between China and other countries allows China to learn about other countries and the whole world more comprehensively and profoundly. This reveals the false myth of capitalist development intentionally fabricated by some Western developed countries. The increasing mobility and interaction between rural and urban residents has improved social culture and political culture in rural areas. Such mobility also forces people to comprehensively and objectively learn the issue of rural development. Mass media spreads political knowledge in a vast scope, which also real-time publicize political events. The Internet broke up the limit of time and region to provide information, and realized remote communication and stranger communication. Through multiple media, people in different circles achieved direct communication, which allows deep reflections on the fate of the state and nation to be carried out at all levels.

Like all other countries, it is a natural and reasonable demand for the citizens to be concerned about the interests of their own government and nation. While, in the process of modernization, the secularization of people's thinking mode and values makes existing state ideology easier to tolerate the expression and appeal of nationalistic interest. In turn, this also makes civil nationalistic appeal able to be expressed in a more direct pattern compared with the past, so as to reduce the resort to other discourse systems.

VII.3.3. Unreasonable international interest pattern

The trend of nationalism in contemporary China has the elents and implications which surpasses traditional ideology. This is not because that people intentionally blur or ignore the difference in social systems of the world (socialism versus capitalism), but rather related to their feelings in regard to the division and evolution of the structure of the contemporary global economic system, which can be deemed as the profound deep cause for the emergence of the nationalism in contemporary China.

Before the 15th Century, human developed within their own nation and country and the external communications were rare. With the rise of capitalism and the formation of global market, all nations blended into the world actively or passively. Capitalism, on the one hand, has enhanced and promoted the relations and exchanges among all nations of the world by dragging them into the tide of globalization. On the other hand, it marginalized numerous nations by colonization and kept these nations far wary from the center and turned their space into backward regions of the world, i.e. the periphery.

In the middle of the 20th Century, China realized its national independence and liberation, and has overcome its national crisis. Chinese nation recovered its national pride and confidence and started the new course of national revival. Since the early 1980s, China's Reform and Opening-up went ahead with a constant fierce attack by Western peaceful evolution. During the communication, cooperation, competition and struggle with Western developed countries, the interest divisions were deepened and contradiction became intensified. Some scholars indicated that, "like in Western countries, the nationalism in China is also a product of modernity. Specifically, it is a result of modernity. Although the Western nationalism naturally formed in the modernization of Western nations, Chinese nationalism was generated passively during the communication and conflict between China and the West."[50]

As a country with the largest population in the world, China has rapidly stood up, which has disturbed those major privileged Western countries which possess massive vested interests in the current pattern of global resource distribution. Some westerners argue that the growth of China and the general improvement of the living standards of the Chinese people will pose a threat and put a strain on other countries of the world, since China will fight for energy and other economic resources to satisfy such living standard. Affected by such narrow interest minded political thinking, some Western countries have started to apply numerous pressures on China. In their opinion, in post-Cold War era, China had lost its value as a factor to restrict and balance the expansion or threat posed by the Soviet Union. Their attempt to use China as a trump card against the Soviet Union or exploit China for their narrow interests have just activated the profound nationalist emotions among the Chinese people, which has its past stock from the 19th Century humiliation, till the new China period.

Since the arrival of 21th Century, the conflict between China and Western countries became more prominent. In the initial stage of the Reform and Opening-up, the institutional structure and values of Western society have made significant effects on China. At that time, although China was hostile against the West in respect to its ideology, there was no frequent specific

---

50   Zhang Rulun, *Study on Contemporary Chinese Ideology*, Shanghai People Press, 2001, p. 111.

interest conflicts, especially economic interest conflicts. Under such circumstances, the West was mainly deemed as an admirable and remote object to follow. For Chinese people, the West meant developed material, energetic and rational spirit, rigorous and reasonable arrangement, advanced technology and abundant capital. As Chinese economy had further merged into the international society, the West had turned from a remote object to follow in the initial stage of modernization to a realistic competitor. When people hopefully entered the global market, they suddenly found that this market was not as ideal as in their imagination and detected there existed an unreasonable international economic order. Thus, the issue of state interest in the unreasonable international economic order became an unavoidable topic.

As Kissinger said, "the world has become smaller and smaller, but countries are not becoming closer. Paradoxically, when we must acknowledge that we need interdependency to solve the most serious problem, nationalism emerges."[51] The manifestation of nationalism is proportional to the stress of survival condition faced by the nation. Trend of nationalism will be enhanced with the increasingly growing strength of China. The trend of nationalism in current China will continue to exist and develop.

VII.3.4. The motive of seeking political legitimacy

In the 1990s, China has launched its large-scale system transformation. In such a era of deep change, the political center needed to have due legitimacy resource so as to keep the stability of the political order and maintain cohesiveness among the people during such transformation. The basic principles of the dominant ideology has played an irreplaceable role for the maintenance of the order of social life. Besides, the achievement in the reform and economic development also constantly contributed to the legitimacy of the regime. But neither could provide enough restraint and regulation in respect of development direction, rights and obligations among social members, distribution of rare resource, and the pursuit of spiritual life and ideal. "Therefore, there are two issues in the modernization of China. First, the historical trend of secularization based on market economy makes the idea of equalitarianism and the theory of class struggle in original ideology corresponding to the old system's loss of its attractive and integrative effect in the social political life. Secondly, the above mentioned patriotism based on marginal cultural factors and with the nature of opposition to traditional dominant culture obviously lacks due national cohesion as it is short of profound and abundant historical and cultural resources, such as

---

51   Karl W. Deutsch, *International Relation Analysis*, The Commercial Press, 1992, p. 349.

"national nature". The modernization promoted by the political center has been faced a puzzle, namely how to avoid ideology from becoming empty and poor as a result of the lack of necessary supplement. Just because of this, under the new historical conditions, it has been a major issue faced by the Chinese modernization drive: how to find and establish new resource of legitimacy for the leading authority so as to maintain cohesiveness and unity among people during such transformation."[52] In order to solve this issue, we need to find a more profound base for identity. In modern China, there existed three theories or ideal patterns about such base. One is the value system represented by freedom and democracy. Another theory tries to adopt traditional culture as the core value, such as the Five Moralities proposed by Liang Suming. The last is notion of nationalism contained in Marxism and Leninism. Under current conditions, the former two theories evidently could not form a value identity in the whole nation. In current commercial society, what can be such an integrating force? "Many people believe that it is the interest of national state, plus the emotion of national community based on this. This may be a basic element for social cohesion and also a fundamental precondition for the formation of nationalism in contemporary China."[53]

Faced by the issue of political legitimacy, the trend of nationalism in contemporary China attempts to undertake two key tasks: the salvation and enlightenment. On the one hand, the trend should absorb the advanced Western experience in respect of social economic life-especially econom- ics- and receive the baptism of Western modern civilization, so as to change idea and realize the localization of it. On the other hand, in real politics, this trend should firmly hold the standpoint of criticizing the West and keep highly vigilant and resistant attitude to any political or cultural infiltration from the Western world.

VII.4. Analysis on the nationalism thought trend in contemporary China

Based on the description above, it can be concluded that, in order to un- derstand the trend of nationalism in contemporary China, we should both look into the knowledge about the pedigree of nationalism in the West,

---

52 Xiao Gongqin, *Nationalism and the Ideology during Chinese Transition Period*, Recorded in *Intellectual Standpoint: Nationalism and Destiny of China during Transformation Period*, The Time Literature and Art Press, 2000, p. 445.
53 Wang Hui, Zhang Tianwei, *Culture Critical Theory and the Issue of Contemporary Chinese Nationalism*, Recorded in *Intellectual Standpoint: Nationalism and Destiny of China during Transformation Period,* The Time Literature and Art Press, 2000, p. 400.

and transcend beyond the dominant values of the West and discuss concrete questions in the concrete, specific context. The core of any social thought trend is its political demand an political colors. Undeniably, the nationalism thought trend is still multi-sense and relatively vague in contemporary China. This trend not only faces the difficulty to communicate with the dominant ideology, but also clashes with, even conflicts with other discourse systems. Below, we will analyze and discuss it from different perspectives.

VII.4.1. Nationalism trend in contemporary China is a marginal ideology

If we evaluate the configuration pattern of the ideological sphere of the superstructure in contemporary China, the trend of nationalism is a marginal ideology on the whole, as one component of non-dominant ideologies. As a non-dominant thought, the trend of nationalism has certain difference and asymmetry with the dominant mainstream ideology and it has evident autonomous and folk qualities. In real life, the popularization of nationalism requires certain realistic factors, such as national crisis and secession threat against the state and its terrritores, which has long faded away in contemporary China. Under new circumstance, the manifestation of all these traditional factors has also changed greatly. Therefore, the emergence of the nationalism trend often aroused confusion by making people question its rationality. It seems like an actor who gets on the stage in wrong order and is booed by the audience. The mainstream discourse also cautiously avoided talking about this topic. As time goes and openness increases, the contact and conflict between China and the world grew increasingly. By the end of the middle and late 1990s, the nationalism trend started to attract an extensive attention from intellectual circles and ordinary people in China. Even so, although the trend has an extensive grassroots basis, it is, to a large extent, still remains at a marginal position in the field of ideology in contemporary China and keeping certain distance from the dominant ideology.

The nationalism as a social thought trend. This fact reminds us that, we must demonstrate those generalized social emotions and thought trends and correctly deals with the relationship between the dominant ideology and non-dominant ideologies; besides, we should guide those non-dominant ideologies so as to do well in ideological work and improve the governing ability of the CPC in the field of ideology.

VII.4.2. Contemporary Chinese nationalism trend has a relatively strong sense of critique

Generally speaking, any social thought trend has its critical colors, and it is the contradictory unity of criticism and constructivism. Criticism often points to the history and real social life practices and proposes theoretical concepts which reflect the practical experience. This is the distinctive feature of the social thought trends, and non-critical social thought trends which are basically non-existent.

From the above analysis, the formation of the contemporary Chinese nationalism itself has been a process of negation, it is inherited and developed in the process of negation, and it has grown through the understanding and criticism of the established system of power discourse. Looking from the historical perspective, either the Western modern nationalism or the Chinese modern nationalism has existed as a kind of critical discourse. The birth and development of contemporary Chinese nationalism is determined by the development of social political and economic life, and it is of the strong atmosphere of reflection and reconstruction with a strong sense of criticism. Superficially, the main critical object of the contemporary Chinese nationalism is the liberal thought trend, which is the questioning and challenge to the discourse of liberalism all over the world. In the Western mainstream discourse interpretation system, the contemporary Chinese nationalism became a potential form debuting during the desolation period of the international communist movement to resist the order and values of the Western world, and even a new opponent in the "clash of civilizations". The ideological orientation of the contemporary Chinese nationalism in theory is to protect the interests of its own nation, and advocates "us" and should at least be equal to "them". In the view of international mainstream ideology, the demands for "equality" and "fairness" are the legacy of "Cold War" era and the period of the national liberation movement, and the evil excuse the "fig leaf" of the rogue states and failed states. Therefore, the nationalist thought trend is mostly attacked by the camp of domestic liberal discourse. Wang Xiaodong, wrote: "In the contemporary China, nationalism has been abused by some so-called mainstream intellectuals. They have roughly two arguments against nationalism: first, it is the era of global village, compared with this beautiful world, the nationalism is "narrow" and "closed" (there are many of these words in contemporary China, once labeled with this kind of hat, you will become a pariah regardless of the contents); Secondly, the nationalism uses and underlines the concept of sovereignty to repress and diminish the issue of human rights, and it has been the tool in the hand of autocratic rulers."[54] Some scholars have put forward "nationalism is a kind of emotion in essence, not a set of systematic theory. The solution to the problem is to resort to uninhibited human emotions, rather than a resort to the rational endowments of human beings that is originally very limited", "nationalism is the factor to endanger national security, and it is the most unstable and difficult to control, nationalist sentiment is easy to stir up hatred and discordance in different ethnic groups", "choosing and supporting nationalism means the choice of the blood and sword", "nationalism emphasizes the absolute sovereignty of a nation and excludes the autonomy of the individual, which may suppress, deprive the individual rights, resulting in the political sovereignty of the absolute monarchy with no restriction domestically and internationally", "although the nationalism deems national interests as supreme, it cannot provide effective means for the realization of national interests except in the field of culture."[55] We think this is a typical critical evaluation of the trend of nationalism.

VII.4.3. Contemporary Chinese nationalism is not equal to national separatism

In the discussion of the trend of nationalism, worries expressed are that the trend of nationalism will turn into a wholly separatist nationalism trend and lead to the division of the nation, which is the prominent point of view, among others which express doubts and take a wait-and-see attitude towards the contemporary nationalism. Therefore, the relationship between the contemporary nationalism and national separatism needs to be carefully analyzed.

The growth of any kind of nationalism thought trend is not the result of people's subjective will. Since the 1990s, often the establishment of a new nation-state by a nationality which has separated from a multi-ethnic country was not caused by the principle of national self-determination and also not caused by the "one-nation, one-state theory" we have discussed earlier, instead the deep causes point to some major fundamental changes regarding the social, political and economic structures of the world. Analyzing, from both historical and logical realistic aspects, nation-state idea and nationalism are never built on purely ethnic and blood relationship, but on self-understanding and self-regulation by specific economic, social, cultural and

---

54   Wang Xiaodong, *Nationalism and Democracy*, Recorded in *Intellectual Standpoint: Nationalism and Destiny of China during Transformation Period*, The Time Literature and Art Press, 2000, pp. 90-91.

55   Liu Junning, *Comprehensive Description on Nationalism*, Recorded in *Intellectual Standpoint: Nationalism and Destiny of China during Transformation Period*, The Time Literature and Art Press, 2000, pp. 13-14, 17.

political groups. This kind of self-understanding and self-regulation does not emerge and develop merely due to the will by an individual or by a group of people but has a complex and profound historical, social, cultural, psychological and political roots. Ethnic divisions in a multi-ethnic country have a more complicated background. The specific analysis should be carried out according to the specific circumstances, and we cannot generally say that the advocacy of nationalism should not necessarily contain the ideological elements of ethnic-national separatism. From the previous analysis, the main body of the interests which is emphasized by the trend of the contemporary Chinese nationalism is the whole Chinese nation and the Chinese nationalism of the whole Chinese nation, and emphasizes the unity of the Chinese nation and the mutual commonality of interests. There are obvious contrasts between the core values and the theoretical pursuit of the contemporary Chinese nationalism and the demands of national xenophobism or national isolationism. If we compare the national separatism with the contemporary Chinese nationalism and we can see that the contemporary Chinese nationalism opposes national separatism, and the "national consciousness" does not constitute its basic theory and we can see the that theory of "one nation, one state" as the theoretical basis of national separatism and xenophobism is obviously rejected. Motives and the theoretical basis of national separatism is completely different from the motives and the theoretical basis of contemporary Chinese nationalism, thus their theories and practical demands completely contrast each other. We should emphasize that our study in this book involves the thought trend of contemporary nationalism, not the national separatism trend. The contemporary nationalism is essentially different from the trend of contemporary Chinese national separatism. The essence of contemporary Chinese nationalism is positive patriotism, reversely the national separatism contrasts the fundamental interests of the Chinese nation, thus the contemporary Chinese nationalism is different from and opposes national separatism.

The reasons why it is easy to link the contemporary Chinese nationalism with national separatism are as follows: Firstly, there is the lack of in-depth research on the contemporary nationalism, thus it is regarded on a par with the Western nationalism and national separatism. Secondly, there is the understanding of the contemporary nationalism, but it is deliberately equated with national separatism in order to achieve the purpose of curbing or even eliminating it.

Although we can conclude that the contemporary Chinese nationalism is not equal to the trend of national separatism, advocating nationalism in contemporary China is indeed likely to cause misunderstanding, even mislead people in their analysis, and this will be used by people who have ulterior motives, and this problem needs to be paid attention to.

VII.4.4. Contemporary Chinese nationalism trend to a certain extent is the contemporary version of modern Chinese nationalism with the same theme

The birth and development of contemporary Chinese nationalism have not only a realistic basis, but also has historical origins. The specific issues of state and nation with which the contemporary nationalism faces are different from the history, but the essence of the subject is the problem of the survival and development of the nation and the state. The history of modern China is a history of humiliation, and it is a bloody history of oppression, exploitation and oppression by the Western powers. This is the deep root of the emergence, development and expansion of Chinese nationalism. In this sense, the trend of the contemporary Chinese nationalism is the nationalism of the stimulative and reflective type. On the surface, the contemporary Chinese nationalism thought trend is inspired by the disintegration of the Soviet Union and the transformation of the US strategy to China from strategy to the strategic courting. In fact, a more profound reason lies in the memories of the past modern history of China, wherein "learning from Britain and the US" was advocated. "Learning from Britain and the US" was a thought and practice in the modern Chinese history, which had encountered repeated frustrations, I can say that this thought and practice has greatly inspired the growth and popularity of a variety of trends of social thoughts including Marxism and nationalism. In the view of contemporary Chinese nationalism, the social practice of Reform and Opening-up is gradually developing within a process of constant exploration, and the widespread implementation of the market economy causes the resurgence of the concept of "learning from Britain and the US" and causes its charm among the people, once more. As a result, for the first time, the current Western-oriented policies, cultural orientation and system of China have become objects of critique and questioning by the nationalism thought trend. This kind of questioning becomes the spiritual element of the modern Chinese nationalism trend to reflect "the Western style modernization" mode.

With the deepening of China's Reform and Opening-up, the contemporary Chinese nationalism has been one thought trend, which longs and seeks further development and enhancement of China's comprehensive national strength. Since the 1990s, the collapse of the Soviet Union has transformed socialistic China into an imaginary enemy for the West. In China, some of the intellectuals have a profound sense of intellectual kinship with the

West, echoing the penetration of Western ideology, after the reform went deeper, many contradictions emerged and there have been many roadblocks on the road of modernization while the Chinese situation has been quite different from that at the beginning of Reform and Opening-up and even the whole 1980s. Someone uses "a group of enemies around and the interior affairs should be cultivated" to describe the current Chinese situation. In the new century, as for how to further enhance the national integrity, cultivate the national spirit and help the Chinese nation overcome the difficulties in the new century with the abundant essence, energy and spirit, the nationalism thought trend offers solutions to this problem. The trend of "fighting against enemies and cultivating inner democracy" has gradually become the consensus of nationalistic intellectuals.

VII.4.5. Contemporary Chinese nationalism trend is an expression of nationalist discourse in the context of globalization

Globalization and nationalism are in mutual contradiction and conflict with each other. There are obvious differences in the attitudes of Chinese intellectuals towards globalization. The different attitudes towards globalization delineate nationalism and liberalism. "Only the globalization wherein the nations hold their political fate in their hand can be beneficial."[56] "Another distinctive attitude towards globalization is liberalism, or 'cosmopolitanism' which advocates that globalization is not just the mode of economic exchanges, but also a political, economic and cultural process, it is the globalization of the whole capitalist mode of production, thus the national interests should be weakened and overwhelmed by global interests, and that the human rights can surpass the rights which originate from being members of a nation and can exist independent of nations."[57]

In particular, globalization has strengthened the status of the nation-state. As Lenin wrote in the article on the Criticism of National Issues: "Developing capitalism knows two historical tendencies in the national question. The first is the awakening of national life and national movements, the struggle against all national oppression, and the creation of national states. The second is the development and growing frequency of international intercourse in every form, the break-down of national barriers, the creation of the international unity of capital, of economic life in general,

---

56   Zhang Wenmu, The National Interests of China in the Process of Globalization, Journal of Strategy and Management, 2002(1).

57   He Jiadong, The Differences between Human Rights and Nationality: What is the True Spirit in Nationalism?, *Journal of Strategy and Management* 1998(3).

of politics, science, etc."[58] This phrase demonstrates that on one hand, the development of capitalism promotes globalization, and on the other hand, it further clarifies the boundaries of the nation states. The nation-state has not weakened with the advance of globalization. A remarkable character-istics of globalization is that it brings uneven development to the world, and greatly increases the gap between the rich and the poor. Due to their unfavorable position in world economic competition, the vast majority of developing countries have allowed laissez-faire and excessive opening-up to such a limit that, this situation may lead to the loss of their national inter-ests, and even endanger their survival.

These latecomer developing countries have to maintain and defend their own economic and political interests by emphasizing their national character. The developed capitalist countries have been the promoters of globalization, but the benefits of globalization are not globally shared, the developed capi-talist countries—in order to grab the maximum profit brought by the expan-sion of capital—they also need to endow the state with "national" colors in order to resist the loss of their privileged interests, profits and maintain their monopoly position. It can be seen that globalization has strengthened the at-tributes of the nation-state, without breaking the nation-state. Thus the judg-ment that "end of nation-state" rhetoric is ridiculous and one-sided.[59] So far, the development process of globalization is still the development with the nation-states as its basic units, globalization is not a development wherein all mankind as its basic unit, and this will remain so in the foreseeable future. On the premise that this basis remains intact, the basic principle of international political operations, will not change, that is, that is, using the national power of the state— as much as possible—in order to defend the interests of its own people–will not change. This shows that the real effect of globalization is the fragmentation and division of the world and this fragmentation makes the role of the nation-state more prominent. Globalization "is a profound and lasting challenge to the traditional international relations, and threatens na-tional sovereignty rights and other rights, and the rules of the people's ac-tivities identified by the national boundaries."[60] This challenge strengthens the national feelings and nation-state consciousness among the peoples. The critical explanation of globalization should be an important innovation in the theory of contemporary Chinese nationalism. According to the contemporary Chinese nationalism trend, the development of China in the current political

---

58   *Selected Works of Lenin,* Vol. 2, People's Publishing House, 1995, p. 30.
59   Yang Xuedong, *Globalization, Frontier of Western Theory,* Social Sciences Academic Press (China), 2002, p. 155.
60   Wang Yizhou, Modern Reflection on the Concept of Nationalism, *Journal of Strategy and Management,* 1994(3).

and economic order of the world tends to be restricted, this nationalism is definitely not in favor of China's seclusion, but it discusses the most optimal way of its participation to the world system. That is, in the era of globalization, the interests of the nation needs to be paid attention to, "and we should be fully aware that the current era is not the era with peace and development as the theme, but the world still has a long way to go before achieving the necessary conditions for peace and development."[61] The process of globalization is a process of homogenization. According to the contemporary Chinese nationalism, homogeneity is only a kind of fragmentation, and it is the same in the form and split in the interests. With the further improvement of comprehensive national strength of China, people more ardently expect the arrival of the national revival. Under the condition of globalization, the developed countries will allow some late developer countries to enhance their national strength and the nation in the local and specific time periods in order to maintain the smooth running of the global capital. But the steady and healthy development of China with a population of 1.3 billion has caused an alarming feeling in the developed countries. China Threat Theory and the arguments calling to contain China are on the rise at this logical starting point. The "Universal Harmony", "Land under Heaven" and "Cosmopolitanism" become feebly high-profile in the face of the grim reality. In order to survive and develop, in order to effectively and efficiently strive for the external space for development, it achieve the goal of national rejuvenation, social solidarity, people's happiness and world peace and development to the greatest extent only through starting from the position of the nation and developing its economic, political and military strength. It can be said that the process of globalization is an important external cause to promote the fermentation of the modern nationalism trend. Perhaps it is true to say that the "most of 'Chinese nationalists' know that the Boxer[62] style anti-Western sentiment cannot not meet the national interests of China, instead China needs to keep a good relationship with the West, but China should also have the consciousness to protect its interests, and it is only the latter point that differs 'Chinese nationalists' from the Chinese intellectuals who approach the Westerners."[63]

---

61   Zhang Wenmu, *The National Interests of China in the Process of Globalization*, *Strategy and Management*, 2002(1).
62   Boxer, movement peasant uprising of 1900 that attempted to drive all foreigners from China.
63   Qin Hui: *What is the Conjunction Point between Liberalism and Nationalism?*, recorded in: *Intellectual Standpoint–Nationalism and Destiny of China during Transformation Period*, The Time Literature and Art Press, 2000, p. 337.

VII.4.6. Contemporary Chinese nationalism trend is not a bourgeois ideology

In the 1980s, people held the real hopes and great expectations for the West. At that time, there was no place for the nationalist discourse. Even in the world, due to the existence of the two camps in the context of the Cold War, in those days nationalism in the world was not been so prominent as in the 1990s. Thus, the views of the Chinese academia and the mainstream ideology in the 1980s towards nationalism were based on the analysis of Western history and nationalism in reality, so they basically thought that nationalism was a bourgeois ideology. For example, Mr. Chen Yongling, the editor of the National Dictionary, wrote in it: "'nationalism, also known as bourgeois nationalism' is the bourgeois views of the nation and its program and policy to handle ethnic-national issues."[64] As the volume of the Encyclopedia of China for the Nationality issue said: "Nationalism is a reflection of the landlord and bourgeois ideology in regard to ethnic-national relations, and the guiding principles, programs and policies for these classes to deal with the issue of nationality."[65]

The Chinese dictionary Ci Hai wrote: "nationalism is the principles, programs and policies for the bourgeoisie and petty bourgeoisie to deal with national problems and national relations, and it had already existed before the emergence of capitalist society. It had developed into a complete ideological system up to the capitalist era, so it is also known as the "bourgeois nationalism".[66] These relatively authoritative interpretations positioned the nationalism issue with the characteristics of bourgeoisie. Whether this kind of definition of nationalism can be applied to the contemporary Chinese nationalism in the 1990s or not is a question that must be clarified in the process analyzing of contemporary Chinese nationalism.

Marx and Lenin both dialectically and historically viewed the liberation of the nations and their struggle for an independent state. In the times of Marx and Lenin, the criticism against bourgeoisie and imperialism was very thorough, and it was also revealed that the capitalist class maintained its own rule by the banner of nationalism. Marx, indeed, had affirmed the progressive nature of the bourgeoisie, and thought that the colonial rule had made historical progress. That does not mean that Marx simply regarded the nationalism of oppressed nations as a thing to reject the advanced productive forces and the modern civilization. Lenin advocated the right of

---

64 *National Dictionary*, Shanghai Lexicographical Publishing House, 1987, p. 347.
65 *Encyclopedia of China Nationality*, Encyclopedia of China Publishing House, 1986, p. 330.
66 *Ci Hai*, Shanghai Lexicographical Publishing House, 1989, p. 47.

oppressed nations to obtain their national self-determination through the struggle of nationalism. In Lenin's view, even if the nationalism of the oppressed nations was advocated by their bourgeois classes, it would also be a progressive development.

We should say that the contemporary Chinese nationalism trend is the expression of a nationalist discourse in the new historical conditions which is completely different from the Western ethnic nationalism under the conditions of globalization, and does not have the character of the bourgeoisie. In general, in the process of rapid development of the contemporary China, some intellectuals have seen China as increasingly hit and contained by some international forces in the process of development, while someone domestically echoed, and they counterattack this kind of public opinion and overall Westernization and psychology of worshipping the foreign power through the discussion of nationalism. In addition, through the over 50 years of socialist construction, China became a major world power, and the its poor and weak nation status was vanished, which has elevated the dignity of the Chinese nation, and the socialist motherland. Some intellectuals have made the induction and generalization of "nationalism" for a valuable emotion in theory. These scholars have repeatedly stressed that Chinese "nationalism" can be evaluated as limited moderate and rational one, and they have argued that it strives to establish a concept of nationalism with Chinese characteristics.

VII.4.7. The essence of contemporary Chinese nationalism trend is patriotism

We can see that the core idea of the contemporary Chinese nationalism trend is still the national spirit and patriotism to elevate the Chinese nation. National spirit and patriotism is historical, specific, exists at any time, thus it is the inherent spirit quality of our nation, and it is wrong to say that we do not have a national pride and dignity until we have the nationalism. Therefore, it is not reasonable to advocate nationalism and replace patriotism with nationalism in China. We have never had an evil history like Western countries which practiced colonialism by the name of nationalism in the process of the formation and development of capitalism. For a long time, we have realized national independence and liberation and realized the development and prosperity of our motherland in the course of the combination of Marxism with the reality in China, we can say that, practically it will be difficult to cultivate such a "new" nationalism unique to China. If we remember that the current situation of the ideological sphere of China is quite complex, it would be unwise and unessential to establish such an ambiguous concept of nationalism which plays different roles in different cases and aims to replace the established ideology of Chinese patriotism.

Some scholars have argued that in the past the meaning of the concepts of nationalism and patriotism used to be quite close and similar, but there has been a trend that the word patriotism has indeed assumed a vulgar character in recent years. A lot of patriotic education makes people only think of some superficial forms of nationalism, but people lack its real meaning and concerns and ignore the explore the new content it has gained.[67] In recent years, the trend of simple, formal, and even vulgar patriotism education in China, especially in the educational institutions has been a real problem, that has displayed itself. This has led to a practical and secular deformation of patriotic education, the forms of teaching has gained diversity and some richer, contents but its essence is quite weak. But this is a minor aspect of the problem, the patriotism and patriotic education cannot be denied and the patriotism should not be confused by nationalism based on it, patriotism is irreplaceable.

In general, what the contemporary Chinese nationalism thought trend reflects is not an aggressive or offensive mindset and not a sense of external hegemonism, but an expression of anxiety or concern for the destiny of the country and the nation, and it demonstrates a kind of vigorous expression of patriotic feelings. In today's international situation which demonstrates certain degree of turmoil and turbulence and that the international situation is in a period of "major transformations and adjustments", the existence of such anxiety can be deemed as normal. The trend of the contemporary Chinese nationalism cherishes and defends the dignity of the Chinese nation, defends its survival and development rights which were established in 1949. Regarding this point, we can say that, although there are biases in its expression, contemporary nationalism thought trend—to some degree—can surpass its the new doctrinarism, dogmas and its rigid aspects state, thus become an important and effective force to integrate and highlight the spirit of Chinese nation.

As a result, this book argues that the contemporary nationalism thought trend is also the unity of the social psychology and ideology, which is based on real interests, which takes the patriotism as its core value and embodies consciousness and concern for the country, nation and includes relevant cognitive elements.[68]

---

67 Wang Xiaodong, Discussion on Contemporary Chinese Nationalism, *Journal of Strategy and Management*, 2000(5).

68 The author discussed the trend in his work *Study on the Nationalism Thought Trend*. This article refers to the important viewpoints of this book, hereby noted. Fang Ning, Wang Bingquan, *Study on the Nationalism Thought Trend*, Higher Education Press, 2004.

CONCLUSION

Guiding the Social Thought Trends

The 6th Plenary Session of the 16th CPC Central Committee, proposed for the first time, major proposition of "erecting socialist core value system", and summarized it from four aspects. That is the guiding role Marxism in the ideological field, the common ideal of socialism with Chinese characteristics, patriotism-centered national spirit and the spirit of times, centered on reform and innovation and fourthly socialist concept of honors and disgraces. It clearly proposes, "adherence to guide the social ideological trend with the socialist core value system, show tolerance and respect for differences and diversity, and strive to form social and ideological consensus."[1]

This has been a major theoretical innovation by our party in the ideological and cultural construction, and an important strategic task set by our party based on profound summary of historical experience and scientific analysis of the current situation. The party's 17th and 18th National Congress have stressed using study and education into the socialist core value system in guiding the social trends of thought, which is not only a major strategic task of our party's ideological work, but has also served as an important starting point for the study of social thought, in our book.[2]

By strictly adhering to the importance and urgency of guiding social trends of thought, we can consciously strengthen our understanding on the socialist core value system; thus constantly improve our ability to guide social trends of thought, we can effectively guarantee that major tasks of the country can be carried out well; enhance the pertinence of guiding social trends of thought, we can enhance the effectiveness of this task; show tolerance and

---

1   *Selected Important Documents Since the 16th National Party Congress* (Volume II), Central Party Literature Press, 2008, p. 661.
2   As mentioned earlier, this book does not make a detailed distinction between social thought trends and political thought trends. It unfolds the formulation "Guiding social trend of thought" in the Document of the Central Authorities and does not specifically discuss the issue of guiding the political thought trends.

respect for differences and diversity, and can strongly resist all kinds of errors and decadent ideas, all these are vivid basic principles for guiding the social ideological trend with the socialist core value system. Therefore, in order to guide social trends of thought by using the socialist core value system, we must clearly recognize the importance and urgency of the socialist core value system, constantly improve our ability to guide social trends by socialist core value system, strengthen the pertinence of guiding social thoughts, actively implement the principle of " showing tolerance and respect for differences and diversity" and resolutely resist erroneous and decadent ideas.

C.1. Adhering to the importance and urgency of guiding the social thought trends

Adhering to the principle of guiding social ideology is an important issue in the field of ideological work, which is critical in the construction of harmonious socialist society and for enhancing the governing capacity of the party.

C.1.1. Important issues in the field of ideology

Work in the ideological field is critically important for our party. Since in the early days of the building of the CPC, the Party included education and publicity of Marxism as an important task in its the agenda. The "Resolution on Education and Propaganda Issues" adopted by the 1st Plenary Session of the 3rd CPC Central Committee, in November 1923, has stressed the education of the basic principles of Marxism, that the Party should adopt various forms to strengthen party member's ideas, and use the world outlook of dialectical materialism and collectivism to educate Party members, intellectuals and masses. Later in the courses of revolution, socialist transformation and construction, our party has repeatedly stressed the ideological and educational work among the masses and proposed to strengthen the education of Party cadres with Marxist theories, which laid a favorable foundation of public opinion for the victory of the new democratic revolution and successful completion of the socialist transformation and construction. It can be said that attaching importance to the ideological work served as an important condition for the party to achieve the victories in the revolution and completion of the socialist transformation and construction.

Following the Reforms and Opening-up, our party has continued to attach great importance to the ideological work, in particular, the occurrence and development of the social thought, especially tracking the study of occurrence and influence as an important aspect of ideological work, all of which have a direct impact and relationship with the current situation of social trend of thought. In the period after the founding of new China and until the period of Reform and Opening-up, our country has passed through a highly centralized period, in the fields of politics, economics and culture. Since the Reform and Opening- up, people have showed active participation in the field of ideology and culture and a variety of social trends thought have appeared, many of which are favorable for the promotion of spreading Marxist ideological theory in China. In order to strengthen and improve the party's ideological work, we should carefully trace and research the occurrence and development of certain erroneous thoughts.

Several generations of our party's central collective leadership have maintained a high degree of vigilance against the wrong ideological trends. Before the Reform and Opening-up, although the variety of social trend of thought was relatively restricted, the party's first generation of central collective leadership led by Comrade Mao Zedong paid high attention to the challenges that emerged in the ideological field, and launched large-scale theoretical education movements targeting various non-Marxist thoughts in the period of socialist transformation and construction. Despite some errors in handling the struggle against non-Marxist thoughts, and all these practices above have provided a lot of experience and lessons for our vigilance and in fighting against erroneous ideological trends, in the proceeding periods. After the Party's the 3rd Plenary Session of the 11th CPC Central Committee, in 1978, Deng Xiaoping, in his many speeches has stressed, the need to pay attention to and study the social trend of thoughts. The party's third generation of the CPC central collective leadership with Comrade Jiang Zemin as the core held high the great banner of Deng Xiaoping theory, attached great importance to understanding and identification of social thoughts, and closely integrated the research on social thoughts with the construction of socialist spiritual civilization. The CPC Central Committee with Comrade Hu Jintao as the general secretary strengthened the construction of the mainstream ideology, repeatedly emphasized the need to guide social thoughts with socialist core value system, and implemented a series of policies and measures to correctly guide ideological and culture spheres and guide public opinions. The resolution issued by the Party during the 6th Plenary Session of the 16th CPC Central Committee clearly stated "to guide the social thoughts with socialist core value system, respect for divergence, allow diversity, maximize efforts to attain social consensus."[3] The report of the 17th Party Congress repeated the need to guide social trends of thoughts, emphasized undertaking the ideological work, well, and said: "We will

---

3 *Selected Important Documents since the 16th National Party Congress* (Volume II), Central Party Literature Press, 2008, p. 661.

explore effective ways of letting the system of socialist core values guide trends of thought and take the initiative in ideological work, respecting divergence and allowing diversity while effectively resisting the influence of erroneous and decadent ideas"[4], and stressed the need to strengthen China's cultural soft power. The 18th Congress of the CPC again stressed that: "Core socialist values are the soul of the Chinese nation and serve as the guide for building socialism with Chinese characteristics. We should carry out thorough study of and education in these values and use them to guide social trends of thought and forge public consensus."[5] In order to ensure this guiding work achieves actual effect, a series of corresponding, specific policy initiatives have been introduced. For example, to strengthen research and construction of the Marxist theories by promoting the creativity, persuasion and appeal of Marxism in the Party's ideological and theoretical work; use Sinicized Marxist theories in order to educate the entire party and people, continue the education of ideals, beliefs, values of socialism and patriotism, constantly enhance people's belief and confidence in the leadership of the CPC, the socialist system, the Reform and Opening-up, the goal of building a prosperous society in an all-round manner. To build and develop a modern cultural industry and new cultural undertakings and cultural enterprises to ensure the healthy development of cultural industry and undertakings while persisting in putting social interest first, persisting in unifying social interest and economic interest, abiding by cultural development rules, adapting to the requirements of socialist market economy development, continue to implement the "One Batch of Four" talent training project and invigorate the system of national cultural creativity, and cultivate creative young talents who can harmoniously work with the ruling party and the government in the fields of art, culture, journalism, art- literature and publishing industry, etc.

Since the 18th Party Congress, the CPC Central Committee, with comrade Xi Jinping as the general secretary, launched a series of new concepts and modes regarding governance, which emphasized the improvement of the work style of the Party, maintaining close ties with the masses, rigorously fighting against extravagance, implementing effective anti-corruption efforts and promoting integrity, improving the conduct of the Party and government, further enhancing nation's cohesion centripetal force and

---

4   Hu Jintao: *Hold High the Great Banner of Socialism with Chinese Characteristics and Strive to Build a Moderately Prosperous Society in an All-round Way–Report to the 17th National Congress of the Communist Party of China*, People's Publishing House, 2007, p. 34.
5   Hu Jintao: *Advance Firmly along the Road of Socialism with Chinese Characteristics and Strive to Build a Well-off Society in an All-round way–Report at the Eighteenth National Congress of the Communist Party of China*, People's Publishing House, 2012, p. 31.

further strengthening confidence in path, theory, and system of socialism with Chinese characteristics which have all laid a solid foundation for improving the work regarding guiding social thought trends.

C.1.2. The significance of guiding the social thoughts

After the third Plenary Session of the 11th CPC Central Committee, especially in recent years, with the further deepening of Reform and Opening-up development, several social thoughts at home and abroad have been stirred up; the ideological field has become more diverse. This provides a good opportunity for strengthening the construction of socialist core value system. At the same time, it also challenges the dominant and guiding position of the Marxism in the field of ideology and social consciousness. The necessity and importance of the socialist core value system to guide the social trend of thought has become increasingly prominent. In view of prevalent importance and necessity of this issue, the academic circles have carried on deeper debates.

Overall, the existing research results mainly discusses the significance of guiding of social trends by the socialist core value system from two aspects. Many scholars have analyzed the significance of guiding social thought trends from the perspective of building a harmonious socialist society. They point out that guiding social thoughts with the socialist core value system is an important political task required by the party in leading people to build a socialist harmonious society. The socialist core value system is the common ideological foundation of cohesion and banner for common struggles of the people of all ethnic groups in China. Consequently, it should play a controlling and guiding function in guiding the contemporary social trend of thought. Some theorists believe that under the background of economic globalization, political multi-polarization trend, cultural diversity and information networking, a new stage of building a socialist harmonious society and the condition of diversified economic and social life and people value orientation, guiding contemporary social trend of thoughts with socialist core value system has a specific significance for the formation of spiritual strength of the people and strengthen the spiritual bond of unity and harmony. To guide people in pushing forward the great cause of building a socialist harmonious society, our party must take the political responsibility of guiding the social thought trends with socialist core value system, based on governing the nation and people.[6]

---

6   Deng Xiaoping Theory and "Three Represents" Thought Research Center in National Defense University: Adhere to Guide the Social Thought Trends with Core Socialist Values, *Guangming Daily*. Dec. 16th, 2006.

Some scholars have summarized the significance of guiding work from the perspective of profound changes in social structure and from the aspect of adjustments we have made on the pattern of interests in the society during the Reform and Opening-up. They argue that the period of great social transformation, firmly guided by the socialist core value system, was the inevitable link that consolidated the whole nation and the whole society to make progress with the spirit of solidarity and harmony; a positive response to the impacts and challenges posed by ideological and cultural changes in the world today; an important way to realize the theoretical innovation of our party; an important way in which our party can better understand the public opinion in the society; a precondition for our party to formulate correct theories, lines, program and policies; an important condition to continuously enhance the ability of the party to remain in power.[7] This book has summarized the significance of adhering to the socialist core value system in guiding the social trends.

The socialist core value system has the ability to guide. The resolution of the CPC Central Committee "On Major Issues Regarding the Building of a Socialist Harmonious Society" issued by the 6th Plenary Session of the 16th CPC Central Committee pointed out that guiding position of Marxism, the common ideal of socialism with Chinese characteristics, patriotism-centered national spirit and the spirit of times centered on reform and innovation, and advocating socialist maxims of honor and disgrace are the basic content of the socialist core value system. The socialist core value system is the essence of socialist ideology and the inner spirit and vital soul of the socialist system, which has a dominant position in China's various cultures and values. It is the essence of our party's ideological and cultural achievement in guiding the people through long-term practice, and a common ideological basis for unity and struggle by the people of all ethnic groups in China, it includes socialist as well as the most precious values, we have inherited from the history of mankind. The socialist core value system represents the society's development direction. Socialist core value system also has a wide range of applicability and embodiment which reflects broad requirements regarding ideological and moral construction. The socialist core value system also reflects the different levels of the masses' ideological situation, and covers different demands of different social groups and social classes. Therefore, socialist core value system is not only the spiritual prop of constructing a harmonious society and not only the spiritual leverage which bonds different nationalities and classes, but also the great

---

7   Zhang Lihai: Adhere to Guide the Social Thought Trends with Socialist Core Values. *Journal of Xi'an Institute of Political Sciences*, 2006(6).

banner of guiding social thought with a strong ability to integrate and guide.

Guiding the social trend of thoughts with socialist core value system is a requirement to promote social harmony. Social trend of thought is a specific consciousness phenomenon, which is a reflection of social existence in a certain period; a "barometer" of the political life and acts as a "wind-vane" (shows the main direction of development) of the society, and a mirror to judge the whole state of ideological super structure in a certain period of time. We have witnessed this in the new century with the deepening of Reform and Opening-up, especially the profound changes in the social structure and especially adjustments made regarding the pattern of interests, a variety of ideological and cultural interactions, changes in people's ideology, moral consciousness, the new changes have increasingly strengthened independence, selectivity, diversification and differentiation of people's mind activity and value orientation, variability and difference among various thought trends have increased. The field of social consciousness presents a complicated situation. Social thought trends have become more complex and dynamic. The difference and diversity of social trends of thought has become an objective existence. In addition, a variety of ideological and cultural exchanges have become more frequent across the world. Facing the new situation, we need to carefully observe the "barometer" and grasp the "wind vane", i.e. the main direction of the current development, and adhere to guiding and integrating social thoughts with socialist core value system, increase both cohesion and charm of socialist ideology under the background of diversification in social consciousness so as to provide strong spiritual support for advancing reform, development, and stability. It can be seen that adhering to the principle of guiding social trend of thoughts with the socialist core value system is the objective requirement in the field of social consciousness to have a profound change and the reality requirements of ideological and moral basis to achieve the construction of a harmonious culture, and consolidation of social harmony.

Adhering to guiding social trend of thoughts with socialist core value system can improve the party's governance capability in the ideological field. Ideological superstructure is a reflection of economy and politics in the field of social consciousness, which in turn affects their development. It is our party's fine tradition and political advantage plus its important ruling experience to attach great importance in the ideological work and give it full play, to mobilize the masses, unite the whole party, fight for the realization of the great goal. In the new historical period, our party should unite and lead people from all nationalities to achieve our goal and gain a firm foothold in the complex international situation. We must continue to attach great importance in the ideological work and enhance the party's ruling ability in the field of ideology. In order to guide social thought trends with socialist core value system, we should profoundly understand the contradictions among different thoughts and ideologies, scientifically analyze their impact on the dominant ideology and actively resolve conflicts, in order to enhance the ability of the ruling party in this field. Therefore, as an important aspect of the party's ideological work, guiding social thoughts with socialist core value system is an important practice to improve its ruling ability in the new period.

C.2. Constantly improving the ability of guiding the social thought trends

The ability to guide must be improved in order to strengthen and improve the work of guiding the social trends of thought as well as getting positive results. It requires us to further emancipate and develop the productive forces which means enhancing the material foundation of guiding social thoughts; to further strengthen research and construction of the Marxist theory, and we should constantly consolidate the ideological basis of guiding social thoughts, further strengthen the leadership of the party, and strengthen the political guarantees of guiding social trends.

C.2.1. Constantly enhancing the material base of guiding the social thought trends

Marx once said "people are fighting for everything that is related to their interests."[8] The thought once separates itself from interests will make a fool of itself. Similarly, the ideological construction work also cannot be aloof from the actual needs of the masses. Therefore, ideological construction work must connect solving problems with interests of the masses. Deng Xiaoping pointed out: "After all, from the historical materialist point of view, correct political leadership should promote the growth of productive forces and the development of material and cultural life of the people."[9]

Only through the continuous development of productive forces and the improvement of people's material life, superiority of the socialist system can be fully reflected, the socialist core value system be consolidated, the material foundation for guiding social thoughts be strengthened and all kinds of wrong thoughts effectively be curbed and eliminated. If there is no development in social productive forces for decades, no improvement in

---

8   *Complete Works of Marx and Engels*, Vol. I, People's Publishing House, 1995, p. 187.
9   *Selected Works of Deng Xiaoping*, 2nd edition, Vol. II, People's Publishing House, 1994, p. 128.

people's living standard, the socialist core value system cannot be consolidated and developed, and will not be recognized and disseminated by majority of the people. So, vigorous development of social productive forces are the strong basis of guiding social thoughts with core socialist values.

In line with the requirements of releasing and developing the productive forces, we must uphold and improve the basic economic system, with public ownership playing a dominant role and diverse forms of ownership developing side by side. It is necessary to firmly consolidate and develop public sector economy, at the same time, encourage support and guide the non-public ownership economy. Deng Xiaoping pointed out: "the socialist economy is based on public ownership."[10] Public ownership and state-owned enterprises are the material and economic basis of the socialist core value system. If the dominant position of public ownership is weakened, the socialist core value system will become a rootless tree. Therefore, in the process of developing productive forces, we must constantly consolidate the dominant position of the socialist public ownership, vigorously develop state-owned economy and improve the state owned enterprises. Individual businesses, private and other forms of non-public economy is an important component of the socialist market economy. Non-public sector of the economy plays an important role in mobilizing the enthusiasm of people from all quarters, accelerates the development of productive forces, and in this way the non-public and public sector of economy can work in unity for the basic realization of socialist modernization.

With the development of social productive forces, we should continue to adhere to the process of building a socialist harmonious society which is people-oriented, fully reflect the value and the basic requirements of Scientific Outlook on Development, reflect the dialectical relationship between overall development of the people and economic and social development, adhere to the principles of development for the people and development depending on people and the fruits of development to be shared by the people, and promote all-round development of people so as to realize harmonious social development.

C.2.2. Constantly consolidating the thought basis of guiding the social thought trends

Our country is a socialist country. Marxism is the fundamental guiding ideology of our party, it is the banner of socialist ideology. Marxism, as our guiding ideology, is the soul of socialist core value system, and determines its nature and orientation. The fundamental principle of constructing and

---

10   Ibid.

establishing socialist core value system, in the society is to adhere to the guiding position of Marxism. By strengthening research and construction of Marxist theory of thought trend and ideology, we can further develop the unifying role of our guiding ideology, Marxism, in establishing the system of socialist core values, greatly enhance the theoretical basis to guide social thoughts with socialist core value system, so that the core value system can demonstrate its strong truth and powerful logic in the process of guiding the social trend of thought.

Currently, the whole party is seriously implementing the "Opinions of the Central Committee of the CPC to Further Prosperity and Development of Philosophy and Social Sciences" and "The Opinions of the Central Propaganda an Ideological Work Guiding Group on the Implementation of Marxist Theory Research and Construction Project". This is an important measure to deepen the study of Marxism, consolidate and expand the contingent of theoretical workers in the sphere of Marxism, thus further consolidate its guiding position. In order to strengthen the research and construction of Marxist theory, the following important measures must be carried out in the long run. The studies on Scientific Outlook on Development should be promoted and strengthened. Scientific Outlook on Development is the product of combination of Marxism with contemporary Chinese reality and the characteristics of times. It is a concentrated expression of the Marxist world outlook and methodology with regard to development. This theory provides new scientific answers to major questions on what kind of development China should achieve in the new environment of the world and how to achieve it. Consequently, proposition of Scientific Outlook on Development has played an important role in answering major theoretical and practical problems of China's modernization, it possesses great practical value in guiding our work and demonstrates theoretical power of Marxist theory.

In order to strengthen the research and construction of Marxist theory, we should produce solutions to important practical questions that lay before us, i.e. we must adhere to principle of being problem oriented and strengthen our problem consciousness in our study. Deng Xiaoping said: "A true Marxist-Leninist must understand, carry on and develop Marxism-Leninism in light of the current situation."[11]

Jiang Zemin added: "If we disregard realities and the development of times, it becomes meaningless to talk about Marxism. There is no sense to study Marx doctrine and be separated from vivid development in real life

---

11   *Selected Works of Deng Xiaoping*, Vol. III, People's Publishing House,1993, p. 291.

in a static and isolated way."[12] Marxist theory is the scientific reflection of social practice; in order to strengthen the research and construction of Marxist theory, we must be deeply concerned about the situation at home and abroad, pay attention to the new developments in the contemporary world, study new situations and new problems in capitalist countries, inter-act with China's actual situation in Reform and Opening-up and socialist modernization construction, study new conditions, explore new challenges, strengthen the study of practical problems, avoid speaking empty words, clichés and nonsense, and make scientific nature and militancy of Marxist theory settle on reality.

C.2.3. Constantly strengthening the political guarantee of guiding the social thought trends

The Communist Party of China is the leading core of the cause of so-cialism with Chinese characteristics. Comrade Jiang Zemin pointed out: "Without putting millions of people's thoughts and strength together in order to advance our common goal of building socialism with Chinese characteristics, no unified leadership of the Communist Party of China can be envisaged."[13] That the ideological sphere being led by the party is an important principle in the long-term practice. It is an important aspect of upholding the party's leadership and cannot be shaken at any time and place. Constructing the socialist core value system and guiding social trend of thoughts with socialist core value system cannot be separated from the mighty leadership of the party. To strengthen the party's leadership means safeguarding socialist core value system in guiding social thought trends. However, due to various reasons, the ability of some leading cadres' grasp and application of the scientific outlook on development lacks adequate strength. Some party organizations at the grass-roots level are weak and lax, and a minority among the party cadres has shaky ideals and beliefs and pale consciousness. They are divorced from the masses, indulged with serious bureaucracy and formalism, laziness and corruption; their world outlook, outlook on life and values seriously deviate from the socialist core value system, which seriously affects their effectiveness in guiding social trends of thought. Strengthening the effectiveness of socialist core value system in guiding social trends of thought, we must purify the cadre ranks of the, con-stantly improve their abilities and level of governance capacity. First of all, the efforts to maintain the party's advanced nature and efforts to maintain is purity should be strengthened, which is extremely important to uphold the socialist core value system. This kind of education activities should guide

12   *Selected Works of Jiang Zemin*, Vol. II, People's Publishing House, 2006, p. 12.
13   Ibid., p. 262.

majority of the Party members to learn Marxism, improve their ideological and theoretical quality, so that they consciously practice socialist core values, and become models in the construction of socialist core value system in the whole society. Secondly, we should strengthen anti-corruption efforts. Corruption is the product of an exploitation system in class societies. The corrupt behavior of some party members and cadres in the party both contrasts the cause and principles of the party and also core socialist values. These bad conducts seriously corrode the party's healthy body and damages the group and relationship between cadres and the masses. Strengthening our anti-corruption efforts and improving the party's credibility in people's hearts will persuade them to affirm the leading model role of party members and cadres in building the socialism system, so that greater achievements can be achieved in the system construction.

C.3. Accurately grasping the basic pattern of social thought trends

Grasping the basic pattern of the social trends of thought, the basic pattern of main trend of thought and the overall development trend is an essential requirement in enhancing effectiveness in our leading work.

C.3.1. The basic situation of social thought trends in current China

Currently, after 30 years of Reform and Opening-up and socialist modernization, China's economic strength, comprehensive national strength and people's living standards have greatly improved, but at the same time, we should clearly see that China is still in the primary stage of socialism and will remain so for a long time. The principal social contradiction active in our society is still the one between the ever-growing material and cultural needs of people and the backward social production. Lately, China has entered a critical period of reform and development by deepening the transformation of its economic system, social structure, pattern of interests and ideas. All these changes necessities us to consider and accord different interests, which is a difficult and arduous task. The unprecedented social changes not only inject great vitality to the development and progress of our country but also inevitably brings a variety of new contradictions and challenges. A variety of study fruits on social trend of thought make different evaluations even in a similar historical period. The evaluations differ in form, content and in naming them which are determined by research standpoints and starting points.

However, a great deal of research results regarding a certain social thought trend can arrive basically identical conclusions and conceptions regarding its content. This stems from the fact that social thought trends enjoy an objective existence which cannot be altered by man's will. Like the science and humanism trend that surged in the era of western modernization and the scientific socialism and the liberalism trend of thought that formed after the May Fourth Movement in China.

In the recent decades, our academy has achieved abundant research fruits on social trend of thoughts, especially regarding neo-liberalism, democratic socialism, historical nihilism, civil society, universal values, "Constitutionalism", "neo-Confucianism (revivalism)"; contemporary Chinese nationalism and the new left thought trends. These thought trends which have emerged and formed since the mid-to-late 1990s are indeed unique in the new period of Reform and Opening-up.

C.3.2. The basic characteristics of social thought trends in the new period

The social trends of thoughts of different times have distinctive characteristics when compared with the trends of thoughts of the former eras, consequently thought trends formed in the new era of Reform and Opening-up have the following important features:

Firstly, they are very active and vigorous. A social trend of thought always have its roots in a certain economic base, more specifically it reflects the contradictions between a certain social economic status and people's interests after an adjustment of these interests, thus a trend of thought reflects demands, emotions and desires belonging to a certain class or stratum. The 30 years of Reform and Opening-up is a very important historical period in the contemporary history of China. The report to the 17th National Congress of the CPC pointed out: "Our party held the 3rd Plenary Session of the 11th CPC Central Committee with a great historical significance in 1978, which opened the new era of Reform and Opening-up. Since then, with indomitable enterprising spirit and innovative practice, the Communist Party and the Chinese people have created a new epic of unremitting self-improvement and pioneering spirit of the Chinese nation. Historic changes have taken place in China, among Chinese people and the China Communist Party."[14] This argument clearly defines the 30 years of Reform and Opening-up as

14   Hu Jintao: *Hold High the Great Banner of Socialism with Chinese Characteristics and Strive to Build a Moderately Prosperous Society in an All-round Way–Report to the 17th National Congress of the CPC*, People's Publishing House, 2007, p. 6.

a "new era", and points out that the new era of radical shocking changes have taken place in China. If we examine specific historical conditions of the formation and development of new social trends of thought, we see that in the new era of Reform and Opening-up, extensive and profound changes have occurred in the spheres of economy, politics and culture. These changes have provided a rich soil for the upsurge of social thoughts in the new era. A variety of social thoughts were formed around the questions faced by China, on how to reform and carry out the construction of modernization construction and other issues which come to the forefront of history, consequently these thoughts have actively expressed realistic propositions from their own theoretical point of view and from different stands, and we have observed their mode of motion has been very active. This is mainly reflected in the following aspects:

Firstly, numerous thoughts have formed. In a certain historical stage, an important symbol of activeness of social trend of thought are demonstrated in their numbers. In the period of revolutions or great reforms, social trends of thought tend to be more active. The convening of the 3rd Plenary Session of the 11th Central Committee of the CPC has been a strong call for the cause of China's modernization. It has awakened different socio-psychological, ideas and concepts, has promoted the generation of new ideas. The deepening of Reform and Opening-up practice, continuously affect social psychology and ideology, like the spring rain. In this new historical period, social trends have continued to surge, the number of social thoughts have been numerous and diverse, the interactions between various thoughts have been frequent, they continuously adjust their value concepts with the changes of specific social and historical conditions. Secondly, the rise and fall of the trend of thoughts. Generally speaking, a specific social trend has a life cycle of occurrence, development, decline and disappearance. In the active period of social thoughts, they are relatively in a full-blown stage in the said life cycle. In China and abroad we can observe that due to time changes, some social thought trends have perished, some flourished and some saw a greater transformation. Within a short span of more than 30 years of reform and opening era the ups and downs of certain social thoughts has been clearly observed by the people, this fact demonstrates that a lot of adjustments in social production and social life during this period have provided an opportunity for thought trends to fully display themselves.

Secondly, they have strong sense of theoretical basis. Any social trend of thought can affect people's ideas and social economic and political life in varying degrees. But, in different historical periods, their impact is strong and the magnitude (degree) of their affection, in addition to other reasons, the affection is also related to the inner logic of the thought itself. If its inner logic has a strong theoretical consistency, the magnitude of their affection can be stronger and long standing.

In the new era of Reform and Opening-up, some of the major thought trends, theoretically have more strong systematic character and their inner logic are more consistent, which can better express the demands and requirements of their core values, also their theoretical origin have a strong past tradition, which they have inherited, which means they have a more mature core theory, and they are closely linked with the real social life. The contemporary new liberal ideological trend in China is a good example for this: it has not only transplanted the ideological system of western liberalism, but also inherited the liberalism trend of China which had been to a degree effective in the 19th Century and 1920s and 1930s, thus it possesses relatively a more complete theoretical system.

Realistic political prominence: Many social thoughts do not only have their direct roots in the reform and opening practice as their realistic basis but they also play an active role in the reform and opening process, they have influenced the direction and the practice of the reform and opening. With changes in social economic and political situation, these thought trends have constantly adjusted their specific demands and their expressions. Their ideas are closely related to the major social realities and represent different expectations, they have ideas on how to undertake reform, on the design of the reform, and each trend embodies a different view regarding the reform process. Some of the social trends aim to achieve a "revolution", in the fundamental system of China, some trends aim to realize a change in the operation or mechanism of the system. With the continuous adjustments made by the leadership regarding socialist reform and the continuous restructuring of the central tasks of reform, these thought trends are impacted, their focus and emphasizes change also their order of appearance changes. For example, in the process of economic system reform, the activity and performance of liberalism thought becomes more prominent, while the performance of democratic socialist thought trend becomes more prominent when we push forward the political system reforms.

C.3.3. The development trend of social thought trends

According to the emergence and development of social trends of thought, and combined with the current domestic and international complex situation of China, the development of these new thought trends have the following basic trends:

Firstly, these social trends of thoughts continue to develop and play their roles, the fundamental reason is that the social and historical conditions that promote their development continue to exist in China. The 17ᵗʰ National Congress of the Communist Party of China proposed that today's world and contemporary China are undergoing extensive and profound changes. Against the background of this era characteristics, China's social structure, the form of social groups in the society and the pattern of social interests have undergone profound changes and these changes have obviously enhanced the independence, selectivity, diversity and difference in people's ideological activities. Although people have similar fundamental interests, interests of various social groups continue to differentiate. Thought trends are the representation of interests, the trend of thoughts of reflecting different interests groups and their demands will be accordingly produced and developed because of the differentiation of social interests. In other words: "in such a society, the expression of various interest demands becomes a common social phenomenon"[15], it seems that these thought trends will also exert a social impact in a larger and wider range.

Some key figures of social trend of thought are able to affect them and push them, so as to exert greater influence. These leading figures of a trend are very active and an important component part of a trend of thought. They control the "right to speak" in some fields and with the deepening of China's reform, they take initiative and they promote the further development of thought trend, regarding the pace of development of this thought trend, and with successful initiative of these leading figures this thought trend may spread to political, economic, legal, historical, cultural and social fields, thus may a greater impact in these different fields. Some trends of thoughts encounter changes with the changes in real life conditions, will gain access to public opinion and media space, and will have a greater impact. For example, the new liberalism thought, part of intellectuals being its core subject may join hands with some "strong" groups which have larger social and economic resources in order to express the growing political demands of this group, and thus these intellectuals will become the "spokespersons" of thought in the public opinion field. The times of changes in the economic and social structure and differentiation of interests also make the mass of ordinary people, to grow their class consciousness more sharply. So they also need to have their own mouthpiece to express their interests and their desires. Some people will sympathize and defend the interests of ordinary workers and vulnerable groups. Their thoughts and activities

---

15   Sun Liping: Construction of Institutional Arrangement Based on Power, *Southern Weekend*. Jan. 1st, 2004.

will also combine further with social reality to promote the development of some thought trends.

Secondly, the development of thought trends makes the situation in the ideological field more complex. With the entering of China into the new century and stage, new profound changes have taken place in the international situation, the trend toward multi-polarization and economic globalization in the world has continued to develop in twists and turns, scientific and technological progress advances forward in with each passing day, competition among countries based on their overall national strength is becoming increasingly fierce. Various ideologies and cultures are stirring up with each other and all kinds of contradictions are becoming more complicated, we still face pressures and restrictions coming from developed countries in the fields of economy, science and technology, etc. Against this background when China's reform and development is at a critical period, and it has entered deeper waters, the social interest relationships among groups in the society has become more complex and social interest have become more diversified, thus new situations and new problems emerge endlessly. In such a situation, the relationships between different thought trends, and the relationships between the thought trends and the mainstream ideology has become further complex. The situation of differentiation and opposition among them will become more and more obvious. First of all, opposition among trends of thoughts will be highlighted. The reason is that if these thought trends further obtain resources to develop, thought trends will inevitably have a relatively large rally in the entire field of social consciousness and other trends of thoughts that oppose against these rising thought trends will also make a corresponding response accordingly. What is more important is that those thought trends, which are contrary to the mainstream ideology, will have a greater impact on the mainstream ideology. They will continue to integrate and consolidate their power and compete with mainstream ideology in many ways to win the masses to compete against mainstream ideology, will try to infiltrate their ideas into the economic, political and cultural life practices.

C.3.4. Deepening research on concrete thought trends

With a further and deeper studies on various specific thought trends our work of guiding them will be more effective, we will better know what should be respected and what to accommodate and tolerate with them and our efforts will be more conscious and targeted. When studying a specific trend of thought, we must first distinguish between primary and secondary issues identify the key points of concern for us, i.e. we should focus on those social trends that have a great social impact. These thoughts are often the "major trends" among many other thought trends and also have a strong influence on other thought trends, we think "major trends" need more attention.

Research on specific thought trends cannot be separated from analytic research on their representative figures and/or schools of thoughts they are related with. Representative figures or schools of thoughts are the supporters of thought trends, they are disseminators and propagators of the trend of thought; their words and deeds to a certain extent reflect the aspirations and nature of the social thoughts they represent, their specific situation has a direct impact on the spread and impact of social thought trends. In order to grasp a specific trend of thought in an all-round and profound way, we need to analyze its standpoint, viewpoint and method, its particular representative figures and its related school of thought. The analysis and study of the representative figures or related school of thought is the inherent study requirement when studying them. When studying specific thought trends, we should also pay attention to the relationship between different thought trends. There is a close connection between different thought trends, and the relations among different trends of thoughts in the same historical period show a certain common nature. The relations among different trends of thoughts from different historical periods show another nature. And the relations among different domestic trends of thoughts and international trends of thoughts, etc., all show complex situations. Social trends of thoughts with similar nature or having different nature also differ from another, and different types of thought trends also have different social functions. Only through a comprehensive understanding of the relationships among different trend of thoughts can the essence of the social trend of thought be understood more deeply.

C.4. Showing tolerance and respecting for differences and diversity

"Showing tolerance and respecting for differences and diversity" are important concepts proposed by the 6th Plenary Session of the 16th CPC Central Committee while discussing the building of a harmonious socialist society and culture, which is a major guideline and fundamental way of guiding social thoughts with the core socialist value system. Showing tolerance and respect for differences and diversity, and emphasizing seeking common ground in diversity, upholding the dominant position of Marxism in the diversity of thoughts and adhering to grasp the correct direction when faced by various kinds of changes in the environment, all these are the keys to persist in when guiding the trend of thoughts with core socialist values system.

To clarify the policy, measures and ways, of how socialist core value system can guide the thought trends guide is the main aspect of the study of the socialist core value system. Some scholars believe that, on the one hand, "showing tolerance and respecting for differences and diversity" itself is the proper meaning of the question of guiding. While on the other hand, other scholars argue that the policy of "showing tolerance and respecting for differences and diversity" is the important prerequisite when insisting on using socialist core value system to guide thought trends. Based on these, we should consider the two points above and—on the premise of upholding the leading position of the socialist core value system, we must strive to create a social and cultural environment in which showing tolerance and respecting for differences and diversity is prevalent, and at the same time focus our efforts on maximizing of the formation of social (societal) consensus. In order to maximize the formation of social consensus, we should—within the overall situation—find the focus point of how to guide thought trends with the socialist core value system, secondly, in order to maximize the formation of social consensus, we should define the fields and channels how to promote the overall work of how to guide thought trends with the socialist core value system, it is extremely necessary to constantly enhance the persuasive vigor and charisma of the socialist core value system so as to guide the social thought trends.[16]

There are also some scholars who have pointed out that: in order to guide the social trend of thought with the socialist core values, one needs to grasp the following principles: firstly, correctly handle the relationship between monism and pluralism; secondly, insist in guiding the social thought trends with positive and healthy thoughts; thirdly, correctly deal the relationship between ideal and reality; fourthly, improve the ability to predict social trends, so as to prevent the formation of wrong thoughts to the maximum extent and to take preventive measures and nip them in the bud, when they are weaker.[17]

Respect for difference and diversity is a specific application of our party's policy of "letting a hundred flowers blossom, let hundred schools of thought contend." In February 1957, Mao Zedong put forward: "the policy

16 Deng Xiaoping Theory and "Three Represents" Thought Research Center in National Defense University: Adhere to Guiding the Social Thought Trends with Socialist Core Values. *Guangming Daily*, Dec. 16th, 2006.

17 Zhang Jun: Adhere to Guiding the Social Trend of Thoughts with Core Socialist Values, *People's Daily*, Jan. 19th, 2007.

of "letting a hundred flowers blossom, let hundred schools of thought contend" to promote the flourishing of the arts and the progress of science
policy, thus advance China's socialist cultural prosperity."[18] This article
emphasizes: "different forms and styles of art should freely develop and
different schools of science should freely argue," and emphasizes: the use
of administrative power to enforce a style or a school of thought or banning
a style, or a different school of thought will harm the development of art
and science."[19] Therefore, "in the sphere of arts and sciences, we should
maintain a cautious attitude, and encourage free discussion and should not
arrive reckless and hasty conclusions."[20] In the field of cultural thoughts,
we should not adopt simple methods to solve it, we must adhere to the
"double hundred policy" and try guide the broad masses of people in recognizing and solving these problems, and we should correctly treat different
voices with Marxist standpoints, Marxist views and methods.

Adhering to the "double hundred policy" does not mean to weaken the
guiding position of the Marxism, instead it will strengthen its guiding role.
We respect differences, tolerance and diversity, with the purpose of maximizing the formation of social consensus, which is fully consistent with the
"double hundred policy." Visibly, "showing tolerance and respecting for
differences and diversity" is a scientific attitude when guiding the social
trend of thoughts with the socialist core value system.

Actively implementing the principle of "showing tolerance and respecting
for differences and diversity" is an objective requirement so that diversity
and pluralism can exist in the field of social consciousness department of superstructure of our socialist society. With deepening Reform and Opening-up
and deepening of the socialist market economy, China's economic structures,
forms of economic organization and operation, ways of employment, and
policy and methods of distribution have increasingly diversified. Accordingly,
there are many differences between different ideas and concepts, the process
of spiritual life of people have become more complicated, the differences and
diversity between various social consciousness have become more obvious,
consequently the differences and diversity are manifested through various
thought trends in a great extent.

Numerous social thought trends not only have different natures, but also
have differences regarding historical period of development, differences regarding geographical spread, thinking and focus of field, social influence,

18   *Selected Important Documents since the Founding of the Country* (Vol. X), Central
Party Literature Press, 1994, p. 88.
19   Ibid.
20   Ibid.

differences regarding their manifestations and also differences in the scope of dissemination. In this context, we must profoundly understand the mutually dependent relationship between the principle socialist core value system guides thought trends that are in diversity and variance and the principle of "showing tolerance and respecting for differences and diversity" in order to construct the socialist harmonious culture, and in order to promote further prosperity and development of China's science and culture.

Mao Zedong pointed out that "relying on the majority and considering the overall situation is our premise."[21] In the process of guiding social thoughts with socialist core value system, "showing tolerance and respecting for differences and diversity" is the guiding line for our party in order to uphold Marxism in the field of social consciousness (superstructure) and the principle of "double hundred" is the means to apply this guiding line and a means to enable fully tapping and encouraging different sectors of society, the positive and progressive spirit implied by different social groups, and a means to enable maximizing the formation of consensus of thoughts, and a means to increase cohesion and strength so as to promote concerted efforts to build socialism with Chinese characteristics.

To carry out the principle of "showing tolerance and respecting for differences and diversity" we must cultivate and create an open, and a relaxed cultural atmosphere. Without an open, and a relaxed cultural atmosphere, "showing tolerance and respecting for differences and diversity" cannot be achieved and will lose its premise and foundation. "Showing tolerance and respecting for differences and diversity" cannot work without an open, relaxed and benign cultural atmosphere.

This requires us that on the basis of upholding the leading position of the socialist core value system, we should follow the principle of "letting a hundred flowers bloom and a hundred schools of thought contend," promote equal footing and candid discussions, try to persuade people with rational arguments, and we should also respect diverse cultural trends and diverse thought trends, we should promote that different thought trends reach common cultural ideals, we should encourage that all kinds of thought trends will adhere to dominant status of the socialist core value system, on the basis of their own complementary advantages, and on the basis of both their separate self-development and coordinated development at the same time, so as to implement the principle of "Showing tolerance and respecting for differences and diversity" to foster and create a benign democratic atmosphere. Some people have argued that the principle of "showing tolerance

---

21   *Selected Works of Mao Zedong,* 2nd edition, Vol. I, People's Publishing House, 1991, p. 264.

and respecting for differences and diversity" means avoiding debates and arguments, and some people bring an "abstract interpretation" and argue that the principle of "showing tolerance and respecting for differences and diversity" means we should guide different thought trends generously and loosely, we should relax the management of the cultural environment.

Of course, in the process of guidance, the principle of "showing tolerance and respecting for differences and diversity" embodies our respect for the rich and colorful traditional culture, and respect for humankind's benign achievements and embodies the idea of "flowers" with infinite colors. When guiding various harmless or favorable thought trends it is necessary to show tolerance to different views and opinions and adopt an open and embracing attitude. However, we should also beware that "showing tolerance and respecting for differences and diversity" is not unprincipled harmony. Giving play to the guiding role of the socialist core value system with regard to thought trends, not only includes guiding various thought trends and enhancement of the attraction and cohesive effect of socialist ideology, but also includes resisting all kinds of situations and thought trends that endanger the stability and unity and the harmony in the society.

Deng Xiaoping stressed that: "serious criticism is necessary for all kinds of erroneous tendencies"[22], "we cannot undermine and lose the weapon of criticism", "we should make great efforts to fight against those thought trends which doubt the Four Cardinal Principles"[23]. And only by having a clear-cut stand and by fighting against the various wrong and anti-Marxist ideas can the social thought be guided. Reversely, if we allow free dissemination of wrong ideas, they will afflict and upset the socialist core value system. The decisive and resolute attitude of Comrade Deng Xiaoping towards mistaken thought trends was exemplary, when he was acutely aware of a wrong thought trend, that could potentially oppose the "Four Cardinal Principles" he suggested that, we should start launching timely critiques, conduct active and effective debates, against them when these thoughts are just in their fermenting stage.

Avoiding unnecessary debates, does not mean we should give up debating against wrong thought trends. During the late 1970s, a weirs argument of "Two Whatevers" had appeared in China, which was a major departure from the basic principles of Marxism and our benign study tradition of "practice is the sole criterion for truth" was turned upside down; against this background, it was necessary to restore, our benign study tradition, and

---

22   *Deng Xiaoping's Selected Works.* 2nd ed., Vol. II, People's Publishing House, 1994, p. 390.
23   *Ibid.,* p. 166.

defend the standpoint that only by all-encompassing argument can we solve major issues. Historical facts and later developments have proven that, the nation-wide big debate on the "sole criterion for testing truth" which was started May 1978 onwards has been very timely and absolutely necessary. Without this argument, the party's ideological line based on Marxist tenets would not be restored. In the new historical period, we should also determinedly debate against various kinds of dogmas.

When resisting an erroneous thought trend, we should carefully take into account, its ideas, concepts, cultural aspects and focus into its development laws. Social thought trends should be categorized under social ideology, consequently the struggle against the wrong social thought trends is an important aspect of ideological work task, which necessities that we should carefully take into account the nature and laws of people's thinking and understanding. Engels had pointed out: "But a philosophy is not disposed of by the mere assertion that it is false."[24] Mao Zedong, when talking on handling the issues of world view, pointed out: "It is only by using discussion, criticism and reasoning that we can really foster correct ideas, overcome wrong ideas and really settle issues."[25] From this point, respecting the characteristics and development laws of thought, concept and culture is a necessary practice. When fighting against wrong ideas we should apply the method of solving the problems, method, which includes: "letting a hundred flowers blossom, let hundred schools of thought contend", see that reasoning or debates replace simple and crude coercion and finally, we should advocate democratic discussion, equal exchanges, and convince people by fair reasoning. Not only we need to have clear-cut criteria to go by and adhere to correct methods, but also need to assume a gentle style of criticism and opt for positive publicity. And when criticizing erroneous views and wrong ideas we should combine the two: absorbing positive ideas in a critique and refute the wrong ones in it.

---

24   *Collected Works of Karl Marx and Frederick Engels*, Vol.26, p.55.
25   *Selected Works of Mao Zedong*, Vol.VII, People's Publishing House, 1999, p. 232 and see https://www.marxists.org/reference/archive/mao/selected-works/volume-5/mswv5_58.htm.

Postscript

A major part of my research work is to follow and study important thought trends in the ideological field of contemporary China. The seething social practices and great changes in contemporary China provide fertile soil for the spiritual life of the people. Since my master degree study period till today, the qualities of political thoughts as having extensive social psychological basis and their possessing of certain degree of depth in regard to social consciousness and ideology have entered into my research vision. After a long-term access to and study on numerous thoughts, and through written or online dialogues and exchange of ideas with many scholars, the idea of seeking for the commonness of these thoughts burgeoned in my brain.

Part I of the book is the fruit of my accumulated thoughts over long years of studies. To dig out and reveal the so-called commonness and regularities of political thought trends might not be difficult for some scholars, but this exploration has racked my brains greatly. This can be attributed to my Marxist philosophy study, since my early studentship, which has made to explore the categories of social consciousness and pursue to grasp the development law of thought trends from the view of historical materialism.

Part II of the book comments on and evaluates several political thought trends, here my judgements might seem humble or sometimes inevitably incorrect, but here I have intended to break the conventional "either-or" analysis method in political thoughts research, and applied my advocate of a more comprehensive view angle when observing and examining these influential political thoughts. Prof. Tian Xinming, an expert from the Department of Social Sciences attached to Ministry of Education, has offered valuable recommendations and guidance regarding the key issues in this book. Dr. Wang Yin from China Social Sciences Press offered selfless help in the editing and publication of the book. Herein I extend my sincere gratitude to both of them.

Due to the limitations in theoretical attainments and academic vision, there might be some lapses in the book. Your criticism and comments will be highly appreciated.

Wang Bingquan
May, 2013

References

I. Reference books

Selected Works of Marx and Engels, Vol. 1-4, People's Publishing House, 1995, 2nd edition.

Articles in the German and French Yearbooks, Marx and Engels, Vol. 1, People's Publishing House, 1956.

Holy Family, Marx and Engels, Vol. 2, People's Publishing House, 1957.

Article, The Situation in Prussia, Marx and Engels, Vol. 12, People's Publishing House, 1962.

Lenin, A Talk with Defenders of Economism, in: Lenin Complete Works, Vol. 5, People's Publishing House, 1986, 2nd edition.

Lenin, Tasks of the Revolutionary Youth, in: Lenin Complete Works, Vol. 7, People's Publishing House 1986, 2nd edition.

Lenin, Inflammable Material in World Politics, in: Lenin Complete Works, Vol. 17, People's Publishing House, 2nd edition.

Book Review, in Collected Works of Lenin, Vol. 25, People's Publishing House, 1988.

Under the Banner of Others, in: Lenin Collected Works, Vol. 26, People's Publishing House 1988, 2nd edition.

Mao Zedong Selected Works, 1-4 Vol., People's Publishing House, 1991, 2nd edition.

Mao Zedong Collected Works, Vol. 7, People's Publishing House, 1999.

Mao Zedong's Letter to Cai Hesen (December 1920), in: Mao Zedong Selected Letters, Central Literature Publishing House, 2003.

Mao Zedong's Excerpts, Central Literature Publishing House, 2003.

Anthology of Deng Xiaoping, Vol. 1-2, People's Publishing House, 1994.

Anthology of Deng Xiaoping, Vol. 3, People's Publishing House, 1993.

Anthology of Jiang Zemin, Vol. 3, People's Publishing House, 2006.

Plekhanov's Selected Works on Philosophy, Vol. 1, Life & Reading Series, New Knowledge Joint Publishing House, 1959.

Plekhanov's Selected Works on Philosophy, Vol. 2, Life & Reading Series, New Knowledge Joint Publishing House, 1961.

Plekhanov's Selected Works on Philosophy, Vol. 3, Life & Reading Series, New Knowledge Joint Publishing House, 1962.

Anthology of Li Dazhao, People's Publishing House, 1959.

Anthology of Qu Qiubai, People's Publishing House, 1985.

Zhong Limeng, Yang Fenglin (Co-editors in chief): Chinese Modern Philosophy History, Compilation of Materials, Episode 1, Vol. 1, Department of Philosophy of Liaoning University, 1981 (Unofficial Publication).

Zhong Limeng, Yang Fenglin (editor in chief): Chinese Modern Philosophy History, Compilation of Materials, Episode 1, Vol. 1, Department of Philosophy of Liaoning University, 1981 (Unofficial Publication).

Cai Shangsi (editor in chief): History of Thoughts in Modern China, Compilation of Materials, Vol. 1, Zhejiang People's Press, 1982.

Reader of the Report to the 17th Congress, People's Publishing House, 2007.

Building A Socialist Core Value System – Major Reference, Red Flag Press, 2007.

Theoretical Bureau of the CPC Central Committee Propaganda Department: Selected Marxist Theoretical Research and Construction Reference Materials – Year 2006, Learning Publishing House, 2007.

Liang Zhu, Zhang Shoumin, et al.: The Primary Stage of Socialism and the Four Cardinal Principles, People's Publishing House, 2002.

Mei Rongzheng, Zhang Xiaohong: On the Thought Trend of Neo-liberalism, Higher Education Press, 2004.

Zhou Xincheng, et al.: Comment on the Humanitarianism of Democratic Socialism, China Renmin University Publishing House, 1998.

Tian Xinming, Guo Baoping: Contemporary University Students' Social Thoughts, Shaanxi People's Publishing House, 1990.

Tian Xinming: Reflection of Cognition, People's Publishing House, 2000.

Cao Changsheng et al.: Research of the Ideological Sphere in the Evolution Process of the Soviet Union, People's Publishing House, 2004.

He Bingmeng: Neo-Liberalism, People's Publishing House, 2004.

Liu Shulin: On the Trend of Democratic Socialism, Higher Education Press, 2004.

Wang Ji: Marxism and Contemporary Social Thoughts – A Reflection on Current Social Trends, Renmin University of China Press, 1994.

Wu Yannan: China's Modern Social Trends (Four Volumes), Lake Southern Education Press, 1998.

Chen Zhenming: Political Science, China Social Science Press, 1999.

Kong Qingdong: On Language Education in Secondary Schools, Shantou University Press, 1999.

Zhang Lei, Kong Qingrong, co-ed: Mechanics of National Cohesion in China, China Social Science Press, 1999.

Yu Jianhua, Nationalism – The Historical Heritage and the Trend of Times, Social Science Literature Press, 1999.

Social Transformation: Multi-cultural and Multi-ethnic Society, Special Issue of the Journal of Social Sciences in China, Social Science Literature Press, 2000.

Cheng Ren: Perspectives on the 20th Century Nationalist Thought Trends, Xiyuan Publishing House, 2000.

Wang Lixin: US Foreign Policy and the Chinese Nationalist Movement During 1904-1928, The National Social Science Press, 2000.

Hu Fengxiang: Social Change and Cultural Tradition - Research On Modern Chinese Cultural Conservatism), Shanghai People's Publishing House, 2000.

Su Songxing, Hu Zhenping, co-ed: Differentiation and integration – The Value of Contemporary Chinese Youth, Shanghai Academy of Social Sciences Press, 2000.

Li Shitao: The Position of Intellectuals - Nationalism and the Fate of Transitional China, Times of Literary and Art Publishing House, 2000.

Li Shitao: The Position of Intellectuals – Pendulum between Radicalism and Conservativism, Times of Literature and Art Publishing House, 2000.

Li Shitao: The Position of Intellectuals – The Struggle between Liberalism and Chinese Thoughts, Times of Literature and Art Publishing House, 2000.

Kuang Xinnian: The Voice of Silence, Anhui Literature and Art Publishing House, 2000.

Hu Angang, Yang Fan, co-ed: Great Power Strategy, Liaoning People's Publishing House, 2000.

Wang Yan: Liberalism and The Contemporary World, Sanlian Bookstore, 2000.

Collective Compilation: Contemporary Trends in the World, CPC Central Party School Press, 2000.

Liu Hong, Shen Shan, Shi Shuhua, co-ed: Dream of Hundred Years: Changes of Economic and Social Trends in the 20th Century, Xiyuan Publishing House, 2000.

Bai Jiancheng: The Ideal Nation, Law Press, 2000.

Xu Datong: Contemporary Western Political Trends since the 1970s, Tianjin People's Publishing House, 2003.

Wang Ke: Nation and Nationality - Genealogy of Multi-ethnic Cohesion in China, National Social Science Press, 2001.

Luo Zhitian: Chaos Floods - Nationalism and Republican Politics, Shanghai Ancient Books Publishing House, 2001.

Cao Jinqing, Chen Baoping, co-ed: Seven Questions of China, Shanghai Science and Technology Education Press, 2002 Annual edition.

Fang Ning, Wang Bingquan, Ma Lijun, Co-ed; Rising, Developing China – A Study of Family Awareness among Contemporary Chinese Youth, People's Publishing House, 2002.

Fang Ning, Wang Bingquan, Co-ed, On the Nationalist Trend of Thought, Higher Education Press, 2004.

Gao Lan, Compilation work: The Specters of the Yasukuni Shrine Visits – Be Vigilant against the Resurrection of the Japanese Militarism, Military Science Press, 2002.

Guo Hanmin: Research on Social Thought Trends in the Late Qing Period, China Social Science Press, 2003.

Xing Ben Si, Li Xiaobing: Contemporary World Trends, The CPC Central Party School Press, 2003.

Zhang Zhicang: Marxism and Social Thought Trends in the Contemporary West, Shanghai People's Publishing House, 2003.

Gu Su, Zhang Fengyang: Contemporary Social Thought Trends in the West, Shandong Education Press, 2004.

Duan Zhongqiao: Contemporary Social Thought Trends in the Western World, China Renmin University Press, 2004.

Wang Min: A Review on Contemporary Western Thought Trends, Zhejiang University Press, 2005.

Ma Tianxiang: Buddhism of Late Qing Dynasty Period and Modern Social Thought in This Era, Henan University Press, 2005.

Yu Zuhua, Zhao Huifeng: Social and Cultural Thought Trends in Modern China, Shandong University Press, 2005.

Wang Zhiwei: The Main Trends and Schools of Modern Western Economics, Higher Education Press, 2005.

Zhang Hao: The Times of Change in the Intellectual History of Modern China, Academic Thoughts Series edited by Chen Yu Shui, China Encyclopedia Publishing House, 2005.

Wan Bin, Zhang Yinghang, co-ed: Contemporary Western Thought Trends from Marxist Perspective, Zhejiang University Press, 2006.

Feng Song, editor in chief: Selected Lectures on Contemporary Social Trends, China Communication University Press, 2006.

Liu Lihong: Cultural Conservatism during May Fourth Movement, China Social Science Press, 2006.

Zhang Weibo: A Study on the Thought Trend of Respecting Confucianism, in the Early Period of Republican China, People's Publishing House, 2006.

Chen Liyang: Russian Nationalism after the Disintegration of the Soviet Union, Chongqing Press, 2006.

Zhang Taiyuan: "Independent Critique" and the Political Thought Trends of the 1930s, Social Sciences Literature Press, 2006.

Yin Xu Yi: Democratic Socialism, Central Compilation and Translation Press, 2007.

Xu Chongwen: Democratic Socialism, Chongqing Press, 2007.

Xu Juezai: History of Socialist Schools, Shanghai People's Publishing House, 2007.

Xiang Qing: Contemporary Japanese Nationalism, Social Science Literature Publishing House, 2007.

Gong Pengcheng: Contemporary Thoughts and Figures, Zhonghua Book Company, 2007.

Hu Weixi: Cross Street and Tower – Liberal Trend of Thought in Modern China, Shanghai People's Publishing House, 1991.

Han Zhen: Research on Socialist Core Value System, People's Publishing House, 2007.

Chen Yajie: Building A Socialist Core Value System, People's Publishing House, 2007.

Jin Zhao: A Reader for Socialist Core Value System Education, Central Literature Publishing, 2007.

Yang Liying, Zeng Shengcong: Globalization, Network situation and Socialist Ideology: Research on the Construction of Contemporary Chinese Political Thoughts, People's Publishing House, 2007.

Li Shenzhi, He Jiadong: China's Path, Nanfang Daily Press, 2000.

Mao Yushi: Who Has Prevented Us from Achieving Prosperity, Guangdong Economic Publishing House, 1999.

Qian Liqun: Reject To Forget - Anthology of Qian Liqun, Shantou University Press, 1999.

Xu Jilin: Infinite Perplexity, Shanghai Joint Publishing House, 1998.

Zhu Xueqin: Revolution in the Study, Changchun Publishing House, 1999.

Tao Dongfeng: Contemporary Social Transformation and Intellectuals, Shanghai Sanlian Books, 1999.

Zhang Ruren: Research on Modern Chinese Thought, Shanghai People's Publishing House, 2001.

Xu Youyu: The Liberal Discourse, Changchun Publishing House, 1999.

Qin Hui: Problems and Doctrines, Changchun Publishing House, 1999.

He Qinglian: We Are Still Looking at the Stars, Lijiang Publishing House, 2001.

Xiao Gongqin: Farewell and Political Romanticism, Hubei Education Press, 2001.

Wang Dingding: My Thoughts of Economics, Life & Reading Series, New Knowledge Joint Publishing House, 1997.

Zheng Yifu: Cost Theory – A New Perspective of Sociology, Life & Reading Series, New Knowledge Joint Publishing House, 1995

Ma Licheng, Ling Zhijun: The Belligerence of Thinkings: A Record – Three Ideological Emancipations in Contemporary China, China Today Press, 1998.

Jing Wu: China's Discourse, China Procuratorial Press, 1999.

Wilbur Schramm: Introduction to Mass Communication, Xinhua Publishing House, 1984.

Michelle Beaud: History of Capitalism 1500-1980, Oriental Publishing, 1986.

Shmuel Noah Eisenstadt: Modernization: Protest and Change, China Renmin University Press, 1988.

Theotonio Dos Santos: Imperialism and Dependence, Social Science Literature Publishing House, 1988.

Ashton Carter, William Perry: Pre-emptive Defense: A New Security Strategy of the US, Shanghai People's Publishing House 2000 edition.

Anthony Giddens: The Third Way – Renewal of Social Democracy, Peking University Press, 2000.

Andrew Vincent: Modern Political Ideologies, Jiangsu People's Press, 2005.

Yael Tamir: Liberal Nationalism, Shanghai Century Publishing Group, 2005.

Anthony Smith: Nationalism: Theory, Ideology, History, Shanghai Century Publishing Group, 2006.

Martyn Frampton: The Long March: The Political Strategy of Sinn Fein, 1981-2007, Fortmills, Basingstoke, Hampshire; New York: Palgrave Macmillan, 2008.

Mingyan Lai, Nativism and Modernity: Cultural Contestations in China and Taiwan under Global Capitalism, State University of New York Press, 2008.

Andreas Kalyvas, Ira Katznelson: Liberal Beginnings: Making a Republic For The Moderns, Cambridge University Press, New York, 2008.

Ge Xiao, Ann Arbor, The Chinese Consumers' Changing Value System, Consumption Values and Modern Consumption Behaviors, UMI, 2006.

Yan Geling, Ha Jin, Maureen F. McHugh, co-ed: The Conceptions of Freedom in Contemporary Chinese and Chinese American Fiction, Kent State University Press, 2003.

II. Academic Papers and Journals

Wang Ruisheng: Preliminary Exploration of Social Thought Trends, Dongyue Forum, 1981(3).

Liu Defu: A Brief Examination on "Social Thought Trends", Journal of Seeking Truth, 1988(1).

Mei Rongzheng: "Pluralism" or Abstract Humanitarian Monism? – An Evaluation on the Theoretical Basis of the Reform in the Ideological Field Made by the Contemporary Democratic Socialism, Journal of Theoretical Reference, 1992(2).

Zhang Shujun: Social Thought Trends and General Social Consciousness and Their Relationship, Journal of Philosophical Research, 1992(3).

Zhang Shujun: On the Generation Mechanism of Social Thought Trends, Journal of Northeast Normal University, 1992(3).

Liu Jianjun: On the Genesis, Development and Perishment of Social Thought Trends, Academic Monthly, 1995(2).

Xiao Jinquan: On the Conception of Social Thought Trend as Level of Social Consciousness, Modern Philosophy, 1997(1).

Wang Jiazhong: The Origin of Social Trends, Their Development Process and Functions, Academic Journal of Qilu, 1997(2).

An Analysis of Comment on the Liberalism of the 90s, A research by Deng Xiaoping Theory Research Center attached to the Ministry of Education, Journal of Academic Theoretical Front, 2000(11).

Zhang Xiaohong: New Liberalism in Globalization, Journal of Marxism Studies, 2002(1).

Mei Rongzheng: An Analysis on Critique of Bourgeois Democracy by Marxist Classics and Their Contemporary Significance, Journal of Socialism Research, 2002(6).

Sha Jiansun: Adhere to the Guiding Position of Marxism When Fighting Against Western Dogmatism, Journal of Marxist Studies, 2004(5).

Zhang Xiaohong: Analysis of the Reasons of the Decline of Neo-liberalism in The West, Journal of Ideological and Theoretical Education, 2004(5)

Zhang Xiaohong: Adhere and Consolidate the Guiding Position of Marxism in the Field of Ideology, When Fighting Against Bourgeois Liberalism, Journal of Seeking Truth, 2004(5).

Mei Rongzheng: The Neo-liberal Pedigree, Change and Influence, Journal of Contemporary World Socialism, 2005(1).

Zheng Dahua: Historical Study of Chinese Cultural Conservatism, Journal of Seeking, 2005(1).

Sha Jian Sun: Scientifically Study and Propagate Glorious Struggle History of the Party and People - Comments On Historical Nihilism, Theoretical Front of Colleges and High Schools, 2005(2).

Mei Rongzheng, Zhou Zhiping: What kind of Thought trend is the "Civil Society Theory"?, Theoretical Front of Colleges and High Schools, 2005(2).

Mei Rongzheng, Yang Jun: An Examination on the Re-emergence of Historical Nihilism, Journal of Marxism Studies, 2005(5).

Zhang Xiaohong: Comment on the Neo-Liberal View of History, Journal of Exploration, 2005(6).

Mei Rongzheng, Wang Bingquan: Several Problems in the Overall Study of Social Thought Trends, Journal of Ideological and Theoretical Education, issue 2005(10).

Mei Rongzheng, Wang Bingquan: On the Dissemination and Leading of Social Thought Trends, Journal of Seeking Truth, 2005(11).

Zhang Xiaohong: Strengthen the Study of Contemporary Social Thought Trends in China, Journal of Hubei Social Sciences Learning, 2005(12).

Zhao Cunsheng, Yu Wenli, Wang Yonghao: Review of Recent Studies on the Advance Culture, Journal of Theoretical Front of Colleges and High Schools, 2006(2)

Liang Zhu: The Important Role of Culture in Building the Harmonious Socialist Society, Journal of Theoretical Front of Colleges and High Schools, 2007(2).

Chen Xianda: Practical Interpretation of the Sinization of Marxism, Journal of Studies on Socialism with Chinese Characteristics, 2007(4).

Zhao Yao: Vigorously Promote the Construction of the Socialist Core Value System, Journal of Red Flag Manuscript, 2007(12).

Zhang Guozuo: On the Issue of Guiding Diverse Social Thought Trends, Journal of Seeking Truth, 2007(14).

Wei Zhaogei: Be Vigilant Against Historical Nihilism, Guangming Daily, March 5th, 2005.

Zhu Xueqin: "1998, Liberal Discourse", Weekly Southern Weekend, December 25th, 1998 (12).

Zhu Xueqin: "What Is the Difference between Liberalism and the "New Left"? Contained in the Anthology of Zhu Xueqin, in part: Reform in the Study, Changchun Publishing House, 1999.

Xu Youyu: Contemporary China and Liberalism, Journal of Open Times, in: 1999(3).

Tao Dongfeng: The Debate of the Century: The New Left and Liberalism, Science Times, 1999(9).

Lu Jianjie: The History of Relations between Chinese Liberalism and Chinese Marxism, the Current Situation and Prospects, Journal of Philosophical Research, 1999(11).

Lin Jinfeng: On the Prediction and Guiding Social Trend Thoughts, Journal of Modern Philosophy, 2001(2).

Xie Yong: "Do We Have No Liberal Tradition?", Contained in the book, "Research on Contemporary Chinese Political Thoughts", Vol. I, published for the commemoration of the 90th year, China Social Science Press, 2001.

Wan He: Interest Groups, the Reform Path and Legitimacy, Journal of Strategy and Management, 2002(2).

Sun Liping: Building A Law Based Institutional Arrangement, Weekly Journal of Southern Weekend, January 1st, 2004.

www.ingramcontent.com/pod-product-compliance
Lightning Source LLC
Chambersburg PA
CBHW031137020426
42333CB00013B/419